Billing & Coding
Clear & Simple

A Medical Insurance Worktext

Billing & Coding Clear & Simple

A Medical Insurance Worktext

Nancy I. Gardner, CPC, CMA (AAMA)
Adjunct Instructor, Business and Technology
Des Moines Area Community College
Ankeny, Iowa

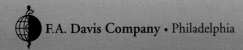 F.A. Davis Company • Philadelphia

F. A. Davis Company
1915 Arch Street
Philadelphia, PA 19103
www.fadavis.com

Printed in the United States of America

Last digit indicates print number: 10 9 8 7 6 5 4 3 2 1

Acquisitions Editor: Andy McPhee
Developmental Editor: Elizabeth LoGiudice
Manager of Content Development: George W. Lang
Art and Design Manager: Carolyn O'Brien

As new scientific information becomes available through basic and clinical research, recommended treatments and drug therapies undergo changes. The author(s) and publisher have done everything possible to make this book accurate, up to date, and in accord with accepted standards at the time of publication. The author(s), editors, and publisher are not responsible for errors or omissions or for consequences from application of the book, and make no warranty, expressed or implied, in regard to the contents of the book. Any practice described in this book should be applied by the reader in accordance with professional standards of care used in regard to the unique circumstances that may apply in each situation. The reader is advised always to check product information (package inserts) for changes and new information regarding dose and contraindications before administering any drug. Caution is especially urged when using new or infrequently ordered drugs.

Library of Congress Cataloging-in-Publication Data

Gardner, Nancy I.
  Billing & coding clear & simple / Nancy I. Gardner.
       p. ; cm.
  Billing and coding clear and simple
  Includes bibliographical references.
  ISBN-13: 978-0-8036-1718-6
  ISBN-10: 0-8036-1718-6
  1. Nosology--Code numbers. 2. Clinical medicine--Code numbers. 3. Medical fees. 4. Health insurance claims. I. Title. II. Title: Billing and coding clear and simple.
  [DNLM: 1. Forms and Records Control--methods--United States. 2. Insurance Claim Reporting--United States. W 80]
  RB115.G767 2011
  651.5'04261--dc22

2010038147

Several years ago I decided to write a billing and coding book that would be easy to understand and follow. Little did I know what a major undertaking that would be. This book would have never existed without all the great support from my family, friends, students, and colleagues.

First I need to say "Thank You" to my husband, Tim, and my children, Ben and Erin. Their patience and encouragement have been unending. You guys are the greatest!!! My family and friends have always found time to listen and encourage me.

My students have been my greatest resources over the years. I appreciate all of your efforts and ideas.

The editors and the staff at F. A. Davis have been very patient. This has taken me much longer than anyone hoped, but they have remained patient and helpful. Thank you!

And last but not least, I must thank Diane VanderPloeg, an instructor at Des Moines Area Community College where I work as an adjunct instructor. Diane thought of me when F.A. Davis contacted her for recommendations for people who might consider writing this text. Thank you, Diane, for believing in me.

Preface

The majority of the patients seen in a medical office today are covered by some type of insurance policy. Because of this, nearly all of a physician's income is from insurance payments. The prompt filing of medical insurance claims is necessary in order for a physician to be able to meet the monthly expenses of running an office. Salaries, medical supplies, office supplies, equipment, rent, utilities all depend on the cash flow generated by the filing of the insurance claims.

The medical coder, the person responsible for filing the insurance claims in a physician's office, should be fluent in medical terminology, as well as the proper methods of claim submission and follow-up. Besides communicating with patients and other health-care workers, the medical coder must be able to code the patient's diagnoses and procedures accurately according to the universal coding systems used by all insurance companies and federal agencies for statistical purposes. **All** claim payments depend on the accurate coding of all diagnoses and procedures. Precise coding and claim completion will determine if the procedures submitted are "medically necessary" and a "benefit" or "payment" will be issued.

It is the responsibility of the medical coder in every physician's office to review the insurance payments, checking for calculation errors, missed codes, or errors in claim processing.

ORGANIZATION

The objective of this text is to provide a practical approach to coding and medical insurance billing. Emphasis will be placed on *Current Procedural Terminology* (CPT) and *International Classifications of Diseases, Ninth Revision, Clinical Modification* (ICD-9-CM) used to facilitate proper coding in claim submission. Pertinent billing tips will be offered for filing Medicare, Medicaid, and various private insurance claims.

Unit 1 introduces the student to the medical coding profession (Chapter 1), the legal considerations in medical coding and billing (Chapter 2), and the Health Insurance Portability and Accountability Act (HIPAA) (Chapter 3), which has far-reaching implications in the modern medical office.

Unit 2 includes coverage of the two main coding systems, ICD-9-CM (Chapter 4) and *Current Procedural Terminology* (Chapters 5 and 6) and provides instruction on the applications of both code sets to patient records and insurance claims.

Unit 3 presents the different types of health insurance plans that are currently in effect in the United States and the proper procedures related to claim submission.

- Commercial Health Insurance (Chapter 7)
- Medicare (Chapter 8)
- Medicaid (Chapter 9)
- Managed Care (Chapter 10)
- TRICARE/CHAMPVA (Chapter 11)
- Worker's Compensation (Chapter 12)

In addition, there is coverage about insurance payments and claim follow-up (Chapter 13), two essential responsibilities for a medical coder.

KEY FEATURES

This book has several key features to promote student learning.

- Key terms and definitions highlighted within the text give context for important terminology.
- Examples throughout the text illustrate practical application of coding and billing guidelines.
- *ICD-10 Notes* within the chapters provide insight into upcoming government changes.
- Resource lists at the end of each chapter show references and Web links to key source material for easy access.
- Chapter review exercises reinforce important concepts and provide practical application.

INTERACTIVE CD-ROM

The bound-in CD contains patient cases for practice, complete with patient data and related claim forms. These cases allow students to test their critical thinking skills to answer questions about insurance information, patient demographics, and denied claims.

WEB RESOURCES

More resources are included at the Davis*Plus* website at http://davisplus.fadavis.com. This companion site provides a resource for students and instructors for new information, content updates, and other helpful information related to coding and billing.

The coding and health insurance industry changes constantly but the basics remain the same. Accurate diagnoses and procedure coding skills make the coder. I hope you enjoy coding as much as I do.

Nancy I. Gardner, CPC, CMA (AAMA)

Reviewers

Eudelia M. Aillon, AA, CMA (AAMA), LMT
Adjunct Faculty
Medical Assisting
El Centro College
Dallas, Texas

Ellen Anderson, RHIA, CCS
Assistant Professor
Health Information Technology
College of Lake County
Grayslake, Illinois

Karen Baker, CPC-I, CPC, CPC-H, PCS, FCS
Instructor
Documentation/Coding
Cooper University Hospital
Cherry Hill, New Jersey

Darlene Boschert,
    BS, CPC, CMA (AAMA), CMT
Vice President
Allied Health
Career Institute of Florida
Holiday, Florida

Koreen L. Byrns, BA, MA, PhD
Byrns Chiropractic
Greensburg, Pennsylvania
Westmoreland County Community College
Youngswood, Pennsylvania

Sheryl S. Chambers, CBCS
Instructor
Medical
Indiana Business College
Bowling Green, Indiana

Emoy E. Goodridge, CPC, CPC-H
Medical Records Instructor
Adult Education
Oswego County BOCES
Mexico, New York

Leah A. Grebner, MS, RHIA, CCS, FAHIMA
Director
Health Information Technology
Midstate College
Peoria, Illinois

Bonnie J. Hair, RHIT
Adjunct Faculty
Health Information Technology
West Virginia Community College
Wheeling, West Virginia

Kathy Kneifel
Instructor
Business Technology
Everett Community College
Everett, Washington

Susan M. Lewis, MBA, CMA (AAMA)
Associate Lecturer
Healthcare Office Management
University of Akron
Navarre, Ohio

Ann K. Minks, AAMT, WAMT, GPSC
Instructor
Health Sciences
QualData
Bellevue, Washington

Pat G. Moeck, PhD, MBA, BA, CMA (AAMA)
Director
Medical Assisting
El Centro College
Dallas, Texas

Kay A. Nave, CMA (AAMA), MRT
Program Director
Medical Assisting
Hagerstown Business College
Hagerstown, Maryland

Eva Oltman, CPC, CMA (AAMA), EMT, MS
Department Chair, Professor
Allied Health
Jefferson Community and Technical College
Louisville, Kentucky

Barbara Parker, CCS-P
Professor
Medical Assisting
Olympic College
Bremerton, Washington

Ona Schulz, CMA (AAMA)
Instructor, Coordinator
Medical Assisting
Lake Washington Technical College
Kirkland, Washington

Corinne M. Smith, MBA, RHIA, CCS
Associate Professor, Clinical Coordinator
Health Information Management
Montgomery College
Tacoma Park, Maryland

Jacqueline Thelian, CPC, PMCC
Coding
Medco Consultants, Inc
Fresh Meadows, New York

Barbara Tietsort, MEd
Associate Professor
Office Information Technology
University of Cincinnati—Raymond Walters
Blue Ash, Ohio

Marilyn M. Turner, RN, CMA (AAMA)
Program Director
Medical Assisting
Ogeechee Technical College
Statesboro, Georgia

Twila J. Wallace, MEd
Instructor
Business Technology
Central Community College
Columbus, Nebraska

Ann Wening, RHIT
Instructor
Health Information Management
Portland Community College'
Portland, Oregon

Carole A. Zeglin, MS, BS, RMA
Director
Medical Assisting
Westmoreland County Community College
Youngwood, Pennsylvania

Table of Contents

Introduction

Chapter Outline

I. Medical Billing and Coding Overview
II. Insurance Claims and the Medical Office
III. Coding for Insurance Claims
IV. Types of Insurance
V. Summary

OBJECTIVES

- Define Key Terms
- Explain the role of insurance claims in the medical office
- List the different types of insurance plans and an example of each type
- Differentiate between a diagnosis and a procedure
- Identify potential responsibilities for a medical coder

MEDICAL BILLING AND CODING OVERVIEW

Employment opportunities in medical billing and coding, filing medical insurance, and related jobs are increasing in the United States. The U.S. Department of Labor's Bureau of Labor Statistics (BLS) claims, "Employment is expected to grow much faster than the average. Job prospects should be very good; technicians with a strong background in medical coding will be in particularly high demand. New jobs are expected in offices of physicians as a result of increasing demand for detailed records, especially in large group practices. Technicians with a strong background in medical coding will be particularly high demand."[1]

INSURANCE CLAIMS AND THE MEDICAL OFFICE

In most medical offices, nearly all of a physician's income is from insurance payments related to patient care/visits. Salaries, medical supplies, office supplies, equipment, rent, and utilities all depend on the cash flow generated by the filing of the insurance claims. Prompt and accurate filing is necessary to meet those monthly expenses running a medical office. This is the main role of the medical coder.

To properly file the insurance claims, a medical coder must navigate the ever-changing world of health-care administration. As new technologies are adopted, systems become more complex, increasing the complexity at every level. Most payers of health-care claims have their own standards for timely claim

[1]Bureau of Labor Statistics, U.S. Department of Labor, Occupational Outlook Handbook, 2008-09 Edition, *Medical Records and Health Information Technicians,* on the Internet at http://www.bls.gov/oco/ocos103.htm (visited January 19, 2009).

submission and reimbursement transactions. Inaccurate billing and coding increases administrative costs for providers and delays or denies reimbursement altogether. The medical coder must remain knowledgeable about new information and regulations to prevent incorrect billing and reimbursement.

■ CODING FOR INSURANCE CLAIMS

Insurance companies offer a variety of policies that determine the coverage a patient may have. For most plans, the insurance claim begins with the medical documentation about the patient encounter or visit. The general rule of thumb in the medical insurance and billing industry is: "IF IT ISN'T DOCUMENTED, IT WASN'T DONE, AND THEREFORE IT ISN'T PAYABLE."

A medical coder relies on the entries in the patient's medical chart to document the diagnosis or reason for the service or procedure provided. This information is then converted into codes that represent the diagnosis and examination, surgery, procedure, treatment, or a diagnostic service that the patient received. For example, a patient visiting the office for an examination of a rash would have a diagnosis code assigned for the rash, which is the reason for the visit. A procedure code would be assigned for the examination, which is the service provided. The proper diagnosis and procedure are determined from the medical documentation generated from the patient's visit.

All claim payments depend on the accurate coding of all diagnoses and procedures. The diagnosis and procedure codes on each submitted claim form tell the insurance company what, where, and why a service was performed. The insurance company then decides if the patient's insurance plan covers the rendered service for the reason given on the claim. Precise coding and claim completion will determine if the procedures performed will be considered "medically necessary" by the insurance company, if the service rendered is considered a "benefit" covered by the patient's insurance plan, and ultimately if a "payment" will be issued.

The procedure and diagnostic codes used on claims and various patient encounter forms are alpha and/or numeric. The *International Classification of Diseases, 9th Revision, Clinical Modification*, or ICD-9-CM, is used to represent the diagnosis in a patient encounter.

For example: the ICD-9-CM code 782.1, represents a rash.

The World Health Organization (WHO) maintains the ICD codes, and uses the codes to determine trends in morbidity (death) and mortality (illness) on a global level. Updates to the ICD-9-CM are released throughout the year to keep up with changes and discoveries in illness and disease.

Codes for services or procedures provided in the physician's office are taken from the *Current Procedural Terminology* (CPT), which is developed and maintained by the American Medical Association (AMA). The AMA releases annual updates to the CPT, similar to the ICD-9-CM updates, to keep the codes current with medical advancements and new procedures.

In some cases, additional codes are needed for medical supplies, injectables, and other services not listed in CPT. These codes can be found in the Healthcare Common Procedure Coding System (HCPCS). HCPCS codes are alphanumeric codes maintained by the Centers for Medicare and Medicaid Services (CMS), the same organization responsible for the CPT, and are used in conjunction with ICD-9-CM codes on insurance claims.

For example the CPT code 10060 represents an incision and drainage of an abscess. The HCPCS code J1470, represents an injection of gamma globulin, intramuscular, 2 cc.

Diagnosis and procedure coding will be addressed in detail in Chapters 4, 5, and 6.

■ TYPES OF INSURANCE

Approximately 84% of all patients seen in a medical office today have some type of insurance policy (Fig. 1). Patients may be covered under a government insurance plan, a commercial insurance plan, or a managed care plan. The more common health insurance plans currently in effect in the United States include the following:

■ Medicare—a government insurance plan for the disabled or elderly persons.

■ Medicaid—a government insurance plan for the low-income persons.

■ Group Insurance—a commercial insurance plan offered by an employer or organization.

- Individual Insurance Plans—a personal, commercial insurance plan.
- Health Maintenance Organization (HMO)—a managed care plan.
- Preferred Provider Organization (PPO)—a managed care plan.
- TRICARE/CHAMPVA—medical insurance for active military or veterans and their families.
- Workers' Compensation—a program that requires an employer to cover medical expenses and lost wages for their workers who become injured on-the-job.
- Short- and Long-Term Disability—an insurance plan offered to employees for partial replacement of wages lost as a result of prolonged illness or injury.

Most insurance claims are filed using a universal claim form called the CMS-1500. Additional information and specific guidelines for completing the CMS-1500 will be discussed in Chapter 7.

Despite using the same claim form, the coverage issues and the rules and regulations of insurance change constantly. Understanding and keeping current on the different rules and regulations and codes is a difficult job, but that is what makes the role of medical coder interesting and rewarding.

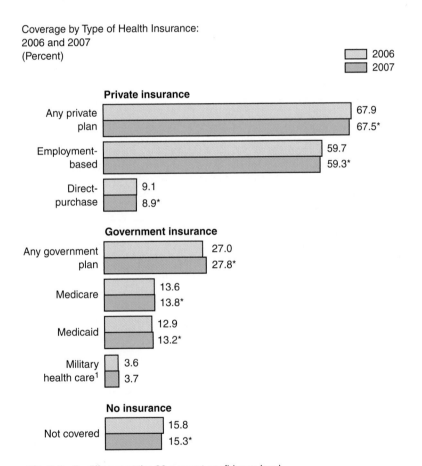

Coverage by Type of Health Insurance:
2006 and 2007
(Percent)

2006
2007

Private insurance

Any private plan	67.9 / 67.5*
Employment-based	59.7 / 59.3*
Direct-purchase	9.1 / 8.9*

Government insurance

Any government plan	27.0 / 27.8*
Medicare	13.6 / 13.8*
Medicaid	12.9 / 13.2*
Military health care[1]	3.6 / 3.7

No insurance

Not covered	15.8 / 15.3*

*Statistically different at the 90-percent confidence level.

[1]Military health care includes CHAMPUS (Comprehensive Health and Medical Plan for Uniformed Services)/Tricare and CHAMPVA (Civilian Health and Medical Program of the Department of Veterans Affairs), as well as care provided by the Department of Veterans Affairs and the military.

Note: The estimates by type of coverage are not mutually exclusive; people can be covered by more than one type of health insurance during the year.

Source: U.S. Census Bureau, Current Population Survey, 2007 and 2008 Annual Social and Economic Supplements.

FIGURE 1: Coverage by Type of Health Insurance: 2006 and 2007. (Source: U.S. Census Bureau, Current Population Survey, 2007 and 2008 Annual Social and Economic Supplements.) http://www.census.gov/prod/2008pubs/p60-235.pdf.

Although the job of being a medical coder in a physician's office may look like a job dealing with a "sea of paperwork," most new employees find they quickly master the process of coding and filing claims. Therefore, it is important for all newcomers who do this work to believe in the POWER OF POSITIVE THINKING—it IS possible to master the art of filing accurate insurance claims!

RESOURCES

American Medical Association (AMA)
http://www.ama-assn.org

American Health Information Management Association (AHIMA)
http://www.ahima.org/medicalcoding/medical_coding_certification.asp

The Bureau of Labor Statistics (BLS)
http://www.bls.gov/oco/ocos103.htm

Centers for Disease Control and Prevention (CDC)
http://www.cdc.gov

Centers for Medicare and Medicaid Services (CMS)
http://www.cms.hhs.gov

Department of Health and Human Services (DHHS)
http://www.dhhs.gov

National Center for Health Statistics
http://www.cdc.gov/nchs

U.S. Census Bureau
http://www.census.gov/prod/2008pubs/p60-235.pdf
http://www.medicalcodingandbilling.com/
http://www.medicalbillingandcoding.net/

Medical Coding Basics

1

A Career in Medical Coding

Chapter Outline

I. The Medical Coder in the Physician's Office
   A. Key Responsibilities
II. The Necessary Tools of the Trade
   A. Patient Data
      1. Personal Information
      2. Referred By
      3. Employment/Student Status
      4. Insurance/Benefit Information
      5. Responsible Parties
      6. Authorizing Signatures
   B. Patient's Medical Records
   C. Insurance Card
   D. Encounter Forms
   E. Computer Skills
      1. Office Statistics
      2. Electronic Claim Forms
   F. Communication Skills
      1. Written Correspondence
      2. Telephone Communication
      3. E-mail Communication
   G. Accuracy
   H. Basic Accounting Skills
   I. Deposit Slips
   J. Coding and Insurance Manuals
      1. CPT, HCPCS, and ICD-9-CM Manuals
      2. Medical Dictionary
      3. Insurance Manuals
III. Professional Credentials
   A. Certification Examinations
   B. Continuing Education
IV. Get Set—Code!

OBJECTIVES

- Define key terms.
- List and describe coding responsibilities.
- Give examples of tools needed.
- Define the components of a patient's medical record and name the two types.
- Understand the importance of an insurance card.
- Describe the make up of an encounter form.
- Name the advantages of a computerized office.
- Develop and practice good communication skills.
- Recognize the importance of accuracy.
- Interpret the need for basic accounting skills.
- List the coding manuals used by the medical coder.
- Define professional credentials.

MEDICAL ASSISTING COMPETENCIES

ABHES

1h. be courteous and diplomatic
1i. conduct work within scope of education, training, and ability
2q. allied health professions and credentialing
3e. locate resources and information for patients and employers
5g. monitor legislation related to current healthcare issues and practices

CAAHEP

IV.C.8. Recognize elements of fundamental writing skills
IV.C.9. Discuss applications of electronic technology in effective communication
IV.P.7. Demonstrate telephone techniques
IV.A.1. Demonstrate empathy in communicating with patients, family and staff
IV. A.7. Demonstrate recognition of the patient's level of understanding in communication
V.C.6. Describe various types of content maintained in a patient's medical record
VI.A.1. Demonstrate sensitivity and professionalism in handling accounts receivable activities with clients

---

KEY TERMS

Assignment of Benefits

Coding Manuals

Electronic Data Interchange (EDI)

Electronic Medical Record

Encounter Form/Route Slip/Superbill

Fiscal Agents

Guarantor

Insurance Card

Insurance Identification Number

Insurance Manuals

Patient Demographics

Patient Ledger

Third-Party Carrier

■ THE MEDICAL CODER IN THE PHYSICIAN'S OFFICE

A medical coder's position could be considered the main artery of any medical office. Knowledge of medical terminology and good communication skills are mandatory for the person responsible for the incoming revenue in the medical practice. In addition to communicating with patients and other health-care workers, this person must be able to correspond with insurance companies and **third-party carriers**. A medical coder conveys information to the insurance companies. That information consists primarily of the patient's diagnoses and procedures performed. The medical coder learns how to transform diagnoses and procedures into alpha-numerical codes that are recognized as the universal coding system used by all insurance companies and federal agencies.

! KEY TERM

THIRD-PARTY CARRIER—An organization that pays or insures health or medical expenses.

The medical coder can be referred to by many different titles, depending on the environment in the medical office. Some of the more common titles include:

- Medical insurance specialist
- Medical coding specialist
- Medical biller
- Insurance billing specialist
- Insurance coding specialist
- Health insurance specialist
- Coder

No matter what the position title, the responsibilities for this position are usually similar.

Key Responsibilities

The size of the office can determine the scope of responsibilities a medical coder may have. In a large practice, there may be specific personnel responsible for posting charges and payments, filing insurance claims, or billing and collections. In a smaller practice, those tasks can be performed by just one person.

Every profession has terms or jargon specific to the nature of the work involved. Medical coders must become skilled at both medical and insurance terminology. They must first be able to understand the language used in medical records to determine a patient's diagnosis and treatment, both of which are needed to properly file an insurance claim. When an insurance company makes or denies a payment for a service provided, the coder must also be able to interpret the information and instructions sent from the insurance company and perform steps to ensure that the services were reimbursed correctly. In this role, it is important to understand all terminology for both fields, along with key abbreviations and acronyms.

In addition to dealing with medical charts and insurance claims, the medical coder often needs to explain insurance benefits and filing procedures to patients. Communication skills can be put to the test when dealing with individuals who are ill or who are under the impression that their insurance policy covers everything. It may be up to the medical coder to explain coverage (or lack of coverage) to patients or their family members. A friendly disposition and precise information is vital.

The medical coder is faced with the challenge of accurately preparing and filing all types of medical and disability claims for the office. The patient's pertinent medical records along with statistical information or demographics, such as address, date of birth, insurance coverage, and place of employment, must be abstracted from the patient's charts and properly recorded on the claim forms. The claim forms are submitted to the insurance companies for reimbursement.

In addition to the patient demographics, the medical coder must be able to comprehend the patient's medical records. Information regarding the rendered services and the reason for those services is recorded in every patient's medical record or chart. As the Introduction has already discussed, that information is converted to medical codes and placed on a claim form by the medical coder. Using the same example of the patient treated for a rash, the medical coder must abstract the exact diagnosis and procedure from the medical record. Based on that information, the coder assigns a diagnosis code and a procedure code. Insurance payments and patient's benefits also must be reviewed, to ensure the proper payment of the submitted claims.

An up-to-date and precise bookkeeping system is critical to a successful practice. The coder must stay current with the latest filing guidelines, rules, and regulations for the major insurance programs in the area. Many of the major insurance programs offer policy manuals to each physician's office. There should be a system to organize this information and make it readily available for reference as often as needed. As new information is received, outdated information should be removed. New information and regulations should be shared with all personnel, including the physicians. When everyone is kept current and a good reference system is in place, everyone, including the patient, benefits. The patient receives the best coverage their insurance plan has to offer and the medical practice receives optimal reimbursement for the services rendered.

The medical coder uses the office bookkeeping system to accurately post all charges, payments, and adjustments to the patient's accounts and accounts receivable journals. Medical services are rendered daily. Payments for these services are received on a daily basis as well, and it is imperative that these transactions be recorded and accounts balanced daily. Monitoring claim reimbursement is the key to proper reimbursement. A request for a payment review for all underpaid claims must be made as soon as they are found.

Insurance rules and regulations change constantly and it is impossible to learn and remember every one of them. Medical coders should take advantage of training seminars offered to them that keep information up-to-date. The local Medicare, Medicaid, commercial insurance, and medical societies often offer ongoing training and continuing education. Private organizations also offer a variety of seminars that educate coders about new insurance and medical coding information. Many of these specific rules and regulations are discussed in later chapters.

■ THE NECESSARY TOOLS OF THE TRADE

To properly complete medical insurance claims, the medical coder needs specific information and material from various sources.

❗ KEY TERM

PATIENT DEMOGRAPHICS—Personal and financial information (e.g., address, date of birth, or insurance coverage) obtained from the patient and kept on file for the billing and processing of claims.

Patient Data

The first time a patient is seen in an office, he or she will be asked to complete a patient information form (Fig. 1–1). This information is crucial to accurate claim filing and should be verified for changes every time the patient is seen. This is the information commonly referred to as the **patient's demographics** and includes the following.

■ **Personal Information**
  ■ Patient's full name
  ■ Gender
  ■ Marital status
  ■ Address and telephone number
  ■ Date of birth
  ■ Social security number
  ■ A contact person in case of an emergency
  ■ Who referred the patient to the physician

Patient Information Form

Please complete information in the spaces provided. Be sure to complete and sign the statement at the bottom of this form.

Patient		
Last Name	First Name	M.I.

Home Address			
Street	City	State	Zip

Phone Numbers & E-mail			
Home	Work	Cell	E-mail

Identity Information	
Social Security Number	Date of Birth

Primary Insurance	
Company Name	Phone Number
Billing Address	
Name of Insured	Relation to Patient
Insured's ID Number	Group Number

Secondary Insurance	
Company Name	Phone Number
Billing Address	
Name of Insured	Relation to Patient
Insured's ID Number	Group Number

Emergency Information		
Emergency Contact Name	Relation	Phone

I authorize the release of any medical or other information necessary to process this claim.
I hereby authorize payment of medical benefits billed to my insurance to John Smith, DO. I hereby accept
responsibility for payment for any service(s) provided to me that is not covered by my insurance. I agree
to pay all co-payments, coinsurance, and deductibles at the time the service is rendered.

_____   _____

Signature of Patient or Guardian   *Date*

FIGURE 1–1: Sample patient information or patient registration form.

■ **Employment/Student Status**

　　■ If the patient is a full- or part-time student

　　■ If employed, the name of the employer

　　■ If married, the spouse's name and employer

■ **Insurance Benefit Information**

　　■ If insured, the name of the insurance company(s) and the identification number(s), and
　　the name of the policyholder

■ **Responsible Parties**

  ■ The name of the person responsible for the bill (referred to as the **guarantor**)

■ **Authorizing Signatures**

  ■ Authorizing signature for information release and benefit assignment

---

⚠ KEY TERM

GUARANTOR—The individual responsible for the payment of the medical bill.

Personal Information

To provide medical services, a physician needs to know personal information about a patient. Key information such as the name of the patient, address, social security number, birth date, and gender are used to identify the patient when filing an insurance claim. It is also advisable to obtain the name of the person(s) who will serve as an emergency contact.

Referred By

If a patient is referred to a physician by another physician this must be documented in the patient's medical record and must be included on the insurance claim form. When a patient is referred to a physician by a friend or family member, that information should not be included on the insurance claim form.

Employment/Student Status

The insurance company will request information regarding the patient's employment or verification if a patient is a student. The insurance company may need to verify that the patient is insured by their plan, and not covered under another insurance plan. For example, if a claim is filed for a female patient who is covered under her husband's insurance plan, the husband's insurance company will want to verify if the female is covered under her own insurance. If that is the case, her plan would be considered the primary plan and would make the first payment toward the services rendered to her. Employment status (full time versus part time) may also indicate whether or not a patient would be offered insurance benefits.

If the patient is a child, the insurance company will need to determine if the child is covered as a dependent under any plan. A child qualifies as a covered dependent if any of the following applies:

■ The child is unmarried and younger than 19 years of age.

■ The child is unmarried, between the ages of 19 and 23 years old, and a full-time student in an accredited secondary school or college.

■ The child is older than 19 years of age but unable to self-support as a result of a mental or physical handicap that began before age 19.

Currently, insurance law does not specify a limiting age for coverage of dependent children. As a matter of common practice, carriers define a dependent child as one who is younger than the age of 19 years, or if the dependent child is enrolled in school as a full-time student, the limiting age is often extended to 23 years.

Insurance/Benefit Information

To properly file an insurance claim, a coder must know the name of the insurance company, who the policyholder is, the insured/policyholder's identification number, and the effective date of the insurance plan. In addition, the coder needs the correct address for sending claims to the insurance company. Much of that information is included on the patient's **insurance card** (Fig. 1–2), and copies of both sides of the card should always be made for the patient's medical record.

⚠ KEY TERMS

INSURANCE CARD—Identification issued to an insured person by his or her insurance company and used to verify or provide information concerning the insured's medical coverage.

INSURANCE IDENTIFICATION NUMBER—The number that appears on the health plan identification card and used in all claims, communications, and inquiries.

| HS | **United Health Systems** |

ID#:   XGA00443   Group #:   4488
Name: **MICHELLE CALABRESE**
Copays: $5 OV, $10 CHIRO, $50 ED

RX: $5

Visit us at: www.UHSystems.com

Member services 1-800-800-1767
Network provider services 1-800-800-1777
Out of network providers 1-800-800-1799

For medical emergencies please dial 911 or go to the nearest emergency room. Please contact your PCP or member services within 24 hours.

For all other care, please contact your PCP.

Refer to your benefit package for coverage descriptions.

Mail Claims to: UHS, Inc., Claims Department
470 Commerce Park
Blueville, CT 06100

UHS rev 12/08

FIGURE 1–2: Front and back of a sample insurance card.

Responsible Parties

In the event that a service is not completely paid for by insurance, the physician's office must know who will be responsible for paying any balance due. This person is considered the **responsible party**, or **guarantor**, and will be required to pay any balance on the patient's account after a visit.

Authorizing Signatures

Most medical offices file the insurance claims for their patients. To release the patient's personal and medical information, the patient (or guarantor, in the case of a minor) must sign a form allowing release of this information. This signature is then referred to as the "signature on file." The release of information authorization is a simple statement that is worded similarly to this:

> **"I authorize the release of any medical or other information necessary for billing purposes."**

This authorization is included on the standard insurance claim form, the CMS-1500 (Fig. 1–3), as follows:

> **"I authorize the release of any medical or other information necessary to process this claim. I also request payment of government benefits either to myself or to the party who accepts assignment below."**

The second sentence in the authorization deals with **assignment of benefits**.

❗ KEY TERM

ASSIGNMENT OF BENEFITS—An agreement signed by the patient directing his or her insurance company to pay the physician or health-care provider directly for any covered service provided.

Assignment of benefits from the patient gives the insurance company the permission to send the payment directly to the physician. This is the second release that patients are asked to sign. The exact wording on the CMS-1500, standard claim form to assign benefits follows:

READ BACK OF FORM BEFORE COMPLETING & SIGNING THIS FORM.
12. PATIENT'S OR AUTHORIZED PERSON'S SIGNATURE I authorize the release of any medical or other information necessary to process this claim. I also request payment of government benefits either to myself or to the party who accepts assignment below.

13. INSURED'S OR AUTHORIZED PERSON'S SIGNATURE I authorize payment of medical benefits to the undersigned physician or supplier for services described below.

SIGNED _____   DATE _____   SIGNED _____

FIGURE 1–3: Boxes 12 and 13 from the CMS-1500 claim form.

> **"I authorize payment of medical benefits to the undersigned physician or supplier for services described below."**

This authorization speeds up the process of reimbursement and relieves the patient from the paperwork involved. However, it does not relieve the patient from the responsibility of paying any balance left after the insurance payment has been received by the physician. This situation is discussed further in Chapter 13. More specific information about proper signature information for the CMS-1500 claims form is presented in Chapter 7.

> **❗ KEY TERM**
>
> ELECTRONIC MEDICAL RECORD—Also known as electronic health record (EHR), is the electronic version of a patient's medical history and demographics.

Patient's Medical Records

The medical records for each patient are commonly referred to as the "patient's chart" or the "patient record." These records can be kept on paper or electronically on a computer. Both types of records have advantages and disadvantages, although more medical offices are moving toward electronic medical records. With any patient records, security and privacy are important issues that must be considered. The Health Insurance Portability and Accountability Act (HIPAA) addresses security and privacy issues and is discussed in Chapter 3.

A patient record is a story of the patient's allergies, symptoms, illnesses, and injuries, and the care given for them. The care given includes examinations, diagnostic procedures, treatments, and surgeries. This information is found in diagnostic and surgical reports, and physician's notes (commonly referred to as progress notes or patient's file). Prescription records and any communication with the patient also should be filed into the patient's chart. The patient records are kept in chronological order, with the latest information always on top. Although every piece of information is important to the quality and continuity of a patient's care, usually the most recent record is the most significant and will be used to properly complete the insurance claim.

Insurance Card

The majority of patients have an insurance identification card (Fig. 1–4), and the card will have the name of the policyholder and an identification number. In some cases, the identification number may be the social security number of the policyholder. Most insurance companies or third-party carriers are adopting their own method of identifying their policyholders. Some may use a set of numbers or

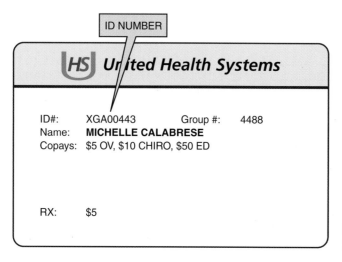

FIGURE 1–4: Front only of insurance card demonstrating ID number.

alphabetic characters or a combination of the two and others may use numbers or letters with a social security number. The numbers or characters are used to identify the policy holder, his or her dependents, and can also be used to establish which group insurance that person is covered under. More information on group and individual insurance coverage can be found in Chapter 7.

The most important thing to remember about a patient's insurance identification card is that a copy of both sides needs to be included with the patient's medical records. In addition to the name of the policyholder and identification number, the card may also contain information about the patient's deductible, copayment, or something specific to the patient's plan. In most cases, the address and phone number of the insurance company will also be provided.

> ### ❗ KEY TERM
>
> ENCOUNTER FORMS (also known as Route Slips or Superbills)—A preprinted list of commonly performed procedures, their fees, and the most common diagnoses of the patients seen in an office.

Encounter Forms

In most medical offices, a form is generated every time a patient receives a service. This form is known as an encounter form, a superbill, a route slip, or a charge slip (Fig. 1–5). The form is preprinted with lists of procedure and diagnosis codes commonly used by the physician's office. It accompanies the patient throughout the office, tracking the diagnosis given and services rendered to the patient. A service is checked to indicate what was provided and a diagnosis to warrant the service. There is usually an area to write in a service, procedure, or diagnosis that is not already printed on the form and an area for any additional patient information, such as when the patient should return for a recheck.

At the end of the patient's visit, the encounter form should be returned to the front office and given to the coder. The information on the form shows the patient's diagnosis (the reason for the visit) and what service(s) were provided. This information is then applied (or "posted") to the patient's account, and is used to generate an insurance claim form.

Computer Skills

Many medical offices today have found the computer to be a most effective tool in billing, filing claims, making appointments, and other recordkeeping tasks. Using a computer, an office can keep track of all of their patient's demographics and financial information. All of the charges and payments made can be recorded in accounts set up for each patient or third-party payer.

Information can even be sent in between computer stations in the office, insurance carriers, or other medical vendors. **Electronic Data Interchange (EDI)** is the process of sending health-care related information from one site to another by computer. Information like health insurance claims, referrals, and precertifications can all be sent by computer networks, limiting the need for administrative paperwork. To protect health information, EDI has very specific privacy and security guidelines, which are discussed in Chapter 3.

> ### ❗ KEY TERM
>
> ELECTRONIC DATA INTERCHANGE—The exchange of claims and other health-care related information by means of computers.

Office Statistics

In addition to lessening office paperwork, the following are just a few of the statistics that can be kept track of with computerized reports:

- Generation of revenue
- Services rendered
- Geographical area the office is serving
- Bad debt collections

Date of service:			
Patient name:		Insurance:	
		Subscriber name:	
Address:		Group #:	Previous balance:
		Copay:	Today's charges:
Phone:		Account #:	Today's payment: check#
DOB: Age: Sex:		Physician name:	Balance due:

Office visit	New	Est
Minimal		99211
Problem focused	99201	99212
Expanded problem focused	99202	99213
Detailed	99203	99214
Comprehensive	99204	99215
Comprehensive (new patient)	99205	
Significant, separate service	−25	−25

Well visit	New	Est
< 1 y	99381	99391
1–4 y	99382	99392
5–11 y	99383	99393
12–17 y	99384	99394
18–39 y	99385	99395
40–64 y	99386	99396
65 y +	99387	99397

Medicare preventive services	
Pap	Q0091
Pelvic & breast	G0101
Prostate/PSA	G0103
Tobacco counseling/3–10 min	G0375
Tobacco counseling/>10 min	G0376
Welcome to Medicare exam	G0344
ECG w/Welcome to Medicare exam	G0402
Flexible sigmoidoscopy	G0403
Hemoccult, guaiac	82270
Flu shot administration	G0008
Pneumonia shot administration	G0009

Inpatient hospital care	
Initial hospital care	99221
Problem focused subsequent hospital care	99231
Expanded problem focused sub. hosp. care	99232
Detailed subsequent hospital care	99233

Other services	
After posted hours	99050
Evening/weekend appointment	99051
Home health certification	G0180
Home health recertification	G0179
Post-op follow-up	99024
Prolonged/30–74 min	99354
Special reports/forms	99080
Disability/Workers' comp	99455

Radiology	

Diagnoses	
1	
2	
3	
4	

Next office visit

Recheck	Prev	PRN	_____ D W M Y

Instructions:

Referral

To:

Instructions:

Physician signature

X _____

Office procedures		
Anoscopy		46600
Audiometry		92551
Cerumen removal		69210
Colposcopy		57452
Colposcopy w/biopsy		57455
ECG, w/interpretation		93000
ECG, rhythm strip		93040
Endometrial biopsy		58100
Flexible sigmoidoscopy		45330
Flexible sigmoidoscopy w/biopsy		45331
Fracture care, cast/splint	29 ____	
Site: _____		
Nebulizer		94640
Nebulizer demo		94664
Spirometry		94010
Spirometry, pre and post		94060
Tympanometry		92567
Vasectomy		55250

Skin procedures		Units
Burn care, initial	16000	
Foreign body, skin, simple	10120	
Foreign body, skin, complex	10121	
I&D, abscess	10060	
I&D, hematoma/seroma	10140	
Laceration repair, simple	120 ___	
Site: _____ Size: _____		
Laceration repair, layered	120 ___	
Site: _____ Size: ____		
Lesion, biopsy, one	11100	
Lesion, biopsy, each add'l	11101	
Lesion, excision, benign	114 ___	
Site: _____ Size: ____		
Lesion, excision, malignant	116 ___	
Site: _____ Size: ____		
Lesion, paring/cutting, one	11055	
Lesion, paring/cutting, 2–4	11056	
Lesion, shave	113 ___	
Site: _____ Size: ____		
Nail removal, partial	11730	
Nail removal, w/matrix	11750	
Skin tag, 1–15	11200	
Wart, flat, 1–14	17110	
Wart, plantar, single	17000	
Wart, plantar, each add'l	17003	

Medications		Units
Ampicillin, up to 500 mg	J0290	
B-12, up to 1,000 mcg	J3420	
Epinephrine, up to 1 ml	J0170	
Kenalog, 10 mg	J3301	
Lidocaine, 10 mg	J2001	
Normal saline, 1,000 cc	J7030	
Phenergan, up to 50 mg	J2550	
Progesterone, 150 mg	J1055	
Rocephin, 250 mg	J0696	
Testosterone, 200 mg	J1080	
Tigan, up to 200 mg	J3250	
Toradol, 15 mg	J1885	

Miscellaneous services	

Laboratory	
Venipuncture	36415
Blood glucose, monitoring device	82962
Blood glucose, visual dipstick	82948
CBC, w/ auto differential	85025
CBC, w/o auto differential	85027
Cholesterol	82465
Hemoccult, guaiac	82270
Hemoccult, immunoassay	82274
Hemoglobin A1C	85018
Lipid panel	80061
Liver panel	80076
KOH prep (skin, hair, nails)	87220
Metabolic panel, basic	80048
Metabolic panel, comprehensive	80053
Mononucleosis	86308
Pregnancy, blood	84703
Pregnancy, urine	81025
Renal panel	80069
Sedimentation rate	85651
Strep, rapid	86403
Strep culture	87081
Strep A	87880
TB	86580
UA, complete, non-automated	81000
UA, w/o micro, non-automated	81002
UA, w/o micro, automated	81003
Urine colony count	87086
Urine culture, presumptive	87088
Wet mount/KOH	87210

Vaccines	
DT, <7 y	90702
DTP	90701
DtaP, <7 y	90700
Flu, 6–35 months	90657
Flu, 3 y +	90658
Hep A, adult	90632
Hep A, ped/adol, 2 dose	90633
Hep B, adult	90746
Hep B, ped/adol 3 dose	90744
Hep B-Hib	90748
Hib, 4 dose	90645
HPV	90649
IPV	90713
MMR	90707
Pneumonia, >2 y	90732
Pneumonia conjugate, <5 y	90669
Td, >7 y	90718
Varicella	90716

Immunizations & Injections		Units
Allergen, one	95115	
Allergen, multiple	95117	
Imm admin, one	90471	
Imm admin, each add'l	90472	
Imm admin, intranasal, one	90473	
Imm admin, intranasal, each add'l	90474	
Injection, joint, small	20600	
Injection, joint, intermediate	20605	
Injection, joint, major	20610	
Injection, ther/therapeutic	20526	
Injection, trigger point	20552	

Supplies	

FIGURE 1-5: Sample encounter form. This form is sometimes called a superbill.

Infectious and Parasitic Diseases

053.9	Herpes zoster, NOS
054.9	Herpetic disease, uncomplicated
075	Mononucleosis
034.0	Strep throat
079.99	Viral infection, unspec.
078.10	Warts, all sites

Neoplasms

Benign Neoplasms
239.2	Skin, soft tissue neoplasm, unspec.
216.9	Skin, unspec.

Endocrine, Nutritional and Metabolic Disorders

Endocrine
250.01	Diabetes I, uncomplicated
250.91	Diabetes I, w/unspec. complications
250.00	Diabetes II/unspec., w/o complications, not uncontrolled
250.90	Diabetes II, w/unspec. complications
242.90	Hyperthyroidism, NOS
244.9	Hypothyroidism, unspec.

Metabolic/Other
274.9	Gout, unspec.
272.0	Hypercholesterolemia
272.2	Hyperlipidemia, mixed
272.1	Hypertriglyceridemia
278.01	Obesity, morbid
278.00	Obesity, NOS
278.02	Overweight

Blood Diseases

285.9	Anemia, other, unspec.

Mental Disorders

300.00	Anxiety state, unspec.
314.00	Attention deficit, w/o hyperactivity
290.0	Dementia, senile, NOS
311	Depression, NOS

Nervous System and Sense Organ Disorders

Nervous System Diseases
354.0	Carpal tunnel
345.90	Epilepsy, unspec., w/o status
346.90	Migraine, unspec., not intractable

Eye Diseases
372.30	Conjunctivitis, unspec.
368.10	Visual disturbance, unspec.

Ears Diseases
380.4	Cerumen impaction
389.9	Hearing loss, unspec.
380.10	Otitis externa, unspec.
382.00	Otitis media, acute

Circulatory System

Arrythmias
427.31	Atrial fibrillation

Cardiac
413.9	Angina pectoris, NOS
428.0	Heart failure, congestive, unspec.
414.9	Ischemic heart disease, chronic, unspec.
424.1	Valvular disorder, aortic, NOS

Vascular
796.2	Elevated BP w/o hypertension
401.1	Hypertension, benign
458.0	Hypotension, orthostatic
443.9	Peripheral vascular disease, unspec.
451.9	Thrombophlebitis, unspec.
459.81	Venous insufficiency, unspec.

Respiratory System

Lower Respiratory Tract
493.90	Asthma, unspec.
466.0	Bronchitis, acute
496	COPD, NOS
486	Pneumonia, unspec.

Upper Respiratory Tract
462	Pharyngitis, acute
477.9	Rhinitis, allergic, cause unspec.
461.9	Sinusitis, acute, NOS
465.9	Upper respiratory infection, acute, NOS

Digestive System

564.00	Constipation, unspec.
562.10	Diverticulosis of colon
562.11	Diverticulitis of colon, NOS
535.50	Gastritis, unspec. w/o hemorrhage
558.9	Gastroenteritis, noninfectious, unspec.
530.81	Gastroesophageal reflux, no esophagitis
455.6	Hemorrhoids. NOS
564.1	Irritable bowel syndrome
578.1	Melena

Genitourinary System

Urinary System Diseases
592.9	Calculus, urinary, unspec.
595.0	Cystitis, acute
599.7	Hematuria
593.9	Renal insufficiency, acute
599.0	Urinary tract infection, unspec./pyuria

Male Genital Organ Diseases
607.84	Impotence, organic
302.72	Impotence, psychosexual dysfunction
601.9	Prostatitis, NOS
257.2	Testicular hypofunction

Breast Diseases
611.72	Breast lump

Female Genital Organ Diseases
616.0	Cervicitis
622.10	Dysplasia, cervix, unspec.
625.9	Pelvic pain, unspec. female disease
616.10	Vaginitis/vulvitis, unspec.

Disorders of Menstruation
626.0	Amenorrhea
627.9	Menopausal disorders, unspec.
626.2	Menstruation, excessive/frequent
625.3	Menstruation, painful
626.6	Metrorrhagia

Pregnancy, Childbirth

641.90	Hemorrhage in preg., unspec.
V24.2	Postpartum follow-up, routine
V22.2	Pregnant state, incidental
V22.0	Prenatal care, normal, first pregnancy
V22.1	Prenatal care, normal, other pregnancy

Skin, Subcutaneous Tissue

706.1	Acne
702.0	Actinic keratosis
682.9	Cellulitis/abscess, unspec.
692.9	Contact dermatitis, NOS
691.8	Eczema, atopic dermatitis
703.0	Ingrown nail
110.1	Onychomycosis
709.9	Other skin disease, unspec.
696.1	Psoriasis, other
695.3	Rosacea
706.2	Sebaceous cyst
702.19	Seborrheic keratosis, NOS
707.9	Ulcer, skin, chronic, unspec.
708.9	Urticaria, unspec.

Musculoskeletal and Connective Tissue

General
716.90	Arthropathy, unspec.
729.1	Fibromyositis
715.90	Osteoarthrosis, unspec.
733.00	Osteoporosis, unspec.
714.0	Rheumatoid arthritis
727.00	Synovitis/tenosynovitis, unspec.

Lower Extremity
729.5	Pain in limb
728.71	Plantar fasciitis

Spine/Torso
724.4	Back pain w/ radiation, unspec.
723.9	Cervical disorder, NOS

Upper Extremity
726.32	Lateral epicondylitis
726.10	Rotator cuff syndrome, NOS

Perinatal (Infant)

779.3	Feeding problem, newborn

Signs and Symptoms

789.00	Abdominal pain, unspec.
795.01	Abnormal Pap, ASC-US
719.40	Arthralgia, unspec.
569.3	Bleeding, rectal
786.50	Chest pain, unspec.
786.2	Cough
787.91	Diarrhea, NOS
780.4	Dizziness/vertigo, NOS
787.2	Dysphagia
788.1	Dysuria
782.3	Edema, localized, NOS
783.3	Feeding problem, infant/elderly
780.6	Fever, nonperinatal
271.9	Glucose intolerance
784.0	Headache, unspec.
788.30	Incontinence/enuresis, NOS
782.2	Localized swelling/mass, superficial
785.6	Lymph nodes, enlarged
780.79	Malaise and fatigue, other
787.02	Nausea, alone
787.01	Nausea w/ vomiting
719.46	Pain, knee
724.2	Pain, low back
785.1	Palpitations
788.42	Polyuria
782.1	Rash, nonvesicular, unspec.
782.0	Sensory disturbance skin
786.05	Shortness of breath
780.2	Syncope
788.41	Urinary frequency
787.03	Vomiting, alone
783.21	Weight loss

Injuries and Adverse Effects

Dislocations, Sprains, and Strains
845.00	Sprain/strain: ankle, unspec.
845.10	Sprain/strain: foot, unspec.
842.10	Sprain/strain: hand, unspec.
844.9	Sprain/strain: knee/leg, unspec.
847.0	Sprain/strain: neck, unspec.
840.9	Sprain/strain: shoulder/upper arm, unspec.
842.00	Sprain/strain: wrist, unspec.

Other Trauma, Adverse Effects
919.0	Abrasion, unspec.
924.9	Contusion, unspec.
919.4	Insect bite
894.0	Open wound, lower limb, unspec.
884.0	Open wound, upper limb, unspec.

Supplemental Classification

V72.32	Confirm norm Pap after initial abn
V25.01	Contraception, oral
V25.02	Contraception, other (diaphragm, etc.)
V25.2	Contraception, sterilization
V58.30	Dressing change, nonsurgical
V01.9	Exposure, infectious disease, unspec.
V72.31	Gynecological exam
V06.8	Immunization, combination, other
V06.1	Immunization, DTP
V04.81	Immunization, influenza
V70.0	Well adult check
V20.2	Well child check

FIGURE 1–5: cont'd

By tracking this information, a medical office can make better decisions about patient care, financial practices, and the internal revenue cycle. A computer system can easily pull important data from patient records, and provide reports to the office staff of important statistics.

! **KEY TERM**

FISCAL AGENT—An association contracted to provide a system for processing data, claim processing, and the administrative duties for Medicare or Medicaid.

Electronic Claim Forms

The biggest time-saving measure office computerization can offer is *claim form generation*. Started in the early 1980s by Medicare fiscal agents, electronic claims submission has become the practical way to submit claims to any insurance company or **fiscal agent** that has the capability of accepting them. Claims submitted electronically contained fewer errors and omissions than those on paper. These claims also mean less handling, clerical work, postage, and sorting for insurance personnel. Electronically submitted claims improve the cash flow of the office. Payment of electronic claims can be expected in 2 weeks or less, whereas payment for a paper claim can take from 4 to 6 weeks to receive.

To file a claim electronically, the medical coder enters the data for the service and diagnosis of each patient encounter. The computer completes the claim forms, tracks claims for reimbursement, and generates claims for any secondary insurance or claim needing to be resubmitted. However, even though this method is more efficient overall, specific billing standards have been developed for proper electronic claims submission. Chapter 3 explains in detail the implications of standardized health insurance billing.

Communication Skills

Everyone has been taught the importance of good oral and written communication skills, but not everyone may know the importance of those learned skills. A medical coder communicates with many different individuals on many different levels. It is important to realize that the coder is representing the physician and the practice. He or she will be judged by the way in which personal ideas, thoughts, and opinions are conveyed and this judgment has an effect on the outcome of the exchange and on the reputation of the medical practice.

A great deal of human communication comes from unspoken gestures that often help make a statement comprehensible. During communication, a message is verbally communicated and nonverbally transmitted. Nonverbal communication is conveyed through vocal tones and facial expressions. In the medical office, communication may be face to face, but a medical coder is more likely to communicate on the telephone, through written correspondence, or by e-mail. This means a medical coder must be clear in all verbal and written communications and cannot rely on nonverbal cues to convey the message.

For the medical coder, most communications focus on requesting information from other professionals such as physicians or other coders and with insurance companies or Medicare/Medicaid carriers. Conversations with patients may deal with matters that range from insurance coverage to a past-due account or who is liable for the bill when the parents of a child have been divorced. In all of these communications, it is important to remember that customer satisfaction is a key responsibility for any office staff member.

Citing data from a national poll, Table 1–1 illustrates customer satisfaction in medical and dental offices and shows good manners are a key element to patient happiness. Only 45% of the patients polled felt that the overall office had good manners and only 38% felt that the front office staff was courteous. There is a lot of room for improvement in this area! (See Box 1–1.)

Written Correspondence

Formal written correspondence, such as letters and accounting statements, should always have proper grammar and spelling. The use of computer-generated documents makes proofing material for spelling errors very easy, but spell check will not correct grammatical errors and may miss usage errors for correctly spelled words. Because of this, it is extremely important to get into the habit of using a basic dictionary and a medical one, and to always read over any piece of correspondence before sending it out.

TABLE 1–1:   Customer Satisfaction in Medical and Dental Practices

Patients Rate Dental and Medical Practices	% of Patients Who Agree
1) Front office team is courteous	**38**
2) Clinical team is courteous	**49**
3) Overall, the entire team displays excellent manners toward patients	**45**
4) Team behaves professionally toward each other	**44**
5) Patients are treated with respect in the office	**48**
6) Office runs on time for appointments	**16**
7) Doctor is attentive and listens	**54**
8) Patient places high trust in the doctor	**57**
9) Excellent clinical care is provided by the office	**47**
10) Fees are reasonable	**35**

Source: National Poll, 2002, Suzanne Boswell Presentations.
Source Unmasking the Patient Perspective, Suzanne Boswell.
Suzanneboswell.com/HealthcarePicture.pdf.

BOX 1–1: The Importance of Courtesy

Being courteous doesn't just pertain to your patients. You also need to extend that to *any* insurance carrier you deal with. Michael T. Myers, Jr., MD, MBA, served as the Medicare carrier for Part B in Maine, Massachusetts, New Hampshire, and Vermont from 1995 through 1998. Here is what he wrote about being courteous:

   "Coding professionals are generally the first (and sometimes the only) point of contact between the physician/hospital and the Medicare intermediary (carrier). Nerves are frayed . . . and it can sometimes be tempting to let that so-and-so on the phone from Provider Relations (department at Medicare) really have a good piece of your mind due to the frustration that attends Medicare billing. But before you let loose, remember this little piece of advice from my grandmother, 'Let your manners be superb'."

   He goes on to say, "More than ever you need a strategy for dealing with your Medicare intermediary, one that will get you the assistance, and maybe some inside information, that will help you cope with your Medicare billing. . . . Don't wait until you have a problem to get in contact with your Medicare intermediary. Find an excuse (inquire about an upcoming carrier-sponsored seminar or ask a question about something you read in the newsletter) to make human contact with someone in Provider Relations, Utilization Management, or even the Carrier Medical Director. The point here is to develop a relationship with someone at the intermediary so that when a problem does arise you have ally who can help you negotiate the maze inside the Medicare contractor's resources."

From Myers MT Jr. Working With Your Medicare Intermediary: Let Your Manners Be Superb, *AAPC Coding Edge, January 2002.*

Telephone Communication

Effective telephone communication is an important element of quality medical services provided in a physician's office. Even though the majority of calls the medical coder handles deal with patient's accounts and insurance coverage, proper telephone etiquette should be observed at all times. The coder's own personal attitude on the phone establishes the tone of the call and the how the person on the other end responds. The impression given on the phone reflects on the physician's practice, not just the medical coder.

   Remember, the person on the other end of the phone may be a patient who is not feeling well, someone who may be hard of hearing, or someone worried or upset over his or her account. Always take into account who is on the call and use the words and terms that are familiar to the person on the other end. Information commonly discussed in the medical office may be unfamiliar to the patient and may be confusing if not explained properly.

   Be prepared to make or take calls. In most cases, this means having paper and a writing implement ready to make notes or document the call. Always note the date, name, and nature of the call. These notes make follow-up easier, and may even become part of the patient record, if the information is deemed important to a patient's care.

For many people, e-mail is now a standard way of communicating with others literally around the world. Most businesses have also adopted the use of e-mail to communicate with customers and business partners. An individual may receive thousands of e-mails each year, and millions of e-mails are sent every day. Most people give very little thought to the contents of an e-mail message, but the same attention should be given to an e-mail as is given to a written document sent out from the medical office. Messages with careless wording can cause problems for the medical coder and even the physician.

Like telephone communication, an e-mail message does not come with facial expressions or gestures that would be present in a face-to-face conversation, and there is no tone of voice to interpret. Be very clear with messages because subtleties can be lost or completely misunderstood. Remember this, too, when reading e-mails from others. Their choice of words, or haste in writing the e-mail, may give it a "virtual attitude" that may seem offensive or unfriendly.

Remember that it can be difficult to express irony and humor in e-mail, and to think about how e-mails are worded before sending them. Many people use smiley faces such as ":)" to indicate humor, but not everyone is familiar with e-mail shorthand, and it may not be appropriate to use shorthand in business situations. If someone makes a mistake, a spelling error, asks an unintelligent question, or gives an unnecessarily long answer, remember to have patience. Read over the message again and be sure the message is not misinterpreted.

Be sure to not be offensive, threatening, or abusive in e-mail communication. Ask, "Would I say this to the person's face?" If the answer is no, rewrite the message until it is something that would be said in a live conversation. Being professional and having good manners are indispensable here.

E-mail systems in the work place can be set up to be backed up onto tape and those tapes can be archived to allow access to mail that you had previously thought was gone forever. There have been several instances in which archived e-mails have been recovered and used in legal cases.

Accuracy

The accuracy of the information submitted to insurance companies and the payment received from the insurance claims depends on the accuracy of the medical coder. More than likely, the coder is recording the patient's data in the medical record, whether on computer or on paper. No matter the method, missing even one number when entering a patient's **insurance identification number** will either generate a claim that is denied payment by the insurance company or a claim on a totally different person, who may not be a patient. These types of errors could result in a number of violations of privacy and unethical procedures, and health-care providers can be held accountable for using and disclosing patient's health information improperly. More discussion of these laws and violations is in Chapter 3.

! **KEY TERM**

PATIENT LEDGER—An individual financial document of the patient's services, charges, balance, and payments.

Basic Accounting Skills

Basic math and accounting skills are required to efficiently manage the financial aspects of the medical coder position. The importance of an orderly, legible medical record has already been discussed, and the patient's financial account also needs to be orderly and legible, for many of the same reasons.

There are several ways in which an office may organize a patient's financial record. There may be one account for each patient or there may be one account for an entire family; the organization depends on the patient management system used in the medical office.

Each service provided in the office has a fee determined. Each separate service is recorded into the patient's account and submitted on a claim form; the insurance company pays on each of those services separately. If an office is computerized, that information is automatically included on an electronic claim form to be sent to the insurance company.

A computerized accounts receivable program acts like a calculator. As services received by the patient are entered in the program, it adds those amounts to the patient's balance, and as payments are recorded (or "posted") to the patient's record, it automatically deducts the payment amounts from the account. The computer program also can generate a bill or statement that is printed out and sent to the patient, showing all of the monthly activity on an account.

If the office is using paper recordkeeping, the services and corresponding fees are manually written on what is called a **patient ledger** card. A ledger card is a financial document of the patient's services, charges, balance, and payments, and the medical coder may be responsible for the accuracy of the financial information included on the ledger card. Without the computer, the office staff has to manually make entries every time there is a service or a payment made on the account, maintain an accurate balance, and make a copy of each ledger card to be sent to the patient.

When an insurance payment is made toward the service received by the patient, accounting skills also are used. The amount generated by a service rendered is posted to the patient's account, creating a new balance, and, depending on the payment received, another amount may need to be subtracted from the balance. A computerized or a manually produced statement is then generated and sent to the patient.

Deposit Slips

After all payments from the insurance companies and from the patients have been posted to the appropriate accounts, the medical coder may be responsible for completing a bank deposit slip (Fig. 1–6), depending on the policies of the medical office. All checks must be endorsed before they can be deposited, usually by a standardized stamp that has been created to represent the physician's practice. The checks and cash received for the day must be totaled and verified for accuracy, and the deposit slip should be the same amount of the payments posted to the patient's accounts.

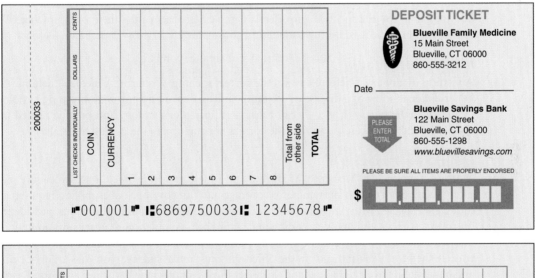

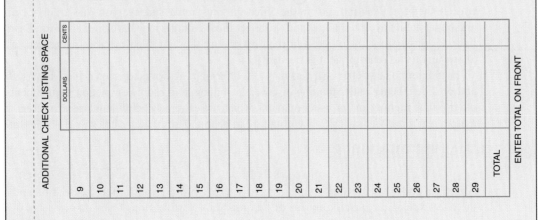

FIGURE 1–6: Deposit slip.

! KEY TERMS

CODING MANUALS—Guidebooks containing the alpha/numerical codes used to represent medical procedures, services, and patient diagnoses.

INSURANCE MANUALS—Guidebooks maintained by an insurance company containing the coverage, billing, and claims processing regulations followed by that company.

Coding and Insurance Manuals

Of all the tools needed to perform the job of a medical coder, the job cannot be completed without the following:

- A Current Procedural Terminology (CPT) manual
- A current International Classification of Diseases 9th Revision Clinical Modification (ICD-9-CM)
- A current edition of Healthcare Common Procedure Coding System (HCPCS) manual
- A medical dictionary
- Insurance carrier/company manuals and informational publications

CPT, HCPCS, and ICD-9-CM Manuals

The CPT manual, which contains the numeric codes that represent the medical services, is revised every year, along with the HCPCS manual. These new editions *must* be used for all services rendered after the first of every new year.

The ICD-9-CM is also updated every year and is usually available in late summer or early fall, allowing time for the medical providers to implement them into their own practice. The current ICD-9-CM must be used on the patient's diagnoses, for all services rendered on October 1 and after.

Medical Dictionary

A medical dictionary is helpful beyond the correct spelling of a term. A medical dictionary provides a better understanding of a disease or condition and an explanation of anatomy and physiology. Entries in a medical dictionary (Fig. 1–7) can clarify confusing terminology and provide related information that a medical coder can use to find the correct information in the coding manuals.

Insurance Manuals

Many carriers such as Medicare, Medicaid, and Blue Cross Blue Shield have procedure manuals that offer specific information pertaining to coverage and noncoverage issues, billing requirements, procedures, and policies. Most carriers also send out newsletters and publications that provide information on coverage issues and updates, coding and claim form completion requirements, and any additional information that will help aid in the billing/payment process. The medical coder is often responsible to educate the physicians and staff in the office and must make sure everyone has an opportunity to read and understand any new changes and the affect those changes may have on their work. Distribute these bulletins throughout the office, and then make sure they are filed or cross-referenced in a way that allows anyone to refer to them as needed.

In addition to newsletters, carriers may also offer training workshops to keep medical staff up-to-date and provide a better understanding of coverage, billing, and claim completion requirements. Medicare offers online training and provider manuals, which are extremely helpful and easy to access. More information regarding Medicare's online training can be found at www.cms.hhs.gov/MLNGenInfo.

PROFESSIONAL CREDENTIALS

A medical coder has the opportunity to certify with a professional coding association and can choose the right type of certification for his or her job. Some certifications focus on physician office coding, others cover facility-based coding, and still others deal specifically with the payers involved in medical insurance claims. Choosing the right certification depends on the type of office and the type of work the medical coder is doing.

opment of a localized area of the skin, usually on the scalp. The area is usually covered by a thin, translucent membrane.

thymic a. A sometimes fatal disorder in which the thymus fails to develop, causing a deficiency of gamma globulin. There is a deficiency of lymph tissue throughout the body. SYN: *thymic alymphoplasia.*

Apley's compression/distraction test (ăp′lēz) A test for differentiating knee pain caused by meniscal injuries from pain caused by ligament sprains. The test is performed with the patient prone and the knee flexed to 90°. With the femur stabilized, the leg is distracted and rotated internally and externally. An axial load is then applied to the leg while the tibia is again internally and externally rotated. Pain produced only when the leg is compressed indicates a meniscal lesion; pain produced only when the leg is distracted indicates ligament trauma.

Apley's scratch test (ăp′lēz) A test of shoulder function with several variations designed to detect asymmetries in range of motion observed during adduction, flexion, extension, internal rotation, and external rotation. The patient performs instructed movements involving positioning the hand to touch the opposite shoulder in the scapular region from behind the back and over the shoulder.

APMA. *American Podiatric Medical Association.* Formerly called the American Podiatry Association.

APN *Advanced practice nurse.*

APNA American Psychiatric Nurses Association.

apnea (ăp-nē′ă) [″ + *pnoe,* breathing] Temporary cessation of breathing and, therefore, of the body's intake of oxygen and release of carbon dioxide. It is a serious symptom, esp. in patients with other potentially life-threatening conditions. SEE: *apnea monitoring; Cheyne-Stokes respiration; sleep apnea; sudden infant death syndrome.*

central a. Absence of breathing during sleep that occurs when the respiratory center of the brainstem does not send normal periodic signals to the muscles of respiration. Observation of the patient reveals no respiratory effort, that is, no movement of the chest, and no breath sounds.

deglutition a. Cessation of breathing while swallowing.

a.–hypopnea index A measure of sleep-disordered breathing based on the number of episodes of apnea or periods of inadequate ventilation during sleep.

mixed a. Dysfunctional breathing during sleep that combines elements of obstructive and central sleep apneas.

obstructive a. Absent or dysfunc-

tional breathing that occurs when the upper airway is intermittently blocked during sleep. Observation of the patient reveals vigorous but ineffective respiratory efforts, often with loud snoring or snorting.

a. of prematurity ABBR: AOP. A condition of the premature newborn, marked by repeated episodes of apnea lasting longer than 20 sec. The diagnosis of AOP is one of exclusion, made when no treatable cause can be found. Increased frequency of apneic episodes directly relates to the degree of prematurity. AOP is not an independent risk factor for sudden infant death syndrome. Apneic episodes may result in bradycardia, hypoxia, and respiratory acidosis.

TREATMENT: There is no specific treatment; however, initial efforts should begin with the least invasive method possible. Tactile stimulation is often successful with early recognition. When gentle stimulation does not produce a response, bag and mask ventilation is initiated. Methylxanthines such as caffeine, theophylline, and aminophylline are helpful.

PATIENT CARE: Care should include maintenance of a neutral thermal environment, avoidance of prolonged oral feedings, use of tactile stimulation early in the apneic episode, and ventilatory support as needed. The infant who has experienced and survived an episode of apnea is maintained on cardiac and respiratory monitoring devices. Before discharge, parents are taught cardiopulmonary resuscitation, use of monitoring equipment, and how to recognize signs of medication toxicity if medications are used.

sleep a. Sleep apnea.

apnea alarm mattress A mattress that is designed to sound an alarm when the infant lying on it ceases to breathe. SEE: *apnea monitoring; sudden infant death syndrome.*

apnea monitoring Monitoring the respiratory movements, esp. of infants. This may be done by use of an apnea alarm mattress, or devices to measure the infant's thoracic and abdominal movements and heart rate. SEE: *sudden infant death syndrome.*

apnea test A test used to determine whether a comatose person receiving life support has suffered brain death.

PATIENT CARE: The patient's ventilator is set to deliver no breaths per minute, and the carbon dioxide level of the blood is allowed to rise above 60 mm Hg. If apnea (no spontaneous breathing) occurs, brain death is confirmed. The test should not be performed if the person has recently received sedative, narcotic, or paralytic drugs; those drugs

FIGURE 1–7: An entry from a medical dictionary can provide extra information that will help interpret the information from the medical record.

The benefits of being a certified coder make it worth the invested time and effort. With similar experience, certified coders receive a higher salary than noncertified coders, and certification is preferred for many employment opportunities. Being certified shows knowledge of the subject matter and a dedication to the coding profession, making certified coders in higher demand by physicians, facilities, and payers.

Certification Examinations

The American Academy of Professional Coders (AAPC) offers three certification examinations. The Certified Professional Coder (CPC), available for people working in a physician's office/clinic, Certified Professional Coder-Hospital (CPC-H) for outpatient facility coders and the Certified Professional Coder-Payer (CPC-P). The AAPC also offers specialty credentialing to their certified coders. Those applicants who are successful in passing the certification examination, but have not met the required "coding work experience," will be awarded the initial designation "CPC-A", "CPC-H-A", or "CPC-P-A." Visit the AAPC website at: www.aapc.com for information and guidelines about the different examinations.

The American Health Information Association (AHIMA) offers three examinations. The Certified Coding Associate certifies a new coder just entering the field. The Certified Coding Specialist (CCS) certifies your knowledge in ICD-9-CM and CPT surgery coding as well as patient documentation, data integrity, anatomy, physiology, and pharmacology. The Certified Coding Specialist-Physician-based (CCS-P) certifies your expertise in multi-specialty CPT, ICD-9-CM, and HCPCS National Level II coding. Information regarding AHIMA and its examinations can be found at: www.ahima.org.

The Alliance of Claims Assistance Professionals (ACAP) also offers several certification examinations: the Certified Claims Assistance Professional (CCAP), the Certified Electronic Claims Professional (CECP), and the Claims Assistance Professional (CAP). For more information, contact the ACAP at www.claims.org.

Continuing Education

Each certification has continuing education requirements and the medical coder is responsible for keeping up with those requirements. Depending on the organization, a certified coding specialist may need to take specific courses, attend annual seminars, or complete online coursework. These requirements ensure that certified coders are up-to-date with new information and material.

■ GET SET—CODE!

Chapter 1 lays the ground work for billing and coding. The following chapters provide detail and insight into coding procedures and diagnoses, completing claim forms and posting insurance payments for various third-party carriers. The financial success of a medical practice is dependent on this knowledge. The medical coder must stay informed and use the tools and references discussed in Chapter 1. This is not a profession where an individual can ever know all of the answers or memorize all of the codes. The job is to know where to find the correct answers and implement them accordingly.

RESOURCE LIST
For information regarding coding:

American Medical Association (AMA)
515 N. State Street
Chicago, IL 60610
(800) 621-8335
  www.ama-assn.org

AHA Central Office
American Hospital Association
1 North Franklin
Chicago, IL 60606
Phone: (312) 422-3366
  www.hospitalconnect.com/ahacentraloffice/index.html

Centers for Medicare and Medicaid Services
7500 Security Boulevard
Baltimore, MD 21244
   www.cms.gov

For information regarding coding certification:

The American Academy of Professional Coders (AAPC)
2480 South 3850 West, Suite B
Salt Lake City, Utah 84120
(800) 626-CODE(2633)
   www.aapc.com

The American Health Information Association (AHIMA)
233 N. Michigan Avenue, 21st Floor
Chicago, IL 60601-5800
(312) 233-1100
   www.ahima.org

The Alliance of Claims Assistance Professionals (ACAP)
873 Brentwood Drive
West Chicago, IL 60185-3743
   www.claims.org

For information regarding Internet etiquette and writing:
   www.albion.com/netiquette
   http://www.dynamoo.com/technical/etiquette.htm

Netiquette, Virginia Shea, Albion Books, 1994.
   Garner's Modern American Usage, 3ed. Bryan A. Garner, Oxford University Press, USA, 2009.
   Taber's Cyclopedic Medical Dictionary, 21st ed. Philadelphia: FA Davis Company, 2009.

Chapter Review Exercises

1. List and describe coding responsibilities.

   _____

   _____

   _____

   _____

   _____

2. Name four tools used by the medical coder.

   a. _____

   b. _____

   c. _____

   d. _____

3. Name the two types of medical records.

   a. _____

   b. _____

4. The patient's medical record is more commonly referred to as (name one):

   _____

5. What is the most important thing to remember about a patient's insurance card?

   _____

   _____

   _____

6. An Encounter Form can also be referred to as: _____

7. Name two advantages of a computerized office

   a. _____

   b. _____

8. Reimbursement from third party carriers can be made to the medical provider via:

   1) _____ 2) _____

9. E-mail can be used in court.   **True or False** (circle one)

10. Recordkeeping for a medical office may use a paper or computerized system to conduct all transactions.   **True or False** (circle one)

11. List and describe the coding books used by the medical coder

    _____

    _____

    _____

    _____

    _____

12. In which coding book will you find diagnoses codes? _____

13. Name the two sources where a coder will find procedure codes.

_____

_____

14. Five years of in-office training must be completed in order to obtain credentials as a certified coder. **True or False** (Circle one.)

15. Information that is transferred to an insurance company after a patient has received a medical encounter consists of two things. Name two:

a. _____

b. _____

The Legal Aspect of Coding and Billing

Chapter Outline

OBJECTIVES

● List the contents of the patient's medical record
● Explain the difference between subjective and objective information in a patient's record
● State the reasons for keeping patient records
● Describe the procedures for corrections or additions to a medical record
● Recognize the importance of patient privacy
● Explain record storage and the destruction of records
● Cite the legal use of the telephone, facsimile, and e-mail

MEDICAL ASSISTING COMPETENCIES

ABHES

1b. maintain confidentiality at all times
1d. be cognizant of ethical boundaries
1i. conduct work within scope of education, training, and ability
2d. serve as a liaison between Physician and others
2e. use proper telephone techniques
2p. professional components
3b. prepare and maintain medical records
3e. locate resources and information for patients and employers
5b. document accurately
5c. use appropriate guidelines when releasing records or information

CAAHEP

IV.P.2. Report relevant information to others succinctly and accurately
IV.A.8. Analyze communications in providing appropriate responses/feedback
IV.A.9. Recognize and protect personal boundaries in communication with others
V.C.5. Identify systems for organizing medical records
V.C.6. Describe various types of content maintained in a patient's medical record
IX.C.2. Explore issue of confidentiality as it applies to the medical assistant
IX.P.1. Respond to issues of confidentiality
IX.P.2. Perform within the scope of practice
IX.P.7. Document accurately in the patient record
IX.P.8. Apply local, state and federal health care legislation and regulation appropriate to the medical assisting practice setting
IX.P.1. Demonstrate sensitivity to patient rights
IX.P.2. Demonstrate awareness of the consequences of not working within the legal scope of practice
IX.P.3. Recognize the importance of local, state and federal legislation and regulations in the practice setting
X.C.1. Differentiate between legal, ethical, and moral issues affecting healthcare
X.P.1. Report illegal and/or unsafe activities and behaviors that affect health, safety and welfare of other is proper authorities
X.A.1. Apply ethical behaviors, including honesty/integrity in performance of medical assisting practice
X.A.2. Examine the impact personal ethics and morals may have on the individual's practice

KEY TERMS

Administrative Disclosure

Assessment

Audit

Authorization

Compliance

Confidentiality

Consent

Disclaimer

Judicial or Statutory
Disclosure

National Correct Coding
Initiative (NCCI)

Office of Inspector
General (OIG)

Problem-Oriented Medical
Record (POMR)

Sanctions

SOAP Notes

Voluntary Disclosure

INTRODUCTION

Thorough and detailed medical records are essential to providing optimal care for each patient in the medical office. The records are a chronicle of each patient's progress, treatment, and therapy, from the first encounter in the office to the last.

Keeping accurate medical records is important for three main reasons:

1. Accurate records provide continuity of the patient's care. A patient's personal, family, and social histories, past surgeries, and previous treatment outcomes all play an important role in future treatment plans. A medical record that is kept accurately and complete provides this valid information and allows for appropriate judgment and treatment plans for ongoing care.

2. Accurate records prevent legal problems. If a patient involves a physician in a lawsuit, the patient's medical records will either tell an accurate story of the proper course of treatment or indicate wrong doing on the part of the physician and their staff.

3. Accurate records provide documentation during an **audit**. Insurance companies, Medicare, and Medicaid all perform periodic audits on providers to ensure services were rendered according to billing records. The medical record must document that the services billed to the insurance company were actually provided to the patient. One of the most important things to remember in the medical office: **If it isn't documented, it didn't happen, and therefore, it is not billable.**

! KEY TERM

AUDIT—To examine patient records, accounts, and claims for accuracy and verification.

MEDICAL RECORDS

There are several ways an office keeps medical records in order. Generally, the contents are as follows:

1. A Patient Information Sheet that contains information on a current address, a responsible party, current insurance information, **authorization** to release medical information to an insurance company, and authorization for the insurance company to pay the physician's office directly (Fig. 2–1).

2. A copy of the patient's current insurance card, front and back. This provides the office with the patient's identification number and the proper address to submit insurance claims.

3. A signature or receipt documenting the patient reviewed the office's privacy practice for Health Insurance Portability and Accessibility Act (HIPAA) **compliance**.

4. Progress notes that contain a chronological order of conditions, diagnostic services, and treatment plans (Fig. 2–2).

Patient Information Form

Please complete information in the spaces provided. Be sure to complete and sign the statement at the bottom of this form.

Patient		
Last Name	First Name	M.I.
Smith	John	J

Home Address			
Street	City	State	Zip
47474 Anystreet	Anycity	Anystate	21212

Phone Numbers & E-mail			
Home	Work	Cell	E-mail
XXX-XXX-XXXX	XXX-XXX-XXXX	XXX-XXX-XXXX	jjsmi@email.com

Identity Information	
Social Security Number	Date of Birth
XXX-XX-XXXX	4-15-XXXX

Primary Insurance	
Company Name	Phone Number
UR Covered	XXX-XXX-XXXX
Billing Address	
4567 Allstreets Anycity, Anystate 55666	
Name of Insured	Relation to Patient
Same	Same
Insured's ID Number	Group Number
235689	1234

Secondary Insurance	
Company Name	Phone Number
None	
Billing Address	
Name of Insured	Relation to Patient
Insured's ID Number	Group Number

Emergency Information		
Emergency Contact Name	Relation	Phone
Eve Smith	Wife	Cell=XXX-XXX-XXXX

I authorize the release of any medical or other information necessary to process this claim.
I hereby authorize payment of medical benefits billed to my insurance to John Smith, DO. I hereby accept responsibility for payment for any service(s) provided to me that is not covered by my insurance. I agree to pay all co-payments, coinsurance, and deductibles at the time the service is rendered.

John Smith
_____
Signature of Patient or Guardian

5 /XX /XXXX
_____
Date

FIGURE 2-1: Patient Information.

Progress Note	
Name:	
Date:	

FIGURE 2-2: Progress Note.

5. Laboratory, pathology, and radiology reports that show results of diagnostic tests done on the patient.

6. Prescription medication dispensed to the patient. The patient's medical record should contain a notation every time a medication is dispensed or refilled for the patient, along with dosage and directions given.

7. Operative Reports for any surgical procedures done during the treatment of the patients. These reports should always be included in the record.

8. An immunization record for children.

9. All correspondence with the patient. This can include letters or documentation of any phone calls.

10. All correspondence with other health-care providers involved in the patient's care. This can include anything from consultation reports to correspondence with insurance carriers on the patient's behalf.

⚠ KEY TERMS

AUTHORIZATION—1. A patient grants the medical provider permission to release medical records to a third party or grants the third-party carrier permission to pay the insurance company directly. 2. Issued by a third-party carrier after determining that a service is medically necessary.
COMPLIANCE—To follow the rules.

Consent and Authorization

Medical records are legal documents that belong to the individual or facility that created them, such as a physician or hospital. However, the information contained in medical records belongs to the patients, and they have the right to the information the records hold. This is why **confidentiality** and protecting patients' right to privacy are key issues in a medical office.

The physician and office staff cannot legally disclose patient information without **consent** from the patient or authorized guardian (or otherwise required by law). Within the medical practice, patient information can be shared among staff members, provided the staff members have the right to the information under the practice's confidentiality policy. Box 2–1 lists guidelines for the release of medical records.

Authorization for Insurance Claims

Every patient and/or guardian must sign an authorization to release confidential information. This authorizes the processing of claim forms without a patient's actual signature appearing on each form. The phrase "signature on file" is sufficient, but it must be typed in block 12 of each CMS-1500 claim form filed.

BOX 2–1: General Rules on the Release of Medical Records

1. Always obtain a written or a signed authorization before releasing records to third parties. This includes other physicians unless a medical emergency exists.
2. All releases should include the date released, the patient's request for release, who or where the records will be released to, and the patient's or legal guardian's signature.
3. A copy of the authorization or a notation regarding the release should be entered into the patient's medical record.
4. Photocopies of the requested records should be given. Original records should not be released.
5. A reasonable charge for the cost of copying the records may be charged to the third party.
6. Medical records cannot be withheld because of an account balance.
7. The patient's health or insurance payment may depend on the release of records. All requests should be honored without delay.
8. Legal counsel should be notified if the request for records is malpractice related.

CONSENT—To give or obtain permission.

CONFIDENTIALITY—To protect and keep secret personal and medical information of patients revealed during the course of treatment.

The following signed statement is all that is needed for patient information to be released to an insurance company for claim filing:

> **I authorize the release of any medical or other information necessary to process this claim.**

Exceptions to this requirement are patients who are covered by Medicaid or Workers' Compensation. When a patient applies for Medicaid, they sign an authorization for the release of medical information. As explained in Chapter 12, any person making a claim for Workers' Compensation benefits agrees to release all information concerning the employees' physical or mental condition related to the claim. The patients waive any privilege for the release of medical records.

Another exception involves the filing of insurance claims for services rendered in a hospital or facility setting. These patients sign an authorization for treatment and an authorization for release of medical information at the hospital before a provider sees them. This release includes the release of information from the hospital *and* the treating physicians. Claims may then be submitted by the physician's office (in addition to the hospital or facility) without having a separate medical information release.

Additional information about patient consent and privacy is covered in Chapter 3.

Disclosing Medical Information

As with the filing of insurance claims, confidential medical information from a patient record cannot be released without the consent of the patient. However, there are times when a physician may recommend the patient to a consulting physician. Because this consultation is part of the patient's care under the original physician, separate authorization is not required for information to be exchanged between the providers. A physician also may discuss a case with a colleague without the knowledge of the patient, but if patient confidentiality is preserved, a separate authorization is not necessary.

If a patient decides to obtain an alternate opinion from another provider, this would not be part of the patient's care under the original physician. A separate authorization is required to release confidential information about the patient to the new provider because the new physician is not bound by the confidentiality agreement of the original physician's practice.

HIV/AIDS Authorization

Patients who are tested or treated for HIV infection must sign additional authorization releasing information regarding his or her HIV status.

Mental Health Information

State laws concerning the disclosure of mental health information are complex. In most states, the law prohibits the release of records unless any of the following three exceptions exists:

1. **Voluntary Disclosure** through written authorization by the patient.

2. **Judicial and Statutory Disclosure** to comply with any civil or criminal judicial proceedings.

3. **Administrative Disclosure**

   - For claims administration.
   - For employees or agents of the same mental health facility to provide professional services.
   - For the collection of a fee to a person or an agency providing collection services.
   - For scientific research.

Substance Abuse

A separate authorization must be signed to release information about drug or alcohol abuse.

Even after signing the consent form, the patient has the option of revoking the consent at any time, provided information has not been disclosed while the consent was in effect. If a patient does not specifically revoke consent, the authorization has a set termination date that must be included in the consent statement.

Drug or alcohol abuse information may be revealed for the following reasons:

■ Audit and evaluation purposes

■ In the case of suspected child abuse or neglect, under state reporting laws

■ To law enforcement personnel, if directly related to the patient's commission of a crime at the treatment facility or against treatment program personnel

■ To medical personnel, in a medical emergency

■ To research personnel, if the researchers prove protection of patient confidentiality

■ Under a court order

■ By written consent by patient

Transferring Records

Patients may not stay with the same medical practice throughout their lives, making it necessary to transfer records. Specific authorization is required when transferring records to a different provider or practice. In most cases, a separate authorization form must be signed by the patient to complete the transfer.

The Office Staff's Role in the Medical Record

A medical office may have many employees, all of whom have different roles in the care of a patient. However, each member of the medical office is responsible for the upkeep and accuracy of the patient's medical record. Every time a patient receives a service in the office, whether it is laboratory tests, an injection, wound check, or blood pressure check, the outcome of the visit must be documented by the attending staff member and an appropriate claim must be generated for the office to obtain reimbursement or payment for the rendered services.

When a patient visits the medical office, the receptionist (or front office staff) immediately begins the claim process by ensuring that the patient information sheet, insurance information, and authorizations are in place and current.

Next the medical assistant, nurse, or technician documents the reason for the patient's encounter by listing the patient's complaints, concerns, or reason for the visit. Depending on the purpose of the visit, the patient's vital signs may be taken and recorded for review. The physician then describes the examination and/or treatment provided to the patient. This information documents what services were rendered and the reason for them. The physician may write this information directly into the patient's chart (by hand or by computer) or may dictate this information for a transcriptionist.

A transcriptionist records the dictated information either as a paper document (filed into the patient's chart) or directly into an electronic medical record. The transcriptionist may be an office employee or an outside individual or business contracted by a medical office. The office employee, third-party transcriptionist or business are all held accountable for their role in the accuracy and confidentiality of medical records working in or outside of the medical office.

No matter who is entering the information into a patient's chart, accurate and detailed entries are essential. The entries tell the story of the patient's complaint or concern: the reason for the visit. They describe the patient's history, examination, and the medical decision making process that was provided to the patient. The records can also document the outcome of the patient's treatment and compliance with the medical advice given. The medical coder relies on all of this information to bill the patient or the insurance company.

Record Formats

! KEY TERMS

PROBLEM-ORIENTED MEDICAL RECORD (POMR)—A process of documenting patient health status information in a problem-solving system.

SOAP NOTES—A process of documenting patient health status information in a patient's chart.

The most widely used format is the **Problem-Oriented Medical Record** (POMR), which is commonly referred to as the **SOAP Note** (Fig. 2–3). This standardized format was developed by Lawrence Weed, MD, a professor of medicine at the University of Vermont, as part of a system for organizing medical records. Previously, the patient records were kept according to their source, such as a physician, laboratory, x-ray, nurse, or technician. This type of format had no connection between the resources, which could allow for inconsistencies, errors, and even malpractice. Dr. Weed's POMR (or SOAP) format eliminated these issues, and provided a more comprehensive system of organization for medical records.

! KEY TERM

ASSESSMENT—The patient evaluation provided by the physician.

SOAP is an acronym. Each of the letters represents a section of the patient's record:

S stands for Subjective

O stands for Objective

A stands for **Assessment**

P stands for Plan

Subjective is the information gathered from the physician's interview with the patient during the history taking and the establishment of the patient's complaints. This can include the following:

- Chief complaint(s)
- Past surgeries

Progress Note	
Name:	Barbara Edwards
Date:	11/11/20XX
	CHIEF COMPLAINT (SUBJECTIVE): Patient states she has pain and
	numbness in her left hand, primarily her thumb. Examination
	(OBJECTIVE) reveals pain when grasping and bending of the left wrist.
	Loss of strength is also noted. Right wrist remains within normal
	limits and range of motion. (ASSESSMENT) The patient suffers from
	carpal tunnel syndrome. (PLAN) Patient is advised that surgery to
	release the carpal tunnel is advised. Patient consents and will be
	set up for surgery next week.

FIGURE 2–3: SOAP Note.

- Past conditions/diseases
- Present conditions/diseases
- Recent diagnostic tests
- Recent surgery

Objective is the observations of the patient by the physician during the examination. It is used to plan the patient's treatment. This section includes the following:

- Vital signs
- General appearance
- Notations during each system review
- Results of diagnostic tests

Assessment is the diagnoses of the patient given by the physician. Included is any information related to:

- Diagnoses
- Suspected conditions

Plan is the plan of treatment. This section can include the following:

- The treatment the patient will receive
- The location of treatment
- The treatment progression
- The equipment/prescription the patient will need
- Patient and family education
- Referral to other sources
- Plans for return visit or discharge

Although the SOAP format is the most widely used, other formats also are used to maintain the integrity of information in the medical record. Regardless of the format, the information in the record must be accurate and organized to provide the best care to the patient and ensure the practice can deal with any legal issues that arise.

Abbreviations

Abbreviations are used as a time and space saver while writing notes. To ensure that everyone can understand them, most offices use the common, approved abbreviations in their medical records (Fig. 2–4). If other abbreviations are conceived, a list of those abbreviations and their meanings should be created by the front office and back office personnel and kept and available upon request from the patient, the insurance review board, the Office of Inspector General, and/or the Insurance Commissioner's office. It is best to stick with the standard abbreviations to avoid problems and audit situations.

! KEY TERM

OFFICE OF INSPECTOR GENERAL—The Office of the Inspector General (OIG) conducts independent investigations, audits, inspections, and special reviews of United States Department of Justice programs to detect fraud, abuse, and misconduct, and to promote efficiency within the Medicare program.

FIGURE 2–4: Abbreviations in the medical records.

DOS = date of service	RX = prescription
DOB = date of birth	TX = treatment
Pt = patient	PT = physical therapy
PX = physical	CC = chief complaint

■ LEGALITIES OF MEDICAL RECORDS

Corrections

As previously stated, the accuracy of medical records is extremely important, and some records may require corrections, if errors are made. The correction must be obvious, because it should be clear that there is no question about the record's accuracy. If medical records are reviewed in court or in an audit, the accuracy would affect the outcome of the review.

When making a correction to a medical record, erasing or covering up content is prohibited. Errors made in a handwritten or typed entry should be struck out by drawing a line through the original content, and the correct information should be placed above or immediately following the error. Corrections should always be initialed and dated.

Electronic records can be corrected by inserting an addendum that contains the necessary correction. As with corrections to paper records, the addendum should be signed and dated.

Storage

Filing systems can store medical records alphabetically by patient's last name or chronologically by the patient's account number. The files should not be accessed by anyone other than the authorized staff. Some filing systems can be locked or secured to prevent unauthorized access.

Due to the volume of records an office may have, the process of keeping current files readily available and storing files of previous patients is an ongoing process. Most offices will mark the patient's chart with a sticker showing the current year to indicate that the patient has been treated recently. The charts of the patients not seen in a set amount of years will then be pulled and stored in another location.

Retention

If storage space is not a problem, a physician's office can retain all records from current and past patients. However, most offices have too many records to consider and may set up a retention procedure for older records.

State law determines the retention of most medical records. In the absence of a state statute, the Department of Health and Human Services' Centers of Medicare and Medicaid recommends 7 years from the last contact with the patient. The government can take criminal or civil action up to 7 years into the past. For minors, records are generally retained until the patient becomes of legal age. After that time period, older records can be destroyed. Records should always be retained if there is a continuing medical need for them.

In addition, records must be retained for a certain period of time in case of an audit. The entries made in the patient's record indicate the reason for the patient's treatment and what kind of treatment was rendered. That documentation proves the necessity of each service and indicates each service that was provided. When an audit is scheduled for an office, a sampling of patient records will be reviewed. The information entered in each chart must then prove that the services billed were indeed performed and the diagnoses provided justify the need for those services. Any discrepancies will be handled through refund to the insurance carrier and/or monetary penalties.

Records should also be retained in the case of malpractice claims. State laws differ, but most state regulations say malpractice actions must begin within a set amount of time (e.g., within 2 years) after the date of injury or death to be claimed.

If space is a concern, medical records can be stored on a computer, microfilmed, or microfiched to conserve space. Records also may be stored off premises in a secured facility. Most importantly, records should be kept so that they are easily accessible. A log of records that have been archived should be kept for retrieval, and the appropriate members of the office staff should be trained on retrieval procedures.

Destroying Medical Records

When medical records are destroyed, their confidentiality must be protected. Procedures should be established in each office that describe the manner in which the records are destroyed. Detailed records should be kept to identify the items destroyed, with the date of destruction, the reason for destruction, the method of destruction, and the name of the individual who performed the destruction documented. Shredding or burning (where permitted) is the best method of destroying medical records no longer in use.

The Future of Medical Records

Medical records from both front and back offices are currently changing from paper records to electronic records. At the front desk a paper appointment book was used to keep track of patients' appointments and times when the physician would not be in the office—while in surgery, on vacation, in meetings, or working in another clinic. The patient's financial and medical records were kept on paper in paper files.

Information technology, or IT as it is commonly referred to, is the computer hardware and software that supports the electronic business. It is responsible for changing the use of all that paper to electronic records. Electronic medical records (EMRs), or electronic health records (EHRs) which they are commonly called, are so much easier to store and can be accessed from a remote site. The advantages are great for both front and back offices as seen from the examples in Box 2–2.

Although the benefits seem enormous, medical offices are slow to make the change. The major hold up mostly likely is the cost to convert from paper to EMR. The time and money spent on employee training and the cost of the hardware and software may not seem worthwhile to small practices.

Confidentiality also may cause hesitancy. The transmission, storage, and accessibility of any medical record must be taken into account. With the implementation of HIPAA, it is mandatory that medical offices follow the rules and regulations of confidentiality. Patient confidentiality must be protected at all times throughout the handling, the retention, and the storage of medical records. HIPAA will be addressed in Chapter 3.

■ LEGALITIES OF THE TELEPHONE, FACSIMILES, AND E-MAIL

Telephones, faxes, and e-mail are all part of the modern medical office. Protecting the patient's confidentiality in each type of correspondence is very important and requires the medical coder to be very careful when dealing with private information. More specifics about patient confidentiality are discussed in Chapter 3.

Telephone

Never give out confidential information over the phone unless it is verified that the caller is entitled to the information. A common practice is to ask the caller for some key identifying information before giving out any information. This information may be an address, date of birth, middle name, initials, or

---

BOX 2–2: EMR Use in the Medical Office

Front Office EMR Use
- Patient scheduling and reminders
- Creating and transmitting electronic medical claims
- Receiving electronic payments and statements
- Maintaining patients financial records
- Billing the patients
- Creating financial reports
- Creating patient demographic reports
- Transcription

Back Office EMR Use
- Maintaining a list of doctors the patients are referred to and from
- Creating a list of businesses called upon, such as laboratories, pharmacies, pharmaceutical representatives, medical suppliers, for example
- Prescribing medicine, ordering tests, or receiving results
- Dictating/recording all patient encounters
- Research, current medical news

a separate security question agreed upon in advance. Many medical offices have patients sign a separate permission statement that documents how and with whom a message can be left regarding the patient. For example, the patient can allow the office to leave confidential information on an answering machine or with another person, something that would not be done without specific permission from the patient.

When a phone call is received from a patient, a note (or transcript) of the phone call should be placed into the patient's medical record. For example, if the patient's call was about a treatment plan, test results, or upcoming surgery, a notation could be made in the record about the patient's questions and any advice given over the phone.

Administrative phone calls also should be documented, even if the patient is not part of the call. Whenever the medical coder discusses information about insurance coverage, authorizations, debt collection, payment status, or any other topic related to patient finances over the phone, the date, nature of the call, and who the call was with should be noted in the patient's financial records.

Facsimiles

Facsimile, or fax, transmissions have become an integral part of all offices, including medical offices. Faxes can expedite the exchange of medical records and other important information, saving time, money, and providing better care to patients. However, as with other types of correspondence, safeguards must be taken to ensure the confidentiality of the patient is always maintained (Box 2–3 and Box 2–4).

To ensure confidentiality, a cover sheet should be used for all transmissions. An example of what can be found on a typical cover sheet includes the following:

1. Time and date of transmission
2. Name, address, and telephone and FAX numbers of sender *and* recipient
3. Name of authorized receiving individual
4. Number of pages transmitted
5. Instructions to verify receipt
6. Confidentiality warning (see Box 2–3)
7. Reliability disclaimer (see Box 2–4)

The local medical society can direct the medical coder and/or office staff of the requirements in their state.

❗ KEY TERM

DISCLAIMER—A measurement taken to protect the sender. The notice explains the intentions of the fax sent and relieves the sender of any responsibility for the condition of the information sent.

BOX 2–3: Confidentiality Warning

The information contained in the facsimile message is privileged and confidential information intended only for the review and use of the individual or entity named above. If the reader of this message is not the intended recipient, you are hereby notified that any disclosure, dissemination, distribution, or copying of this communication or the information contained herein is strictly prohibited. If you have received this communication in error, please immediately notify us by telephone and return the original message to us at the above address.

BOX 2–4: Reliability Disclaimer

These records have been sent by facsimile transmission at the request of, for the convenience of, and under the sole responsibility of the recipient. Because of possible transmission errors or illegibility, medical records sent by facsimile should not be exclusively relied upon for medical diagnosis or treatment. Photostatic copies of the original records (will/will not) be forwarded by mail.

E-mail

Despite being quick and easy to use, e-mail is treated like any other paper correspondence in the eyes of the law. Anything written in an e-mail is subject to guidelines and regulations similar to those pertaining to letters or faxes. In addition, the electronic transmission of e-mail can make it easier to access than other types of correspondence.

To protect the patient's privacy and release of patient information, the medical office must set up a control over the use of e-mails. Secured servers and networks can be used to guarantee the safekeeping of information transmitted. Each employee should have a personal login and password to send and receive e-mails, and only authorized users should send e-mail over the office network. A Confidentiality Warning and Reliability Disclaimer, similar to those used on faxes, can be attached to each e-mail to indicate its intended use.

COMPLIANCE IN CLAIM FILING AND CODING

There are specific regulations and guidelines for coding medical records and filing insurance claims. Insurance carriers and government agencies are responsible for maintaining, updating, and enforcing these policies and ensuring compliance among health-care providers. A provider must adhere to the procedures set forth in these regulations, or may face monetary penalties, insurance limitations, or the closing of the medical practice.

Many offices have compliance programs or an internal audit procedure that reviews office billing practices. The purpose of a compliance program is to provide quality care to the patient while maintaining accurate claim submission and recordkeeping and reducing errors. Medical offices need to confirm that patient records contain enough documentation to justify the services that have been billed for, or the providers may find themselves in violation of carrier regulations. As part of the compliance program, periodic chart audits may be performed. Internal audits can be done periodically by a specific staff member, or external audits can be done by a third party (Box 2–5).

No matter who completes the audit, the auditor reviews a sample of patient charts and compares the documented services to the billing records. If errors are found, monetary penalties can be charged and the office must return any overpayments. When dealing with the aftermath of an audit, having a compliance program in place can help establish that the errors were not intentional.

Audit Red Flags

Any private insurance company or government organization (Medicare or Medicaid) that has a contract with a physician has the right to perform an audit of the physician's medical records. The carriers also have the right to request refunds, and, if fraud or abuse is discovered, impose penalties.

There are certain coding and filing habits that may trigger an external audit of a medical office. Some suspicious billing practices include the following:

1. Billing for excessive diagnostic tests
2. Always billing for the highest level of care
3. Overpayments never returned
4. Changing dates of service to coincide with a patient insurance coverage

Proper coding and billing practices will be discussed in later chapters.

BOX 2–5: Surviving an Audit

If a physician's office is notified that an audit will be done the medical billing specialist needs to prepare by:

1. Notifying the office staff
2. Cooperating with all requests
3. Supplying the auditors with all of the supporting documentation needed or requested; never altering or tampering with medical records that are in the audit

National Correct Coding Initiative (NCCI)

To promote correct coding techniques on a national scale, The Centers for Medicare and Medicaid (CMS) formed the **National Correct Coding Initiative** (NCCI). The NCCI also provides guidelines regarding improper coding, which often results in improper payment on insurance claims. The CMS developed its coding policies based on coding conventions defined in the American Medical Association's CPT manual, national and local policies and edits, coding guidelines developed by national societies, analysis of standard medical and surgical practices, and a review of current coding practices. The CMS website maintains an updated version of the CCI Coding Policy Manual. The CCI Coding Policy Manual should be used as a general reference tool to help explain the rationale for CCI edits.

Office of Inspector General (OIG)

The **Office of Inspector General** was formed under Public Law 95-452 to protect the Department of Health and Human Services (DHHS) programs and the beneficiaries of those programs. A national network of audits, investigations, and inspections is used by the OIG to regulate billing and coding practices in physician offices. The OIG is responsible for reporting any audit discrepancies to the Secretary of DHHS and to Congress, along with the measures to correct them.

In addition to alerting government entities to improper activities, the OIG releases Special Fraud Alerts to the health-care industry whenever a fraudulent or abusive act has been discovered. The Special Fraud Alerts notify other health-care providers that certain abusive practices were discovered and will indicate a plan to track and take legal action, as appropriate. The alerts also remind members of the health-care industry to examine their own practices to avoid future **sanctions**.

State Medical Societies

If questions or problems arise, the medical coder should not hesitate to contact the local Insurance Commissioner's office or local medical society. A list of medical societies can be found on the companion website.

■ LEGALLY SPEAKING

"An ounce of prevention is worth a pound of cure." "A stitch in time saves nine." These ancient proverbs are words to live by for the medical coder. The accuracy of the work performed provides reliable record management and office revenue, and prevents legal consequences. Medical records, claim filing and coding, authorizations, phone, fax, and e-mail are all part of the coder's daily routine.

Understanding and following the rules of coding and billing is a full-time job in itself. No one could possibly be aware of all of the rules and regulations. The medical coder must rely on good resources to be successful.

Current coding manuals and insurance guidelines must always be used. The local Medicare and Medicaid office, the state medical society, participation in coding seminars, and membership in the local professional coding chapter can provide exposure to the necessary information and provides a network a medical coder can always refer to.

RESOURCES

Center for Medicare and Medicaid (CMS)
www.cms.hhs.gov/

Iowa Medical Society
www.iowamedical.org

Kansas Medicare
www.kansasmedicare.com/

Office of Inspector General
www.oig.hhs.gov/

Chapter Review Exercise

1. Name the three exceptions to releasing medical records without the patient's written authorization:

   _____

   _____

   _____

2. The release of HIV/AIDS information requires an additional authorization. **True or False** (circle one)

3. It is illegal to fax medical records. **True or False** (circle one)

4. Under federal regulations, medical records must be retained for _____ years.

5. The health-care provider must abide by (state) or (federal) law regarding the retention of medical records. (circle one)

6. Electronic records can be corrected by inserting an addendum that contains the necessary correction. **True or False** (circle one)

7. Cite one suspicious billing practice:

   _____

   _____

8. List the four sections of a patient's problem-oriented medical record.

   1. _____
   2. _____
   3. _____
   4. _____

9. List five contents of a patient's medical record:

   1. _____
   2. _____
   3. _____
   4. _____
   5. _____

10. A health-care provider may charge the patient for a copy of their medical records. **True or False** (circle one)

HIPAA: The Health Insurance Portability and Accountability Act

Chapter Outline

LEARNING OBJECTIVES

- Define key terms
- Name the covered entities
- Identify the components of administration simplification
- Define electronic transactions and code sets requirements
- List and describe the privacy, security, and national identifier requirements

MEDICAL ASSISTING COMPETENCIES

ABHES

  1b. maintain confidentiality at all times

  1d. be cognizant of ethical boundaries

  2d. serve as a liaison between physician and others

2h. receive, organize, prioritize, and transmit information expediently
3b. prepare and maintain medical records
5a. determine needs for documentation and reporting
5b. document accurately
5c. use appropriate guidelines when releasing records or information
5g. monitor legislation related to current healthcare issues and practices

CAAHEP

IV.C.6. Differentiate between subjective and objective information
IV.C.13. Identify the role of self boundaries in the health care environment
IV.2. Report relevant information to others succinctly and accurately
IV.A.5. Demonstrate sensitivity appropriate to the message being delivered
IV.A.8. Analyze communications in providing appropriate responses/feedback
IV.A.9. Recognize and protect personal boundaries in communicating with others
V.C.5. Identify systems for organizing medical records
V.C.6. Describe various types of content maintained in a patient's medical record
V.C.11. Discuss principles of using Electronic Medical Record (EMR)
V.P.3. Organize patient's medical record
V.P.4. File medical records
V.P.5. Execute data management using electronic healthcare records such as the EMR
IX.C.2. Explore issue of confidentiality as it applies to the medical assistant
IX.C.3. Describe the implications of HIPAA for the medical assistant in various medical settings
IX.P.1. Respond to issues of confidentiality
IX.P.3. Apply HIPAA rules in regard to privacy/release of information
IX.P.7. Document accurately in the patient record
IX.A.1. Demonstrate sensitivity to patient rights
IX.A.2. Demonstrate awareness of the consequences of not working within the legal scope of practice
IX.A.3. Recognize the importance of local, state, and federal legislation and regulations in the practice setting

---

KEY TERMS

Certification and Authorization

Compliance

Coordination of Benefits

Covered Entity (CE)

Disclosure

Electronic Data Interchange

Electronic Data Transmission

Electronic File Interchange (EFI)

Electronic File Interchange Organization (EFIO)

Electronic Protected Health Information (EPHI)

Employer Identification Number (EIN)

Health-Care Clearinghouse

Health-care Provider

Identifiers

Intelligence-free

National Provider Identifier (NPI)

Privacy Officer

Protected Health Information (PHI)

Remittance Advice

◼ HIPAA OVERVIEW

HIPAA is the acronym for the Health Insurance Portability and Accountability Act. Since its inception, this law has had a major influence on **health-care providers** and their patients. This chapter will explain mandated requirements under Titles I and II, the two major components of the HIPAA law and how the requirements affect the job of the medical coder. These two titles provide the basic framework for the more specific areas of the law.

HIPAA became a law when it was passed by Congress in 1996 and was finally implemented in all medical offices and facilities in 2003. Congress passed this law for three major reasons:

1. To provide consumers with greater access to health-care insurance

2. To promote more standardization and efficiency in the health-care industry

3. To protect the privacy of health-care data

HIPAA actually consist of five parts or titles.

◼ **Title I: Insurance Reform:** Protects health-insurance coverage for workers and their families when they change or lose their jobs.

◼ **Title II: Administration Simplification:** Requires the Department of Health and Human Services to establish national standards for electronic health-care transactions and national **identifiers** for providers, health plans, and employers. It also addresses the security and privacy of health data.

◼ **Title III: Tax Related Health Provisions:** Sets certain deductions for medical insurance, and makes other changes to health-insurance law.

◼ **Title IV: Application and Enforcement of Group Health Plan Requirements:** Sets conditions for group health plans regarding coverage of persons with pre-existing conditions, and modifies continuation of coverage requirements.

◼ **Title V: Revenue Offsets:** Defines provisions related to company-owned life insurance, treatment of individuals who lose U.S. citizenship for income tax purposes, and repeals the financial institution rule to allocation of rules.

❗ KEY TERMS

HEALTH-CARE CLEARINGHOUSE—An entity that standardizes health information data into a standardized billing format.

COVERED ENTITY—Refers to an organization, in this case a health-care provider, a health-care clearinghouse, or a health plan. For purposes of the HIPAA Privacy Rule, health-care providers include hospitals, physicians, and other caregivers, and researchers who provide health care and receive, access, or generate individually identifiable health-care information.

IDENTIFIERS—Number used in the administration of health care to identify health-care providers, health plans, employers, and individuals (patients).

Covered Entities

The law applies directly to three main groups referred to as covered entities (CE).

◼ **Health-Care Providers:** Any provider of medical or other health services or supplies who transmits any health information in electronic form.

◼ **Health Plans:** Any individual or group plan that provides or pays the cost of health care.

◼ **Health-Care Clearinghouses:** Any entity that conducts health-care transactions, such as processing insurance claims.

In addition, all hired personnel who perform work for any of the three types of covered entities are subject to HIPAA jurisdiction.

HIPAA also indirectly affects many others in the health-care field. For example, software billing vendors and third-party billing services that do not qualify as clearinghouses or some other covered entity are not covered by HIPAA. However, these businesses may need to alter operations if they are trading partners or business associates of a covered entity.

TITLE I: INSURANCE REFORM

The health insurance portability side of HIPAA is often referred to as "insurance reform." It is intended to offer continuous, "portable," access to health-insurance coverage for employees and their dependents when they change jobs or employers.

Health-Care Access

HIPAA guarantees that an individual cannot be denied enrollment in a group health-insurance plan on the basis of his or her health status. An individual cannot be charged a higher premium because of poor health. However, an individual may be subject to a *pre-existing condition exclusion*. A pre-existing exclusion is the period of time that a health plan will not cover and is not responsible for the treatment costs of the pre-existing condition. HIPAA defines a pre-existing condition as any health condition, physical or mental, for which a patient has been treated within 6 months before the start of coverage under a new plan. HIPAA allows exclusion periods but limits them to no more than 12 months for first-time enrollment in a health plan and 18 months for a late enrollment in a plan.

Title I also established the concept of *creditable coverage*. This gives the insured and dependents credit for the amount of time they were insured by one plan, which is called *prior coverage*. Prior coverage is applied to the pre-existing condition exclusion period of a new insurance plan as long as the gap in coverage is not more than 62 days. To make this easier to understand, look at the following example:

> A patient was receiving treatment for diabetes and was covered under an employer's group plan for 10 months before being laid off. The patient did get a new job right away and enrolled in the new employer's plan 24 days later. The new plan had a 12-month pre-existing exclusion. The HIPAA law allowed the patient to deduct the 10 months of prior coverage from the 12-month exclusion period of the new insurance plan. The patient was only responsible for 2 months of uncovered costs for the diabetes treatment before full coverage began again. The patient was covered for any other illness or injury immediately after signing up for the new insurance.

In the example, 10 months of coverage "travels" with the covered individual to the next insurance plan, even though the coverage is through a new employer. The concept of "portable" coverage is the major reform brought about by Title I and one of the key contributions of HIPAA.

TITLE II: ADMINISTRATIVE SIMPLIFICATION

Title II of HIPAA, Administrative Simplification, was developed to promote standardization and efficiency in the health-care industry. It also is intended to protect or be "accountable" for the privacy of the health-care data. The Privacy Rule sets standards for accessibility to **Protected Health Information (PHI)**, which can be in electronic, oral, or paper format. The Security Rule sets standards for the access of **Electronic Protected Health Information (EPHI)** and does not cover the transmission of PHI orally or in writing.

! KEY TERMS

PROTECTED HEALTH INFORMATION (PHI)—Any information that identifies an individual. The information includes past, present, and future physical and mental health information and payment for health care.

ELECTRONIC PROTECTED HEALTH INFORMATION (EPHI)—Any protected health information (PHI), which is generated, maintained, sent, and received electronically.

Standardization and Efficiency

Title II of HIPAA was designed to streamline the administration of health care. This section of the law promotes uniformity by establishing standards for several types of electronic health information transactions.

According to The Centers for Medicare and Medicaid (CMS), "About 26 cents of every health-care dollar is spent on administrative overhead," which can include beneficiary enrollment, premium payments, claims filing, and related activities. By creating provisions for standardization in health-care administration, HIPAA has already improved administrative efficiency and generated considerable financial savings on overhead costs. CMS estimates "that full implementation of these provisions could save as much as $9 billion per year on administrative overhead, while improving efficiency and enhancing the quality of health-care services."

As part of HIPAA, different insurers can no longer have unique claim processing requirements. Every medical facility under the jurisdiction of HIPAA is required to provide the same information and to use standard formats for claims processing, payments, data maintenance, and **electronic data transmission**.

In the past, there were more than 400 different ways to submit a claim. Since HIPAA, there is only one way to properly submit an insurance claim. With these standards in place, the entire reimbursement process is easier, faster, and less costly. The requirements mandated by HIPAA also help health-care providers take advantage of new technologies and, ultimately, improve their overall business practices.

! KEY TERM

HEALTH-CARE PROVIDER—Any individual or business entity that furnishes health-care services, or bills for and is paid for those services.

Electronic Transaction Requirements

Transactions are activities involving the transfer of health-care information for specific purposes. Under Title I of HIPAA, a health-care provider must comply with certain standards for specific types of transactions. HIPAA requires every provider who does business electronically to use the same health-care transactions, code sets, and identifiers. The following transactions need to be compliant with **electronic data interchange** (EDI) for the transmission of health-care data:

- Claim form or equivalent encounter information
- Payment and **remittance advice**
- Inquiries and responses about claim status
- Inquiries and responses about eligibility
- Inquiries and responses regarding referral **certification and authorization**
- Enrollment and disenrollment in a health plan
- Health plan premium payments
- **Coordination of benefits**
- Claims attachments

! KEY TERMS

CERTIFICATION AND AUTHORIZATION—Process that determines whether or not a service is medically necessary and/or covered under a patient's health-care plan

COORDINATION OF BENEFITS—Process of managing benefits when an individual is covered under more than one health-insurance plan.

ELECTRONIC DATA TRANSMISSION—The transfer or exchange of data using computers.

Each of these standard transactions streamlines the process of electronic claims and accelerates reimbursement for services.

Code Sets Standards

Code sets are any alpha characters or numbers used to indicate data such as specific diagnoses and clinical procedures on claims and encounter forms. The Current Procedural Terminology (CPT) and International Classification of Diseases, 9th revision, Clinical Modification, (ICD-9-CM) codes are examples of code sets for procedure and diagnosis coding. Other code sets adopted under the Administrative Simplification provisions of HIPAA, include codes used for medical supplies, dental services, and drugs (see Chapter 5 for more information).

HIPAA refers to code sets as either medical codes (clinical codes) or nonmedical codes (nonclinical codes). Medical code sets are used in transactions to identify a medical condition, diagnosis, treatment, procedure, and any medical supplies related to the patient's encounter.

The medical code sets that have been approved for use by HIPAA include:

- **ICD-9-CM:** Diagnosis codes used to identify the physician's diagnosis of the patient's condition.
- **CPT:** Procedure codes used to identify the service provided to the patient during the encounter.
- **NDC:** National Drug Codes used to identify drugs and pharmaceuticals.
- **CDT:** Current Dental Terminology used with dental services and procedures.
- **HCPCS:** Healthcare Common Procedures Coding System applies for all other equipment, supplies, and items used in health care. (HCPCS will be addressed in detail in Chapter 5.)

Nonmedical code sets represent administrative information rather than medical conditions or services. Some types of nonmedical codes that pertain to patient data include:

- Zip codes, street address, county, precinct, or state abbreviations
- Telephone and fax numbers
- Electronic mail addresses
- Social Security numbers
- Medical record or account numbers

Other nonmedical code sets are used for specific information related to insurance claims (Box 3–1). Some of those code sets include:

- **Claim Adjustment Reason Codes and Remittance Advice Remark Codes:** Codes that indicate the payment policies of the insurance plan.
- **Claim Status Category Codes and Claim Status Codes:** Codes that indicate the status of claims and why claims were denied or adjusted.

Whether medical or nonmedical, every code set involved in electronic claims and reimbursement is standardized under HIPAA legislation. A medical coder should be familiar with the different code sets and know how they are used in the medical office.

National Identifier Requirements

HIPAA requires standard national numbers for health-care providers, health plans, and employers. These standardized numbers serve as identifiers on standard transactions such as claims, eligibility inquiries, claim status inquiries, referrals, and remittance advices (Fig. 3–1).

BOX 3–1: Claim Adjustment and Status Codes Example

- PR, Patient Responsibility—Represents an amount that is billed to the patient or insured, typically the deductible or copayment amount.
- B15—Claim/service denied/reduced because this procedure/service is not paid separately.
- 5—The procedure code/bill type is inconsistent with the place of service.

Source: Understanding the Remittance Advice: A Guide for Medicare Providers, Physicians, Suppliers, and Billers. Centers for Medicare and Medicaid (CMS), 2006. Available at http://www.cms.hhs.gov/MLNProducts/downloads/RA_Guide_Full_03-22-06.pdf.

```
1  EXAMPLE MEDICARE CARRIER                                                       MEDICARE
   PROVIDER #:  999999                          GOODHEALTH GROUP PRACTICE         REMITTANCE
   CHECK/EFT:   00234569        01/28/2003            PAGE 2 OF 2                  NOTICE

   SUMMARY OF UNASSIGNED CLAIMS

   PERF PROV   SERV DATE POS NOS  PROC  MODS   BILLED   ALLOWED    DEDUCT    COINS   GRP/RC   AMT  PROV PD
2  NAME FINE, R. U.        HIC 9999999999 ACNT  FINE7-002      ICN 0202199000150   ASG N         MOA MA28
   123456ABC  0526 052602 11   1  99214        60.47    52.58     0.00     10.52   CO-42   0.00    7.89
   PT RESP       60.47         CLAIM TOTALS    60.47    52.58     0.00     10.52           0.00
   ADJ TO TOTALS:    PREV PD  0.00  INT   0.00 LATE FILING CHARGE     0.00

   NAME LAWN, MOE D.       HIC 9999999999 ACNT  LAWN4-667      ICN 0202199140370   ASG N         MOA MA28
   123456ABC  0222 022202 11   1  99214        60.47    52.58     0.00     10.52   CO-42   0.00    7.89
   PT RESP       60.47         CLAIM TOTALS    60.47    52.58     0.00     10.52           0.00
   ADJ TO TOTALS:    PREV PD  0.00  INT   0.00 LATE FILING CHARGE     0.00

   GROUP CODES:
   PR        Patient Responsibility
   CO        Contractual Obligation
   OA        Other Adjustment

   GLOSSARY:  Group, Reason, MOA, Remark and Adjustment Codes
   CO        Contractual Obligation.  Amount for which the provider is financially liable.  The patient may
             not be billed for this amount.
   PR        Patient Responsibility.  Amount that may be billed to a patient or another payer.
   42        Charges exceed our fee schedule or maximum allowable amount.
   96        Noncovered charge(s)
3  B15       Claim/service denied/reduced because this procedure/service is not paid separately.
             Charges exceed our fee schedule or maximum allowable amount.
   M80       We cannot pay for this when performed during the same session as another approved procedure for
             this beneficiary.
   MA01      (Initial Part B determination, carrier or intermediary)  If you do not agree with what we
             approved for these services, you may appeal our decision.  To make sure that we are fair to you,
             we require another individual that did not process your initial claim to conduct the review.
             However, in order to be eligible for a review, you must write to us within 6 months of the date
             of this notice, unless you have a good reason for being late.  (An institutional provider, e.g.,
             hospital, SNF, HHA may appeal only if the claim involves a medical necessity denial, a SNF
             recertified bed denial, or a home health denial because the patient was not homebound or was not
             in need of intermittent skilled nursing services, and either the patient or the provider is
             liable under 1879 of the Social Security Act, and the patient chooses not to appeal.)  NOTE:  If
             you are a member of the telephone review demonstration, or if telephone reviews are expanded,
             add the following to the end of the description for MA01.  If you meet the criteria for a
             telephone review, you may phone to request a telephone review.
   MA07      The claim information has also been forwarded to Medicaid for review.
   MA28      Receipt of this notice by a physician who did not accept assignment is for information only and
             does not make the physician a party to the determination.  No additional rights to appeal this
             decision, above those rights already provided for by regulation/instruction, are conferred by
             receipt of this notice
   50        Late Filing Reduction
   FB        Forwarding Balance
```

FIGURE 3–1: Medicare remittance advice.

REMITTANCE ADVICE—A form issued from a third-party carrier indicating any claims processed for a health-care provider.

THE NATIONAL PROVIDER IDENTIFIER (NPI)—The NPI is a unique identification number for covered health-care providers. The NPIs must be used in the administrative and financial transactions adopted under HIPAA. The NPI is a 10-digit number, intelligence-free numeric identifier. The numbers do not carry other information about health-care providers, such as the state in which they live or their medical specialty.

This standardization helps eliminate paperwork and simplifies activities such as enrollment in health plans, payment of health insurance premiums, the processing of health-care claims, and the coordination of medical benefits.

The **National Provider Identifier (NPI)** is a 10-digit, **intelligence-free**, identification number that remains with a health-care provider regardless of job or location changes. All health-care providers that are HIPAA-covered entities, whether they are individual health-care providers (e.g., physicians, dentists, chiropractors, pharmacists) or organizations (e.g., hospitals, clinics, nursing homes, pharmacies), must obtain an NPI to identify themselves in any HIPAA standard transactions.

EMPLOYER IDENTIFICATION NUMBER (EIN)—The EIN is also known as a Federal Tax Identification Number and is used to identify a business entity. Most businesses need an EIN.

INTELLIGENCE-FREE—Identifiers that do not carry specific identifying information such as the state or medical specialty of the medical practice.

The Centers for Medicare and Medicaid Services (CMS) contracted with Fox Systems, Inc., to serve as the NPI Enumerator. An enumerator is responsible for dealing with health plans and providers and issuing the NPIs. **Electronic file interchange (EFI)**, also referred to as "bulk enumeration," is a process by which physicians and other health-care providers can have an organization (the "EFIO") apply for NPI on their behalf. Rather than a provider or group of providers submitting an application for each and every health-care organization they participate with, the EFIO obtains an NPI for them.

An EFI can contain hundreds or thousands of providers' applications. By submitting these applications both simultaneously and electronically, the administrative and financial responsibilities for both the health-care providers and the Department of Health and Human Services (HHS) are significantly reduced.

! KEY TERMS

ELECTRONIC FILE INTERCHANGE (EFI)—The process in which a provider can fill out one application for a **National Provider Identifier (NPI)** through one organization, called an **Electronic File Interchange Organization (EFIO)** and that organization will grant the provider an NPI and then submit the NPI to Medicare, Medicaid, and all health-care insurance organizations.

NPIs were designed to last up to 200 years, allowing for growth in the number of health-care providers.

Privacy Requirements

In addition to simplifying the administration in the medical office, HIPAA regulations also set national standards for the privacy of health information. The Office of Civil Rights states, "The major purpose of the Privacy Rule is to define and limit the circumstances in which an individual's protected health information (PHI) may be used or disclosed by covered entities"[1] Under the law, health information is considered:

- Any information that identifies an individual and is exchanged electronically
- Any information printed from a computer
- A covered entity may not use or disclose protected health information, except:
    - When requested by the individual patient or his or her representative.
    - When requested by the Department of Health and Human Services as part of an investigation, review, or enforcement action.
    - When needed for internal review, credentialing, or by another governing body (e.g., police, World Health Organization).

Covered entities can use and release, or disclose, health information with the patient's consent. A consent form (Fig. 3–2) must specifically name the information that may be released and who it is released to.

In some cases, the covered entities also are allowed to release health information without patient authorization for the purpose of utilization review, quality assurance, and or credentialing. Other ways health information can be released without the patient's consent include:

- Emergencies affecting the life or the safety of the patient
- Research
- Judicial proceedings
- Law enforcement
- Giving information to the next of kin
- Government health data systems
- To identify a body or for the cause of death
- For hospital facilities
- To process payment for health care by a financial institution

---

[1]http://www.hhs.gov/ocr/privacysummary.pdf.

AUTHORIZATION FOR RELEASE OF PROTECTED HEALTH INFORMATION

Josefina Marie Simms   _8/16/54_   _876-32-1234_
Patient name   Date of birth   Social security #

> PATIENT'S NAME, DATE OF BIRTH, AND SOCIAL SECURITY NUMBER ARE INCLUDED.

I, _Josefina Marie Simms_ , authorize the use or disclosure of my protected health information by
     PATIENT NAME

Dr. Robert Greer as specified below. I understand that signing this authorization is voluntary and that Dr. Greer may
not require me to sign this authorization before Dr. Greer provides me with treatment. I understand that I have the
right to revoke this authorization at any time by providing a signed, written notice of such revocation to Dr. Greer. I
understand that a description of my rights to revoke my authorization is set forth by Dr. Greer.

> RIGHT TO REVOKE THE PERMISSION TO DISCLOSE IS INCLUDED.

Notice of Privacy Practices: I understand that information is being released pursuant to this authorization at my request
and that the information may no longer be protected by law or regulation and may be redisclosed by the recipient.

Please use or disclose the following information:
☒ The entire medical record
☐ The following limited health information

> INFORMATION TO BE DISCLOSED IS SPECIFIED AND THE REQUEST IS REASONABLE. (FOR EXAMPLE, A REQUEST FOR 45 YEARS OF A MEDICAL RECORD IS AN UNREASONABLE REQUEST.)

The following information cannot be disclosed without specific authorization. Please initial next to each item below that
you specifically authorize the release of health information relating to the testing, diagnosis, or treatment for:

JMS HIV or AIDS

JMS Drug and alcohol abuse

JMS Mental health or psychiatric disorders

> BECAUSE INFORMATION REGARDING HUMAN IMMUNODEFICIENCY VIRUS (HIV) STATUS, MENTAL HEALTH HISTORY, AND SUBSTANCE ABUSE HISTORY ARE CONSIDERED HIGHLY SENSITIVE, AUTHORIZATION TO RELEASE THAT INFORMATION MUST BE EXPLICITLY OUTLINED.

Please specify the time period for the information you described to be disclosed:
☐ All information maintained at this time by Dr. Greer
☒ Information maintained by Dr. Greer from _10/8/2004_ to _2/28/2005_

Please specify who may receive the information requested by this authorization:

Carla J. Simmons
Attorney at Law
211 Main Street
Lovely, CT 06111

> THE PERSON OR AGENCY (LAW OFFICES) WHERE THE INFORMATION IS TO BE RELEASED IS SPECIFIED AND THE ADDRESS OF THE AGENCY IS INCLUDED.

By signing below, I understand and acknowledge the following:
• I have read and understand this authorization
• I am authorizing Dr. Greer to use or disclose the health information to the person(s) identified in this authorization.
If I have any questions about disclosure of my protected health information pursuant to this authorization, I may contact
Anthony Campbell, Paralegal, law offices of:

Carla J. Simmons
Attorney at Law
211 Main Street
Lovely, CT 06111

> THE DOCUMENT IS SIGNED AND DATED.

Josefina Marie Simms   _Josefina Marie Simms_   _5/24/2008_
Printed name of patient   Signature of patient   Date

FIGURE 3-2: Sample of a consent/authorization form, for release of medical record information.

⚠ KEY TERM

DISCLOSURE—Release of protected health information from one entity to another.

NOTICE OF PRIVACY PRACTICES

THIS NOTICE DESCRIBES HOW MEDICAL INFORMATION ABOUT YOU MAY BE USED AND DISCLOSED AND HOW YOU CAN GET ACCESS TO THIS INFORMATION. PLEASE REVIEW IT CAREFULLY.

We respect our legal obligation to keep health information that identifies you private. We are obligated by law to give you notice of our privacy practices. This Notice describes how we protect your health information and what rights you have regarding it.

TREATMENT, PAYMENT, AND HEALTHCARE OPERATIONS

The most common reason why we use or disclose your health information is for treatment, payment or healthcare operations. Examples of how we use or disclose information for treatment purposes are: setting up an appointment for you; testing or examining your eyes; prescribing glasses, contact lenses, or eye medications and faxing them to be filled; showing you low vision aids; referring you to another doctor or clinic for eye care or low vision aids or services; or getting copies of your health information from another professional that you may have seen before us. Examples of how we use or disclose your health information for payment purposes are; asking you about your health or vision care plans, or other sources of payment; preparing and sending bills or claims; and collecting unpaid amounts (either ourselves or through a collection agency or attorney). "Health care operations" mean those administrative and managerial functions that we have to do in order to run our office. Examples of how we use or disclose your health information for health care operations are: financial or billing audits; internal quality assurance; personnel decisions; participation in managed care plans; defense of legal matters; business planning; and outside storage of our records.

We routinely use your health information inside our office for these purposes without any special permission. If we need to disclose your health information outside of our office for these reasons, [we will] [we usually will not] ask you for special written permission.

We will ask for special written permission in the following situations: _____.

USES AND DISCLOSURES FOR OTHER REASONS WITHOUT PERMISSION

In some limited situations, the law allows or requires us to use or disclose your health information without your permission. Not all of these situations will apply to us; some may never come up at our office at all. Such uses or discloses are:

- when a state or federal law mandates that certain health information be reported for a specific purpose;
- for public health purposes, such as contagious disease reporting, investigation or surveillance; and notices to and from the federal Food and Drug Administration regarding drugs or medical devices;
- disclosures to governmental authorities about victims of suspected abuse, neglect or domestic violence;
- uses and disclosures for health oversite activities, such as for the licensing of doctors; for audits by Medicare or Medicaid; or for investigation of possible violations of health care laws;
- disclosures for judicial and administrative proceedings, such as in response to subpoenas or orders of courts or administrative agencies;
- disclosures for law enforcement purposes, such as to provide information about someone who is or is suspected to be a victim of a crime; to provide information about a crime at our office; or to report a crime that happened somewhere else;
- disclosure to a medical examiner to identify a dead person or to determine the cause of death; or to funeral directors to aid in burial; or to organizations that handle organ or tissue donations;
- uses and disclosures for health-related research;
- uses and disclosures to prevent a serious threat to health or safety;
- uses or disclosures for specialized government functions, such as for the protection of the president or high-ranking government officials; for lawful national intelligence activities; for military purposes; or for the evaluation and health of members of the foreign service;
- disclosures of de-identified information;
- disclosures related to worker's compensation programs;
- disclosures of a "limited data set" for research, public health, or health care operations;
- incidental disclosures that are an unavoidable by-product of permitted uses or disclosures;
- disclosures to "business associates" who perform health care operations for us and who commit to respect the privacy of your health information;
- [specify other uses and disclosures affected by state law].

Unless you object, we will also share relevant information about your care with your family or friends who are helping you with your eye care.

APPOINTMENT REMINDERS

We may call or write to remind you of scheduled appointments, or that it is time to make a routine appointment. We may also call or write to notify you of other treatments or services available at our office that might help you. Unless you tell us otherwise, we will mail you an appointment reminder on a postcard, and/or leave you a reminder message on your home answering machine or with someone who answers your phone if you are not home.

FIGURE 3-3: Sample of HIPAA privacy statement.

OTHER USES AND DISCLOSURES
We will not make any other uses or disclosures of your health information unless you sign a written "authorization form." The content of an "authorization form" is determined by federal law. Sometimes, we may initiate the authorization process if the use or disclosure is our idea. Sometimes, you may initiate the process if it's your idea for us to send your information to someone else. Typically, in this situation you will give us a properly completed authorization form, or you can use one of ours.

If we initiate the process and ask you to sign an authorization form, you do not have to sign it. If you do not sign the authorization, we cannot make the use or disclosure. If you do sign one, you may revoke it at any time unless we have already acted in reliance upon it. Revocations must be in writing. Send them to the office contact person named at the beginning of this Notice.

YOUR RIGHTS REGARDING YOUR HEALTH INFORMATION
The law gives you many rights regarding your health information. You can:
- ask us to restrict our uses and disclosures for purposes of treatment (except emergency treatment), payment or health care operations. We do not have to agree to do this, but if we agree, we must honor the restrictions that you want. To ask for a restriction, send a written request to the office contact person at the address, fax or E-mail shown at the beginning of this Notice.
- ask us to communicate with you in a confidential way, such as by phoning you at work rather than at home, by mailing health information to a different address, or by using E-mail to your personal E-mail address. We will accommodate these requests if they are reasonable, and if you pay us for any extra cost. If you want to ask for confidential communications, send a written request to the office contact person at the address, fax or E-mail shown at the beginning of this Notice.
- ask to see or get photocopies of your health information. By law, there are a few limited situations in which we can refuse to permit access or copying. For the most part, however, you will be able to review or have a copy of your health information within 30-days of asking us (or 60 days if the information is stored off-site). You may have to pay for photocopies in advance. If we deny your request, we will send you a written explanation, and instructions about how to get an impartial review of denial if one is legally available. By law, we can have one 30-day extension of the time for us to give you access or photocopies if we send you a written notice of the extension. If you want to review or get photocopies of your health information, send a written request to the office contact person at the address, fax or E-mail shown at the beginning of this Notice.
- ask us to amend your health information if you think that it is incorrect or incomplete. If we agree, we will amend the information within 60 days from when you ask us. We will send the corrected information to persons who we know received the wrong information, and others that you specify. If we do not agree, you can write a statement of your position, and we will include it with your health information along with any rebuttal statement that we may write. Once your statement of position and/or our rebuttal is included in your health information, we will send it along whenever we make a permitted disclosure of your health information. By law, we can have one 30-day extension of time to consider a request for amendment if we notify you in writing of the extension. If you want to ask us to amend your health information, send a written request, including your reasons for the amendment, to the contact person at the address, fax or E-mail shown at the beginning of this Notice.
- get a list of the disclosures that we have made of your health information within the past 6 years (or a shorter period if you want). By law, the list will not include: disclosures for purposes of treatment, payment or health care operations; disclosures with your authorization; incidental disclosures; disclosures required by law; and some other limited disclosures. You are entitled to one such list per year without charge. If you want more frequent lists, you will have to pay for them in advance. We will usually respond to your request within 60 days of receiving it, but by law we can have one 30-day extension of time if we notify you of the extension in writing. If you want a list, send a written request to the office contact person at the address, fax or E-mail shown at the beginning of this Notice.
- get additional paper copies of this Notice of Privacy Practices upon request. It does not matter whether you have one electronically or in paper form already. If you want additional paper copies, send a written request to the office contact person at the address, fax or E-mail shown at the beginning of this Notice.

OUR NOTICE OF PRIVACY PRACTICES
By law, we must abide by the terms of this Notice of Privacy Practices until we choose to change it. We reserve the right to change this notice at any time as allowed by law. If we change this Notice, the new privacy practices will apply to your health information that we already have as well as to such information that we may generate in the future. If we change our Notice of Privacy Practices, we will post the new notice in our office, have copies available in our office, and post it on our Web site.

COMPLAINTS
If you think that we have not properly respected the privacy of your health information, you are free to complain to us or the U.S. Department of Health and Human Services, Office for Civil Rights. We will not retaliate against you if you make a complaint. If you want to complain to us, send a written complaint to the office contact person at the address, fax or E-mail shown at the beginning of this Notice. If you prefer, you can discuss your complaint in person or by phone.

FOR MORE INFORMATION
If you want more information about our privacy practices, call or visit the office contact person at the address or phone number shown at the beginning of this Notice.   NF/03

ACKNOWLEDGEMENT OF RECEIPT

I acknowledge that I received a copy of_____O.D., Notice of Privacy Practices. Date_____

Patient name_____Signature_____

FIGURE 3-3: cont'd

Providers are required to provide every patient with a written Notice of Privacy Practices (NPP) (Fig. 3–3) regarding the privacy policy of the office. Patients are required to sign a statement that documents their receipt of the privacy information. Information in the notice will define the patient's right to:

1. Request restrictions on certain uses and **disclosures** of PHI
2. Request confidential communications
3. Access, inspect, and obtain a copy of their PHI
4. Request an amendment of their PHI
5. Receive a record that details disclosures of their PHI

Security Requirements

Prior to HIPAA, there were no universal requirements for security standards that protected the health information in the health-care industry. Since that time, new technology has moved health care away from paper and toward computers to pay claims, answer eligibility questions, and administer health information. Health-care providers can now access patient medical records, review test results, and place patient care orders online. Although this allows the medical providers to be more efficient, it has also increased potential security risks. The availability of electronic health records has made it necessary to protect the confidentiality of the Electronic Protected Health Information (EPHI) and maintain the appropriate access and use of that information. The security regulations within Title II of HIPPA require medical offices to adopt administrative, technical, and physical standards and safeguards. The security regulations prevent unauthorized access to protected health-care information.

Administrative Security Safeguards

Administrative security safeguards make up half of the Security Rule's standards. These standards require documented policies and procedures for day-to-day operations. There are standards for managing the conduct of employees with PHI, and for managing the selection, development, and use of security controls. The specific standards of the administrative safeguards include:

- **Security management process:** The purpose of this standard is to establish policies and procedures that a covered entity would use to avoid, identify, control, and resolve security violations in their daily business.

- **Assigned security responsibility:** A single individual must be designated to have overall responsibility for the security of a covered entity's (CE's) EPHI. This security official or also referred to as the **privacy officer** is responsible for the development and implementation of the policies and procedures of the covered entity.

❗ KEY TERM

PRIVACY OFFICER—Person who is responsible for implementing and adhering to HIPAA policies and procedures and the handling of privacy complaints.

- **Workforce security:** Policies and procedures need to ensure that employees have only appropriate access to EPHI and to prevent anyone else from getting that protected health information.

- **Information access management:** Policies and procedures for authorizing access to EPHI must be put into operation. Covered entities must determine what protected information is appropriate for each employee to have access to.

- **Security awareness and training:** A training program for a CE's entire workforce must be in place. The training standards cover log-in monitoring and password protection and management.

- **Security incident procedures:** Created policies and procedures to handle any security incidents.

- **Contingency plan:** Policies and procedures must be established to provide a plan that will manage an emergency or other occurrence that damages systems containing EPHI.

- **Evaluation:** Periodic monitoring and evaluation must occur to ensure the CE's security policies and procedures meet the ongoing requirements of the Security Rule.

- **Business associate contracts and other arrangements:** A covered entity may permit a business associate to "create, receive, maintain or transmit" EPHI on its behalf. But it may do so only if there are "satisfactory assurances" that the business associate will appropriately safeguard the PHI. Written contracts or other arrangements documenting such assurances are one of the administrative safeguards required by the Security Rule.

All of the standards and implementation specifications found in the Administrative Security Safeguards deal with the policies and procedures that must be in place to establish, manage, and maintain the requirements mandated by Title II of HIPAA.

Physical Security Safeguards

The physical security safeguards are measures meant to protect a CE's electronic information systems, buildings, and equipment from natural hazards, environmental hazards, and unauthorized use. The measures include both administrative policies and physical controls. The specific standards of the physical safeguards include:

- **Facility access controls:** Policies and procedures must be implemented to limit physical access to electronic information systems and the actual premises where they are stored, while making sure that appropriate, legitimate access is permitted.

- **Workstation use:** Policies and procedures must be put into place that identify appropriate workstation use. In HIPAA, a workstation refers to a desktop computer, laptop computer, or any other device that performs similar functions. The policies must identify the appropriate work to be done on a workstation, the manner in which the work should be carried out, and the characteristics of the actual physical surroundings of workstations regardless of where the workstation is located. Something as ordinary as logging off before leaving a workstation for an extended amount of time or using antivirus software is common practice.

- **Workstation security:** Safeguards must be set up for all workstations that limit access of EPHI to only authorized users.

- **Device and media controls:** Policies and procedures for the receipt and removal of hardware and electronic media that contain EPHI and the movement of those items within a CE are mandatory. This standard covers the proper handling of electronic media including receipt, removal, backup, storage, reuse, disposal, and accountability.

Technical Security Safeguards

The technical security safeguards category under HIPAA is made up of several security measures that specify how a CE can use technology to protect and control access to EPHI. The specific standards of the technical safeguards include:

- **Access control:** Policies and procedures for electronic information systems containing EPHI to only allow access to persons or software programs that have appropriate access rights must always be in place. A good example of access control is the assignment and use of unique user identification, such as a name or number.

- **Audit controls:** Hardware, software, and/or procedural mechanisms to record and examine activity in information systems that contain or use EPHI must be implemented. These controls are useful for examining and recording user activity and also can determine if a security violation has occurred.

- **Integrity:** Policies and procedures must be set to protect EPHI from improper modification or destruction by either a user or electronic medical errors or failures.

- **Person or entity authentication:** Any persons or entities seeking access to EPHI must be able to verify who or what they claim to be.

- **Transmission security:** Security measures must prevent unauthorized access to EPHI that is being transmitted over an electronic communications network.

Technical security policies and procedures apply to all EPHI. The measures protect and control access to all EPHI, ensuring that the covered entities will protect the confidentiality and availability of EPHI.

■ THE CODER'S ROLE

A medical coder may be required to provide information, file medical claims, and/or maintain patient accounts using standard formats for processing claims and payments. The maintenance and transmission of electronic health-care information and data must also follow the standard format. Knowledge of HIPAA requirements is essential to these duties and other potential duties related to the medical office, its patients, and its business contacts. All of these responsibilities ensure that the health-care provider is in **compliance** with the law. The coder needs to stay current with regulations and new provisions related to HIPAA legislation (Box 3–2).

When dealing with patient records and insurance coverage, the medical coder may be faced with questions regarding the benefits and limitations of coverage in a patient's policy. Patients may have concerns regarding their pre-existing condition(s) and how the current services rendered to them will or will not be covered under their existing insurance plans. The medical coder may need to contact an insurance company and verify coverage for a patient. Financial arrangements with patients may need to be established for any balances due after insurance payments or as a result of no coverage for a particular service. Understanding the concept of creditable and prior coverage provides the medical coder the opportunity to inform the patient of his or her options. When patients understand the options afforded them, they are better able to make informed decisions regarding their health care. This provides patient satisfaction and helps secure proper reimbursement for the services rendered to a patient.

A coder will have access to the confidential records of their patients and the financial matters of the medical practice they work for. This information cannot be revealed, unless proper authorization is obtained, either by the patient, the covered entity, or a governing body. Violation of the patient-doctor relationship is extremely unethical. If a patient asks a question about medical care, he or she should be referred to the medical assistant, nurse, or the physician. Practicing medicine is not the role of the coder.

The coder must have knowledge of, comply with, and remain current with the security standards in the workplace. All passwords, EPHI, PHI, and appropriate work principles must be protected and preserved. In addition, the coder may be responsible for applying for and maintaining the health-care provider's national provider identifiers. This work must be done in compliance with HIPAA guidelines.

Even though each medical office is different, compliance with HIPAA regulations is a universal standard for working in the health-care field. Medical coders must correctly apply HIPAA guidelines to their daily work, for the protection of the medical office, the patients, and themselves.

 KEY TERM

COMPLIANCE—To accept and work within the rules and regulations of HIPAA.

BOX 3–2: Dos and Don'ts List

1. Do educate and remain educated with current HIPAA guidelines and regulations.
2. Do keep all PHI and EPHI secure and accessible *only* to those authorized.
3. Do provide a private area that enables patients to discuss their personal matters.
4. Do have all patients sign an authorization to release their PHI and EPHI as appropriate.
5. Do review or examine your office policies and procedures routinely to maintain compliance with the law.
6. Don't give out any unauthorized PHI or EPHI in any format.
7. Don't leave out any PHI or EPHI where an unauthorized individual can view it.
8. Don't give out your password.
9. Don't give out PHI over the phone without verifying to whom you are speaking.
10. Don't allow confidential conversations or materials to be overheard or seen by an unauthorized individual.

■ CONCLUSION

- ■ HIPAA was created to provide continuous health insurance coverage to individuals and their dependents when they change or lose their jobs.
- ■ HIPAA also provides standardization guidelines to improve the efficiency of the exchange of health-care data and was designed to protect the privacy of that health-care data.
- ■ Covered entities must comply with standards and the regulations of HIPAA.
- ■ While the detailed rules and regulations may seem overwhelming, common sense can prevail.
- ■ Stay current with all rules and regulations involved.
- ■ Remember the principals of medical ethics.
- ■ Provide medical services to your patients with respect and dignity and their best interest in mind at all times.

RESOURCE LIST

Center for Medicare and Medicaid CMS
> http://www.cms.hhs.gov/hipaa/hipaa2

CMS HIPAA Hotline at 1-866-282-0659
> askhipaa@cms.hhs.gov

Office for Civil Rights
> http://www.hhs.gov/ocr/hipaa

> http://www.hhs.gov/ocr/privacy/index.html

Office of Inspector General
> http://oig.hhs.gov/Quick Guide to HIPAA for the Physician's Office by Brenda Burton

Workgroup for Electronic Data Interchange (wedi)
> http://wedi.org

Federal Register
> http://www.gpoaccess.gov/fr/

What Physician Executives Need to Know about HIPAA by J. Michael Fitzmaurice, PhD, and Jeffrey S. Rose, MD
> www.ahrq.gov/data/hipaa1.htm

HIPAA Compliance Rule Standards
> www.hipaa-101.com/hipaa-rules.htm

American Academy of Professional Coders (AAPC). *Coding Edge.* 2003;5(7); and 2005; 9(3).

Versel N. The Truth About HIPAA. *CMA Today.* 2004;5:26.

Chapter Review Exercises

1. Name the four parts to HIPAA's Administrative Simplification section:

   _____

   _____

   _____

   _____

2. A covered entity includes all of the following except:
   a. A physician
   b. Health insurance plan
   c. Health-care clearinghouse
   d. A patient

3. CPT and ICD-9 codes are code sets.   **True or False** (circle one)

4. A patient's payment of his or her medical bill is part of Protected Health Information. **True or False** (circle one)

5. As the coder, you are allowed to turn over a patient's medical records to a court of law. **True or False** (circle one)

6. Under what circumstances are you allowed to give out Protected Health Information over the telephone?

   _____

   _____

7. **A good example of access control within the Technical Security Safeguards is:**
   a. User identification
   b. Screen savers
   c. Prohibit the use of e-mail
   d. File insurance claims weekly

8. HIPAA refers to code sets as _____ and _____.

9. Match the acronym with the correct term

   a. PHI   _____ Electronic Protected Health Information

   b. EDI   _____ Protected Health Information

   c. EPHI   _____ Electronic File Interchange Organization

   d. EFIO   _____ National Provider Identifier

10. Patients are required to sign a statement regarding the receipt of the office privacy policy. **True or False** (circle one)

Coding Systems

Diagnostic Coding

OBJECTIVES

● Understand the significance of accurate diagnosis coding

● Comprehend the difference between Volumes 1, 2, and 3 of ICD-9-CM

- Identify and follow the format, instructional terms, punctuation, abbreviations, and symbols used in the ICD-9-CM manual
- Locate and verify diagnoses in Volumes 1 and 2 of ICD-9-CM
- Compare the difference between principal, primary, and concurrent diagnoses
- Explain basic coding rules
- Accurately code all diagnoses using the ICD-9-CM coding manual

MEDICAL ASSISTANT COMPETENCIES
ABHES
1d. be cognizant of ethical boundaries
1i. conduct work within scope of education, training, and ability
2d. serve as a liaison between Physician and others
2h. receive, organize, prioritize, and transmit information expediently
3v. perform diagnostic coding
3w. complete insurance claim forms
5a. determine needs for documentation and reporting
5b. document accurately
5c. use appropriate guideline when releasing records or information
8b. implement current procedural terminology and ICD-9-CM coding
8c. analyze and use current third-party guidelines for reimbursement

CAAHEP
IV.C.11. Define both medical terms and abbreviations related to all body systems
IV.P.2. Report relevant information to others succinctly and accurately
IV.P.3. Use medical terminology, pronouncing medical terms correctly, to communicate information, patient history, data and observations
V.P.5. Execute data management using electronic healthcare records such as the EMR
V.P.6. Use office hardware and software to maintain office systems
VI.P.3. Utilize computerized office billing systems
VIII.C.1. Describe how to use the most current procedural coding system
VIII.C.3. Describe how to use the most current diagnostic coding classification system
VIII.P.2. Perform diagnostic coding
VIII.A.1. Work with physician to achieve the maximum reimbursement

KEY TERMS

Acute versus Chronic Condition
Adverse Effects of Drugs
Category
Classifications
Codes
Concurrent Diagnosis
Current Procedural Terminology (CPT)
Diagnosis, diagnoses
Disease
E Code
Formulary
ICD-9-CM
Late Effects
Manifestation
Metastasis
Morphology
Mortality
Neoplasm
Nonessential Modifiers
Not Elsewhere Classified (NEC)
Not Otherwise Specified (NOS)
Poisoning of a Drug
Primary Diagnosis
Principal Diagnosis
Puerperium
Subcategory
Subclassification
Secondary Diagnosis
Tabular
Uncertain Behavior
V Code

■ HISTORICAL BACKGROUND

To gather data on **mortality** (cause of death) rates, a statistician in 17th century England developed a system for recording the causes of death. Since that time, the original reporting system evolved into a numeric system used for the cataloging of all **diseases** and conditions, occurrences, morbidity (severity) rates, and mortalities. The World Health Organization (WHO) began administration of this system in 1948, now known as the International Classification of Diseases (ICD). Revisions were made as new diseases and conditions were discovered. The ICD is the international standard coding system.

> **! KEY TERMS**
>
> MORTALITY—The cause of death.
>
> ICD-9-CM—*The International Classification of Diseases, 9th Revision, Clinical Modification* (ICD-9-CM) is a coding system used by health-care providers to represent diagnoses, collect data, and communicate with third-party carriers.
>
> DIAGNOSIS, DIAGNOSES (PLURAL)—The cause, disease, or condition a person is identified with.
>
> DISEASE—A condition marked by subjective complaints, a specific history, and clinical signs, symptoms, and laboratory or radiographic findings. (Source: Taber's Cyclopedic Medical Dictionary, 21st ed. FA Davis Company, 2009.)

In the 1970s, the ICD was in its ninth revision. The United States National Center for Health Statistics (NCHS) was responsible for modifying the existing ICD system into a system that would describe the patient's actual conditions rather than just record health statistics and trends. This modification was known as the Clinical Modification (CM), and the first official **ICD-9-CM** was published in 1979. The clinical modification of the coding system was used to transform the verbal or written descriptions of conditions, diseases, and injuries in the medical record into a numerical code, to track health statistics. These standardized **codes**, which are easily read by computers, also were applied to insurance claims, making it easier to process claims and exchange information throughout the health-care revenue cycle.

> **! KEY TERM**
>
> CODES—A collection of 3-, 4-, and 5-digit numbers that convert the verbal description of diseases or conditions into a numerical system.

In 1989, the federal government made the use of ICD-9-CM mandatory for *all* diagnostic coding on *all* Medicare and Medicaid claims. Following the government's lead, private and public insurance companies soon adopted similar diagnostic coding requirements for all submitted claims. Through the ICD codes on insurance claims, government agencies and health-care organizations gather statistics on diseases and injuries and determine future changes in Medicare, Medicaid, and other insurance programs.

> **★ ICD NOTE**
>
> ICD-9-CM codes are also used to analyze health-care costs, trends, and the utilization of health-care facilities.

The following four parties cooperate to maintain the codes and provide the guidelines for the ICD-9-CM:

- National Center for Health Statistics (NCHS): A component of the Centers for Disease Control and Prevention (CDC), the nation's principal health statistics agency.
- Centers for Medicare and Medicaid Services (CMS): U.S. federal agency that administers Medicare, Medicaid, and the Children's Health Insurance Program (CHIP).

■ American Hospital Association (AHA): The national organization that represents and serves all types of hospitals, health-care networks, and their patients and communities.

■ American Health Information Management Association (AHIMA): The association of health information management (HIM) professionals who provide effective management of health data and medical records.

Official guidelines were developed to assist the coder with the proper use of ICD-9-CM. They should be used in conjunction with the instructions provided within ICD-9-CM itself. The instructions within ICD-9-CM take priority over the guidelines. The cooperating parties review and update the guidelines as needed.

The ICD-9-CM is revised every year in October by the United States National Center for Health Statistics and the CMS. The current ICD-9-CM codebook must be used for dates of service that occur on and after October 1st of every year.

ICD-10-CM

The WHO owns the international version of ICD. In 1992, the WHO released the 10th revision of ICD. Many countries already use this version. The United States has not yet adopted the clinical modification of the 10th revision, although adoption is expected in the near future. ICD-10-CM provides more categories for diseases and conditions than ICD-9-CM. ICD-10-CM is much more specific. The ICD-10-CM codes are up to 7 digits long to provide for greater specificity and for the expansion of new codes. ICD-9-CM codes are only up to five-digits long and future additions are limited. Tips and comparisons to ICD-9-CM will be made throughout Chapter 4. More information regarding ICD-10-CM can be reviewed on the Davis*Plus* website.

■ THE CODING PROCESS

The source of a patient's **diagnosis** may come from the patient's verbal complaints or concerns or a diagnosis may be determined through the examination of the patient or as a result of a diagnostic test or a surgery. The physician (health-care provider) will determine the patient's current diagnosis and convey that information in the patient's medical record and on the patient's super bill, encounter form, or route slip. These are returned to the front office where the patient's total charge for services will be calculated. The medical coder transforms the verbal or written description of diseases, injuries, and procedures into numerical codes and then posts or applies these codes to the patient's personal account.

The coder uses diagnosis codes to document the reason for the services rendered to the patient and procedure codes (discussed in Chapters 5 and 6) to describe the actual services rendered to the patient. These codes and the charges, dates of service, and patient demographics are transmitted to the appropriate insurance company via paper or electronic insurance claims for reimbursement.

It is important that every coder develop an understanding of the ICD-9-CM terminology and format. Understanding the format, abbreviations, punctuation, and symbols of ICD-9-CM is essential to accurate coding.

■ ICD-9-CM FORMAT AND TERMINOLOGY

Currently, the ICD-9-CM contains three volumes of 3- to 5-digit codes. Volumes 1 and 2 contain diagnosis codes and Volume 3 contains procedure codes. All health-care providers use volumes 1 and 2 to assign diagnosis codes, and hospitals and skilled nursing facilities use Volume 3 codes to assign procedure codes for rendered services. In the case of physician's offices, **Current Procedural Terminology (CPT)** codes are used to record the services provided. CPT codes will be discussed in detail in Chapters 5 and 6.

! KEY TERM

CURRENT PROCEDURAL TERMINOLOGY (CPT)—A manual containing the 5-digit numerical codes used to report medical services and procedures.

ICD-10 NOTE

ICD-10 contains just two volumes. ICD-10-PCS replaces ICD-9-CM's third volume of procedure codes. The "PCS" stands for Procedure Coding System.

ICD-10 codes are alphanumeric and include all letters except U. The letter U has been set aside for new diseases of undetermined etiology. Codes can be up to seven characters.

! KEY TERM

TABULAR—A list of diagnosis codes arranged in a numerical sequence.

Volume 1 of ICD-9-CM is referred to as the **"Tabular"** or the "numerical index" of diseases and injuries, and final diagnosis codes are assigned from this section. Volume 2 is the alphabetical index of diseases, injuries, and functions like a standard index. Volume 3 contains a tabular index and an alphabetical index, but for procedures instead of diseases and injuries. This text will focus only on Volumes 1 and 2.

■ CONVENTIONS

ICD-9-CM uses a set of abbreviations, symbols, and punctuations known as conventions to provide understanding and instruction to the coder. These conventions may be found in either the tabular or numerical listings. Explanations of the commonly used conventions follow.

Abbreviations

The ICD-9-CM tabular list, Volume 1, uses two important abbreviations, **NEC, Not Elsewhere Classified** and **NOS, Not Otherwise Specified**, to direct the coder and provide instructions.

! KEY TERMS

NEC—NOT ELSEWHERE CLASSIFIED—This abbreviation appears after a subterm in Volume 1. If a code has a NEC designation, it means that ICD-9-CM does not provide a more specific code for this diagnosis, even though the diagnostic statement in the medical record may be more specific. The code may be classified as "other."

NOS—NOT OTHERWISE SPECIFIED—This abbreviation appears next to code descriptions in Volume 1 and indicates the code is unspecified or generic. The coder should use a NOS code when the diagnosis from the patient's medical record does not give any definite information or specifics for an exact code to be used.

ICD-10 NOTE

ICD-10 uses the abbreviations NEC and NOS.

! KEY TERM

NONESSENTIAL MODIFIERS—Supplementary words added to a diagnosis that do not change the code assignment.

Punctuation

ICD-9 uses punctuation to save space, and each punctuation mark has a special meaning.

[ ] Brackets are used in Volume 1 to enclose synonyms, alternative wordings or codes, explanatory phrases. For example, code 460, Acute nasopharyngitis in Volume 1. Brackets enclose the term "common cold," a synonym for the medical term "nasopharyngitis."

[ ] Slanted brackets used in Volume 2, the alphabetic index, designate codes that require an additional code be used to describe the patient's condition.

( ) Parentheses are used to enclose **nonessential modifiers**, which are supplementary words that do not affect the code assignment. Nonessential modifiers may be present in the statement of a disease, but are not required to assign the correct diagnostic code. In Volume 2, see the entry for "Symptoms." The word "general" is in parentheses. Further down the list of Symptoms, the coder will find the codes for joint symptoms, specifically of the shoulder. The word "region" is also in parentheses. Those terms will not affect the selection of the correct code, which is why they are considered nonessential. Parentheses appearing in Volume 1 enclose the codes of underlying diseases or conditions and direct the coder to assign that code as the primary code.

: Colons are used in Volume 1, after an incomplete term. As an example, see diagnosis code 780.0 in Volume 1. The word coma under the main term, *Alteration of consciousness* is followed by a colon and a list of types of comas, diabetic, hepatic, and originating in the perinatal period.

{ } Braces may be used in Volume 1 to enclose or connect a list of terms that the medical coder might find in the patient's medical record describing the type of condition. For example, 786.59 Other (Chest Pain). Found below the term "Other" is a list of adjectives describing chest pain:

Discomfort
Pressure   in chest
Tightness

Not all publishers use braces in their version of the ICD-9-CM. In the case that braces are *not* used, the list of terms is printed beneath the main term.

> ★ **ICD-10 NOTE**
> The same conventions are used in ICD-9-CM and ICD-10-CM with the exception of braces and brackets.

Instructional Notes

The instructional notes indicated in Table 4–1 require the coder to read the directions and follow the instructions given by ICD-9 if they are applicable to the patient's condition.

VOLUME 1: THE TABULAR INDEX

Volume 1 of ICD-9-CM contains 17 chapters of numerical listings of diseases and injuries, two sections of additional codes known as "V" and "E" codes and four appendices (Table 4–2). The first 10 chapters are dedicated to each major organ system and the next seven chapters are devoted to specific types of conditions that can affect the body.

> ★ **ICD-10 NOTE**
> The first character of every ICD-10-CM code is a capital letter.

> ❗ **KEY TERM**
> CATEGORY(S)—A three-digit code used to represent a particular disease or condition is termed a category.

> ❗ **KEY TERM**
> SUBCATEGORIES—Most three-digit categories have been expanded to 4- or 5-digit codes that provide more specific information regarding the disease or condition. The fourth digit of an ICD-9-CM code is called a subcategory.

TABLE 4–1: Instructional Notations

Type of Notation	Purpose and Location
Includes	Appears immediately under a three-digit code title to further define or give an example of the contents of the category.`
Excludes	Terms following the Excludes instruction are to be coded elsewhere as instructed or in addition to the code they modify.
Notes	Provide instructions or guidelines. Volume 2 notes are boxed and further define terms, clarify information, or list choices for additional digits.
See	Directs you to a more specific term to find the correct code.
See also	Additional information available elsewhere that may provide an additional diagnostic code.
See category	Review the entire category specified before assigning a code.
See condition	Directs you to refer to a main term rather than looking for a code by an anatomical site or by an adjective describing the condition. If you look up the actual word "condition," you will only find subterms for psychiatric and respiratory conditions and be directed to look for the actual disease.
Code first underlying disease	Used in categories not intended to be the primary diagnosis. The code, its title and instructions appear in italics. The note requires that the underlying disease (etiology) be recorded first and the particular manifestation second.
Use additional code	Appears in categories where you must add further information to give a more complete picture of the diagnosis.

Structure of Chapters

As mentioned earlier, Volume 1 is composed of 17 chapters, each containing diagnostic codes pertaining to a type of disease or disorder or an anatomical part of the human body. Each chapter is then broken down by:

- ■ **Sections:** Groups of three-digit code numbers representing a set of similar conditions.
- ■ **Categories:** Three-digit code numbers representing each of those conditions.
- ■ **Subcategories:** Four-digit code numbers listed under three-digit categories.
- ■ **Fifth-digit subclassifications:** Five-digit code numbers listed under three- and four-digit categories. Five digits provide even more information regarding cause, site, **manifestation**, characteristic signs, symptoms, or secondary processes of an illness.

For example, all codes have at least three digits. The fourth or fifth digits that apply to a particular code adds detail to the condition, see code 780, General symptoms (Fig. 4–1). It is the first **category** in the Symptoms (780–789) section of Chapter 16, SYMPTOMS, SIGNS, AND ILL-DEFINED CONDITIONS (780–799).

Just below 780 and indented is the four-digit code, 780.0, called a **subcategory**. A subcategory is three numbers and a decimal point, followed by a fourth digit; the decimal point separates the first three digits from its subcategory.

The fourth digit makes the code more specific, because it tells the coder that 780.0, is alteration of consciousness. Most categories (three-digit codes) have four digits that make the category codes more specific. These digits indicate a site (area of the body), a cause or source, and/or a manifestation. Whenever a fourth digit is present, that four-digit code must be used—do not use the three-digit code preceding it.

(continued on page 72)

TABLE 4–2:   Chapter Listings for Volume 1, Tabular List

Chapter	Classification of Diseases	Range of Codes
Chapter 1	Infectious and Parasitic Diseases	001–139
Chapter 2	Neoplasms	140–239
Chapter 3	Endocrine, Nutritional, and Metabolic Disease, and Immunity Disorders	240–279
Chapter 4	Diseases of the Blood and Blood-Forming Organs	280–289
Chapter 5	Mental Disorders	290–319
Chapter 6	Diseases of the Nervous System and Sense Organs	320–389
Chapter 7	Diseases of the Circulatory System	390–459
Chapter 8	Diseases of the Respiratory System	460–519
Chapter 9	Diseases of the Digestive System	520–579
Chapter 10	Diseases of the Genitourinary System	580–629
Chapter 11	Complications of Pregnancy, Childbirth, and the Puerperium	630–677
Chapter 12	Diseases of the Skin and Subcutaneous Tissue	680–709
Chapter 13	Diseases of the Musculoskeletal System and Connective Tissue	710–739
Chapter 14	Congenital Anomalies	740–759
Chapter 15	Certain Conditions Originating in the Perinatal Period	760–779
Chapter 16	Symptoms, Signs, and Ill-Defined Conditions	780–799
Chapter 17	Injury and Poisoning	800–999

Supplementary Classifications

V Codes	Classification of Factors Influencing Health Status and Contact with Health Services	V01–V89
E Codes	Classification of External Causes of Injury and Poisoning	E800–E999

Appendices

Appendix A	**Morphology of Neoplasms**
Appendix B	Glossary of Mental Disorders (Removed from FY 2005 ICD-9-CM)
Appendix C	Classification of Drugs by American Hospital Formulary Service, Lists Numbers and Their ICD-9-CM Equivalents
Appendix D	Classification of Industrial Accidents According to Agency
Appendix E	List of Three-Digit Categories

❗ KEY TERMS

MANIFESTATIONS—The demonstration of the presence of a sign, symptom, or alteration, especially one that is associated with a disease process. (Source: Taber's Cyclopedic Medical Dictionary, 21st ed. FA Davis Company, 2009.)

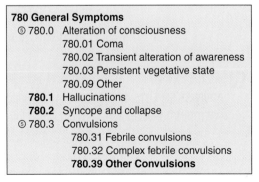

780 General Symptoms
Ⓢ 780.0 Alteration of consciousness
          780.01 Coma
          780.02 Transient alteration of awareness
          780.03 Persistent vegetative state
          780.09 Other
  780.1 Hallucinations
  780.2 Syncope and collapse
Ⓢ 780.3 Convulsions
          780.31 Febrile convulsions
          780.32 Complex febrile convulsions
          780.39 Other Convulsions

FIGURE 4–1: General Symptoms in the Tabular List.

A fifth digit is available on many codes and adds even more specific information to the description of the condition. A fifth digit is called a subclassification. To the left of 780.0, there is a symbol that indicates a fifth digit should be used (see Fig. 4–1). This means there is a fifth digit **subclassification** present and use of the fifth digit is *mandatory.* To choose a valid ICD-9-CM code for an alteration of consciousness, the coder must choose from the fifth-digit subclassifications, 780.01, 780.02, 780.03 or 780.09, listed beneath the subcategory, 780.0. Remember, the coder should use three digits *only* when there is not a more specific fourth digit available, and use a four-digit code *only* when there is not a more specific, fifth digit available. Fifth-digit subclassifications also may appear in Volume 1 immediately below a three-digit category (Fig. 4–2).

! KEY TERM

SUBCLASSFICATION—A fifth digit added on to a four-digit ICD-9-CM code is called a subclassification. The fifth digit provides even greater details regarding the condition.

★ **ICD-10 NOTES**

ICD-10-CM codes can be expanded to as many as seven digits offering greater detail.

A decimal should not be added to diagnosis codes that are only three-digits long.

! KEY TERM

V CODES—Diagnosis codes that begin with the letter V and represent a circumstance other than diseases or injuries as a diagnosis or problem.

V Codes

V codes (V01–V82) are officially known as the Classification of Factors Influencing Health Status and Contact with Health Services (Table 4–3). Each numeric code is preceded by a capital "V." These codes are used for patients who are not currently ill but a health service is called for to address another need. A V code should be assigned when a patient is:

■ Acting as a donor of an organ or other tissue.

■ Receiving a vaccination or immunization.

■ Discussing a problem or concern that is not considered a disease or an injury, such as family planning.

■ Receiving a general examination.

■ Receiving a specific treatment, such as chemotherapy or dialysis.

■ Exposed to a situation or a substance that can affect the status of their health but is not a current illness or injury yet.

V codes are discussed in detail a little later on in this chapter.

! KEY TERMS

ADVERSE EFFECTS OF DRUGS—Any unwanted side effect or reaction to a drug taken properly.
POISONING OF A DRUG—A toxic reaction to a drug taken improperly.

TABLE 4–3: V Code Listings

Categories	V Code Range
Persons with Potential Health Hazards Related to Communicable Diseases	V01–V06
Persons with a Need for Isolation, Other Potential Health Hazards, and Prophylactic Measures	V07–V09
Persons with Potential Health Hazards Related to Personal and Family History	V10–V19
Persons Encountering Health Services in Circumstances Related to Reproduction and Development	V20–V29
Liveborn Infants According to Type of Birth	V30–V39
Persons With a Condition Influencing Their Health Status	V40–V49
Persons Encountering Health Services for Specific Procedures and Aftercare	V50–V59
Persons Encountering Health Services in Other Circumstances	V60–V69
Persons Without Reported Diagnosis Encountered During Examination and Investigation of Individuals and Population	V70–V82

---

789 Other symptoms involving abdomen and pelvis
   The following fifth-digit subclassification is to be used for codes 789.0, 789.3, 789.4, 789.6
   0   **unspecified**
   1   **right upper quadrant**
   2   **left upper quadrant**
   3   **right lower quadrant**
   4   **left lower quadrant**
   5   **periumbilic**
   6   **epigastric**
   9   **other specified site**

⑤ **789.0 Abdominal pain**
   789.1 Hepatomegaly
   789.2 Splenomegaly
⑤ **789.3 Abdominal or pelvic swelling, mass, or lump**
⑤ **789.4 Abdominal rigidity**

FIGURE 4–2: Fifth-digit subclassifications.

E Codes

E codes (E800–E999) are officially known as the Supplementary Classification of External Causes of Injury and Poisoning. These alpha/numeric codes each begin with the capital letter "E." E codes are used to capture how an injury occurred, the intent, (accidental or intentional), and the place where the injury occurred, such as a fall on ice or allergic reaction to a drug. These codes are not used to diagnose the cause of a disease and can never be used for the primary diagnosis. They are only used in addition to the ICD-9-CM codes 001 through V codes and should never be used alone.

The alphabetic E code index (Table 4–4) is organized by main terms, which describe the accident, circumstance, event, or specific agent that caused the injury or other adverse effect. The categories for nature and cause of injury provide information in relation to industrial medicine, insurance underwriters, national safety programs, and public health agencies. Unless mandated by an insurance carrier regulation or a state mandate, the use of most E codes is optional. Health-care providers are encouraged to report E codes for all of the initial treatment of injuries to provide information for the study and assessment of injuries and their prevention. However, the use of E codes is mandatory for the reporting of the adverse effect of drugs in therapeutic use, E930–E949. E codes are also assigned for Late Effects (Table 4–5).

More explanation is provided later in the chapter in the section on E codes.

TABLE 4–4: E Codes

E Code Range	Coverage
E800–E848	Transport Accidents—Any accident involving a device designed or used primarily for carrying persons or goods from one place to another; includes aircraft, spacecraft, watercraft, motor vehicles, railway, and other road vehicles
E849	Optional category used only with categories E850–E869 and E**0-E928 to indicate the place where the accident or poisoning occurred
E850–E858	Accidental Poisoning by Drugs, Medicinal Substances and Biologicals
E860–E869	Accidental Poisoning by Other Solid and Liquid Gases and Vapors
E870–E876	Misadventures to Patients During Surgical and Medical Care
E878–E879	Surgical and Medical Procedures as the Causes of Abnormal Reaction of Patient or Later Complications Without Mention of Misadventure at the Time of Procedure
E880–E888	Accidental Falls
E890–E899	Accidents Caused by Fire and Flames
E900–E909	Accidents Due to Natural and Environmental Factors
E910–E915	Accidents Caused by Submersion, Suffocation, and Foreign Bodies
E916–E928	Other Accidents
E929	Late Effects of Accidental Injury
E930–E949	Drugs, Medicinal, and Biological Substances Causing Adverse Effects in Therapeutic Use
E950–E959	Suicide and Self-Inflicted Injury
E960–E969	Homicide and Injury Purposely Inflicted by Other Person
E970–E979	Legal Intervention
E980–E989	Injury Undetermined Whether Accidentally or Purposely Inflicted
E990–E999	Injury Resulting From Operations of War

TABLE 4–5: E Codes for External Causes of Late Effects

E Code Range	Late Effect
E929	Late Effects of Accidental Injury
E959	Late Effects of Self-Inflicted Injury
E969	Late Effects of Injury Purposely Inflicted by Other Person
E977	Late Effects of Injuries Due to Legal Intervention
E878–E879	Late Effects of Surgical and Medical Complications and Misadventures
E989	Late Effects of Injury, Undetermined Whether Accidentally or Purposely Inflicted
E999	Late Effects of Injury Due to War Operations

★ **ICD-10 NOTE**

The codes that represent Factors Influencing Health Status and Contact with Health Services and Classification of External Causes of Injury and Poisoning have been included along with all of the codes in ICD-10-CM and are not found in a separate section (Table 4–6). All ICD-10-CM codes are alphanumeric and include all letters except the letter U. The letter U has been held in reserve for new diseases of undetermined causes.

! **KEY TERM**

MORPHOLOGY—The form and structure of a neoplasm.

TABLE 4–6: ICD-10-CM Tabular List

Chapter	Title	Code Range
I	Certain Infectious and parasitic disease	A00–B99
II	Neoplasms	C00–D48
III	Disease of the blood and blood-forming organs and certain disorders	D50–D89
IV	Endocrine, nutritional and metabolic diseases	E00–E90
V	Mental and behavioral disorders	F00–F99
VI	Disease of the nervous system	G00–G99
VII	Diseases of the eye and adnexa	H00–H59
VIII	Diseases of the ear mastoid process	H60–H95
IX	Disease of the circulatory system	I00–I99
X	Disease of the respiratory system	J00–J99
Xi	Disease of the digestive system	K00–K93
XII	Diseases of the skin and subcutaneous tissue	L00–L99
XIII	Disease of the musculoskeletal system and connective tissue	M00–M99
XIV	Disease of the genitourinary system	N00–N99
XV	Pregnancy, childbirth and the puerperium	O00–O99
XVI	Certain conditions originating in the perinatal period	P00–P96
XVII	Congenital malformations, deformations and chromosomal abnormalities	Q00–Q99
XVIII	Symptoms, signs, and abnormal clinical and laboratory findings, not elsewhere classified	R00–R99
XIX	Injury, poisoning and certain other consequences of eternal causes	S00–T98
XX	External causes of morbidity and mortality	V01–V98
XXI	Factors influencing health status and contact with health services	Z00–Z99
XXII	Codes for special purposes	U00–U99

Appendices

Most ICD-9-CM publishers include four appendices to provide the coder with additional information:

■ **Appendix A: Morphology of Neoplasms.** This is a list of five-digit codes, all beginning with the capital letter "M." Morphology is the form and structure of a neoplasm. These codes are for statistical data only and are never used on a physician's claim form. Tumor registrars, pathology departments, and other agencies specializing in cancer use these codes.

 KEY TERM

NEOPLASM—An abnormal development of tissue as in a tumor or growth.

■ **Appendix B: Glossary of Mental Disorders.** This appendix was a reference for the classification of mental disorders, chemical dependencies, dementias, psychoses, and neurotic and psychological disorders. In 2004, the American Psychiatric Association requested that the glossary be removed, because it had not been maintained and was no longer accurate. ICD-9-CM was designated as the only acceptable diagnostic code set when HIPAA regulations went into effect; therefore, ICD-9-CM had to remain current with the clinical terminology changes that had taken place in the field of mental disorders, and chose to delete the appendix.

★ **ICD-10 NOTE**

The mental and behavioral disorder codes in ICD-10-CM are equivalent to the codes found in the *Diagnostic and Statistical Manual of Mental Disorders* published by the American Psychiatric Association.

■ **Appendix C: Classification of Drugs by American Hospital Formulary Services List Number and their ICD-9-CM Equivalents.** The American Hospital Formulary is published by the American Society of Hospital Pharmacists and is a drug index that includes the monographs of each drug. A monograph is used by physicians and pharmacists for information on drug interactions, adverse reactions, contraindications, cautions, therapeutic-specific dosage administration information, and other drug-specific information. The list appears in ICD-9-CM only to classify drugs by types (e.g., antibiotics, antihistamines, or diuretics) and provide a diagnosis code for poisoning from that drug type. For example, the Hospital Formulary listing 4:00 is the classification number for all antihistamine drugs. This classification of numbers is also used to track drug usage for each drug type, but the coder uses the **formulary** list to find the ICD-9-CM codes for the poisoning of drugs that are not listed by name in Volume 2's Table of Drugs and Chemicals. The Poisoning and Adverse Effects section in this chapter will address how to use and find codes from the formulary list.

❗ KEY TERM

FORMULARY—A list of drugs available for routine use at a health-care facility. (Source: Taber's Cyclopedic Medical Dictionary, 21st ed. FA Davis Company, 2009.)

■ **Appendix D: Classification of Industrial Accidents According to Agency.** This appendix is a list of codes used to classify industrial accidents. These occupational hazard codes are not used by the coder and never placed on a CMS-1500 claim form. Instead, these codes are used by state and federal organizations to collect data on industrial accidents.

■ **Appendix E: List of Three-Digit Categories.** This appendix is a summary of all three-digit code categories that appear in each chapter of Volume 1. This list can only be used as an overview of all codes listed in Volume 1 and can never be used to code a claim form. See the explanation of subcategories and subclassifications earlier in the chapter for more information.

■ VOLUME 2: THE ALPHABETIC INDEX

Volume 2, the alphabetic index of diseases, conditions, and injuries, is divided into the following three sections:

1. **The Index to Diseases, Conditions, and Injuries** is listed in alphabetic order. This section index also contains the tables for codes related to hypertension and neoplasms. These tables list specific sites and types of hypertension and neoplasms.

2. **The Table of Drugs and Chemicals** contains an extensive list of drugs, industrial solvents, corrosives, gases, noxious plants, pesticides, and other toxic agents. The table identifies types of poisonings and external causes of adverse effects.

3. **The Alphabetic Index to External Causes of Injuries and Poisonings (E codes)** contains codes that describe how an injury or condition occurred. This section is formatted according to the type of event or accident. Further explanation of E codes is later in the chapter.

 ICD-10 NOTE

ICD-10-CM Volume 2 is organized in the same manner as ICD-9-CM. Codes are listed by main terms.

Layout and Conventions

The layout of Volume 2 is similar to a dictionary. Understanding the format here is critical for an accurate coding selection. Main terms are listed alphabetically and appear in **boldface** type. For an example, when the coder looks up the word "Symptoms" in Volume 2, the main term **"Symptoms"** will be followed by an indented alphabetical list of subterms (Fig. 4–3), indented two spaces below the main term of symptoms ranging from the abdomen to vascular with a four- or five-digit code following each symptom. If the complete entry of the subterm cannot fit on the page, an added line will follow below and indented even further to distinguish it from another subterm (Fig. 4–4).

It is a good idea to use a ruler or straight edge to help line up the subterms and added lines under a main term to allow the coder a clearer perspective.

The coder will find diagnosis codes listed by main terms printed in bold face describing:

■ A disease such as influenza or bronchitis

■ A condition such as a symptom, fracture, or injury

■ A noun such as the name of a disease, disturbance, or syndrome

■ An adjective such as double, kink, or even large

The coder will *not* find codes by anatomical site. Using the example of symptoms, if the coder was looking for an ICD-9-CM code for abdominal symptoms, the word symptoms would be referenced, not the word abdomen or abdominal. The coder will find the appropriate codes by looking under adjectives and nouns that describe the patient's conditions. In most cases, if the coder looks for a code under an anatomical site, they will be directed to *"see also condition."* The ICD-9-CM instruction tells

---

Symptoms, specified (general) NEC 780.99
  abdomen NEC 789.9
  bone NEC 733.90
  breast NEC 611.79
  cardiac NEC 785.9
  cardiovascular NEC 785.9
  chest NEC 786.9
  joint NEC 719.60
    ankle 719.67
    elbow 719.62
    foot 719.67
    hand 719.67

FIGURE 4–3: Subterms for "Symptoms."

Surgery
  cosmetic NEC V50.1
    following healed injury or operation V51
    hair transplant V50.0
  elective V50.9
    breast augmentation reduction V50.1
    circumcision, ritual or routine (in absence of
      medical indication) V50.2
    cosmetic NEC V50.1
    ear piercing V50.3
    face-lift V50.1
    following healed injury or operation V51
    hair transplant V50.0
  not done because of
    contraindication V64.1
    patient's decision V64.2
    specified reason NEC V64.3
  plastic
    breast augmentation or reduction V50.1
    cosmetic V50.1
    face-lift V50.1
    following healed injury or operation V51
    repair of scarred tissue (following healed
      injury or operation) V51
    specified type NEC V50.8

FIGURE 4–4: Added line for subterm.

the coder to look for the diagnosis code under the type of symptom or condition the patient has. It does not imply that the coder reference the actual word "condition."

In addition to typefaces and layout, Volume 2 also contains other conventions, including instructional notes, abbreviations, punctuation marks, and symbols.

ESTABLISHING THE PROPER DIAGNOSIS

Just as specific coding is essential, the other most important aspect of diagnosis coding is coding to the "highest degree of certainty." For example, a patient visits a medical clinic complaining of a headache. During the examination, the doctor notes a questionable weakness on the right side of the body. The doctor orders a CAT or CT scan of the brain to rule out a brain tumor. The correct ICD-9-CM codes for the visit should *only* represent the symptoms noted by the patient and by the physician. The brain tumor is not an established condition—it is only a suspicion until confirmed. A definite diagnosis can never be used with a statement such as "rule out," "suspected," or "probable." The patient's signs, symptoms, and complaints are assigned ICD-9 codes until a definite diagnosis, known as a primary or principal diagnosis, is made.

Primary, Principal, Concurrent Diagnoses

The term **primary diagnosis** refers to diagnoses used in an outpatient setting. It is the condition that is considered the reason the patient was seen. This primary condition is always coded first followed by concurrent diagnoses or conditions. A **concurrent diagnosis** is a condition(s) present at the same time as the primary condition. The **principal diagnosis** refers the diagnoses used in an inpatient setting. The principal diagnosis is determined to be the major cause for the patient's condition. The principal diagnosis is not the admitting diagnosis but rather the diagnosis given after testing or surgery that demonstrates the reason for the hospitalization. Refer to the example of the patient that comes to the doctor complaining of a headache. The *primary* diagnosis for the examination is the headache, 784.0. The concurrent diagnosis is the weakness on the right side, 728.87. The *principal* diagnosis would have to be assigned *after* CAT scan results were reviewed. If a biopsy was taken of the tumor, and/or surgery was performed, the principal diagnosis would change to represent the outcome—whether the tumor was benign, malignant, or of an **uncertain behavior**.

❗ KEY TERMS

CONCURRENT DIAGNOSIS—A condition that is present at the same time as the primary diagnosis.

PRIMARY DIAGNOSIS—A diagnosis or condition in an outpatient setting that indicates the reason the patient was seen. This is always coded first.

PRINCIPAL DIAGNOSIS—A diagnosis determined in an inpatient setting after diagnostic testing or procedures determine the reason for hospitalization.

UNCERTAIN BEHAVIOR—The specimen showed signs of both malignancy and benign cells. The tumor may be changing and additional studies would be necessary to decide the tumor type.

CODING A DIAGNOSIS

Basic Coding Rules

■ When coding a diagnosis, establish the reason for the patient's encounter. In the patient's medical record, find the main term of the diagnostic description or the patient's symptoms or complaints.

■ Always consult the ICD-9-CM Alphabetic Index (Volume 2) first to locate that main term.

 ICD-10 NOTE

The Alphabetic Index also must be consulted first when choosing an ICD-10-CM code.

■ In Volume 2, also refer to any notes and modifiers under the main terms.

■ Refer to any subterms indented under the main term. Remember, these *do* have an affect on the code selection.

■ Verify the code in the Volume 1 (Tabular List). *Never code directly from Volume 2 (Alphabetical Index).*

■ If necessary, use two or more codes to completely classify a diagnosis. The "code also" instructions in Volume 1 (Tabular List) provide the best guide to determining if two codes are necessary.

■ Read and be guided by the inclusions and exclusions that may appear under a particular code, category, section, or chapter.

■ Read any footnotes or notes.

■ If the code matches the patient's diagnosis, assign that code to the patient's medical record and/or insurance forms.

■ Follow any cross-references (terms or instructions) or directions to "*see*" or "*see also.*"

■ Code to the highest level of specificity. Assign three-digit codes *only* when there are no four-digit codes within that category. Assign a four-digit code *only* when there is no fifth-digit subclassification for the category.

Applying V Codes

As discussed earlier, V codes are used when a person who is not currently sick encounters health services for some specific purpose; for example, to receive a vaccination, to discuss a problem that is not in itself a disease or injury, to seek consultation regarding family planning, or to request sterilization.

V codes may show situations that influence a patient's health status but are not a current illness or injury, including the following:

■ Family history or personal history of cancer

■ Counseling for family problems

■ Screening or observation for suspected condition

V codes are appropriate as the primary code to designate the reason for the patient's visit. V codes can be used to identify a patient:

■ Receiving therapy services as part of an ongoing plan of treatment.

■ Receiving routine or screening services.

■ With a history of a disease.

■ Seeking follow-up services.

CMS has given Medicare and Medicaid carriers coding instructions for use of V codes. Medicare and Medicaid set limits on the coverage of routine care and of well physicals, so reimbursement may not be received for some V codes. The local carrier manual should always be consulted for current regulations regarding the use of V codes.

Applying E Codes

E codes show the cause of an injury, event, or circumstance such as the following:

■ How an accident occurred

■ Whether a drug overdose was accidental or purposeful

■ Other circumstances that caused the injury or condition being coded

E codes are located in Volume 1 following the V-code section. An alphabetic index of external causes of injury and poisoning is listed in section 3 of Volume 2. All E codes begin with the capital letter "E" followed by three numeric digits and, in most cases, a decimal point and fourth numeric digit. There are no fifth-digit subclassifications on E codes. The fourth-digit subdivisions add specificity to help identify the injured person or type of accident involved.

E codes can be useful when describing an accident or injury to a worker's compensation company or to an auto insurance company. The coder may use as many E codes as necessary to explain the situation. *Never* list E codes as a solitary code or primary diagnosis on a claim.

E Code Example

A construction worker fell from the roof of a structure and sustained a fractured pelvis. Code the injury first, fractured pelvis, 808.8. The description of the incident will be found in the Alphabetic Index under Fall, falling, from, off, building **E882.**

 ## SPECIAL CONSIDERATIONS

Multiple Coding and Combination Coding

A *combination code* is a single code that either combines two diagnoses or combines a diagnosis with an associated secondary development (manifestation) or complication. Combination codes are identified by looking at the subterm entries in Volume 2 (Alphabetic Index) and by reading the inclusion and exclusion notes in the Volume 1 (Tabular List). The two main terms may be joined together by combination terms such as:

associated with	complicated (by)	due to	during
following	in	secondary to	with/without

The combination code should only be assigned when it fully identifies the diagnostic conditions involved or when instructed by the Alphabetic Index. Multiple codes should not be used if a combination code identifies all of the elements documented in the diagnosis—only a combination code should be used. When a combination code is not specific enough to describe the manifestation or complication, an additional code may be used as a secondary code.

 ### ICD-10 NOTE

ICD-10-CM codes combine etiology and manifestation together and are represented by one code. ICD-9-CM usually requires two codes.

Multiple coding is the use of more than one code to completely identify the entire diagnosis. When "Use additional code" notes are listed in Volume 1, another code may be included, though not mandatory to fully describe a condition and added as the secondary code. For example, directions for the code 590, *Infections of the kidney,* in Volume 1 says, "Use additional code, if desired, to identify organism, such as *Escherichia coli* [*E. coli*] (041.4)." The coder should include the additional code for the organism responsible for the condition when documented in the patient's medical record.

KEY TERM

SECONDARY DIAGNOSIS—A diagnosis used in addition to the main, primary diagnosis.

If any "code first" notes appear in the chosen code and there is an underlying condition present in the medical record, the underlying condition should be sequenced first.

Underlying Cause (etiology) = primary diagnosis

Effect (manifestation) = secondary diagnosis

For example, directions for code, 425.7, *Nutritional and metabolic cardiomyopathy,* in Volume 1 says, "Code first underlying disease, as:

Amyloidosis (277.30–277.39)

Beriberi (265.0)

Cardiac glycogenesis (271.0)

Mucopolysaccharidosis (277.5)

Thyrotoxicosis (242.0–242.9)

Multiple coding is only mandatory when a second code appears in *italics* and inside brackets in the Alphabetic Index (Volume 2) *and* is then found under the code in Volume 1. For example, see Diabetes, diabetic 250.0, in Volume 2 (Fig. 4–5). Many of the subterms listed show codes in italics after the code for the diabetic condition; these italicized codes represent conditions associated with diabetes. For example, see Diabetic neuritis, 250.6x. This condition is listed in Volume 2 as "Diabetes, diabetic, neuritis *[357.2]*." When the code is verified in Volume 1, "polyneuropathy" is listed (357.2) beneath the code, and this signifies that a second code is mandatory. In this case, 250.6 (x-fifth digit required) is assigned for the primary diagnosis and 357.2 is assigned for the secondary one.

ICD-10 NOTE

The medical coder must always remember multiple coding should *not* be used when a combination code accurately identifies the diagnosis.

ICD-10-CM also contains combination codes.

Symptoms, Signs, and Ill-defined Conditions (780–799)

Codes that describe a patient's signs and/or symptoms are used when a definitive diagnosis has not been established or confirmed by the physician.

Diabetes, diabetic (brittle) (congenital) (familial) (mellitus) (poorly controlled) (severe) (slight) (without complication) 250.0

> *Note — Use the following fifth-digit subclassification with category 250:*
> *0 type II or unspecified type, not stated as uncontrolled*
> *fifth-digit 0 is for use for type II patients, even if the patient requires insulin*
> *1 type I [juvenile type], not stated as uncontrolled*
> *2 type II or unspecified type, uncontrolled fifth-digit 2 is used for type II patients, even if the patient requires insulin*
> *3 type I [juvenile type], uncontrolled*

with
    coma (with ketoacidosis) 250.3
     hyperosmolar (nonketotic) 250.2
    complication NEC 250.9
     specified NEC 250.8
    gangrene 250.7 *[785.4]*
    hyperosmolarity 250.2
    ketosis, ketoacidosis 250.1
    osteomyelitis 250.8 *[731.8]*
    specified manifestations NEC 250.8
  acetonemia 250.1
  acidosis 250.1
  amyotrophy 250.6 *[358.1]*
  angiopathy, peripheral 250.7 *[443.81]*
  asymptomatic 790.29
  autonomic neuropathy (peripheral) 250.6 *[337.1]*

FIGURE 4–5: Entry for Diabetes in Volume 2.

Codes 780–799 should be used for the following:

- Cases for which no other more specific diagnosis can be made after a thorough study
- Signs and symptoms existing on initial visit
- Cases that were transferred elsewhere before a definite diagnosis could be made
- Certain symptoms that represent important problems or complications or that further show that treatment is medically necessary

Conditions That Are an Integral Part of a Disease Process

Signs and symptoms that are an integral part of the disease process should *not* be assigned as additional codes. For example: A patient is seen by the physician for a fever and itchy rash. After examination, the physician diagnosed the patient with chickenpox. Fever and itchy rash are common symptoms of chickenpox and are not coded; only the diagnosis of chickenpox is coded.

Conditions That Are Not an Integral Part of a Disease Process

Additional signs and symptoms that may not be associated routinely with a disease process should be coded when present. For example: A patient, who suffers with chronic diverticulitis, presents with diarrhea. Diarrhea is not a typical condition with diverticulitis and would be coded, in addition to diverticulitis.

Suspected Conditions

Many times a patient is seen by their physician because of symptoms they are having that may indicate a certain condition. For example, chronic heartburn may lead to or be the cause of esophagitis; however, the physician can only suggest the diagnosis, until a test actually confirms it. Code *only* the symptoms noted in the medical record until a definite diagnosis is made by the physician. When the medical record states a condition as "rule out," *only* the symptoms the patient is currently having should be coded. The patient with the heartburn may be set up for an esophagogastroduodenoscopy (EGD) specifically to rule out esophagitis, but until the test is completed and the results have been interpreted, the diagnosis is still heartburn.

Acute and Chronic Conditions

If the patient's condition is described as both acute (or subacute) and chronic, and separate codes exist in the Alphabetic Index (Volume 2) at the same indentation level, code both conditions. The acute (or subacute) code should always be listed first. For example:

Appendicitis

acute 540.9

chronic (recurrent) 542

 KEY TERMS

ACUTE versus CHRONIC CONDITIONS—An acute condition strikes quickly with severe symptoms and runs a short course. A chronic condition progresses slowly with little change in symptoms.

★ **ICD-10 NOTE**

ICD-10-CM follows the same guidelines for acute, subacute, and chronic conditions.

KEY TERMS

LATE EFFECT—A remaining condition left after an acute phase of an illness or injury has ended.

Late Effects

A **late effect** is a remaining problem or condition that occurs after the acute phase of the illness or injury. Late effects can occur anytime, even if it's less than a month or more than a year since the acute phase of the illness or injury. In cases that include late effects, two codes will be needed to identify the patient's condition, with three exceptions:

1. When the residual effect is not stated.

2. When no late effect code is provided in ICD-9-CM.

3. When the residual condition follows a cerebrovascular disease. In the third type of case, the fourth and fifth digits of the code 438 (Late effect of a cerebrovascular accident) include the residual conditions.

No matter what type of case, always code the residual condition as the first diagnosis and the cause as the second diagnosis. Remember, the residual condition must be documented by the physician in the patient's medical record in order to code it. To locate the appropriate code for cause of the residual condition, refer to the entry for "Main Term, Late effect(s)" in Volume 2. This list represents *only* conditions that have already occurred. To be considered a late effect, the patient no longer has this condition but is suffering from the effects of the condition.

For example, a patient visits the physician with arthritis in the forearm, due to previous fracture of the elbow that occurred some time ago. The fractured bone has healed now, but arthritis has developed since then. The arthritis should be coded as the primary diagnosis with 716.43; this is the reason the patient is being treated now because of the fracture that occurred. The fracture should be assigned a secondary code from Volume 2 (Fig. 4–6). In this case, the correct code is 905.2, Late effect(s), fracture, extremity, upper.

When the present condition is a result of a previous circumstance, disease, or disorder, the medical coder should *never* code that circumstance, disease, or disorder as if it is a current condition. Coding that same scenario with codes 716.43 (arthritis), 813.80 (fracture) would imply that the patient currently has a fracture.

■ COMPLICATED CONDITIONS

Burns (940–949)

Codes from the 940 through 949 categories are used for coding current burn conditions.

Burns are categorized by location, degree, and cause, such as thermal, chemical, electrical, or radioactive material (represented by an E code). Burns can be classified in three ways:

1. First degree: A superficial burn where damage is just of the epidermis layer and is marked by erythema (redness) and tenderness, such as sunburn. There are no blisters and the area heals without a scar.

2. Second degree: A burn that damages partial thickness of the epidermal and some dermal tissues. This burn forms blisters, is red and painful, and may leave a scar.

3. Third degree: A burn that involves the full thickness of the skin and subcutaneous tissue. The burn is not painful because the nerve cells are destroyed. The skin can be brown, gray, or blackened and scarring will occur.
(Source: Taber's Cyclopedic Medical Dictionary, 21st ed. FA Davis Company, 2009.)

> Late effect(s) (of) – *see also* condition-
>   fracture (multiple) (injury classifiable to 828–829) 905.5
>   extremity
>   lower (injury classifiable to
>   821–827) 905.4
>   neck of femur (injury
>   classifiable to 820)
>   905.3
>   upper (injury classifiable to
>   (810–819) 905.2

FIGURE 4–6: Late effects in Volume 2.

The coder must locate the main term "Burn" in Volume 2 of ICD-9-CM, then find the code indicating the location of the burn, followed by the degree (Box 4–1). The cause is represented by E codes located in the Index to External causes, under the main term, "Burning, burns."

When coding a burn, the extent of the total body surface involved is based on using the "rule of nines" (Fig. 4–7). The head and neck are considered 9%, each arm 9%, each leg 18%, and so on. Based on the rule of nines, a physician may determine that a patient's first degree burns cover 10% of the patient's body surface, second degree burns cover 15%, and third degree burns affect 35%. Added together 60% of the total body surface was burned. Of that 60%, 35% was third degree. In this example, the correct code would be 984.63.

> ★ **ICD-10 NOTE**
>
> ICD-9-CM classifies injuries by type such as sprain or fracture. ICD-10 groups injuries together by anatomical site and then by type.
>
> | **ICD-9-CM** | Injuries | |
> |---|---|---|
> | | Fractures | 800–829 |
> | | Dislocations | 830–839 |
> | | Sprain/rains | 840–848 |
> | **ICD-10-CM** | Injuries to head | S00–S09 |
> | | Injuries to neck | S10–S19 |
> | | Injuries to thorax | S20–S29 |

Fractures (800–829)

A *fracture* is any break of a bone. A patient may suffer from many different types of fractures (Fig. 4–8), such as a hairline fracture or a comminuted fracture. However, identifying the type of fracture and the appropriate care is determined by the physicians and other medical personnel. The coder only needs to know the location of the fracture, whether or not the fracture is open or closed, and whether or not the bones were manipulated back into place.

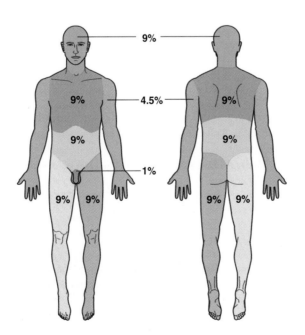

FIGURE 4–7: Rule of Nines percentages. The percentages may be altered to accommodate the size of infants and children. Head and neck equals 9%, each arm equals 9%, each leg equals 18%, the anterior of the trunk equals 18%, and the posterior of the trunk equals 18%.

BOX 4–1: Tips for Coding Burns

1. Each burn site should be coded separately.
2. When burns of different degrees are present in the same local area, only code the burn of the highest degree.
3. Category 948 codes identify the total percentage of body surface that is burned by any degree. The fourth digits in category 948 are classified according to the extent of body surface involved; when the site of the burn is not specified; or there is need for additional data, such as evaluating burn mortality; or when more than 20% of the body surface is involved. The fifth digits identify the total body percentage that has third-degree burns. The fifth digit assigned can never be greater than the total amount of burned surface. A fifth digit of "0" is used when there is less than 10% or when there are *no* third-degree burns present on the patient's body.
4. Burns that do not heal are considered to be acute burns. In cases of acute burns, necrosis of burned skin also may need to be coded.
5. When more than one burn is present, code the most severe or highest degree burn first. If a burn site becomes infected, assign an additional code 958.3, Post-traumatic Wound Infection, not elsewhere classified.
6. The late effects of burns, such as scars or contractures should be coded as the residual or remaining condition, followed by the appropriate late effect code. See "Late Effect (s) (of) – burn (injury classifiable to 948–949)."
7. If necessary, the diagnosis of a late effect of a burn may be coded along with a current burn being treated.

In the case of open and closed fractures, an *open fracture* is one in which the bone penetrates the skin (compound fracture) and a *closed fracture* is one in which the bone does not penetrate the skin. If there is no mention of open or closed in the diagnosis, code the fracture as closed. When a fracture is both closed and open, it should be coded as if it were an open fracture, whereas an injury that involves a fracture-dislocation of the same bone is coded as a fracture. ICD-9-CM describes a closed fracture as one that would include the following terms:

- Comminuted
- Depressed
- Elevated
- Fissured
- Fracture not other specified (NOS)
- Greenstick
- Impacted
- Linear
- Simple
- Slipped epiphysis
- Spiral

ICD-9-CM describes an open fracture as one that would include the following terms:

- Compound
- Infected
- Missile
- Puncture
- With foreign body

To properly code a fracture, the coder must first identify the location of the fracture. For example, 800–804 codes are used strictly for fractures of the skull, including all facial bones. All codes in this section are five-digit codes, and the fifth digit is used to document whether or not the patient lost consciousness. The fourth digit specifies an open or closed fracture and whether or not other factors (e.g., intracranial injury, hemorrhaging) were involved.

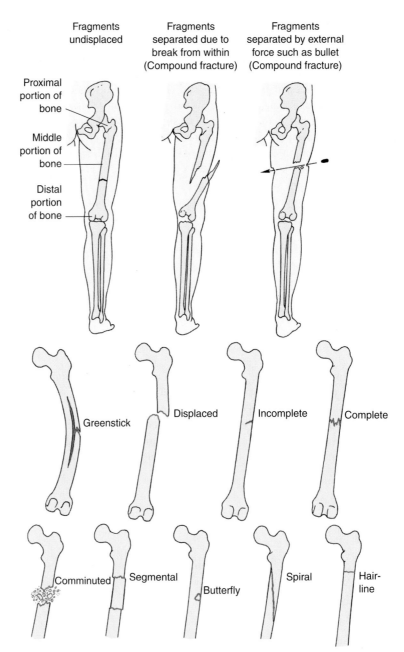

FIGURE 4–8: Types of fractures. (From Taber's Cyclopedic Medical Dictionary, 21st ed. Philadelphia: FA Davis, 2009.)

Pathological fractures involve a bone(s) that is weakened by a disease; they are also referred to as stress fractures. Under normal circumstances, a healthy bone would not sustain a fracture as a result of the incidence or activity at the time. However, due to bone weakness, a fracture occurred. All stress or pathological fractures are always listed as the primary diagnosis and are coded with 733.1 through 733.19. The fourth digit indicates there is an underlying disease and the fifth digit indicates the location of the fracture. In addition, the cause of the fracture should also be included and coded second. The medical coder must never code a pathological/stress fracture as a traumatic fracture.

Injuries (870–897)

When coding injuries, always assign a code for each injury unless there is an appropriate combination code available; the combination code should be used instead. Whenever there are multiple injuries involved, the coder must be as specific as possible and assign each of the injuries separately.

Multiple injury codes are provided in ICD-9-CM, but should be assigned *only* if a specific code is not listed.

To properly assign codes for injuries, code for the most serious injury first. Superficial injuries or abrasions are *not* coded when they are associated with more severe injuries of the same site. Whenever the primary injury involves a *minor* injury to a nerve or blood vessel, the injury should be coded first, followed by the appropriate code for the injury to the nerve or vessel. However, the same does not hold true when it results in a *major* injury to a blood vessel(s) or nerve(s). In that case, the injury to the blood vessel or nerve would be coded as the primary diagnosis, followed by any additional codes. These codes are *not* to be used for normal, healing surgical wounds or to identify complications of surgical wounds.

There is no differentiation between sprains or strains. Except for a few diagnoses, such as eye or physical strain, they are both coded the same and can be found in the Alphabetic Index, Volume 2 as Sprain, strain and then alphabetically by site.

ICD-10 NOTE

Currently, ICD-9-CM classifies injuries by type; for example, dislocation, sprain, or fracture. ICD-10-CM arranges injuries by site and then by the type of injury.

Poisoning (960–979) and Adverse Effects of Drugs

A poisoning is "1. The illness produced by the introduction of a toxic substance into the body. 2. Administration of a noxious substance." (Source: Taber's Cyclopedic Medical Dictionary, 21st ed. FA Davis Company, 2009.)

An adverse reaction is "in pharmacology and therapeutics, an undesired side effect or toxicity caused by a treatment." Adverse reactions may occur as a result of drug therapies, physical therapy, radiation or surgery. The onset of the unwanted *effect* may be immediate or may take days or months to develop. One common type of adverse reaction is an adverse drug reaction. (Source: Taber's Cyclopedic Medical Dictionary, 21st ed. FA Davis Company, 2009.)

To assign the correct diagnosis code in the case of a poisoning or an adverse effect of a drug, an understanding of the ICD-9-CM coding guidelines is necessary.

ICD-9-CM uses the term *"Poisoning"* to refer to drug overdoses and the taking of the wrong substance in error, as follows:

1. Drugs given in error in diagnostic or therapeutic procedures (a tech/nurse giving a patient the wrong medication or the wrong quantity of a medication).

2. Medications given in error by nonmedical personnel (a mother giving a child medication from the wrong bottle, a caregiver giving an incorrect medication).

3. Drugs taken in error by self (taking the wrong bottle off a shelf in the dark or becoming confused about the identity of pills mixed together in a pillbox).

4. Medications (prescription or nonprescription) taken in combination with alcoholic beverages.

5. The combination of a prescription drug with a drug taken by the patient on his own initiative like an over-the-counter substance such as aspirin.

6. Drugs taken in an attempted suicide or drugs given in an attempted homicide.

An *adverse reaction* is classified as a reaction to a correct substance properly administered and would include the following:

1. A drug taken in a therapeutic or diagnostic procedure.

2. A drug taken by oneself or given to another person as prescribed or in recommended dosages.

3. The accumulative effects of a drug sometimes referred to as intoxication of.

4. The interaction of more than one prescribed drug(s).

5. A drug intensifying the effect of another drug.

6. Hypersensitivity to a prescribed drug or one taken in the recommended dose.

7. Side effects to a drug taken as prescribed or in the recommended dose.

The Table of Drugs and Chemicals (Fig. 4–9) is found in Volume 2, following the index of diseases. This alphabetic chart contains the list of drugs and chemical substances in the first column followed by four other columns to the right that identify the external causes of the poisoning: "accidental poisoning," "suicide attempt," "assault," or "undetermined."

The column labeled "Therapeutic Use" is *not* used for poisonings. The codes in the therapeutic use column should be used *only* for adverse reactions to a substance that was properly administered. The codes for the actual adverse effects, such as coma, rash, swelling, can be found in the index of diseases and injuries.

Coding Poisonings

Proper codes in the Table of Drugs and Chemicals can be located using the Alphabetic Index to Poisoning and External Causes of Averse Effects of Drugs and Other Chemicals Substances in Volume 2.

Key Steps for Coding a Poisoning

1. The ICD-9-CM code for Poisoning should be listed first when a drug has been prescribed or administered in error, an overdose of a drug was intentionally taken or administered, or a nonprescribed over-the-counter drug or medicinal agent was taken in combination with a correctly prescribed and properly administered drug.

2. Code the manifestation, the condition resulting from the poisoning, second.

3. Include an E code to indicate the poisoning circumstance if documented in the patient's record, such as accident, suicide attempt, or assault.

4. The external cause is considered "Undetermined" unless the patient's medical record specify otherwise.

5. If a specific drug cannot be found in the table, it can usually be found in Appendix C, Classification of Drugs by American Hospital Formulary.

6. Never use codes in the "Therapeutic Use" column with a Poisoning code.

 E Code Example: A child is brought unconscious into the emergency department after ingesting a bottle of aspirin.

965.1 Poisoning by salicylates.

780.09 Other alteration of consciousness.

E850.3 Accidental poisoning by salicylates.

In this case, poisoning is the primary diagnosis, not the external cause or adverse reaction (noted by the E code). The poisoning is coded as the first diagnosis, the manifestations or conditions resulting from the poisoning are coded as the second diagnosis, and the external causes are coded as the third diagnosis.

 E Code Example: Accidental ingestion of chlorine bleach

983.9 Refer to the Table of Drugs and Chemicals for the Chlorine bleach poisoning.

E864.3 represents the external cause as an accident.

IMPORTANT: The use of E codes is not required and E codes can never be used as a primary diagnosis. The use of E codes is not favorable on Medicare or Medicaid claim forms (the local carrier should be consulted for the applicable rules) *but,* using them on commercial insurance claims can help explain the nature of the adverse effect or poisoning, which can speed up the process of the claim payment.

TABLE OF DRUGS AND CHEMICALS

Substance	Poisoning	Accident	Therapeutic Use	Suicide Attempt	Assault	Undetermined
		External Cause (E-Code)				
Diucardin..974.3		E858.5	E944.3	E950.4	E962.0	E980.4
Diupres..974.3		E858.5	E944.3	E950.4	E962.0	E980.4
Diuretics NEC..974.4		E858.5	E944.4	E950.4	E962.0	E980.4
carbonic acid anhydrase inhibitors.......974.2		E858.5	E944.2	E950.4	E962.0	E980.4
mercurial...974.0		E858.5	E944.0	E950.4	E962.0	E980.4
osmotic...974.4		E858.5	E944.4	E950.4	E962.0	E980.4
purine derivatives................................974.1		E858.5	E944.1	E950.4	E962.0	E980.4
saluretic...974.3		E858.5	E944.3	E950.4	E962.0	E980.4
Diuril...974.3		E858.5	E944.3	E950.4	E962.0	E980.4
Divinyl ether..968.2		E855.1	E938.2	E950.4	E962.0	E980.4
d-lysergic acid diethylamide....................969.6		E854.1	E939.6	E950.3	E962.0	E980.3
DMCT..960.4		E856	E930.4	E950.4	E962.0	E980.4
DMSO..982.8		E862.4	——	E950.9	E962.1	E980.9
DMT...969.6		E854.1	E939.6	E950.3	E962.0	E980.3
DNOC..989.4		E863.5	——	E950.6	E962.1	E980.7
DOCA..962.0		E858.0	E932.0	E950.4	E962.0	E980.4
Dolophine...965.02		E850.1	E935.1	E950.0	E962.0	E980.0
Doloxene...965.8		E850.8	E935.8	E950.0	E962.0	E980.0
DOM..969.6		E854.1	E939.6	E950.3	E962.0	E980.3
Domestic gas — *see* Gas, utility						
Domiphen (bromide) (lozenges)...............976.6		E858.7	E946.6	E950.4	E962.0	E980.4
Dopa (levo)..966.4		E855.0	E936.4	E950.4	E962.0	E980.4
Dopamine...971.2		E855.5	E941.2	E950.4	E962.0	E980.4
Doriden..967.5		E852.4	E937.5	E950.2	E962.0	E980.2
Dormiral...967.0		E851	E937.0	E950.1	E962.0	E980.1
Dormison..967.8		E852.8	E937.8	E950.2	E962.0	E980.2
Dornase...963.4		E858.1	E933.4	E950.4	E962.0	E980.4
Dorsacaine..968.5		E855.2	E938.5	E950.4	E962.0	E980.4
Dothiepin hydrochloride...........................969.0		E854.0	E939.0	E950.3	E962.0	E980.3
Doxapram...970.0		E854.3	E940.0	E950.4	E962.0	E980.4
Doxepin..969.0		E854.0	E939.0	E950.3	E962.0	E980.3
Doxorubicin..960.7		E856	E930.7	E950.4	E962.0	E980.4
Doxycycline..960.4		E856	E930.4	E950.4	E962.0	E980.4
Doxylamine..963.0		E858.1	E933.0	E950.4	E962.0	E980.4
Dramamine...963.0		E858.1	E933.0	E950.4	E962.0	E980.4
Drano (drain cleaner)...............................983.2		E864.2	——	E950.7	E962.1	E980.6
Dromoran..965.09		E850.2	E935.2	E950.0	E962.0	E980.0
Dromostanolone.......................................962.1		E858.0	E932.1	E950.4	E962.0	E980.4
Droperidol..969.2		E853.1	E939.2	E950.3	E962.0	E980.3
Drotrecogin alfa.......................................964.2		E858.2	E934.2	E950.4	E962.0	E980.4
Drug..977.9		E858.9	E947.9	E950.5	E962.0	E980.5
specified NEC......................................977.8		E858.8	E947.8	E950.4	E962.0	E980.4
AHFS List						
4:00 antihistamine drugs......................963.0		E858.1	E933.0	E950.4	E962.0	E980.4
8:04 amebicides 961.5		E857	E931.5	E950.4	E962.0	E980.4
arsenical anti-infectives....................961.1		E857	E931.1	E950.4	E962.0	E980.4
quinoline derivatives.........................961.3		E857	E931.3	E950.4	E962.0	E980.4
8:08 anthelmintics................................961.6		E857	E931.6	E950.4	E962.0	E980.4
quinoline derivatives.........................961.3		E857	E931.3	E950.4	E962.0	E980.4
8:12.04 antifungal antibiotics................960.1		E856	E930.1	E950.4	E962.0	E980.4
8:12.06 cephalosporins.........................960.5		E856	E930.5	E950.4	E962.0	E980.4
8:12.08 chloramphenicol........................960.2		E856	E930.2	E950.4	E962.0	E980.4
8:12.12 erythromycins...........................960.3		E856	E930.3	E950.4	E962.0	E980.4
8:12.16 penicillins.................................960.0		E856	E930.0	E950.4	E962.0	E980.4
8:12.20 streptomycins...........................960.6		E856	E930.6	E950.4	E962.0	E980.4
8:12.24 tetracyclines.............................960.4		E856	E930.4	E950.4	E962.0	E980.4
8:12.28 other antibiotics........................960.8		E856	E930.8	E950.4	E962.0	E980.4
antimycobacterial..............................960.6		E856	E930.6	E950.4	E962.0	E980.4
macrolides..960.3		E856	E930.3	E950.4	E962.0	E980.4
8:16 antituberculars..............................961.8		E857	E931.8	E950.4	E962.0	E980.4
antibiotics...960.6		E856	E930.6	E950.4	E962.0	E980.4

FIGURE 4-9: An excerpt from the Table of Drugs and Chemicals.

Late Effects of a Poisoning

The rules for coding late effects also apply when coding a late effect related to a poisoning. Code any specified effect, such as blindness or deafness, if included in the patient's records, then assign code **909.0**, Late effect of poisoning due to drug, medicinal or biological substance, OR **909.1**, Late effect of toxic effects of nonmedicinal substance. The code **E929.2**, Late effects of accidental poisoning may also be assigned.

Brain damage due to overdose of Methamphetamine in an attempted suicide 2 months ago

348.9 Unspecified condition of brain; **909.0** Late effect of poisoning due to drug, medicinal or biological substance; **E959** Late effects of self-inflicted injury.

Aphasia due to accidental ingestion of lye 3 years ago

784.3 Aphasia; **909.1** Late effect of toxic effects of nonmedicinal substance.

Coding an Adverse Effect

1. First code the problem, the adverse effect (reaction) (vomiting, diarrhea, severe rash, etc.).

2. Then use the E code from the "Therapeutic Use" column to identify the specific drug or substance causing the adverse effect (reaction).

An E code is used to identify the exact drug or substance that caused the adverse reaction. The patient's complaint is the primary diagnosis. Remember, E codes are secondary diagnoses only and never used alone. Although E codes are not required, their use helps to clarify the incident.

Allergic reaction to a prescription of the antibiotic, Amoxicillin

995.20 Unspecified adverse effect of drug, medicinal and biological substance. The diagnosis indicates only the fact that the patient has suffered some sort of reaction to the prescribed drug. The code can be found in Volume 2, under the main term Allergy, allergic (reaction), subterm drug, medicinal substance, and biological (any) (correct medicinal substance properly administered) (external) (internal). Code the reason the patient is seeking medical care first, followed by the cause. **E930.0** A separate code for amoxicillin is not listed in the Table of Drugs and Chemicals for the external cause. The coder will need to proceed to the Classification of Drugs by American Hospital Formulary Service (AHFS) list, Appendix C of Volume 1. Amoxicillin is from the Penicillin family. Under Anti-Infective Agents, "The Penicillins," the AHFS classification number, 8:12:16 will be found. The list classifies drug types and then gives a diagnosis code that represents poisoning from each type of drug, the diagnosis is an adverse effect, and so the ICD-9-CM code 960.0 listed cannot be used. The Table of Drugs and Chemicals in Volume 2 should be referenced. Under the subterm, Drug, find the AHFS classification, 8:12:16. Under the "Therapeutic" column, the code E930.0 will be found and this is the correct code needed for this diagnosis.

> ### ■ E Code Example: Insomnia due to the hypersensitivity of an antidepressant medication
>
> **292.85** Insomnia main term, drug-induced, subterm. In this example there is a named condition to code rather than just an allergic reaction. Remember code the reason, complaint, or condition the patient presents with followed by the cause.
>
> **E939.0** Referring again to the Table of Drugs and Chemicals, the subterm, Antidepressants will be found. Under the "Therapeutic" column, the code E930.0 is the correct code needed for this diagnosis.

Late Effects of Adverse Reactions to Drugs

There is no late effect E code for adverse effects of drugs, according to the Official Coding Guidelines.

Coding Neoplasms

A Table of Neoplasms is located under the term "Neoplasm" in Volume 2 of the ICD-9-CM. This table organizes the code for neoplasms by anatomical site, listing each site in alphabetical order.

There are four different **classifications** of neoplasms presented in the table:

❗ KEY TERM

CLASSIFICATIONS—Groups or types of neoplasms.

1. **Malignant:**

   Primary—the original site of the tumor

   Secondary—a site of **metastasis**

   In situ—confined to the site of origin

2. **Benign:** Noninvasive tumors that remain localized and do not spread.

3. **Uncertain Behavior:** Behavior cannot be determined. Cells may become malignant at a later date. This type of neoplasm should never be considered a neoplasm of unspecified nature, and the diagnosis must make reference to uncertain behavior.

4. **Unspecified Nature:** Diagnosis is so vague that it does not indicate the behavior.

❗ KEY TERM

METASTASIS—1. Movement of bacteria or body cells (especially cancer cells) from one part of the body to another. 2. Change in location of a disease or its manifestations or transfer from one organ or part to another not directly connected. The usual application is to the manifestation of a malignancy as a secondary growth arising from the primary growth in a new location. The malignant cells may spread through the lymphatic circulation, the bloodstream, or avenues such as the cerebrospinal fluid. (Source: Taber's Cyclopedic Dictionary, 21st ed. FA Davis, 2009.)

To properly code a neoplasm, first consult the general alphabetic index in Volume 2 for the term connected with the diagnosis. For example, an adenomyoma is a tumor containing glandular and smooth muscular tissue. The index entry (Fig. 4–10) in Volume 2 contains a note to "see also Neoplasm, by site, benign." Unless the diagnosis is "adenomyoma of the prostate," which is the only diagnosis listed under this entry in Volume 2, the coder must find the anatomical site on the Table of Neoplasms and assign the code from the "benign" column. The note in the index indicates the coder must assume the lesion is benign, unless the written diagnosis states something different.

Volume 2 informs the coder whether or not the term connected with the diagnosis is benign, malignant, or uncertain behavior. Unless the patient's diagnosis states otherwise, the coder should assume the tumor is as stated in Volume 2 and refer to the Table of Neoplasms to search by the anatomical site.

Adenomyoma (M8932/0) – *see also* Neo-
    plasm, by site, benign
  prostate 600.20
    with
      other lower urinary tract symp-
        toms (LUTS) 600.21
      urinary
        obstruction 600.21
        retention 600.21

FIGURE 4–10: Index entry for Adenomyoma.

In addition, an important note about neoplasm classification is at the beginning of the Table of Neoplasms. It states that "Sites marked with the sign * (e.g., face NEC*) should be classified to malignant neoplasm of skin of these sites if the variety of neoplasm is a squamous cell carcinoma or an epidermoid carcinoma and to benign neoplasm of skin of these sites if variety of neoplasm is a papilloma (any type)."

It is important to note the use of V codes when coding neoplasms. If the primary site was previously removed with no evidence of recurrence, a V code should be used as the primary diagnosis, for example, personal history of breast cancer, V10.3. A code from the V58 category also should be used if the primary reason the patient is seen is for chemotherapy or radiation therapy. The secondary diagnosis would now be the cancer code. This is because the patient is still under treatment for the malignancy even if it may have been removed rather than a" personal history of" code.

ICD-10 NOTE

In ICD-10-CM, if the primary site was previously removed with no evidence of recurrence, a code from Z85, Personal history of primary and secondary malignant neoplasm, should be used.

Metastatic Neoplasms

Metastasis in neoplasm greatly affects how codes are applied. Cancer described as "metastatic from" a given site should be interpreted as primary of that site. When the primary site is still present, it should be coded first followed by the secondary site(s) of metastasis.

Cancer described as "metastatic to" should be interpreted as secondary of that site. Metastatic "to" points to the site stated as a secondary malignancy and should be coded as the secondary diagnoses.

 E Code Example: Malignant tumor from the breast

174.9, metastatic to the axillary lymph nodes, 196.3.

In this example, the breast is considered the primary site and the axillary lymph nodes are considered the secondary site.

 E Code Example: Malignant tumor from the breast

174.9, metastatic to the axillary lymph nodes, 196.3 and liver, 197.7.

In this example, more than one site is named in the diagnosis. However, the breast should still be listed as the primary site, with the axillary lymph nodes and the liver listed as two separate secondary sites.

A code for the primary site of the malignancy should be assigned *only* if the malignancy is still present. Use a "personal history of" if the primary site has been removed.

E Code Example: History of malignant cancer of the breast, metastatic to the axillary lymph nodes

196.3 located in the Neoplasm Table as secondary malignancy of the lymph, lymphatic, gland, axillary.
V10.3 located in History, (personal) malignant neoplasm (of) breast.

 E Code Example: A woman with malignant carcinoma of the breast, metastatic to the axillary lymph nodes

174.9 located in the Neoplasm Table as breast (connective tissue) (female) (glandular tissue) (soft parts). If the stated diagnosis specified a particular portion of the breast or that the patient was male, an extensive list is below this general code.
196.3 located in the Neoplasm Table as secondary malignancy of the lymph, lymphatic gland axillary.

Proper Order of Neoplastic Codes

The same rule for designating the primary diagnosis is applied when coding neoplasms. The primary diagnosis is the condition that is considered the reason for the patient's visit. This primary condition is always coded first on the insurance claim and then followed by concurrent conditions.

 ICD-10 NOTE

ICD-10-CM contains a table of neoplasms. The codes have been expanded in this section to allow further specificity of the location of a neoplasm. For example, ICD-10-CM diagnosis codes have been created to include the sides of the body, left or right, called laterality (Table 4–7).

CODING FOR DISEASE CONDITIONS

Circulatory Diseases

Coding disease of the circulatory system can be challenging because of the variety of terms used by physicians or, in many cases, the lack there of. The coder may discover the information regarding a patient's condition in the medical record very generic. To code these conditions accurately, the coder must read and follow all of the conventions and instructions in Volume 1. The use of fifth-digit sub-classifications are often found and determine the accuracy of the code chosen to represent the patient's condition. Chapter 7 of Volume 1, the Tabular List, contains the codes representing diseases of the circulatory system (Fig. 4–11).

TABLE 4–7:   Coding for Neoplasms in ICD-10-CM

	Malignant Primary	Malignant Secondary	Malignant CA in situ	Benign	Uncertain Behavior	Unspecified
Breast Central portion (unspecified)	C50.10	C79.81	D05.90	D24.00	D48.60	D49.3
left side	C50.12	C79.81	D05.92	D24.02	D48.62	D49.3
right side	C50.11	C79.81	D05.91	D24.01	D48.61	D49.3
Ectopic sites (unspecified)	C50.80	C79.81	D05.90	D24.00	D48.60	D49.3
left side	C50.82	C79.81	D05.92	D24.02	D48.62	D49.3
right side	C50.81	C79.81	D05.91	D24.01	D48.61	D49.3
Inner (unspecified side)	C50.80	C79.81	D05.90	D24.00	D48.60	D49.3

7. DISEASES OF THE CIRCULATORY SYSTEM (390–459)
Acute Rheumatic Fever (390–392)
Chronic Rheumatic Heart Disease (393–398)
Hypertensive Disease (401–405)
Ischemic Heart Disease (410–414)
Disease of Pulmonary Circulation (415–417)
Other Forms of Heart Disease (420–429)
Cerebrovascular Disease (430–438)
Disease of Arteries, Arterioles, and Capillaries (440–449)
Disease of Veins, Lymphatics, and Other Disease of the Circulatory System (451–459)

FIGURE 4–11: Sections of the Tabular List covering the circulatory system.

Acute Rheumatic Fever and Rheumatic Heart Disease

Rheumatic fever is caused by untreated streptococcal pharyngitis (strep throat). Rheumatic fever often leads to inflammation of the heart affecting the heart valves. ICD-9-CM lists the codes for rheumatic fever with and without rheumatic heart disease. Codes have been created to differentiate between an acute or dormant fever and whether or not there is heart involvement.

Hypertension

Most high blood pressure is said to be essential hypertension, meaning no identifiable cause. In adults, a blood pressure reading of 140/90 mm Hg or greater is considered high. One thing to be cautious about when coding high blood pressure is there can be a *difference* between high blood pressure and hypertension. A patient may have high blood pressure at the time of a visit or examination because they are nervous, upset, or for any number of reasons. If the diagnosis indicates high blood pressure and *does not* mention hypertension, the coder should code the symptom 796.2, Elevated blood pressure reading without diagnosis of hypertension. The coder can *only code to the highest degree of certainty.* Care must be taken to prevent mislabeling any patient.

 ICD-10 NOTE

A single elevated blood pressure reading that does not mention hypertension is coded as R03.0 in ICD-10-CM.

For coding purposes, hypertension is considered malignant, benign, or unspecified. A table (Fig. 4–12) appears in Volume 2, the Alphabetic Index, under the main term "Hypertension" and contains a list of conditions due to and associated with hypertension. The table has columns that identify three subcategories, Malignant, Benign, and Unspecified.

In most cases, patients are being treated for benign hypertension. This type of hypertension is fairly stable and compatible with a long life. However, if untreated, it can be a major risk factor in coronary heart disease and cerebrovascular disease. It also can be asymptomatic until complications develop.

Malignant hypertension is far less common, occurring in only about 5% of patients with elevated blood pressures. This type of hypertension frequently has an abrupt onset and often ends with renal failure or cerebral hemorrhage.

When coding hypertension, the coder must be as specific as the medical record details, making certain to code the specific type of hypertension, or code "unspecified" if the medical record does not contain an exact description of the hypertension. Because physicians frequently do not specify whether the hypertension is benign or malignant, the coder has to assign unspecified codes.

 ICD-10 NOTE

In ICD-10-CM hypertension is classified as benign, malignant, or unspecified. For example:

ICD-9-CM	401.0 Essential hypertension, malignant
	401.1 Essential hypertension, benign
	401.9 Essential hypertension, unspecified
ICD-10-CM	I10 Essential (primary) hypertension

INDEX TO DISEASES   **Hypertension, Hypertensive**

Hypertension, hypertensive	Malignant	Benign	Unspecified
(arterial) (arteriolar) (crisis) (degeneration) (disease) (essential) (fluctuating) (idiopathic) (intermittent) (labile) (low renin) (orthostatic) (paroxysmal) (primary) (systemic) (uncontrolled) (vascular)	401.0	401.0	401.9
with			
chronic kidney disease..........			
stage I through stage IV, or unspecified....................................	403.00	403.10	403.90
stage V or end stage renal disease	403.01	403.11	403.91
heart involvement (conditions classifiable to 429.0–429.3, 429.8, 429.9 due to hypertension) (*see also* Hypertension, heart)	402.00	402.10	402.90
with kidney involvement—*see* Hypertension, cardiorenal			
renal involvement (only conditions classifiable to 585, 586, 587) (excludes conditions classifiable to 584) (*see also* Hypertension, kidney)	403.00	403.10	403.90
with heart involvement—*see* Hypertension, cardiorenal			
failure (and sclerosis) (*see also* Hypertension, kidney)	403.01	403.11	403.91
sclerosis without failure (*see also* Hypertension, kidney)	403.00	403.10	403.90
accelerated (*see also* Hypertension, by type, malignant)...............	401.0	——	——
antepartum—*see* Hypertension complicating pregnancy, childbirth, or the puerperium			
cardiorenal (disease)	404.00	404.10	404.90
with			
chronic kidney disease			
stage I through stage IV, or unspecified....................................	404.00	404.10	404.90
and heart failure..	404.01	404.11	404.91
stage V or end stage renal disease	404.02	404.12	404.92
and heart failure..	404.03	404.13	404.93
heart failure..	404.01	404.11	404.91
and chronic kidney disease	404.01	404.11	404.91
stage I through stage IV or unspecified	404.01	404.11	404.91
stage V or end stage renal disease	404.03	404.13	404.93
cardiovascular disease (arteriosclerotic) (sclerotic)	402.00	402.10	402.90
with			
heart failure..	402.01	402.11	402.91
renal involvement (conditions classifiable to 403) (*see also* Hypertension, cardiorenal)	404.00	404.10	404.90
cardiovascular renal (disease) (sclerosis) (*see also* Hypertension cardiorenal)...........................	404.00	404.10	404.90
cerebrovascular disease NEC	437.2	437.2	437.2
complicating pregnancy, childbirth, or the puerperium	642.2	642.0	642.9
with			
albuminuria (and edema) (mild)..........................	——	——	642.4
severe	——	——	642.5
chronic kidney disease	642.2	642.2	642.2
and heart disease...	642.2	642.2	642.2
edema (mild)..	——	——	642.4
severe	——	——	642.5
heart disease...	642.2	642.2	642.2
and chronic kidney disease	642.2	642.2	642.2
renal disease...	642.2	642.2	642.2
and heart disease...	642.2	642.2	642.2
chronic..	642.2	642.0	642.0
with pre-eclampsia or eclampsia	642.7	642.7	642.7
fetus or newborn	760.0	760.0	760.0
essential...	——	642.0	642.0
with pre-eclampsia or eclampsia	——	642.7	642.7
fetus or newborn	760.0	760.0	760.0
fetus or newborn	760.0	760.0	760.0
gestational	——	——	642.3
pre-existing	642.2	642.0	642.0
with pre-eclampsia or eclampsia	642.7	642.7	642.7
fetus or newborn	760.0	760.0	760.0
secondary to renal disease	642.1	642.1	642.1
with pre-eclampsia or eclampsia	642.7	642.7	642.7
fetus or newborn	760.0	760.0	760.0
transient..	——	——	642.3
due to			
aldosteronism, primary	405.09	405.19	405.99
brain tumor..	405.09	405.19	405.99
bulbar poliomyelitis.......................................	405.09	405.19	405.99
calculus			
kidney..	405.09	405.19	405.99
ureter..	405.09	405.19	405.99
coarctation, aorta	405.09	405.19	405.99
Cushing's disease	405.09	405.19	405.99
glomerulosclerosis (*see also* Hypertension, kidney)....................	403.00	403.10	403.90

FIGURE 4–12: Excerpt from Hypertension Table.

Myocardial Infarction

A myocardial infarction (heart attack) (MI) is considered as acute at onset and up to 8 weeks after the occurrence. ICD-9-CM codes for acute MI are listed by the site in which it has occurred, such as anterior wall, inferior wall, and lateral wall. A fifth digit is required to state the episode of care, either initial, subsequent, or unspecified (see codes 410.0 through 410.9). An MI is considered old and coded as 412, when the diagnosis is used 8 weeks after the occurrence. If an ECG performed indicates a patient has previously suffered an MI but has no symptoms, the MI is also considered to be old and coded as 412. When a patient presents with symptoms caused by a previous infarction, the code 414.8, Other specified forms of chronic ischemic heart disease, is used as the primary diagnosis code. The symptoms the patient presents with are coded secondly.

Diabetes Mellitus

"Diabetes mellitus is a chronic metabolic disorder marked by hyperglycemia. Diabetes mellitus (DM) results in either the failure of the pancreas to produce insulin (type 1 DM) or from insulin resistance, with inadequate insulin secretion to sustain normal metabolism (type 2 DM). Either type of DM may damage blood vessels, nerves, kidneys, the retina, and in pregnancy, the developing fetus." (Source: Taber's Cyclopedic Medical Dictionary, 21st edition, FA Davis Company, 2009.)

Coding for diabetes mellitus (Box 4–2) must differentiate between:

- **Diabetes mellitus, type 1**—insulin dependent (previously called juvenile diabetes).

- **Diabetes mellitus, type 2**—non-insulin dependent (previously called adult onset).

The codes and guidelines for diabetes mellitus are in category 250 of the ICD-9-CM, and all five digits are necessary for proper code assignment. The fourth digit describes the complication involved and an additional code should be included as the secondary diagnosis (with diabetes as the primary diagnosis). The fifth digit indicates the type and level of control of the disease.

Per the category notes, the following fifth-digit subclassifications must be used with the diagnosis code 250 (diabetes mellitus) for proper coding (see Fig. 4-5):

- **0, type 2 non-insulin dependent type** (NIDDM), adult-onset type or unspecified type, not stated as uncontrolled.

- **1, type 1 insulin dependent type** (IDDM), juvenile type, not stated as uncontrolled.

- **2, type 2 non-insulin dependent type** (NIDDM) adult-onset type, or unspecified type, uncontrolled.

- **3, type 1 insulin dependent type** (IDDM) juvenile type, uncontrolled.

 ICD-10 NOTE

Codes represent the types of diabetes mellitus, body system affected, and complications affecting that body system in ICD-10-CM. There are six areas of code sets for Diabetes versus just one in ICD-9-CM:

E08 Diabetes mellitus due to an underlying condition
E09 Drug or chemical induced diabetes mellitus
E10 Type 1 diabetes mellitus
E11 Type 2 diabetes mellitus
E13 Other specified diabetes mellitus
E14 Unspecified diabetes mellitus

BOX 4–2: Types of Diabetes

Type 1 diabetes is also known as insulin-dependent diabetes mellitus (IDDM) or juvenile diabetes. Usual onset occurs before 30 years of age. Type 1 patients are insulin dependent.

Type 2 diabetes is also known as non–insulin-dependent diabetes mellitus (NIDDM) or adult onset diabetes. Usual onset occurs after 40 years of age. Type 2 patients are non–insulin-dependent.

Diabetes Mellitus and Pregnancy
Diabetes mellitus complicating pregnancy, delivery, or the puerperium is considered the primary diagnosis, instead of a secondary diagnosis as with most other conditions related to diabetes. Codes from the category 648.0x, which apply to current conditions complicating pregnancy, must be placed first and then followed by the appropriate diabetes code.

❗ KEY TERM

PUERPERIUM—The 6 weeks following childbirth.

Diabetes that develops during pregnancy is called gestational diabetes, and is *only* recognized during pregnancy. If a woman has diabetes before she becomes pregnant, she is not considered to have gestational diabetes. The only code for gestational diabetes is 648.8x, which is listed first, followed by the appropriate diabetes mellitus code.

Pregnancy, Childbirth, and the Puerperium

Conditions that affect pregnancy, childbirth, or **puerperium** are assigned codes (630–677) of Chapter 11 in Volume 1 of the ICD-9-CM. To be coded from this section, a condition causes difficulty in the pregnancy or the pregnancy causes difficulty in the condition. These codes are listed first followed by a code(s) from the other chapters that may need to be used to further describe the patient's condition. However, if a woman is seen by her physician for a condition unrelated to her pregnancy, that condition should be coded first, followed by V22.2, Pregnant state, incidental. Diagnosis codes from Chapter 11 must be used to diagnose the mother's condition(s) only. These codes may never be used for the newborn's condition(s).

Fourth- and Fifth-Digit Subclassifications

When coding an encounter dealing with pregnancy, birth, or the puerperium, a fourth digit is added to specify any coexisting complication. The addition of a fifth digit relays information on the current episode of care. The fifth-digit definitions are as follows:

■ **0, Unspecified as to episode of care or not applicable.**

■ **1, Delivered, with or without mention of antepartum condition.** This includes:

  ■ Antepartum condition with delivery.

  ■ Delivery NOS (with mention of antepartum complication during current episode of care).

  ■ Intrapartum obstetric condition (with mention of antepartum complication during current episode of care).

  ■ Pregnancy, delivered (with mention of antepartum complication during current episode of care).

■ **2, Delivered, with mention of postpartum complication.** This includes:

  ■ Delivery with mention of puerperal complication during current episode of care.

■ **3, Antepartum condition or complication.** This includes:

  ■ Antepartum obstetric condition, not delivered during the current episode of care.

■ **4, Postpartum condition or complication.** This includes:

  ■ Postpartum or puerperal obstetric condition or complication following delivery that occurred during previous episode of care or outside hospital, with subsequent admission for observation or care.

 ICD-10 NOTE

ICD-10-CM codes designate what trimester the patient's condition occurs.

Outcome of Delivery (V27.0–V27.9)

V codes V27.0–V27.9 are intended for the coding of the outcome of delivery on the mother's record, in conjunction with delivery codes from the 650–659 range. The delivery codes do not include the outcome of delivery, so V codes in this category should be used with a delivery code to indicate that outcome. The coder also can locate these codes in Volume 2 under the main term, "Outcome of Delivery" (Fig. 4–13).

Liveborn Infants According to Birth (V30–V39)

When coding the birth of an infant, a code from categories V30–V39 must be assigned as the primary diagnosis, according to the type of birth. This includes V30 single liveborn, V31 twin, mate liveborn, and V34 other multiple, mates all liveborn. These codes are *only* assigned at the time of birth, and any conditions that occur after birth are coded separately.

In addition to the main code, fourth and fifth digits are assigned. The following fourth digits are used with codes V30–V39:

.0, Born in hospital.

1, Born before admission to hospital.

2, Born outside hospital and not hospitalized.

The fourth digit .0, requires a fifth digit to document whether or not the delivery was cesarean:

0, Delivered without mention of cesarean delivery.

1, Delivered by cesarean delivery.

V27 Outcome of delivery
  Note: This category is intended for the coding of the outcome of delivery on the mother's record.
  V27.0 Single liveborn
  V27.1 Single stillborn
  V27.2 Twins, both liveborn
  V27.3 Twins, one liveborn and one stillborn
  V27.4 Twins, both stillborn
  V27.5 Other multiple birth, all liveborn
  V27.6 Other multiple birth, some liveborn
  V27.7 Other multiple birth, all stillborn
  V27.9 Unspecified outcome of delivery
      Single birth, outcome to infant unspecified
      Multiple birth, outcome to infant unspecified

FIGURE 4–13: V codes related to delivery.

Late Effect of Complication of Pregnancy, Childbirth, and the Puerperium (677)

Code 677 is used for cases when an initial complication of a pregnancy develops into or results in a condition that requires care or treatment at a future date. This code may be used at any time after the initial postpartum period. Like all late effects codes, 677 should be placed after the code describing the condition at the time of treatment.

Abortions

An *abortion* is termed as the spontaneous or induced termination of pregnancy before the fetus reaches a viable age. Diagnosis codes can be found in Volume 2 under Abortion (complete) (incomplete) (inevitable) (with retained products of conception). The codes for abortions are located in Chapter 11, Complications of Pregnancy, Childbirth, and the Puerperium (630–677) of Volume 1 (Fig. 4–14 and Fig. 4–15).

There are different types of abortion:

■ Complete (fifth digit 2)—An abortion in which the total products of conception have been expelled (637.92).

■ Elective (category 635)—Voluntary termination of a pregnancy for other than medical reasons. The procedure may be recommended when the mother's mental or physical state

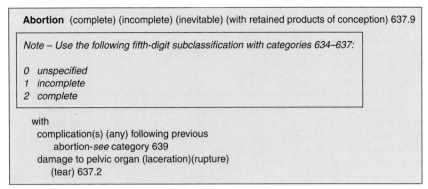

Abortion (complete) (incomplete) (inevitable) (with retained products of conception) 637.9

Note – Use the following fifth-digit subclassification with categories 634–637:

0 *unspecified*
1 *incomplete*
2 *complete*

with
    complication(s) (any) following previous
       abortion-*see* category 639
    damage to pelvic organ (laceration)(rupture)
       (tear) 637.2

FIGURE 4–14: Diagnosis codes for Abortions.

would be endangered by continuation of the pregnancy. It also may be performed as a result of rape or incest (635.92).

■ Incomplete (634.0–637.9, fifth digit 1)—An abortion in which part of the products of conception has been retained.

■ Induced (635–636)—The intentional termination of a pregnancy by means of dilating the cervix and evacuating the uterus (635.92, 636.92).

■ Missed (632)—Abortion in which the fetus has died before completion of the 20th week of gestation but the products of conception are retained in the uterus for 8 weeks or longer.

■ Spontaneous (Category 634)—Abortion occurring without apparent cause also known as a miscarriage.

■ Therapeutic (Category 635)—Abortion performed when the pregnancy endangers the mother's mental or physical health or the fetus has a known condition incompatible with life.

■ Threatened (640.0x)—The appearance of signs and symptoms of possible loss of the fetus.

Official Guidelines for Coding Abortions

1. Fifth digits are required for Abortion categories 634–637.

■ 0, Unspecified used when the patient's medical records do not indicate complete or incomplete.

■ 1, Incomplete, indicates that all of the products of conception have not been expelled from the uterus.

■ 2, Complete, indicates that all products of conception have been expelled from the uterus prior to the episode of care. A code from categories 640–648, Complications Mainly Related to Pregnancy, and 651–657, Normal Delivery and Other Indications for Care in Pregnancy, Labor, and Delivery, may be used as additional codes with an abortion code to indicate the complication leading to the abortion.

■ 3, Assigned with codes from these categories when used with an abortion code because the other fifth digits will not apply.

★ ICD-10 NOTE

In ICD-10-CM, fourth digits under O03, Spontaneous abortion, indicate whether or not the abortion was complete or incomplete and whether it was complicated. ICD-10-CM contains fewer complication codes than ICD-9-CM does.

OTHER PREGNANCY WITH ABORTIVE OUTCOME (634-639)

Note: Use the following fifth-digit subclassification with categories 634–637:

0 **Unspecified**
1 **Incomplete**
2 **Complete**

The following fourth-digit subdivisions are for use with categories 634–638:

.0 **Complicated by genital tract and pelvic infection**
Endometritis
Salpingo-oophoritis
Sepsis NOS
Any condition classifiable to 639.0, with condition classifiable to 634–638

Excludes: urinary tract infection (634–638 with .7)

.1 **Complicated by delayed or excessive hemorrhage**
Afibrinogenemia
Defibrination syndrome
Intravascular hemolysis
Any condition classifiable to 639.1, with condition classifiable to 634–638

.2 **Complicated by damage to pelvic organs and tissues**
Laceration, perforation, or tear of:
Bladder
Uterus
Any condition classifiable to 639.2, with condition classifiable to 634–638

.3 **Complicated by renal failure**
Oliguria
Uremia
Any condition classifiable to 639.3, with condition classifiable to 634–638

.4 **Complicated by metabolic disorder**
Electrolyte imbalance with conditions classifiable to 634–638

.5 **Complicated by shock**
Circulatory collapse
Shock (postoperative) (septic)
Any condition classifiable to 639.5, with condition classifiable to 634–638

.6 **Complicated by embolism**
Embolism:
NOS
Amniotic fluid
Pulmonary
Any condition classifiable to 639.6, with condition classifiable to 634–638

.7 **With other specified complications**
Cardiac arrest or failure
Urinary tract infection
Any condition classifiable to 639.8, with condition classifiable to 634–638

.8 **With unspecified complication**

.9 **Without mention of complication**

⑤ **634** **Spontaneous abortion**
Includes: miscarriage
spontaneous abortion

⑤ **634.0** **Complicated by genital tract and pelvic infection**
⑤ **634.1** **Complicated by delayed or excessive hemorrhage**
⑤ **634.2** **Complicated by damage to pelvic organs and tissues**
⑤ **634.3** **Complicated by renal failure**
⑤ **634.4** **Complicated by metabolic disorder**
⑤ **634.5** **Complicated by shock**
⑤ **634.6** **Complicated by embolism**
⑤ **634.7** **With other specified complications**
⑤ **634.8** **With unspecified complication**
⑤ **634.9** **Without mention of complication**

● Code new to this edition   ▲ Revision of existing code   ④ ⑤ Fourth or fifth digit required

FIGURE 4–15: Fifth digits for use with Abortions.

Codes from the 660–669 series, Complications Occurring Mainly in the Course of Labor and Delivery, are not to be used for complications of abortion.

2. Code 639, Complications Following Abortion and Ectopic and Molar Pregnancies, is to be used for all complications following abortion. Code 639 cannot be assigned with codes from the Abortion code categories 634–638.

3. Abortion and Liveborn Fetus (partial birth abortion)—When an attempted termination of pregnancy results in a liveborn fetus assign code 644.21, Early onset of delivery, with an appropriate code from category V27, Outcome of Delivery. The procedure code for the attempted termination of pregnancy should be assigned.

4. Retained Products of Conception Following an Abortion—Subsequent admissions for retained products of conception following a spontaneous or legally induced abortion are assigned the appropriate code from the Abortion category 634, Spontaneous Abortion, or Legally Induced Abortion, with a fifth digit of "1" (incomplete). This advice is appropriate even when the patient was discharged previously with a discharge diagnosis of complete abortion.

Newborn (Perinatal) Guidelines

For coding and reporting purposes the perinatal period is defined as birth through the 28th day following birth. The codes 760–779, Certain Conditions Originating in the Perinatal Period, can never be used on the maternal record. The following guidelines are provided for reporting purposes. Hospitals may record other diagnoses as needed for internal data use.

General Perinatal Rule

All clinically significant conditions noted on a routine newborn examination should be coded. A condition is clinically significant if it requires:

- A clinical evaluation
- Therapeutic treatment
- Diagnostic procedures
- Extended length of hospital stay
- Increased nursing care and/or monitoring
- Has implications of future health-care needs

Liveborn Infants According to Birth (V30–V39)

When coding the birth of an infant, assign a code from the categories V30–V39, according to the type of birth. A code from this series is assigned as a primary diagnosis, and is assigned only once to a newborn at the time of birth.

Newborn Transfers

If the newborn is transferred to another institution, the V30 series is not used at the receiving hospital.

Observation and Evaluation of Newborns and Infants for Suspected Conditions Not Found (V29)

- Assign a code from the category V29, to identify those instances when a healthy newborn is evaluated for a suspected condition that is determined after the study not to be present. Do not use a code from V29 when the patient has identified signs or symptoms of a suspected problem; in such cases, code the actual sign or symptom.

- A V29 code is to be used as a secondary code after the V30, Outcome of Delivery, code. It may also be assigned as a primary code for readmissions or encounters when the V30 code no longer applies.

Maternal Causes of Perinatal Morbidity and Mortality (760–763)

Codes from categories 760–763 are assigned only when the maternal condition has actually affected the fetus or newborn. The fact that the mother has an associated medical condition or experiences some complication of pregnancy, labor, or delivery does not justify the routine assignment of codes from these categories to the newborn record.

Congenital Anomalies (740–759)

Assign an appropriate code from categories 740–759 as an additional diagnosis when a specific abnormality is diagnosed for an infant. Congenital anomalies also may be the primary or first listed diagnosis for admissions/encounters subsequent to the newborn admission. Such abnormalities may occur as a set of symptoms or multiple malformations. A code should be assigned for each presenting manifestation if the syndrome is not specifically indexed in ICD-9-CM.

Coding of Additional Perinatal Diagnosis

■ Assign codes for conditions that require treatment or further investigation, prolong the length of stay, or require resource utilization.

■ Assign codes for conditions that have been specified by the physician as having implications for future health-care needs. (This guideline should only be used for newborns, *not* adult patients.)

■ Assign a code for Newborn Conditions Originating in the Perinatal Period (categories 760–779), as well as complications arising during the current episode of care classified in other chapters, only if the diagnosis has been documented by the responsible physician at the time of transfer or discharge as having affected the fetus or newborn.

Prematurity and Fetal Growth Retardation

Codes from category 764, Slow Fetal Growth and Fetal Malnutrition, and from 765, Disorders Relating to Short Gestation and Low Birthweight (subcategories 765.0 and 765.1), should not be assigned based solely on recorded birthweight or estimated gestational age, but on the attending physician's clinical assessment of maturity of the infant. *Note:* Physicians may use different criteria in determining prematurity; therefore, do not code the diagnosis of prematurity unless the physician documents the condition.

A code from subcategory 765.2, Weeks of Gestation, should be assigned as an additional code with category 764 and codes from 765.0 and 765.1 to specify weeks of gestation as documented by the physician.

 ICD-10 NOTE

ICD-10-CM codes in Pregnancy, Delivery, and Puerperium designate the trimester in which the condition takes place.

■ ICD-9-CM VERSIONS

The ICD-9-CM is published in a variety of styles by different publishers. The codes also may be obtained directly from the National Center for Health Statistics. The codes can be found on CD-ROM or in print. The printed versions of ICD-9-CM offer the guidelines and coding fundamentals and many even include the official ICD-9-CM guidelines that help the coder understand and code more accurately. Even though there are many different styles, all versions contain the same basic information and can be used to properly assign diagnosis codes. Different publishers may combine all three volumes into one book or offer only Volumes 1 and 2 together. Some editions are color-coded tabbed, whereas others may have Volume 2 (the alphabetical listing) appearing before Volume 1 (the numerical listing of the actual diagnoses). Other versions offer multicolored indicators that identify when an additional digit is required, or when a code is considered to be nonspecific. Some even offer citations for the American Hospital Association's (AHA) *Coding Clinic for ICD-9-CM*, which is the official publication for ICD-9-CM coding guidelines. Each medical coder must decide which publication is most comfortable to use.

■ CONCLUSION

Over the years, diagnosis coding has developed from classifying causes and gathering statistics to supplying the insurance companies with the documentation required to pay a claim. Computer technology demanded a way to transform a written description of a patient's health condition to a numeric one. Accurate diagnostic coding is imperative to document the medical necessity of any service provided to a patient. The medical coder must code only what is recorded, follow any applicable guidelines, and always use the current ICD-9-CM edition.

RESOURCE LIST

ICD-9-CM information at the National Centers for Health Statistics
http://www.cdc.gov/nchs/about/otheract/icd9/abticd9.htm

ICD-10-CM
http://www.cdc.gov/nchs/icd.htm

American Hospital Association
http://www.aha.org/

Centers for Medicare and Medicaid Services
http://www.cms.hhs.gov/

World Health Organization
http://www.who.int/en/

The Workgroup for Electronic Data Interchange (WEDI)
http://www.wedi.org

Chapter Review Exercises

Answer the following questions.

1. What is the three-digit category code for measles? _____

2. What is the subcategory code for measles without mention of complication?

   _____

3. What do the subcategory codes for measles represent? _____

4. What are the subcategories for measles, manifestations, sites, or causes?

   _____

Underline the main term in each of the following:

5. Breast mass

6. Primary hydronephrosis

7. Deviated nasal septum

8. Hemorrhoids in pregnancy

9. Inguinal adenopathy

10. Arteriosclerotic heart disease

Code the following:

11. Bunion _____

12. Cancerphobia _____

13. Hemosalpinx _____

14. Hyperkalemia _____

15. Arteriopathy _____

16. Lame back _____

17. Little-league elbow _____

18. Low hemoglobin _____

19. Pachydermatitis _____

20. Gastrostenosis _____

21. Tension headache _____

22. Suppurative pancreatitis _____

23. Menopausal headache _____

24. Bronchial croup _____

25. Alcoholic gastritis _____

Assign codes to the following conditions:

26. Dysfunctional uterine bleeding _____

27. Severe back pain _____

28. Acute pelvic cellulitis _____

29. Herpes of penis _____

30. Pernicious anemia _____

31. Viral hepatitis with hepatic coma _____

32. Tietze's syndrome _____

33. Staphylococcal toxemia due to food _____

34. Diverticulosis and diverticulitis of ascending colon _____

35. Grave's disease in crisis _____

36. Petit mal epilepsy _____

37. Uncontrolled diabetes, insulin dependent _____

38. Polycystic ovarian disease _____

39. Acute bronchial asthma, status asthmaticus _____

40. Peptic ulcer disease with perforation _____

Assign codes to the following late effects: *
41. Cerebrovascular accident 2 years ago with late effects _____

42. Traumatic arthritis, right ankle, following fracture, right ankle _____

43. Cicatricial contracture of the left hand due to burn _____

44. Brain damage following cerebral abscess 7 months ago _____

45. Neural deafness resulting from childhood measles 10 years ago _____

46. Mononeuritis, median nerve, resulting from previous crush injury to right arm _____

47. Post-traumatic, painful arthritis, left hand _____

48. Residuals of previous severe burn, left wrist _____

*Note numbers 41 and 48 have only one code assigned, 42 through 47 have two.

Assign codes for the following conditions:

49. Ulcerative colitis _____

50. Renal colic due to kinked ureter _____

51. Nervous trouble _____

52. Diabetic neuritis _____

53. Prostatitis with urethritis _____

54. Diffuse chronic cystic mastitis _____

55. Acute cervical adenitis due to staphylococcal infection _____

56. Carpal tunnel syndrome _____

57. Apical periodontal abscess, multiple abscessed teeth _____

58. Ureteral calculus with secondary hydronephrosis _____

59. Acute pyelonephritis due to *E. coli* _____

60. Sliding hiatal hernia _____

61. Staphylococcal pneumonia complicated by pleural effusion _____

62. Pelvic inflammatory disease, acute _____

63. Gross, painless hematuria, cause undetermined _____

Assign V codes to the following:

64. Insertion of intrauterine contraceptive device _____

65. History of allergic reaction to penicillin _____

66. Admission to hospital for colostomy closure _____

67. Evaluation of kidney donor _____

68. Fitting of vaginal diaphragm _____

69. Hospital admission of a 10-day-old infant due to mother's postpartum complications

_____

70. Single liveborn infant born in hospital _____

71. Liveborn twin, mate stillborn, born in the hospital _____

72. Premature twin born in the hospital _____

73. Adjustment to cardiac pacemaker _____

74. Acute anxiety due to stress of a parent-child conflict _____

75. Routine circumcision, 10-year-old male _____

76. Renal dialysis session _____

77. Removal of pin from healed fracture of the humerus _____

Assign codes to the following neoplasms:

78. Generalized carcinomatosis, primary site undetermined _____

79. Hodgkin's disease _____

80. Hepatoma with metastases to both lungs _____

81. Plasma cell leukemia _____

82. Malignant carcinoid of appendix _____

83. Lipoma of kidney _____

84. Osteoma of the mandible _____

85. Monocytic leukemia in remission _____

86. Acute exacerbation of chronic leukemia _____

87. Epidermoid carcinoma of lip _____

88. Metastatic carcinoma of lung and bone from pelvis (requires three codes) _____

89. Uterine leiomyoma, subserous _____

90. Neoplasm of liver _____

91. Carcinoma in situ of cervix _____

92. Epidermoid carcinoma of lung with no evidence of recurrence or metastases _____

Assign codes to the following circulatory conditions:

93. Acute myocardial infarction. Arteriosclerotic cardiovascular disease. _____

94. Arteriosclerotic heart disease with coronary artery insufficiency and angina pectoris

(Requires three codes) _____

95. Syphilitic aortic aneurysm _____

96. Renal and heart disease due to hypertension _____

97. Chest pain originating in chest wall _____

98. Acute cerebrovascular insufficiency with infarction, left middle cerebral artery _____

99. Abnormal electrocardiogram _____

100. Rheumatic carditis, acute. Streptococcal pericarditis. _____

101. Cor pulmonale. Hypertensive left ventricular hypertrophy _____

102. Hypertensive cardiomegaly with acute congestive heart failure _____

103. Endocardial fibroelastosis _____

104. Monckeberg's sclerosis _____

105. Ruptured cerebral aneurysm _____

106. Wolff-Parkinson-White syndrome _____

107. Inferior vena cava syndrome. Thromboangiitis obliterans. Generalized arteriosclerosis.

   (Requires three codes) _____

Assign codes to the following poisonings and adverse effects:

108. Lead poisoning from eating paint _____

109. Accidental ingestion of four Valium tablets _____

110. Carbon monoxide poisoning, car exhaust, attempted suicide _____

111. Digitalis intoxication _____

112. Intentional ingestion of barbiturate overdose _____

113. Accidental ingestion of mother's oral contraceptives. _____

114. Adverse effect from interaction of a prescribed diuretic, 40:28 and self-administered

   over-the-counter Contac pills _____

115. Accidental ingestion of lye _____

116. Adverse effect from dye administered for intravenous pyelogram _____

117. Residuals of severe allergic reaction to chemotherapy (Fluorouracil). Medication

   discontinued 6 months ago. _____

118. Allergic reaction to a prescription of Tetracycline _____

119. Reaction to anticholinergic mydriatic administered during eye exam 6 months

   ago _____

120. Adverse effect to long-term steroid therapy _____

121. Interaction of Elavil and alcohol (Elavil 28:16.04) _____

Procedural Coding: Introduction to CPT and Evaluation and Management

Chapter Outline

I. Introduction

II. Historical Background

III. CPT Format and Conventions

   A. Understanding CPT Content and Format

   B. Contents

   C. Format

   D. Symbols

   E. CPT Index

IV. CPT Code Categories

   A. Category I Codes

   B. Category II Codes

   C. Category III Codes

V. Section I: Evaluation and Management Services

   A. Documentation Guidelines

VI. Assigning E/M Codes

   A. New and Established Patients

   B. Level of Care in the Medical Record

   C. E/M Components

   D. Determining Level of History

     1. Differences in 1995 versus 1997 History Criteria

   E. Determining Level of Examination

     1. Differences in 1995 versus 1997 Examination Criteria

   F. Determining Medical Decision Making

     1. Number of Diagnoses or Management Options

     2. Amount and/or Complexity of Data to Be Reviewed

     3. Risk of Significant Complication, Morbidity, and/or Mortality

OBJECTIVES

- Identify and understand the format, instructional terms, punctuation, abbreviations, and symbols used in the CPT manual
- Understand the meaning of and the use for HCPCS codes
- Understand the difference between new and established patients
- Recognize and describe the components of Evaluation and Management services
- Interpret the elements of each component
- Understand the basic levels of Evaluation and Management services
- Accurately code Evaluation and Management services
- Identify consultations and demonstrate how to code them
- Abstract and code Evaluation and Management services from patient records
- Explain SOAP notes
- Identify the proper use of modifiers

MEDICAL ASSISTING COMPETENCIES

ABHES

2d. serve as liaison between Physician and others
2h. receive, organize, prioritize, and transmit information expediently
3w. complete insurance claim forms
3x. use physician fee schedule
5a. determine needs for documentation and reporting
5b. documents accurately
5c. use appropriate guidelines when releasing records or information
8b. implement current procedural terminology and ICD-9 coding

CAAHEP

IV.C.11. Define both medical terms and abbreviations related to all body systems
IV.P.2. Report relevant information to others succinctly and accurately
IV.P.3. Use medical terminology, pronouncing medical terms correctly, to communicate information, patient history, data and observations
VIII.C.1. Describe how to use the most current procedural coding system
VIII.C.4. Describe how to use the most current HCPCS coding
VIII.P.1. Perform procedural coding
VIII.A.1. Work with physician to achieve the maximum reimbursement

---

KEY TERMS

Add-on Codes

American Medical Association (AMA)

Centers for Medicare and Medicaid Services (CMS)

Chief Complaint

Code Set

Comprehensive

Conscious Sedation

Contributing Factors

Consultation

Coordination of Care

Counseling

Current Procedural Terminology

Department of Health and Human Services (HHS)

Detailed

Documentation Guidelines (DG)

Domiciliary Care Facility

Evaluation and Management Services

Examination

Expanded Problem Focused

Healthcare Common Procedure Coding System (HCPCS)

High Complexity

History

History of Present Illness

Key Components

Level of Care

Levels of Risk

Low Complexity

Management Options

Medical Decision Making

Moderate Complexity

Modifier

Nature of Presenting Problem

New and Established Patients

New/Emerging Technology

Office and Outpatient Services

Performance Measures

Personal, Family, Social History

Preventive Medicine

Problem Focused

Procedures

Review of Systems (ROS)

Straightforward

Supervision and Interpretation

Time

▪ INTRODUCTION

As with diagnostic codes, procedure codes were developed to track health statistics and to facilitate communication between health-care providers and insurance companies. These codes are assigned for all services or treatments provided to the patient during a medical encounter and they follow specific rules.

Procedure codes are routinely checked against the diagnostic codes to ensure reimbursement is only received for those **procedures** that are "medically necessary" for the proper treatment of the stated diagnosis. Therefore, the medical coder must code each procedure separately and make sure the assigned codes accurately reflect the procedures and/or service performed for the patient.

> **❗ KEY TERM**
>
> PROCEDURES—The provision of care or treatment provided to a patient by medical personnel.

▪ HISTORICAL BACKGROUND

In 1966, the first edition of the ***Current Procedural Terminology*** (CPT) was developed by the **American Medical Association (AMA)**. When CPT was first published, codes consisted of four digits. Those codes represented some surgical procedures, with very limited sections on medicine, radiology, and laboratory procedures. More codes were quickly required, and the second edition was published in 1970, with five-digit codes replacing the original four-digit ones. By 1977, when the fourth edition (CPT-4) was published, the **code set** had been expanded to keep up with medical technology and included codes for medical, anesthesia, surgical, radiological, laboratory and pathological, and medicine services.

AMERICAN MEDICAL ASSOCIATION (AMA)—The largest medical organization in the United States, which represents physicians from every specialty. The association helps doctors work together on important professional and public health issues. The AMA is also responsible for maintaining the CPT.

CODE SET—Any set of codes used for coding data such as medical diagnoses or medical procedure codes.

The Health Care Financing Administration (HCFA), now known as the **Centers for Medicare and Medicaid Services (CMS)**, adopted CPT for their **Healthcare Common Procedure Coding System (HCPCS)** in 1983 and mandated the use of CPT and other HCPCS codes for all services billed to the Medicare Part B program. In 2000, CPT was chosen as the national standard for procedural coding by the **Department of Health and Human Services (HHS)**. Under the Health Insurance Portability and Accountability Act (HIPAA), physicians and health-care professionals must use the CPT codes for all financial and administrative health-care business done electronically.

CENTERS FOR MEDICARE AND MEDICAID SERVICES (CMS)—The federal agency that manages Medicare, Medicaid, and Children's Health Insurance Program.

DEPARTMENT OF HEALTH AND HUMAN SERVICES (HHS)—The principal government agency designed to protect the health of all Americans and provide essential human services.

HEALTHCARE COMMON PROCEDURE CODING SYSTEM (HCPCS)—Alphanumeric codes used to represent special services, medical supplies, and certain drug items.

The AMA currently updates and maintains the CPT with the help of the CPT Editorial Panel, the AMA CPT Advisory Committee, and the AMA Health Care Professionals Advisory Committee. Physicians, licensed therapists, and/or members of specialty associations represent each group. All specialties of health care, from adolescent medicine to ultrasound medicine are represented. Medical specialty societies, health insurance organizations and agencies, individual physicians, and other health professionals also may contribute ideas and suggestions for new and improved representation of the medical services within the CPT.

The CPT is now published annually to remain current with the rapidly changing health-care field. The **code set** is now known as CPT of each current year (e.g., CPT 2009). Revisions and new CPT codes are published and available in the fall of each year. Those revisions and new codes must then be used for all services beginning January 1 of the next year. This allows health-care providers and payers time to put the changes into practice. Though some of the annual changes may be found on the Internet (www.ama-assn.org), the AMA does not provide access to their codes without a fee. It is extremely important for the medical coder to obtain and use the new edition of CPT each year for several reasons:

1. Hundreds of changes are made to the book each year.

2. The medical coder would have no way of knowing what revisions were made or what new codes were introduced.

3. The physician's reimbursement would not be optimal without the use of current codes.

4. The medical practice could expose itself to audit liability, by not keeping up with the changes in the definition of the codes.

The medical coder should also follow any new guidelines or rules from the AMA, CMS, or any other organization concerned with procedural coding. The process may change from year to year and it is very important to stay current.

■ CPT FORMAT AND CONVENTIONS

Understanding CPT Content and Format

Codes found in the CPT are to be used by physicians or qualified health-care providers. Listed numerically, each five-digit code describes, in detail, each medical service rendered to a patient.

In addition to the actual procedure codes, CPT lists place of service codes and **modifiers** just inside the front cover. A **detailed** explanation of each CPT modifier also can be found in Appendix A of the CPT manual. The Introduction contains instructions on how to properly use the CPT coding book to locate a code. It explains the format of the terminology, the symbols used, and additional resources that some coders find very helpful.

❗ KEY TERMS

EVALUATION AND MANAGEMENT SERVICES—The medical encounter provided to a patient by a physician. This section of the CPT manual contains codes assigned to describe the examination, history, and medical decision making portion of a patient encounter.

MODIFIER—A two-digit numeric or alphanumeric code that can be added to a five-digit procedure code to describe a circumstance that has occurred and alters the code in some way. Example: modifier 50 added to a code explains that the procedure was performed bilaterally. Procedure code 19303-50 represents a bilateral mastectomy was performed.

NEW/EMERGING TECHNOLOGY—Any up-and-coming medical procedure and/or equipment.

PERFORMANCE MEASURES—The collection of medical data used to evaluate the quality of care a patient receives.

Contents

There are the eight sections within CPT, each with a range of codes:

1. Evaluation and Management Services

2. Anesthesiology

3. Surgery

4. Radiology

5. Pathology and Laboratory

6. Medicine

7. Category II **Performance Measures**

8. Category III **New/Emerging Technology**

Within each section are subsections with anatomic, procedural, condition, or descriptor subheadings.

❗ KEY TERM

SUPERVISION AND INTERPRETATION—To oversee and evaluate a diagnostic procedure.

There are guidelines in front of each section. **Evaluation and Management** guidelines define in great detail the levels of care for office visits, hospital visits, and consultations. Anesthesia guidelines briefly define **time** reporting, materials, multiple procedures and specific Anesthesia modifiers. Surgery guidelines help explain surgical packages follow-up care, multiple and separate procedures. Radiology guidelines describe **Supervision and Interpretation**, while the guidelines for Pathology—Laboratory and Medicine explain the use of separate and multiple procedures.

There are also 14 Appendices to the CPT.

Appendix A	CPT modifiers
Appendix B	Summary of Additions, Deletions and Revisions
Appendix C	Clinical Examples
Appendix D	Summary of CPT **Add-on Codes**
Appendix E	Summary of Codes Exempt from Modifier 51
Appendix F	Summary of Codes Exempt from Modifier 63
Appendix G	Summary of Codes which include **Conscious Sedation**
Appendix H	Index of Performance Measures
Appendix I	Genetic Testing Code
Appendix J	Electrodiagnostic Medicine Listing
Appendix K	Products Pending FDA Approval
Appendix L	Vascular Families
Appendix M	Crosswalk to Deleted Codes
Appendix N	Summary of Resequenced CPT Codes

The AMA has printed the pages of the appendices A through M with a colored outer edge so they can be located quickly.

Format

Like the ICD-9-CM, many of the CPT code descriptions are indented below main terms, instead of repeating common information for each group of codes (Fig. 5–1). The common components are printed once and then followed by a semicolon. Codes below the common components are indented and refer back to the common component. The reason for this is merely to save space.

The medical coder must recognize the placement of the semicolon and where indentation occurs. The common component in the first code listed, should be applied to each of the individual codes listed below it.

Symbols

○ Bull's-eye printed to the left of the code to indicate procedures which used conscious sedation services.

● Dots printed to the left of the code indicate the code is new. It is imperative that these new codes be used each year, beginning with services performed on January 1 of the new year as there is no grace period.

99381	**Initial comprehensive preventative medicine** evaluation and management of an individual... new patient; infant (age younger than 1 year)
99382	early childhood (ages 1 through 4 years)
99383	late childhood (ages 5 though 11 years)
99384	adolescent (ages 12 through 17 years)

FIGURE 5–1: Format of CPT code description.

○ Open circle indicates a code that has reestablished or brought back.

⊘ Precedes codes that are exempt from the use of the -51 modifier.

▲ Triangles printed to the left of the code indicate that the description of the procedure code has been changed since the previous year. You will need to compare the new description to the previous year's to ensure proper use of the code.

▶◀ Arrows appear around new or revised text.

✚ The plus sign appears to the left of the code to indicate services performed in addition to the primary service/procedure.

⚡ The lightning bolt indicates codes for vaccines that are pending the approval of the FDA.

\# Resequenced code. CPT identifies codes that are not in numerical order with the symbol \# to the left of the code. This has allowed CPT to group related procedures together rather than having to delete and/or renumber existing codes.

CPT Index

The CPT index is located in the back of CPT. AMA has printed the index pages with a shaded outer edge so that the medical coder can locate it quickly. The index of the CPT codebook is designed much differently from the index in the ICD-9-CM. The main terms found in the CPT index represent a service or procedure, an anatomical site, a condition, an abbreviation, a synonym, or eponym.

The CPT index, however, is similar to ICD-9-CM in two ways:

1. A main term will be bolded and subterms will be found under the main term and indented to the right.

2. A code should never be chosen directly from the index. The medical coder must verify the code(s) listed in the index is accurate.

Many of the procedures are listed with a range of codes to choose from. Each code should be reviewed in the main section of the CPT to locate the procedure that best represents the service provided to the patient.

CPT CODE CATEGORIES

In addition to the recommendation of the advisory committees, the AMA also accepted the CPT-5 workgroup proposal. The workgroup identified the need to create codes to represent new technologies and data for performance measures. The CPT-5 Executive Project Advisory Group was implemented in 2002, *not* to develop a new coding system, but to allow CPT to evolve with the changes in health care and to comply with HIPAA. To comply with the workgroup's recommendations, CPT developed two additional categories of codes. CPT now contains three categories of codes.

Category I Codes

Category I codes are divided into two levels. Level I is made up of the CPT codes 99021 through 99607, which are located in the six main sections previously listed. This chapter will address the first section of the CPT, Evaluation and Management, and Chapter 6 will address the remaining sections.

Level II is made up of separate HCPCS codes. CMS developed Level II of the HCPCS coding system to cover services not specifically reported by the use of CPT codes. The system provides codes for hearing and vision services, medical supplies, orthotic and prosthetic devices, durable medical equipment, and injections.

Level II HCPCS codes are updated several times a year and published annually and all providers who deal with medical services, vision or hearing services, or supplies must use the correct codes on insurance claims. Every year there are changes made; new codes are added, and some codes are deleted or revised. It is important to use the latest edition of the HCPCS code set. The reimbursement of the health-care practice cannot be optimal without current codes, and the practice is put at risk for incorrect billing without current material. Unlike CPT, the medical coder will find the current list of HCPCS codes online. The alphanumeric HCPCS file can be downloaded from the following website: http://www.cms.hhs.gov/HCPCSReleaseCodeSets/.

Category II Codes

Category II codes are supplemental tracking codes that measure performance and collect test result data. The use of these codes is *optional* because they cannot be substituted for Category I codes and have no reimbursement linked with them. They are four numeric digits followed by an alpha character. The Category II codes are published twice a year on January 1st and July 1st. Go to www.ama-assn.org/go/cpt for the most current listing.

Category III Codes

Category III codes are temporary codes used to track new emerging technology, services, and procedures. Like Category II codes, these are four numeric digits followed by an alpha character. If a Category III code is available, it should be used instead of an unlisted code from Category I's CPT codes. Use of these codes rather than the CPT unlisted procedure codes collect data on new services or procedures to be used to demonstrate a new code may be needed as a permanent Category I code. A list of both Category II and III codes can be found after the Medicine section in CPT and each is preceded by very specific guidelines.

■ SECTION I: EVALUATION AND MANAGEMENT SERVICES

Patient encounters were once categorized as office visits, hospital visits, or house calls, with no standard system to convey more information. Established in 1992, CPT's current Evaluation and Management service codes offer a more precise method of code assignment according to the type of **history**, **examination**, and **medical decision making** involved in diagnosing and treating patients.

❗ KEY TERM

DOCUMENTATION GUIDELINES (DG)—The rules and instructions created to regulate and standardize the coding of the Evaluation and Management services.

Documentation Guidelines

The CMS created guidelines to supplement the CPT definitions of the E/M codes. It is mandatory that the E/M services assigned on the insurance claim reflect the actual work or services that were provided to the patient. To standardize this process, CMS worked with the AMA to develop the first set of **Documentation Guidelines (DG)** and implemented them September 1, 1995. They are referred to as the 1995 DGs. However, many specialist doctors criticized the guidelines because the requirements for a complete single system examination were unclear, and the specialists were not able to meet the documentation guidelines for high-level E/M services, limiting reimbursement. Prompted by this issue, CMS, the AMA, and several medical specialty societies developed an alternative set of DGs that contains ten single system examinations and incorporates different specialties. The alternative DGs were released in 1997 and are referred to as the 1997 DGs. The 1997 DGs were intended to replace the 1995 DGs, but there was strong opposition from health-care practitioners. Some practitioners felt the 1995 guidelines best suited the services rendered, whereas some specialty physicians insisted the 1997 guidelines should be followed. Many physicians thought that both sets of guidelines were too difficult to interpret and felt they would have less time to spend treating their patients.

In 1998, CMS told the Medicare and Medicaid carriers to use either 1995 or 1997 DGs for reviews. Physicians can choose the version that is most advantageous. Since then CMS and the AMA have been working on a simplified version of the 1997 DGs, and two additional sets of guidelines have been developed (1999 and 2000) but no final decision has been made about complete replacement of the older versions. For more information, the official guideline website is: http://cms.hhs.gov/medlearn/emdoc.asp.

■ ASSIGNING E/M CODES

The medical coder must first determine *where* the service was provided, whether in the office/outpatient setting, emergency room, inpatient hospital setting, or nursing facility, for example. The categories within the Evaluation and Management section represent the different locations a service could take place. Once the place of service is determined, patient's status (new or established) must be recognized. And lastly, the patient's *medical record* must be reviewed to determine the **level of care** that was provided.

New and Established Patients

Determining if a patient is new or established must be done to correctly code some E/M services. CPT guidelines state that a new patient is one who has never been seen by a physician or who has not been seen for 3 years. If there is more than one doctor practicing in an office or clinic, the patient is considered established once he or she has been seen by any one of the physicians of the same specialty. If a physician of another specialty in the same practice sees the patient within 3 years, the patient is considered a new patient. A patient will be considered established when a physician from another practice is taking call for a physician and sees an established patient of the absent physician. The physician taking call is acting in the other physician's behalf and the patient is not considered new to the physician.

! KEY TERMS

NEW AND ESTABLISHED PATIENTS—The status of frequency of the relationship between the patient and the physician.

OFFICE AND OUTPATIENT SERVICES—Evaluation and management services performed in a physician's office, outpatient or other ambulatory facility.

The frequently used Office or Other Outpatient Service codes have separate codes for **new and established patients**, along with codes for Domiciliary/Home Care and **Preventive Medicine** Services. Codes used to describe E/M services provided in an inpatient setting (99221–99233) or at a nursing facility (99304–99310) do distinguish between the initial service and subsequent services provided, but the same codes are used for new or established patients.

! KEY TERMS

DOMICILIARY CARE FACILITY—A home that provides care to persons who need help in assisted living as a result of their physical or mental conditions.

PREVENTIVE MEDICINE SERVICES—The routine examination or check-up provided to a patient with no current medical complaint or illness.

Level of Care in the Medical Record

The level of care is determined by the amount of effort or service rendered to the patient and, just as importantly, documented in the patient's chart. Remember the general rule *"If it isn't documented, it wasn't done, and therefore it isn't payable."* The medical coder can only bill what the documentation supports, which is why providers must follow the E/M DGs set up by CMS and the AMA. The medical record *must* confirm and validate the level of care chosen to justify the level of care billed.

! KEY TERM

KEY COMPONENTS—The main elements, history, examination, and medical decision making completed during the evaluation of a patient.

The appropriate level of care is determined using three **key components**—history, examination, and medical decision making—in addition to the **chief complaint**. Some physicians may determine what level of care was performed when treating or seeing the patient and may assign a code. However, the medical coder may have to refer to the patient's record to confirm the physician's code assignment or determine the appropriate code, if the physician did not assign one.

! KEY TERM

PERSONAL, FAMILY, SOCIAL HISTORY—A review of the patient's closely related family's medical events and illnesses, as well as their own and their medications, surgeries, and life routines.

E/M Components

The levels of E/M services include the following seven components, six of which are used in defining the levels of E/M services.

1. History

2. Examination

3. Medical decision making

4. Counseling

5. Coordination of care

6. Nature of the presenting problem

7. Time

The first three components—history, examination, and medical decision making—are considered the key components in selecting a level of E/M service and are required when determining level of care. Three other components or **contributing factors**—**counseling, coordination of care**, and **nature of presenting problem**—help to determine the level of care in some cases. The last component, time, is not used in code assignment unless the majority of the patient's visit is spent on counseling and coordination of care.

! KEY TERMS

CONTRIBUTING FACTORS—Other conditions or situations the patient has that may affect the treatment and outcome or the quality of health.

COORDINATION OF CARE—The steps taken by the physician to provide care that will harmonize with the patient's existing health care.

COUNSELING—The advice and direction the physician provides to his or her patient.

EXAMINATION—To look over or inspect a patient's body and systems to determine the presence or the absence of disease.

HISTORY—A synopsis of the patient's pertinent medical, social, and family events and conditions.

MEDICAL DECISION MAKING—The evaluation of medical data the physician reviews to arrive at a diagnosis and/or treatment.

NATURE OF PRESENTING PROBLEM—The degree of severity of the reason for the medical encounter if the patient's condition is left untreated.

TIME—Average amount of time typically spent with a patient.

When reviewing a record in SOAP format, the different key components are usually included as follows.

Subjective	**History =**	Chief Complaint **(CC)**
		History of present illness **(HPI)**
		Nature of Presenting Problems **(NPP)**
		Past, Family and/or Social History **(PFSH)**
Objective	**Exam =**	Doctor's findings
		Results of diagnostic tests or procedures
Assessment	**Medical Decision**	Diagnoses
Plan of treatment	**Making =**	Management Options

From this information the medical coder will need to follow these steps to insure the proper code selection:

1. Identify the place of service (office, hospital, ER, etc.).

2. Determine if the patient is new or established. Remember separate codes exist for services rendered to a new or established patient for the office and outpatient setting, a patient's home or residence (domiciliary), and for preventive medicine services. The rest of the occasions or types of visits in Evaluation and Management share the same codes and do not differentiate between new or established.

3. Review the instructions if they are present. Under many categories and subsections, CPT has supplied key information for choosing the right code.

4. Review the requirements for the specific levels of care listed.

An experienced medical coder can carry out these first four steps quickly after reviewing the patient's records. Reviewing and qualifying the patient's visit to the actual level of care takes a little more time.

Determining Level of History

A statement in the patient's record that reveals the patient's symptom(s), problem(s), or condition(s) "is usually called the "chief complaint," and is the reason(s) for the patient's visit. Many offices have patients complete paperwork before being seen, and these forms may contain a series of questions about past and current condition(s). A space is usually provided to indicate the reason for the visit. Other offices bring the patient back to an examination room and the medical assistant (or other medical personnel) obtains the necessary information from the patient. Besides the chief complaint, a chronological description of the development of the patient's present illness from the first sign and/or symptom to the present should be noted. The patient's history of illness, diseases, allergies, surgeries, social activities or habits, and pertinent diseases or disorders of family members should also be noted. This documentation is what the medical coder needs in order to choose the correct E/M code and comply with the CPT guidelines.

! KEY TERM

CHIEF COMPLAINT—A patient's reason for seeking medical care.

There are four types of history:

1. **Problem Focused** is a brief report of the patient's present condition or illness.

2. **Expanded Problem Focused** should include a brief statement of the patient's present condition or illness and a review of the relevant system.

3. **Detailed** histories must contain an extensive history of the current illness and a review of the system involved as well as a few additional systems recognized. The detailed history also must include a notation of any past medical, family, and/or social history that coincides with their current condition.

4. **Comprehensive** will also contain an extended history of the patient's current condition. A review of the system involved as well as all of the additional body systems; complete past, family, and social history.

Each of the four types of history should *always* state the patient's chief complaint or concern.

! KEY TERMS

COMPREHENSIVE—A complete history and review of systems along with a report on the patient's current illness or condition.

DETAILED—A more extensive review of systems along with a report on the patient's current illness or condition.

EXPANDED PROBLEM FOCUSED—A report on the patient's current illness or condition along with more information about the affected system.

HISTORY OF PRESENT ILLNESS—A chronological sequence of events defining the patient's current illness.

PROBLEM FOCUSED—A brief report on the patient's current illness or condition.

REVIEW OF SYSTEMS (ROS)—A series of questions asked of the patient and used to provide for an inventory of body systems.

The medical coder also must understand that a complete history includes three areas (Table 5–1):

1. **History of Present Illness (HPI)** presents details related to these *eight* areas: *location, quality, severity, duration, timing, context, modifying factors,* and *associated signs and symptoms* to document the history of the present illness (Table 5–2).

2. **Review of Systems (ROS)** is an inventory of body systems obtained through a series of questions seeking to identify signs and/or symptoms that the patient is currently experiencing. These questions are not a part of the examination and should relate to the specialty of the

TABLE 5–1: Components of a Patient History

Components	Factors/Elements	Number of Elements	Type of History
Chief Complaint (CC)	Reason for visit	Must always be documented	**All**
History of Present Illness (HPI)	Location, quality, severity, duration, timing, context, modifying factors, associated signs or symptoms	One to three elements describing the present illness Four or more	**Brief** **Extended**
Past Medical History (PH)	Prior major illness and injuries Prior operations Prior hospitalizations Current medication(s) Allergies to drugs, foods, other Current immunizations Nourishment/diet habits	At least one specific item reviewed from any of the three areas of history, past, family, or social	**Pertinent** Past, family, and/or social history (PFSH)
Social History (SH)	Smoker/nonsmoker Consume alcohol Any use of street drugs Occupation		
Family History (FH)	Health status of parents, siblings, children Cause of death of parents, siblings, children History of any diseases found in a close relative	Two or all three areas of history reviewed	**Complete** PFSH
Review of Systems (ROS)	Questions asked of patient to identify signs or symptoms of the following systems: • Constitutional (fever, weight loss) • Eyes, ears, nose, mouth, and/or throat • Cardiovascular • Respiratory • Gastrointestinal • Genitourinary • Musculoskeletal • Integumentary (skin or breast) • Neurological • Psychiatric • Endocrine • Hematologic/Lymphatic, • Allergic/Immunological	Just the system directly related to CC Two to nine systems documented 10 or more systems documented	**Problem Pertinent** **Extended** **Complete**

TABLE 5–2: Level of History Using These Key Components

Level of History (N/A = not applicable)	Chief Complaint (CC)	History of Present Illness (HPI)	Past, Family, and/ or Social History (PFSH)	Review of Systems (ROS)
Problem Focused (PF)	CC	Brief HPI	N/A	N/A
Expanded Problem Focused (EPF)	CC	Brief HPI	N/A	Problem Pertinent ROS
Detailed (D)	CC	Extended HPI	Pertinent PFSH	Extended ROS
Comprehensive (C)	CC	Extended HPI	Complete PFSF	Complete ROS

physician. For example, "Do you have frequent urination?" "Have you developed a rash?" "Do you have pain in your joints?" "Have you experienced chest pain, shortness of breath, or experienced frequent episodes of indigestion?"

3. **Past, Family, and Social History (PFSH)** contains a review of the patient's past medical history that includes any illnesses, surgeries, hospitalizations, medications, or allergies. The family history contains information about the health status of the patient's parents and immediate family members. Social histories contain information regarding the patient's past or current activities such as participation in sports or exercise. When age-appropriate, the patient's past and current employment, marital status, use of drugs, alcohol, tobacco, caffeine, or sexual activities.

The following case study is information from a sample medical record. This example will be used to show how to determine the level of history using documentation in the medical record.

CASE STUDY

PATIENT: JOHN DOE

Chief Complaint: Chronic cough and discomfort in the chest

History of Present Illness: This 73-year-old white male states for <u>"the last 6 months,"</u> he feels like he has sinus drainage, but it "feels like things are constantly in his throat." The feeling seems to be "worse about a half hour after eating a meal." The patient really does not have an acid taste, but he does have "moderate discomfort in his mid chest" and "must continually clear his throat or cough." "There is a constant 'tickle' or irritation in the back of his throat." "Antacids have created less coughing for the patient and do relieve the chest discomfort somewhat." The patient states that "spicy foods seem to irritate the symptoms more than blander food." The patient's "weight has not changed much in the last 6 months but his appetite has decreased somewhat."

Medical History: "Tonsils removed at age 5"

Social History: Patient is a retired banker. Married with three grown children, all healthy. He drinks 2–3 cups of coffee every day and enjoys a brandy after his dinner meals. Patient does not currently smoke, however did smoke for 25 years before quitting 20 years ago.

Family History: Mother deceased at age 85 with complications of colon cancer, father deceased at age 79 of cardiac arrest.

Continued

CASE STUDY—cont'd

REVIEW OF SYSTEMS:

General: Patient denies weight loss.
GI: The patient states he has regular bowel movements. Denies hematemesis or hematochezia.
Genitourinary: The patient denies dysuria or hematuria, but does admit to frequency.
Respiratory: The patient admits to a cough, which is nonproductive.
Cardiovascular: Some chest discomfort, which is somewhat relieved by antacids.
ENT: Patient clears throat constantly and feels he has something in the back of his throat. Denies hoarseness.

Rationale
This case study contains four or more elements of the history of the present illness and qualifies as an **extended history of present illness (HPI)**.
Chief Complaint: Chronic cough and discomfort in the chest (CC).
History of Present Illness:
• Duration: "Past 6 months"
• Timing: "Feels like things are constantly in his throat. The feeling seems to be worse about a half hour after eating a meal"
Severity: "Moderate discomfort in his mid chest"
Location: "The back of his throat and his mid chest"
Quality: "Must continually clear his throat or cough. There is a constant 'tickle' or irritation in the back of his throat."
Context: began "last 6 months" and "feeling seems to be worse about a half hour after eating a meal."
Modifying Factors: "Antacids have created less coughing for the patient and does relieve the chest discomfort somewhat. The patient states that spicy foods seem to irritate the symptoms more than blander food."
Associated Signs and Symptoms: "The patient's weight has not changed much in the last 6 months but his appetite has decreased somewhat."
This case study contains all three areas of history review from each of the three areas of history, past, family or social and qualifies as a complete Past family, social history (PFSH).
Medical History: Tonsils removed at age 5
Social History: Patient is a retired banker. He drinks 2–3 cups of coffee everyday and enjoys a brandy after his dinner meals.
Family History: Mother deceased at age 85 with complications of colon cancer, father deceased at age 79 of cardiac arrest.
This case study contains six systems documented and meets the criteria for an extended Review of Systems (ROS): General, GI, Genitourinary, Respiratory, Cardiovascular, and ENT.

LEVEL OF HISTORY   Chief Complaint +
                        Extended HPI +
                        Complete PFSH +
                        Extended ROS
                        DETAILED LEVEL OF HISTORY

Determining Level of Examination

CPT guidelines require a statement that shows each system or area of body of the patient that has been examined by the physician during the visit. The number of areas or systems reviewed/examined is measured by the clinical judgment of the physician performing the examination and on the nature of the patient's presenting problem(s).

There are four types of examinations:

1. **Problem Focused** examinations are limited to the system or area involved in the patient's complaint.

2. **Expanded Problem Focused** examinations are limited to the area or system involved as well as any other systems that may be connected.

3. **Detailed** examinations include an extended examination of the area or system involved as well as any other systems that may be connected.

4. **Comprehensive** examinations are extensive on either multiple systems or a complete examination of the single organ involved.

CPT identifies the body areas as:

■ Abdomen

■ Back

■ Chest (includes the breasts and the axillas)

■ Extremities (each of the four separately)

■ Genitalia (includes the groin and the buttock)

■ Head (includes the face)

■ Neck

CPT defines the organ systems as:

■ Cardiovascular

■ Ears, nose, mouth, and throat

■ Eyes

■ Gastrointestinal

■ Genitourinary

■ Hematologic/lymphatic/immunologic

■ Musculoskeletal

■ Neurologic

■ Psychiatric

■ Respiratory

■ Skin/integumentary

Documentation elements for a general multisystem examination or a single organ system examination are clearly defined by "bullets" in both the 1995 and 1997 DGs. Any physician regardless of specialty may use the general multisystem criteria or a single-organ system examination.

Table 5–3 shows the guidelines for a general multisystem examination and Table 5–4 shows how to apply the guidelines to determine an examination level.

The following excerpt from the previous case study shows how the elements in the medical record are used to establish the appropriate level of the examination and how to interpret the documentation correctly.

TABLE 5–3: Multisystem Examination Documentation Guidelines

System/Body Area	Elements of Examination
Constitutional	• Measurement of **any three of the following seven** vital signs: 1) Sitting or standing blood pressure 2) Supine blood pressure 3) Pulse rate and regularity 4) Respiration 5) Temperature 6) Height 7) Weight (may be measured and recorded by ancillary staff). General appearance of patient (e.g., development, nutrition, body habitus, deformities, attention to grooming)
Eyes	• Inspection of conjunctivae and lids • Examination of pupils and irises (e.g., reaction to light and accommodation, size, and symmetry) • Ophthalmoscopic examination of optic discs (e.g., size, C/D ratio, appearance) and posterior segments (e.g., vessel changes, exudates, hemorrhages)
Ears, Nose, Mouth, and Throat	• External inspection of ears and nose (e.g., overall appearance, scars, lesions, masses) • Otoscopic examination of external auditory canals and tympanic membranes • Assessment of hearing (e.g., whispered voice, finger rub, tuning fork) • Inspection of nasal mucosa, septum, and turbinates • Inspection of lips, teeth, and gums • Examination of oropharynx including oral mucosa, salivary glands, hard and soft palates, tongue, tonsils, and posterior pharynx
Neck	• Examination of neck (e.g., masses, overall appearance, symmetry, tracheal position, crepitus) • Examination of thyroid (e.g., enlargement, tenderness, mass)
Respiratory	• Assessment of respiratory effort (e.g., intercostal retractions, use of accessory muscles, diaphragmatic movement) • Percussion of chest (e.g., dullness, flatness, hyperresonance) • Palpation of chest (e.g., tactile fremitus) • Auscultation of lungs (e.g., breath sounds, adventitious sounds, rubs)

Cardiovascular	• Palpation of heart (e.g., location, size, thrills)
	• Auscultation of heart with notation of abnormal sounds and murmurs
	• Examination of:
	  • Carotid arteries (e.g., pulse amplitude, bruits)
	  • Abdominal aorta (e.g., size, bruits)
	  • Femoral arteries (e.g., pulse amplitude, bruits)
	  • Pedal pulses (e.g., pulse amplitude)
	  • Extremities for edema and/or varicosities

Chest (Breasts)	• Inspection of breasts (e.g., symmetry, nipple discharge) • Palpation of breasts and axillae (e.g., masses or lumps, tenderness)
Gastrointestinal (Abdomen)	• Examination of abdomen with notation of presence of masses or tenderness • Examination of liver and spleen • Examination for presence or absence of hernia • Examination (when indicated) of anus, perineum and rectum, including sphincter tone, presence of hemorrhoids, rectal masses • Obtain stool sample for occult blood test when indicated
Genitourinary	**MALE:** • Examination of the scrotal contents (e.g., hydrocele, spermatocele, tenderness of cord, testicular mass) • Examination of the penis • Digital rectal examination of prostate gland (e.g., size, symmetry, nodularity, tenderness)

TABLE 5–3:   Multisystem Examination Documentation Guidelines—cont'd

System/Body Area	Elements of Examination
	FEMALE:
	• Pelvic examination (with or without specimen collection for smears and cultures) • Examination of external genitalia (e.g., general appearance, hair distribution, lesions) and vagina (e.g., general appearance, estrogen effect, discharge, lesions, pelvic support, cystocele, rectocele) • Examination of urethra (e.g., masses, tenderness, scarring) • Examination of bladder (e.g., fullness, masses, tenderness) • Cervix (e.g., general appearance, lesions, discharge) • Uterus (e.g., size, contour, position, mobility, tenderness, consistency, descent or support) • Adnexa/parametria (e.g., masses, tenderness, organomegaly, nodularity)
Lymphatic	Palpation of lymph nodes in **two or more** areas: • Neck • Axillae • Groin • Other
Musculoskeletal	Examination of gait and station • Inspection and/or palpation of digits and nails (e.g., clubbing, cyanosis, inflammatory conditions, petechiae, ischemia, infections, nodes) • Examination of joints, bones, and muscles of **one or more of the following six** areas: 1) Head and neck 2) Spine, ribs, and pelvis 3) Right upper extremity 4) Left upper extremity 5) Right lower extremity 6) Left lower extremity The examination of a given area includes: • Inspection and/or palpation with notation of presence of any misalignment, asymmetry, crepitation, defects, tenderness, masses, effusions • Assessment of range of motion with notation of any pain, crepitation, or contracture • Assessment of stability with notation of any dislocation (luxation), subluxation, or laxity • Assessment of muscle strength and tone (e.g., flaccid, cog wheel, spastic) with notation of any atrophy or abnormal movements
Skin	• Inspection of skin and subcutaneous tissue (e.g., rashes, lesions, ulcers) • Palpation of skin and subcutaneous tissue (e.g., induration, subcutaneous nodules, tightening)
Neurological	• Test cranial nerves with notation of any deficits • Examination of deep tendon reflexes with notation of pathological reflexes (e.g., Babinski) • Examination of sensation (e.g., by touch, pin, vibration, proprioception)
Psychiatric	• Description of patient's judgment and insight Brief assessment of mental status including: • Orientation to time, place, and person • Recent and remote memory • Mood and affect (e.g., depression, anxiety, agitation)

TABLE 5–4: Examination Elements

Factors/Elements	Number of Elements	Type of Examination
Systems Ears, nose, mouth, and throat Eyes Integumentary Respiratory	Examination of one to five areas or systems items from a single or from multiple system(s) or area(s)	**Problem focused** **(PF)**
Cardiovascular Genitourinary Hematological/ 　　Lymphatic/Immunologic	Examination of six to 11 areas or systems items from a single or from multiple system(s) or area(s)	**Expanded problem focused** **(EPF)**
Musculoskeletal Neurological Psychiatric	Examination of 12 to 17 areas or systems items from a single or from multiple system(s) or area(s)	**Detailed** **(D)**
Areas Abdomen Back Chest (includes the breasts 　　and the axillas) Each of the four extremities Genitalia (includes groin and 　　buttock) Head (includes the face) Neck	Examination of 18 or more items from a single or from multiple system(s) or area(s)	**Comprehensive** **(D)**

CASE STUDY

PATIENT: JOHN DOE

Physical Examination:
Reveals an alert, oriented, 73-year-old white male. Height is 5 feet, 9 inches. Weight is 185 pounds, BP is 130/70, pulse 70, Temperature 98.6.
HEENT exam is unremarkable.
Lungs are CTA.
Heart is a Regular Rate and Rhythm.
Abdomen is soft, bowel sounds are active. There is no tenderness, guarding, or rebound.
Extremities are WNLs.

Rationale
Level of Examination: 10 areas or systems are documented here to qualify for an **Expanded problem focused examination**.
1. Patient is alert (Psychiatric)
2. Patient is oriented (Psychiatric)
3. When three or more patient's vitals are recorded, it equals 1 system or area. (Constitutional)
4. HEENT, Head, Ears, Eyes, Nose, Throat count as 3 systems or areas. (Head, Ears, Eyes, Nose, Throat)
5. Lungs equal one system or area (Respiratory)
6. Heart equals one system or area (Cardiovascular)
7. Abdomen equals 1 area of Gastrointestinal system reviewed. No tenderness equals palpation of abdomen and bowel sounds are active equals auscultation of the abdomen
8. Extremities are within normal limits (Musculoskeletal)

Documentation Guideline

Differences in 1995 versus 1997 Examination Criteria

The 1995 criteria allows the use of both a general multisystem examination or single specialty examination criteria but does not define documentation elements for the single specialty examination. General multisystem examination criteria define the number of elements that must be documented in each type of examination but the content and performance elements are left to the clinical judgment of the physician.

Determining Medical Decision Making

Medical decision making is the process of establishing a diagnosis or treatment to manage the patient's condition. CPT measures the complexity of Medical Decision Making using the following criteria:

1. The number of diagnoses and/or treatment options given to the patient.

2. The quantity and difficulty to review and decipher the patient's medical records, diagnostic tests, and pertinent information.

3. The threat of complications associated with the patient's condition, the risk involved with diagnostic tests or treatment options, and other conditions that could worsen the current state.

This is an extremely objective, gray area when determining the level of decision making performed. This area calls for the medical provider or medical coder to review the data documented and give a "best" estimate. To qualify for a given level only two out of the three elements must be met or exceeded.

! KEY TERM

MANAGEMENT OPTIONS—The options for treatment after an examination is completed and a diagnosis is determined.

Number of Diagnoses or Management Options

The number of diagnoses and/or **management options** is based on the following:

■ The number and types of issues focused on during a visit.

■ The difficulty of making a diagnosis.

■ The management choices made by the physician.

Decision making is usually easier with a diagnosed problem than an undiagnosed problem. The type of and number of diagnostic tests ordered generally indicates the possible number of diagnoses. Improving conditions are less difficult than ones that have not changed or are deteriorating. If advice or **consultation** with another source is needed, it also can indicate the complexity of the decision making.

It is recommended that:

■ One diagnosis or treatment option meets the **Minimal** level.

■ Two diagnoses or treatment options meets the **Limited** level.

■ Three diagnoses or treatment options meets the **Multiple** level.

■ Four diagnoses or treatment options meets the **Extensive** level.

See Box 5–1 for documentation guidelines related to diagnoses and treatment options when determining medical decision making.

Amount and/or Complexity of Data to Be Reviewed

The amount and complexity of data to be reviewed is based on the types of diagnostic tests ordered and evaluated. A decision to obtain and review old medical records and/or obtain history from sources other than the patient increases the amount and complexity of data to be reviewed.

See Box 5–2 for documentation guidelines related to amount and complexity of data when determining medical decision making.

BOX 5–1: Documentation Guidelines for Diagnoses and Treatment Options

- For each encounter, an assessment, clinical impression, diagnosis should be documented. It may be explicitly stated or implied in documented decisions regarding management plans and/or further evaluation.
  - For a presenting problem with an established diagnosis, the record should reflect whether the problem is (1) improved, well-controlled, resolving, or resolved; or (2) inadequately controlled, worsening, or failing to change as expected.
  - For a presenting problem without an established diagnosis, the assessment or clinical impression may be stated in the form of a differential diagnoses or as "possible," "probable," or "rule out" diagnoses.
- If referrals are made, consultations requested or advice sought, the record should indicate to whom or where the referral or consultation is made or from whom the advice is requested.
- The initiation of, or changes in, treatment should be documented. Treatment includes a wide range of management options including patient instructions, nursing instructions, therapies, and medications.

BOX 5–2: Documentation Guidelines for Diagnostic Services

- If a diagnostic service (test or procedure) is ordered, planned, scheduled, or performed at the time of the E/M encounter, the type of service (e.g., laboratory test or x-ray) should be documented.
- The review of laboratory, radiology, and/or other diagnostic tests should be documented. An entry in a progress note such as "WBC elevated" or "chest x-ray unremarkable" is acceptable. Alternatively, the review may be documented by initialing and dating the report containing the test results.
- A decision to obtain old records or a decision to obtain additional history from the family, caretaker, or other source to supplement that obtained from the patient should be documented.
- Relevant finding from the review of old records, and/or the receipt of additional history from the family, caretaker, or other source should be documented. If there is no relevant information beyond that already obtained, that fact should be documented. A notation of "Old records reviewed" or "additional history obtained from family" without elaboration is insufficient.
- If a surgical or invasive diagnostic procedure is ordered, planned, or scheduled at the time of the E/M encounter, the type of procedure (e.g., laparoscopy) should be documented.
- The direct visualization and independent interpretation of an image, tracing, or specimen previously or subsequently interpreted by another physician should be documented.
- The results of discussion of laboratory, radiology, or other diagnostic tests with the physician who performed or interpreted the study should be documented.
- If a surgical or invasive diagnostic procedure is performed at the time of the E/M encounter, the specific procedure should be documented.
- The referral for or decision to perform a surgical or invasive diagnostic procedure on an urgent basis should be documented or implied.

Risk of Significant Complication, Morbidity, and/or Mortality

The risk of significant complications, morbidity, and/or mortality is based on the risks associated with the presenting problem(s), the diagnostic procedures(s), and the possible management options. This is the only part of medical decision making that gives the medical coder a guide to determine the actual risk (Table 5–5) involved in diagnosing and treating the patient.

There is a correlation between the medical decision making risk and the nature of the presenting problem. The medical decision making is measured by the nature and the risk of the patient's presenting problem(s).

See Box 5–3 for documentation guidelines related to risk when determining medical decision making.

! KEY TERM

LEVELS OF RISK—The danger of a patient's existing condition, the danger of any diagnostic tests performed, and the chance a patient takes on the treatment options the physician recommends after examination.

TABLE 5-5: Levels of Risk

Level of Risk	Presenting Problem(s)	Diagnostic Procedure(s) Ordered	Management Options Selected
Minimal	• One self-limited or minor problem, e.g., cold, insect bite, tinea corporis	• Laboratory tests requiring • Venipuncture • Chest x-rays • EKG/EEG • Urinalysis • Ultrasound (e.g., echocardiography) • KOH prep	• Rest • Gargles • Elastic bandages • Superficial • Dressings
Low	• Two or more self-limited or minor problems • One stable chronic illness (e.g., well-controlled hypertension, non–insulin-dependent diabetes, cataract, BPH) • Acute uncomplicated illness or injury (e.g., cystitis, allergic rhinitis, simple sprain)	• Physiologic tests not under stress (e.g., pulmonary function tests) • Noncardiovascular imaging studies with contrast (e.g., barium enema) • Superficial needle biopsies, clinical laboratory tests requiring arterial puncture • Skin biopsies	• Over-the-counter drugs • Minor surgery with no identified risk factors • Physical therapy, occupational therapy • IV fluids without additives
Moderate	• One or more chronic illnesses with mild exacerbation, progression, or side effects of treatment • Two or more stable chronic illnesses, undiagnosed new problem with uncertain prognosis (e.g., lump in breast) • Acute illness with systematic symptoms (e.g., pyelonephritis, pneumonitis, colitis) • Acute complicated injury (e.g., head injury with brief loss of consciousness)	• Physiologic test under stress (e.g., cardiac stress test, fetal contraction stress test) • Diagnostic endoscopies with no identified risk factors • Deep needle or incisional biopsy • Cardiovascular imaging studies with contrast and no identified risk factors (e.g., arteriogram, cardiac catheterization) • Obtain fluid from body cavity (e.g., lumbar puncture, thoracentesis, culdocentesis)	• Minor surgery with identified risk factors • Elective major surgery (open, percutaneous, endoscopic) with no identified risk factors • Prescription drug management • Therapeutic nuclear medicine • IV fluids with additives • Closed treatment of fracture or dislocation without manipulation
High	• One or more chronic illnesses with severe exacerbation, progression, or side effects of treatment • Acute or chronic illnesses or injuries that may pose a threat to life or bodily function (e.g., multiple trauma, acute MI, pulmonary embolus, severe respiratory distress, progressive severe rheumatoid arthritis, psychiatric illness with potential threat to self or others, peritonitis, acute renal failure) • An abrupt change in neurological status (e.g., seizure, TIA, weakness, or sensory loss)	• Cardiovascular imaging studies with contrast with identified risk factors • Cardio electrophysiological tests • Diagnostic endoscopies with identified risk factors • Discography	• Elective major surgery (open, percutaneous or endoscopic) with identified risk factors • Emergency major surgery (open, percutaneous or endoscopic) • Parenteral controlled substances • Drug therapy requiring intensive monitoring for toxicity • Decision not to resuscitate or to de-escalate care because of poor prognosis

EKG, electrocardiogram; EEG, electroencephalogram; BPH, benign prostatic hypertrophy; KOH, potassium hydroxide; MI, myocardial Infarction; TIA, traneschemic attack.

BOX 5–3: Documentation Guidelines for Comorbidities

■ Comorbidities/underlying diseases or other factors that increase the complexity of medical decision making by increasing the risk of complications, morbidity, and/or mortality should be documented.

Using the criteria listed in Table 5–6, there are four levels of medical decision making:

1. **Straightforward** decision making includes minimal diagnoses or treatment plans. The amount of information that was reviewed and the complication risks are minor.

2. **Low Complexity** decision making includes a limited amount of diagnoses or treatment plans. The amount of information that was reviewed also is considered limited and the complication risks are low.

3. **Moderate Complexity** decision making includes multiple diagnoses or treatment plans. A moderate amount of information was reviewed and the complication risks are moderate.

4. **High Complexity** decision making includes extensive diagnoses, management options, and amount of information reviewed. The patient's risk is high if not treated.

⚠ KEY TERMS

HIGH COMPLEXITY—Decision making that includes extensive information and a high risk.

LOW COMPLEXITY—Decision making that includes limited information and a low risk.

MODERATE COMPLEXITY—Decision making that includes several diagnoses or treatments along with a moderate risk.

STRAIGHTFORWARD—Decision making that includes minimal information and very low risk.

The following excerpt from the previous case study shows the medical decision making criteria and how to interpret the documentation correctly.

TABLE 5–6: Medical Decision Making Criteria

Number of Diagnoses Or Management Options	Amount and/or Complexity of Data To Be Reviewed	Risk of Complications and/ or Morbidity or Mortality (see Table 5–5)	Type of Decision Making
Minimal (1)	None or Minimal (the review of written laboratory or radiology reports)	Minimal*	Straightforward
Limited (2)	Limited (same as Minimal)	Low*	Low Complexity
Multiple (3)	Moderate (the review of medical records, EKG rhythm strips, a pulmonary function test, x-rays or other information or results from outside sources that involve interpretation)	Moderate*	Moderate Complexity
Extensive (4 or more)	Extensive (such as performing the actual review or interpretation of complex diagnostics such as MRIs, CT scans, cardiovascular stress tests)	High*	High Complexity

*See Table 5–5.

CASE STUDY EXCERPT

IMPRESSION:

1. Chronic cough with gastroesophageal reflux disease.
2. Family history of colon cancer.

Plan: The patient has a need for an EGD and colonoscopy. Both procedures with the risks and benefits are discussed. The patient is given a booklet entitled "UGI Endoscopy and Colonoscopy" and the anatomy is reviewed. The patient is advised the largest risk of both procedures is perforation of the colon and if this would occur we would have to do surgery and repair it. The other risks and benefits are discussed. The patient understands, consents, and will be set up for the procedure.

Rationale

Level of Medical Decision Making: *Two diagnoses were determined. An endoscopy procedure* documented in the scenario is for an average risk patient and qualifies for a *moderate level* of Medical Decision Making.

Contributory Factors

The next three components—counseling, coordination of care, and the nature of the presenting problem—are considered contributory factors in the majority of encounters. The NPP is generally part of every patient visit, whereas counseling and coordination of care are not expected or required to be part of every patient encounter. A fourth component, time, also may be a factor in more complicated cases, to assign the proper code.

Counseling

Counseling is considered a contributory factor when determining a level of service provided. It is the documented dialogue physicians may have with the patient or the patient's family or caregiver regarding diagnosis, prognosis, treatment or management options, or patient risk. A language or communication barrier may result in working through an interpreter and cause much more work. The discussion will relate to the current or future care of the patient. If the physician's encounter is to discuss one or more of these areas, the nature of the discussion and the length of time spent must be documented to choose an accurate code.

Psychotherapy, the treatment of mental illness or behavior problems is not considered counseling. There are codes designated for this type of care or treatment, found in the Medicine section of CPT.

Coordination of Care

Coordination of care is also considered a contributory factor. Once a plan of treatment has been decided upon, implementing it can be difficult or time consuming. If the treatment must be arranged with other providers of health care, organizing the plan of treatment can be complex, and the effort more than usual. As with Counseling, the nature of the difficulty coordinating care must be documented to show the unusual effort taken to provide the proper treatment.

Nature of Presenting Problem

The Nature of Presenting Problem (NPP) can document the medical necessity of the patient encounter. CPT defines a presenting problem as "a disease, a condition, an illness, injury, symptom, sign, finding, complaint, or other reason for the encounter, with or without a diagnosis being recognized at the time of the encounter." The medical coder should find documentation of the NPP in the history section, usually as part of the patient's complaint, and in the diagnosis, the plan of treatment and management option sections.

CPT lists the following five types of presenting problems:

1. **Minimal**—A problem that may not require the presence of a physician but treatment would be provided under the supervision of a physician.
2. **Self-limited** or **minor** (level 1)—A problem that follows a specific course, is temporary, and is likely not to permanently alter health status. The prognosis is good with management/compliance.
3. **Low severity** (level 2)—A problem in which the risks of morbidity or mortality are low without treatment. A full recovery is expected without any functional damage.
4. **Moderate severity** (level 3)—A problem in which the risks of morbidity or mortality are moderate without treatment. The prognosis is uncertain and the probability of prolonged functional impairment is increased.
5. **High severity** (levels 4 and 5)—A problem in which the risk of morbidity is high to extreme without treatment, the risk of mortality is moderate to high or high without treatment, and the probability of severe, prolonged, functional impairment is high.

In the previous scenario, the patient's problems should follow a specific course of treatment; the risk of morbidity and mortality without treatment is low to moderate. The patient should make a full recovery without functional impairment and his condition should not permanently alter his health status. Depending on the findings from the endoscopies, the prognosis is good with management and patient compliance. The NPP is low to moderate.

Time

The last component, time, is an explicit factor in selecting the most appropriate level of E/M services. When counseling and/or coordination of care is more than half of the face-to-face physician/patient encounter, then time is considered the key or controlling factor. The extent of counseling and/or coordination of care must be documented in the medical record. The ranges of time listed in the CPT descriptions are averages and the correct code assignment depends on the specific circumstances of each patient encounter.

■ SELECTING THE E/M CODE

In order to select the right level of service, the coder will have to determine the:

- Chief complaint.
- Extent of the history.
- Nature of the presenting problem.
- Review of systems performed.
- Detail of the physical examination.
- Complexity of the medical decision making.

The chosen E/M level, represented by a specific code, is calculated by the documented content about each of the key components. According to CPT guidelines, all three key components must meet or exceed E/M level requirements in the following types of services:

- A new patient office visit
- A hospital observation service
- An initial hospital visit
- Any office or an initial inpatient consultation
- An emergency department visit
- Primary care in a nursing facility
- Care provided to a new patient seen at home or a **domiciliary care facility**

Table 5–7 shows the proper levels of care for codes assigned for New Patient Visits and Initial Hospital Visits. Remember, the levels of all three key components must agree for these codes.

TABLE 5–7: Codes for New Patient Visits and Initial Hospital Visits

Service	Codes	PFH	EPFH	DH	CH	PFE	EPFE	DE	CE	SMDM	LCMDM	MCMDM	HCMDM
New Pt	99201	X					X			X			
Visit	99202		X					X		X			
3/3	99203			X					X		X		
	99204				X				X			X	
	99205				X				X				X
Initial	99221			X					X		X		
Hosp Care	99222				X				X			X	
3/3	99223				X				X				X

E/M=Evaluation and Management; CC=Chief Complaint; HPI=History of Present Illness; ROS=Review of Symptoms; PFSH=Past, Family, and Social History; PH=Past History; SH=Social History; FH=Family History; PFH=Problem Focused History; EPFH=Expanded Problem Focused History; DH=Detailed History; CH=Comprehensive History; NPP=Nature of Presenting Problem; MDM=Medical Decision Making; SMDM=Straightforward Medical Decision Making; LCMDM=Low Complexity Medical Decision Making; MCMDM=Moderate Complexity Medical Decision Making; HCMDM=High Complexity Medical Decision Making; PF=Problem Focused; EPF=Expanded Problem Focused; D=Detailed; C=Comprehensive; PFE=Problem Focused Examination; EPFE=Expanded Problem Focused Examination; DE=Detailed Examination; CE=Comprehensive Examination.

According to CPT guidelines, two of the three key components must meet or exceed E/M level requirements in the following types of services:

■ An established patient office visit

■ Subsequent hospital visits

■ Subsequent nursing facility visits/care

■ Care provided to an established patient seen at home or a domiciliary facility

Table 5–8 shows the proper levels of care for codes assigned for Established Patient Visits and Subsequent Hospital Visits. Remember, the level of at least two of the three key components must agree for these codes.

The following text illustrates how to properly assign a code for the scenario that was previously discussed. Two options are provided: one for a new patient and one for an established patient.

In the scenario, the components of the patient visit consist of the following:

Detailed level of history +

Expanded Problem Focused Examination +

Moderate Level of Decision Making +

Low to Moderate Nature of Presenting Problem =

99202 for a new patient visit or a 99214 for an established patient.

The breakdown of each component is shown in Table 5–9.

Consultations

A consultation is an examination requested by the primary physician to obtain another opinion regarding a patient's condition. The need for a consultation must be documented in the patient's medical record. The consulting physician should send a written report of the findings and/or recommendations to the primary physician. A consultation requested by a patient and/or family member, and not requested by a physician, cannot be coded as a consultation.

TABLE 5–8: Codes for Established Patient Visits and Subsequent Hospital Visits

Service	Codes	PFH	EPFH	DH	CH	PFE	EPFE	DE	CE	SMD	LCMD	MCMD	HCMD
Est Pt. Office	99211	No Dr. Contact											
Visit	99212	X				X				X			
2/3	99213		X				X				X		
	99214			X				X				X	
	99215				X				X				X
Subseq	99231	X				X				X			
Hosp	99232		X				X					X	
Visits	99233			X				X					X

E/M=Evaluation and Management; CC=Chief Complaint; HPI=History of Present Illness; ROS=Review of Symptoms; PFSH=Past, Family, and Social History; PH=Past History; SH=Social History; FH=Family History; PFH=Problem Focused History; EPFH=Expanded Problem Focused History; DH=Detailed History; CH=Comprehensive History; NPP=Nature of Presenting Problem; MDM=Medical Decision Making; SMDM=Straightforward Medical Decision Making; LCMDM=Low Complexity Medical Decision Making; MCMDM=Moderate Complexity Medical Decision Making; HCMDM=High Complexity Medical Decision Making; PF=Problem Focused; EPF=Expanded Problem Focused; D=Detailed; C=Comprehensive; PFE=Problem Focused Examination; EPFE=Expanded Problem Focused Examination; DE=Detailed Examination; CE=Comprehensive Examination.

> **! KEY TERM**
>
> CONSULTATION—An examination requested by the primary physician to obtain another opinion regarding a patient's condition.

In order to bill the services as a consultation, the consulting physician may only perform diagnostic services or begin a therapeutic service. Any subsequent encounters or treatments are not considered consultations and must be billed as an established patient office or other outpatient service. If the encounters occur in the hospital of nursing facility the same rule applies. The initial encounter is considered a consultation followed by subsequent hospital or nursing facility codes. If after the initial consultation, a consulting physician begins treating a patient, the physician must bill using an appropriate office, outpatient, or inpatient visit code for any subsequent visits. If a consulting physician begins treating a patient at the initial consultation and continues to care for the patient, the appropriate visit codes should be used. However, this situation would be considered a referral from one physician to another, not a consultation.

According to CPT guidelines, the requirements for a consultation are the same as the requirements for an initial office or outpatient service. This means the level of all three key components must meet the code assignment requirement.

Table 5–10 shows the proper levels of care for codes assigned for Office/Outpatient Consultations and Inpatient Consultations.

TABLE 5–9: Component Breakdown for Proper Code Assignment of the Scenario as an Outpatient Visit

Service	Codes	PFH	EPFH	DH	CH	PFE	EPFE	DE	CE	SMD	LCMD	MCMD	HCMD
Est Pt. Office Visit 2/3	99211	No Dr. Contact											
	99212	X				X				X			
	99213		X				X				X		
	99214			X				X				X	
	99215				X				X				X
New Pt Visit 3/3	99201	X				X				X			
	99202		X				X			X			
	99203			X				X			X		
	99204				X				X			X	
	99205				X				X				X

E/M=Evaluation and Management; CC=Chief Complaint; HPI=History of Present Illness; ROS=Review of Symptoms; PFSH=Past, Family, and Social History; PH=Past History; SH=Social History; FH=Family History; PFH=Problem Focused History; EPFH=Expanded Problem Focused History; DH=Detailed History; CH=Comprehensive History; NPP=Nature of Presenting Problem; MDM=Medical Decision Making; SMDM=Straightforward Medical Decision Making; LCMDM=Low Complexity Medical Decision Making; MCMDM=Moderate Complexity Medical Decision Making; HCMDM=High Complexity Medical Decision Making; PF=Problem Focused; EPF=Expanded Problem Focused; D=Detailed; C=Comprehensive; PFE=Problem Focused Examination; EPFE=Expanded Problem Focused Examination; DE=Detailed Examination; CE=Comprehensive Examination.

TABLE 5–10: Codes for Consultations

Service	Codes	PFH	EPFH	DH	CH	PFE	EPFE	DE	CE	SMD	LCMD	MCMD	HCMD
Office-Out Pt Consult	99241	X				X				X			
	99242		X				X			X			
	99243			X				X			X		
	99244				X				X			X	
	99245				X				X				X
Inpt. Consult	99251	X				X				X			
	99252		X				X			X	X		
	99253			X				X			X		
	99254				X				X			X	
	99255				X				X				X

E/M=Evaluation and Management; CC=Chief Complaint; HPI=History of Present Illness; ROS=Review of Symptoms; PFSH=Past, Family, and Social History; PH=Past History; SH=Social History; FH=Family History; PFH=Problem Focused History; EPFH=Expanded Problem Focused History; DH=Detailed History; CH=Comprehensive History; NPP=Nature of Presenting Problem; MDM=Medical Decision Making; SMDM=Straightforward Medical Decision Making; LCMDM=Low Complexity Medical Decision Making; MCMDM=Moderate Complexity Medical Decision Making; HCMDM=High Complexity Medical Decision Making; PF=Problem Focused; EPF=Expanded Problem Focused; D=Detailed; C=Comprehensive; PFE=Problem Focused Examination; EPFE=Expanded Problem Focused Examination; DE=Detailed Examination; CE=Comprehensive Examination.

Using the previous scenario as a consultation, the code for an outpatient consultation would be assigned as follows:

Table 5–11 shows the levels of the various components.

CONSULTATION

PATIENT: JOHN DOE

Chief Complaint: Chronic cough and discomfort in the chest

History of Present Illness:
1. **Duration:** Sinus drainage the last 6 months
2. **Location:** His throat and chest.
3. **Quality:** Discomfort in his mid chest.
4. **Severity:** Moderate
5. **Timing:** Worse about a half hour after eating a meal
6. **Context:** After eating a meal, spicy foods seem to irritate the symptoms more than blander food
7. **Modifying factors:** Antacids, coughing relieve the chest discomfort somewhat
8. **Associated signs and symptoms:** Must continually clear his throat or cough, constant "tickle" or irritation in the back of his throat, weight has not changed much in the last 6 months but his appetite has decreased somewhat, does not have an acid taste.

Rationale
HPI: This scenario contains *8 total elements* and qualifies as an *Extended HPI*

HISTORY

Medical History: Tonsils removed at age 5
Allergies: No known allergies
Medications: Multivitamin daily, Glucosamine, Calcium and Prilosec OTC daily.
Social History: Patient is a retired banker. Married with three grown children, all healthy. He drinks 2–3 cups of coffee every day and enjoys a brandy after his dinner meals. Patient does not currently smoke, however did smoke for 25 years before quitting 20 years ago.
Family History: Mother deceased at age 85 with complications of colon cancer, father deceased at age 79 of cardiac arrest.

Rationale
History: This scenario contains all three areas of history review from each of the three areas of history, past, family or social and qualifies as a *Complete PFSH.*

REVIEW OF SYSTEMS

General: Patient denies weight loss.
Gastrointestinal: The patient states he has regular bowel movements. Denies hematemesis or hematochezia.
Genitourinary: The patient denies dysuria or hematuria, but does admit to frequency.
Respiratory: The patient admits to a cough, which is nonproductive.
Cardiovascular: Some chest discomfort, which is somewhat relieved by antacids.
ENT: Patient clears throat constantly and feels he has something in the back of his throat. Denies hoarseness.

Rationale
ROS: This scenario contains six systems documented, General, Gastrointestinal, Genitourinary, Respiratory, Cardiovascular, and Ears, Nose, Throat and meets the criteria for an *Extended Review of Systems (ROS).*
Level of History = Chief Complaint + Extended History of Present Illness + Complete PFSH + Extended Review of Systems = *Detailed Level of History.*

CONSULTATION—cont'd

EXAMINATION:

The Level of Examination is the same here as it was for the office/outpatient examination earlier. Eleven areas or systems are documented and qualify for an _Expanded Problem Focused Examination._

Medical Decision Making:
In the scenario, the patient's problems should follow a specific course of treatment; the risk of morbidity and mortality without treatment is _low to moderate._ The patient would most likely make a full recovery without functional impairment and his condition would most likely not alter his health status permanently. Depending on the findings from the endoscopies, the prognosis is good with management/compliance. The NPP is _low to moderate._

Based on all of the information, the components of the Office or Outpatient Consultation consist of:

Detailed Level of History +
Expanded Problem Focused Examination +
Moderate Level of Decision Making +
Low to Moderate Nature of Presenting Problem =
99242

TABLE 5–11: Component Breakdown for Proper Code Assignment of the Scenario as a Consultation

Service	Codes	PFH	EPFH	DH	CH	PFE	EPFE	DE	CE	SMD	LCMD	MCMD	HCMD
Office-	99241												
Out Pt	99242						X						
Consult	99243			X									
3/3	99244											X	
	99245												

E/M=Evaluation and Management; CC=Chief Complaint; HPI=History of Present Illness; ROS=Review of Symptoms; PFSH=Past, Family, and Social History; PH=Past History; SH=Social History; FH=Family History; PFH=Problem Focused History; EPFH=Expanded Problem Focused History; DH=Detailed History; CH=Comprehensive History; NPP=Nature of Presenting Problem; MDM=Medical Decision Making; SMDM=Straightforward Medical Decision Making; LCMDM=Low Complexity Medical Decision Making; MCMDM=Moderate Complexity Medical Decision Making; HCMDM=High Complexity Medical Decision Making; PF=Problem Focused; EPF=Expanded Problem Focused; D=Detailed; C=Comprehensive; PFE=Problem Focused Examination; EPFE=Expanded Problem Focused Examination; DE=Detailed Examination; CE=Comprehensive Examination.

■ E/M MODIFIERS

As defined earlier in the chapter, modifiers are two extra characters, appended to the end of any five-digit CPT code. Their primary purpose is to explain circumstances that affect a procedure or provided service. Some modifiers affect reimbursement, while others are for documentation purposes. Adding a modifier to a code can:

- Further explain what procedure was performed.
- Provide additional information of the procedure performed.
- Indicate what anatomical location the procedure was performed on (left or right).
- Explain why a procedure was performed.
- Show who performed a service.
- Justify why a procedure was performed.

The majority of CPT modifiers are numeric. There also are HCPCS modifiers that are both alpha (e.g., LT = left) and alphanumeric (e.g.., T1 = Left foot, great toe). Modifiers from either section can be used with any code, as long as the use is appropriate. An entire list of all CPT modifiers is located in Appendix A of the CPT manual. CPT also lists modifiers that are generally used with codes in each of the main sections of CPT: Medicine, Anesthesia, Surgery, Radiology, and Pathology/Laboratory.

The modifiers that may be used with E/M procedures are:

24   **Unrelated Evaluation and Management service provided by the same physician within a postoperative time period.** Example: A patient is seen 4 days after an appendectomy for conjunctivitis.

25   **Significant, Separately Identifiable Evaluation and Management service provided by the same physician on the same day of a procedure or other service.** Example: A child falls off a jungle gym and is brought to the emergency room. After evaluation it is determined that the patient has a fractured radius and has a laceration on the back of his head that needs repair. There was a diagnosis at the time the patient was brought in. Only after a thorough examination was it discovered that the child had injuries.

32   **Mandated Services.** A service that has been mandated by a third-party carrier. Example: In order for the insurance company to provide coverage for a procedure, the patient must be seen by another physician to prove medical necessity.

55   **Postoperative Management Only.** This modifier is used when the physician providing the E/M service has not performed the surgical procedure or service. Example: While on vacation the same child who fell from the jungle gym had to have his sutures removed in a local walk-in clinic.

56   **Preoperative Management. Only.** This modifier is used when the physician is providing the E/M service before the surgical procedure but does perform the surgery. Example: A pregnant woman received her prenatal care from one physician, moved away, and was delivered by a completely different physician.

57   **Decision for Surgery.** This modifier is used when during an evaluation and management service it is decided that the patient must have surgery. Example: A patient seen for acute abdominal pain is taken to surgery to have an emergency appendectomy.

Using an E/M Modifier

Many surgical and diagnostic procedures include the E/M services. The medical coder cannot bill separately for an E/M service related to those procedures. For example, if a patient had a major surgery, such as a hysterectomy, any E/M service related to postoperative care of the surgery cannot be billed separately.

Regardless of these billing guidelines, sometimes it is necessary for the physician to provide an E/M service during a postoperative period. If the patient is experiencing problems unrelated to the surgery, a physician may treat the patient and bill for the service provided. The medical coder must indicate that the reason for the patient's visit was for an unrelated condition than the surgery to obtain reimbursement. To indicate that, the medical coder should add modifier 24 to the appropriate CPT code. Modifier 24 indicates that the E/M service was performed within the postoperative time frame but is unrelated to the surgery. The medical coder should also assign a diagnosis code that justifies the service code.

With the addition of a modifier, the medical coder may need to provide additional information with the claim to justify the chosen modifier. Additional information on the use of other modifiers will be discussed in the following chapter.

CONCLUSION

The E/M section of CPT is probably the most challenging section to master. The medical coder may have to assign more E/M codes than the codes from the other sections of CPT. Accuracy is always first and foremost and can be achieved by reviewing the basics: place of service, type of service, and patient status, new or established. After those three factors are established, the coder should review the key components of the service provided: the history, the examination, and the medical decision making. The contributing factors—counseling, coordination of care, the nature of the presenting problem, and time—may be used to help establish the level of the service. Deciding on the level of service is much like working a math equation:

# of components of history + # of components of exam +

# of components of medical decision making + contributing factors = *Level of Care*

Most importantly, the documentation must always be present to support each E/M code and any other CPT code assigned.

RESOURCE LIST

Current Procedural Terminology 2009 (Standard Edition or Professional Edition), American Medical Association

http://www.ama-assn.org

Principles of CPT Coding, American Medical Association

http://www.ama-assn.org

HCPCS codes at the Centers for Medicare and Medicaid Services

http://www.cms.hhs.gov/HCPCSReleaseCodeSets

CHAPTER REVIEW EXERCISES

General CPT Coding Questions

1. Name and describe the three categories of procedure codes:

   Category 1 = _____

   Category 2 = _____

   Category 3 = _____

2. Name the six sections of CPT:

   1. _____

   2. _____

   3. _____

   4. _____

   5. _____

   6. _____

3. A summary of annual changes made to CPT can be found in

   _____

4. A triangle (∆) to the left of a code indicates _____

5. A black dot (•) to the left of a code indicates _____

6. A (+) to the left of a code represents _____

7. Name the seven components that make up the Evaluation and Management codes:

   1. _____

   2. _____

   3. _____

   4. _____

   5. _____

   6. _____

   7. _____

8. Which of the seven Evaluation and Management components is the explicit factor?

   _____

9. A new patient is someone who has not received any services from your physician in 3 years. **True or False** (circle one)

10. When a physician asks another physician to see a patient and render an opinion and/or advise regarding the condition or treatment of the patient, that service is called a

    _____.

New or Established Patient

Determine if the patients in the next sections are considered new or established and circle the appropriate answer of the corresponding number.

11. New or Established in question 21
12. New or Established in question 22
13. New or Established in question 23
14. New or Established in question 24
15. New or Established in question 25
16. New or Established in question 26
17. New or Established in question 27
18. New or Established in question 28
19. New or Established in question 29
20. New or Established in question 30

E/M CPT Coding

Assign codes to the following scenarios.

21. Office visit by a cardiologist, for an initial evaluation of a 63-year-old male with chest pain on exertion. _____

22. Office evaluation by family practice physician for new onset of right lower quadrant pain in a 32-year-old woman, who is an established patient. _____

23. Initial office evaluation by a general surgeon, for a 48-year-old man with recurrent low back pain, radiating to the leg. _____

24. A 73-year-old male with an unexplained 20-lb weight loss is seen for the first time by an oncologist/hematologist. _____

25. Internal medicine physician performs an office visit with an out-of-town visitor who needs a prescription refilled because she forgot her hay fever medication.

_____

26. Initial office visit with a dermatologist for a 16-year-old male with severe cystic acne.

_____

27. An infectious disease specialist provides a follow-up visit for a 65-year-old male with a fever of recent onset, while on outpatient antibiotic therapy for endocarditis.

_____

28. An established patient sees his orthopedist with known osteoarthritis and painful swollen knees. _____

29. A pediatrician sees a 6-year-old established patient with a sore throat and headache.

_____

30. Cursory check in the internal medicine physician's office for an established patient with a

hematoma one day after venipuncture. _____

E/M Codes
Match the E/M code with the description.

31. ____ 99203   A. Domiciliary, rest home, or home care plan oversight

32. ____ 99391   B. Office or other outpatient visit of a new patient

33. ____ 99242   C. Subsequent hospital care

34. ____ 99254   D. Office or other outpatient consultation new or established patient

35. ____ 99236   E. Emergency department visit new or established patient

36. ____ 99282   F. Observation or inpatient care new or established patient

37. ____ 99222   G. Inpatient consultation of a new or established patient

38. ____ 99231   H. Initial hospital care new or established patient

39. ____ 99340   I. Domiciliary, rest home, or custodial care new patient

40. ____ 99336   J. Periodic comprehensive preventive medicine of an established

                                                   patient

E/M Coding
Assign codes to the following scenarios.

41. Inpatient consultation for a 6-year-old female, established patient, with endocarditis and

changing heart murmur. _____

42. Follow-up hospital visit for a 32-year-old patient admitted the previous day for corneal

ulcer. _____

43. Initial hospital consultation for 50-year-old female with incapacitating knee pain due to

generalized rheumatoid arthritis. _____

44. Initial office consultation for a 20-year-old male with acute respiratory tract symptoms.

_____

45. Emergency department visit for a 20-year-old student who presents with a painful sunburn

with blister formation on the back. _____

46. Subsequent visit in a skilled nursing facility with a patient who is 6 months post stroke and

now has a fever and mild cough. _____

47. Initial hospital visit for a 69-year-old female with controlled hypertension, scheduled for surgery. _____

48. Initial inpatient consultation for a 76-year-old female with massive, life-threatening gastrointestinal hemorrhage and chest pain. _____

49. Initial office consultation for evaluation of a 70-year-old male with appetite loss and diminished energy. _____

50. Subsequent hospital visit for a 44-year-old patient with electrical burns to the left arm with ascending infection. _____

Coding Modifiers

Give the appropriate modifier for the following descriptions.

51. Multiple Procedures _____

52. Bilateral Procedure _____

53. Professional Component _____

54. Assistant Surgeon _____

55. Reference (Outside) Laboratory _____

56. Anesthesia by Surgeon _____

57. Multiple Modifiers _____

58. Surgical Care Only _____

59. Unusual Services _____

60. Reduced Services _____

E/M Coding Scenarios

Provide the correct E/M code for each scenario.

61. CONSULTATION COMPLAINT: Severe rectal pain.

HISTORY OF COMPLAINT: This 38-year-old white female who has been referred to me by Dr. BeWell for review. She presents with severe rectal pain that has been going on for a month. She stated it started with some burning, she had some bleeding with a bowel movement and the pain increased in severity. The patient has been using hydrocortisone acetate suppositories but the patient says the pain has become more intense, it's relieved when she's standing and when she's sitting. The patient's pain is incapacitating. The patient did have an exam accomplished by Dr. Robert BeWell, she had some external hemorrhoids and she really couldn't identify fissure, and digital rectal exam was extremely painful.

ALLERGIES: Patient suffers from seasonal allergies. She is allergic to aspirin.

MEDICATIONS: Cetirizine hydrochloride for allergies, metoprolol tartrate for her hypertension, and ibuprofen prn. The patient has been taking stool softeners and fiber and she's also been using suppositories for 2 weeks.

PAST SURGICAL HISTORY: Consists of a C-section at age 28 and another at age 30. The patient has had a left broken ankle as a child but no surgery was required.

FAMILY HEALTH: Her mother is alive at age 67 has high blood pressure and has a pacemaker. The patient's father is alive at age 70 and has high blood pressure and arthritis. There is no family history of breast, stomach, colon cancer, or any bleeding disorders.

SOCIAL: The patient is married; her husband's name is Richard. She has two children who are alive and healthy. The patient is a teacher at ABC Middle School. The patient does not currently smoke, but did smoke for approximately 5 years while in school. She drinks 2–3 cups of coffee a day. She does not report if she drinks alcohol.

PAST MEDICAL HISTORY: Positive for hypertension and hypercholesterolemia.

REVIEW OF SYSTEMS: GI: The patient states that she's having difficulty having bowel movements because of the amount of pain and discomfort that she's having. She denies hematemesis but does report hematochezia on a regular basis. GU: The patient denies dysuria or hematuria. CV: The patient denies cough, shortness of breath, or chest pain. OB/Gyn: Her periods have been regular, her last period was June 25th.

PHYSICAL EXAM: Exam reveals an alert, oriented 38-year-old white female.

Height: 5 feet 0 inches; weight 220 pounds.

HEENT: Unremarkable.

LUNGS: Clear to auscultation.

HEART: Regular rate and rhythm.

GI: Abdomen: soft, bowel sounds are active.
    Rectal: The patient refuses a rectal exam stating that she is too sore to even be examined. The patient is encouraged just to have external anal visualization. Visualization of her anus is accomplished; and is unremarkable except for some small external hemorrhoids.

IMPRESSION:
1. Severe rectal pain with probable anal fissure.
2. External with possible internal hemorrhoids.
3. Hypertension.
4. Hypercholesterolemia.

PLAN: The patient will be placed on a lidocaine based gel and continue with the hydrocortisone acetate suppositories. I will see the patient back in 1 week and see if we're able to perform an anal exam at that time.
    Thank you Bob, for referring this pleasant young woman to me for examination. A follow-up letter will follow after the anal exam can be accomplished.

---

62. CHIEF COMPLAINT: Right inguinal pain.

HISTORY OF COMPLAINT: This 34-year-old male, well known to me and our office, presents with increasing inguinal pain that has occurred this past weekend while out doing yard work. The patient states that he had similar pain 9 years ago when he was diagnosed with an umbilical hernia.

ALLERGIES: NO KNOWN ALLERGIES.

MEDICATIONS: None.

PAST SURGICAL HISTORY: Umbilical hernia repair.

PAST MEDICAL HISTORY: He denies hypertension, diabetes, heart or lung disease.

SOCIALLY: The patient does smoke. The patient drinks a moderate amount of caffeine and a moderate amount of alcohol socially.

FAMILY HEALTH: Both mother and father are alive and in good health. There is no serious family illness. The patient is married and has three living children.

REVIEW OF SYSTEMS: GI - the patient has fairly regular bowel movements. Denies hematemesis or hematochezia. GU - the patient denies dysuria or hematuria. CV - the patient denies cough, shortness of breath, or chest pain.

PHYSICAL EXAM: Alert, oriented 34 year-old male. His temperature is 97, pulse 84, respirations 18, blood pressure 128/58.

HEENT within normal limits

LUNGS are clear to auscultation.

HEART has a regular rate and rhythm.

GI: The patient's abdomen is soft, bowel sounds are present. The patient has tenderness centered directly in the right inguinal region. Palpation of the area reveals a walnut-size hernia quite palpable just beneath the level of the skin. The patient has quite a bit of tenderness in this area. He has slight guarding, no rebound is elicited. Left side is negative for symptoms.

SKIN is warm and dry.

EXTREMITIES are within normal limits.

IMPRESSION:
1. Right inguinal pain
2. Right inguinal hernia

PLAN: This being Monday, the patient will be set up for a right inguinal herniorrhaphy on Friday of this week. This will give the patient time for a pre-op workup to clear him for surgery.

---

63. CHIEF COMPLAINT: Acute cephalgia with fever.

HISTORY OF COMPLAINT: This 56-year-old female was brought to the emergency room at 4 am this morning by her husband. She was complaining of fever and headaches that had started approximately 2 days ago. The patient states that during the night, the pain has become excruciating. On a scale of 10, 10 being the extreme, the patient states her pain is 11. The patient has had no appetite for the last 2 days. Patient has been taking acetaminophen and ibuprofen around the clock with no relief. The patient has been admitted.

ALLERGIES: No known allergies.

MEDICATIONS ON ADMISSION:

1. Metoprolol Succinate
2. Aspirin 81 mg po daily
3. Metformin

PAST SURGICAL HISTORY:

1. Right rotator cuff repair 3 years ago.
2. Back surgery 7–8 years ago for partial laminectomy.
3. The patient had an esophagogastroduodenoscopy and colonoscopy performed by myself on 05/20/05. The patient was found to have gastritis and colonic polyps of the cecum, at 45 cm, 40 cm, and 30 cm. The patient was also found to have gastritis.

FAMILY HEALTH: Her mother is deceased at age 70 of a stroke. The patient's father died at age 62 of a heart attack. There is no family history of colon cancer.

SOCIAL: The patient has five children. The patient is married. She does not smoke or drink coffee. She drinks 1–2 cans of pop a day. The patient averages 1–2 beers a week on average.

PAST MEDICAL HISTORY: Positive for:

1. Hypertension.
2. Diabetes.
3. History of esophageal strictures.

REVIEW OF SYSTEMS:

GI: The patient states that she has had fairly formed stools. Denies hematemesis, hematochezia.

GU: The patient denies dysuria, hematuria.

CV: The patient denies cough, shortness of breath, or chest pain.

The patient does report cephalgia with headaches in frontal region, which have only slightly been relieved with Tylenol or ibuprofen.

PHYSICAL EXAM: Reveals alert, oriented 56-year-old female. Her temperature on admission was 102. Heart rate 95. Respirations 20. Height is 5 feet 3 inches. Weight is 152.5 pounds. The patient's blood pressure was 162/82.

HEENT exam is unremarkable. There is no scleral icterus.

LUNGS are clear to auscultation.

HEART has a regular rate and rhythm. Her abdomen is protuberant but soft. Bowel sounds are active. There is acute epigastric tenderness. No guarding, no rebound is noted. A chest x-ray reveals a normal examination with no interval changes from a chest x-ray of 12/29/03. The patient's flat and upright reveal a nonspecific abdominal gas pattern.

LABORATORY: The patient's laboratory revealed a sodium of 134, BUN 12, creatinine of 0.8, AST 44, ALT 98, GGT of 237, a white blood cell count of 13.1 with hemoglobin and hematocrit of 12.4 and 36.2. She has 78% neutrophils and 9 lymphs. Sedimentation rate is 111.

IMPRESSION:

1. Cephalgia with fevers with possible viral versus spinal meningitis.

2. Diabetes mellitus.

3. Hypertension.

4. History of gastritis and esophagitis.

PLAN: The patient was discussed with her family doctor, Dr. Ed Thompson. I think the immediate concern is for CT scan of the head and consideration for a spinal tap to rule out meningitis with the patient's high fevers. Her therapy will be based on the findings of this. Overall the patient is stable but I think an urgent CT scan of the head is indicated. The CT scan will be performed as soon as possible.

---

64. CHIEF COMPLAINT: Left arm pain, leg pain, and loss of consciousness status post ATV injury.

HISTORY OF PRESENT ILLNESS: This 37-year-old white male was riding a four-wheeler ATV when he lost control. The patient states that he was in a ditch near gravel. There were no trees around. The patient did not have a helmet. The patient lost control. He does not remember the accident. The patient denies drinking alcohol. The patient was trauma packaged at the scene and transported to Medical Center emergency room. The patient was unable to reduce his left arm below his head. The patient did have pulses. There was tingling of the arm present. The patient's left lower leg was not moving at the scene. Since arriving the patient is able to move his leg some.

PHYSICAL EXAM: The patient's HEENT exam reveals pupils to be equal and reactive to light. His extraocular motions are intact. The patient's cranium is grossly intact. There is no blood from his nares. No blood from his ears. The patient has a cervical collar in position. The patient has no clavicular depression. The patient is quite muscular. The patient's lungs are clear to auscultation with some diminished breath sounds at the bases. His heart is regular. The patient's abdomen is soft. Bowel sounds are present. There is no tenderness, guarding or rebound. The patient's pelvis was stable. The patient's extremities reveal good peripheral pulses. The patient is now moving his left leg. The patient's vitals reveal a pulse of 88, respirations 18, blood pressure 132/92; his O2 saturations are 98% on O2 two liters.

The patient had an 18-french Foley catheter placed by myself. The patient had clear urine. The patient's left shoulder was x-rayed and there appears to be posterior dislocation with possible fracture of the humeral head. The quality of x-ray film was poor. Due to the patient's size he was not going to be able to be transported by life support vehicle with the shoulder in the overhead position. The patient was given propofol by anesthesia and the patient's left shoulder reduced. The patient had a good radial pulse, fair sensation of the fingers with a tingly sensation and a strong grip post reduction. The patient did not have a post reduction x-ray obtained. Dr. James was contacted at the University Hospitals and Clinics who accepted the patient in transfer by life support vehicle. The patient was transferred in a serious condition.

---

65. CHIEF COMPLAINT: Anemia.

HISTORY OF COMPLAINT: This 59-year-old female was evaluated by Roger Foster, ARNP last week because of iron deficiency anemia. The patient was evaluated. Her hemoglobin was 6.7. The patient did receive three units of packed red blood cells on an outpatient basis the following day. The patient has been referred back to myself for consideration of repeat colonoscopy and upper GI endoscopy.

ALLERGIES: NO KNOWN ALLERGIES.

MEDICATIONS: Iron 325 mg three times daily
Advair 250 micrograms two times daily
Lexapro 10 mg daily
Singulair 10 mg daily
Pulmicort daily

PAST SURGICAL HISTORY: Right LASIK surgery on the right and left eye 10 years ago. Colonoscopy and gastroscopy by myself just 18 months ago. The patient was found to have gastritis and small hiatal hernia and six sigmoid colon polyps which were hyperplastic.

FAMILY HEALTH: Is one of ten children. Her mother is deceased at age 90. She had breast cancer. Father is deceased at age 82 from heart failure. There is no family history of colon, stomach cancer, or bleeding disorders.

SOCIAL: The patient is not married. She has three children who are alive and healthy. She does live with a significant other. The patient works for ABC Electric Company. The patient does not smoke. She drinks two cans of pop a day but does not drink coffee. The patient drinks alcohol 4–5 times a week.

PAST MEDICAL HISTORY: Positive for asthma, osteoarthritis, and the recently diagnosed anemia.

REVIEW OF SYSTEMS: GI: The patient states she has had fairly regular bowel movements prior to being diagnosed with the anemia. The patient did not notice any blood in her stools and had no hematemesis or hematochezia. She just has been extremely tired ever since having the colonoscopy accomplished. GU: The patient denies dysuria or hematuria. CV: The patient admits to shortness of breath associated with her asthma. Denies cough or productive cough.

PHYSICAL EXAM: Alert, oriented 56-year-old white female. Her height is 5 feet 5 inches. Weight is 205 pounds.

HEENT: Exam is unremarkable.
Lungs are clear to auscultation.
Heart has a regular rate and rhythm.

GI: Her abdomen is protuberant but soft, bowel sounds are active, there is no tenderness, guarding, or rebound.
Extremities are within normal limits.
CBC obtained today revealed a white count of 8.3 with a hemoglobin of 6.7 and MCV of 63, platelets of 770, reticulocyte count was 3.6. Iron studies included a serum iron of 13, total iron binding capacity of 473, and saturations of 3%.

IMPRESSION:

1 Anemia.

2. History of gastritis and hiatal hernia by history.

3. Asthma.

4. Osteoarthritis.

PLAN: I have advised the patient to have a repeat upper and lower GI endoscopy. She also could possibly benefit from a small bowel evaluation. The patient was asking about having a camera evaluation of her GI tract. She is advised that this is not as practical for the upper and lower colon but it is practical for the small bowel. I would recommend a standard colonoscopy. The patient is agreeable to this and will be set up for this.

6

Procedural Coding: Anesthesia, Surgery, Radiology, Pathology and Laboratory, and Medicine

Chapter Outline

VII. Medicine Section

VIII. Conclusion

OBJECTIVES

- Develop an understanding of Anesthesia Guidelines
- Develop an understanding of the Surgery Guidelines
- Identify the general Surgery Section Layout
- Comprehend a global surgical package and pre and post op care
- Define Add-on codes, separate procedure, and 51 modifier exempt codes
- Know what services are included in a surgical code
- Develop an understanding of the Radiology Coding Guidelines
- Understand the difference between supervision and interpretation of radiology services
- Understand the difference of coding laboratory procedures between the physician and the technologists
- Develop an understanding of the Pathology Laboratory Guidelines
- Locate the many subsections in the Pathology Laboratory Section
- Develop an understanding of the Medicine Guidelines
- Identify the many subsections of the Medicine Section
- Locate procedure codes for miscellaneous therapies and diagnostic procedures, physical medicine and rehabilitation, immunizations and injectables

MEDICAL ASSISTANT COMPETENCIES

ABHES

1i. conduct work within scope of education, training, and ability

2d. serve as a liaison between Physician and others

2h. receive, organize, prioritize, and transmit information expediently

3h. file medical records

3w. complete insurance claim forms

3x. use physician fee schedule

5a. determine needs for documentation and reporting

5b. document accurately

CAAHEP

IV.P.2. Report relevant information to others succinctly

V.C.5. Discuss filing procedures

VII.C.7. Describe how guidelines are used in processing insurance claims

VII.C.11. Describe the concept of RBRVS

VIII.C.1. Describe how to use the most current procedural coding system

VIII.C.2. Define upcoding and why it should be avoided

VIII.C.4. Describe how to use the most current HCPCS coding

VIII.P.1. Perform procedural coding

VIII.A.1. Work with physician to achieve maximum reimbursement

IX.P.7. Document accurately in the patient record

KEY TERMS

Multiple Procedures   Physical Status Modifiers

■ INTRODUCTION

The information in Chapter 6 will continue to address accurate coding for anesthesia services, surgeries, radiology, pathology and laboratory and medical procedures that were rendered to the patient.

■ ANESTHESIA SECTION

The Anesthesia section of the CPT provides a list of codes for the "administration of an anesthetic agent," for the performance of surgery. The definition of anesthesia according to *Taber's Cyclopedic Medical Dictionary* is "the partial or complete loss of sensation, with or without loss of consciousness, as a result of disease, injury, or administration of an anesthetic agent, usually by injection or inhalation."

Surgical anesthesia can be classified as:

- Topical—An anesthetic agent applied directly to the surface of the area involved in the surgical procedure.

- Local—An injection of a solution directly into the area involved in the surgical procedure.

- Conscious Sedation—A level of depressed consciousness brought on by an administered analgesic or sedative, which allows the patient to breathe on their own and respond physically and verbally.

- Regional—An anesthetic injected into a nerve or immediately around the nerve supplying sensation to the area involved in the surgical procedure.

- General—An anesthesia that produces complete loss of consciousness.

According to CPT guidelines, the use of any topical, local anesthesia, or conscious sedation is included in the surgical procedure and, therefore, is not separately coded or billed for. However, regional and general anesthesia should be coded and billed for separately from the surgical procedure.

Most of the anesthesia codes are listed by the anatomical site where the surgery will be done. The anatomical sites are arranged from head to toe, with codes for the upper body listed before codes for the lower extremities. Codes for radiological procedures, treatment of burns, obstetrics, and miscellaneous codes are included after codes for the major body sections. Many surgical CPT codes correlate with a single anesthesia code; more than 4000 surgical, medical, and radiology codes are represented by fewer than 300 anesthesia codes.

Anesthesia: Base and Time Units

Anesthesia services are reimbursed differently from other procedure codes. Part of the payment for anesthesia is based on "base units." The base units were created by the American Society of Anesthesiologists (ASA) to determine a fee schedule. They reflect the difficulty of each anesthesia service. The base units range from one to 30. These base units are used by every carrier for reimbursement. The remainder of the payment allowance is based on the anesthesia conversion factor (CF) and time. CMS releases an updated conversion factor schedule annually and it is specific to the geographic location where the anesthesia service is rendered and on the amount of time the patient was "under anesthesia."

The conversion factors can be viewed at any time on the Medicare website, http://www.cms.hhs.gov/center/coverage.asp (under "Browse by Provider Type," choose "Anesthesiologist Center"). Both the base units for each anesthesia code and the annual conversion factors are available.

Time plays an important role in the reimbursement for anesthesia. The medical coder must know the length of time anesthesia was administered in order to properly code and bill for it. First, the actual time is calculated by the minutes the provider is continually in the presence of the patient. Officially, anesthesia time begins when the anesthesia provider begins prepping the patient for the anesthesia and ends when the patient is no longer under the care of the anesthesia provider and can safely be taken into postoperative care. Each minute is considered one unit of service. An hour of anesthesia would be 60 units of service. The units of services are reported on the claim form in Box 24G (Fig. 6–1). (See Chapter 7 for more information on claim form completion.)

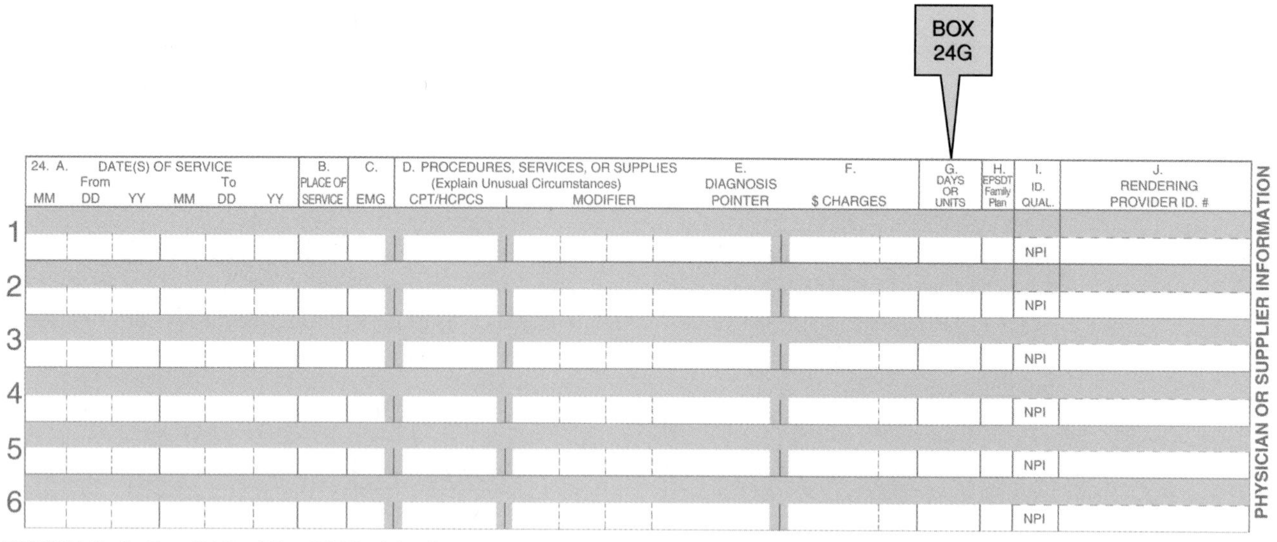

FIGURE 6–1: Box 24G of the CMS claim form.

A third-party carrier will convert the actual amount of time indicated on the claim into time units by 15-minute increments. If the total amount of time when converted is only a fraction of a 15 minute increment the unit is rounded to the nearest increment. The total amount of minutes can also be divided by 15.

For example: 60 actual minutes of anesthesia would be 4 units, $(60 \div 15 = 4)$, but 70 minutes of anesthesia time would be rounded up to the next decimal place and would be considered 4.7 units $(70 \div 15 = 4.6666666666666666666666666666666)$.

The conversion table (Table 6–1) makes calculating easier.

Other carriers simply round to the nearest minute increment. Using the same example, 60 minutes would be considered 4. 70 minutes would be considered 5 units.

TABLE 6–1: Conversion of Minutes to Units

Minutes	Units
1–2	0.1
3	0.2
4–5	0.3
6	0.4
7–8	0.5
9	0.6
10–11	0.7
12	0.8
13–14	0.9
15	1.0
16–17	1.1
18	1.2
19–20	1.3
21	1.4
22–23	1.5
24	1.6
25–26	1.7
27	1.8
28–29	1.9
30	2.0

Reimbursement is calculated by adding the base units and the time units together and then multiplying that amount by the conversion factor. The formula to calculate the allowed amount for anesthesia is:

$$[\text{Base Units} + \text{Time (in units)}] \times CF = \text{Anesthesia Fee Amount}$$

Physical Status Modifiers and Qualifying Circumstances

Anesthesia codes are five-digits long and begin with a zero. Similar to standard CPT modifiers, CPT has developed modifiers that can be used with an anesthesia code. They are referred to as **physical status modifiers** (Table 6–2). These modifiers represent levels of the anesthesia complexity and are located in the Anesthesia Guidelines preceding the actual CPT codes. Some carriers do recognize these modifiers and reimbursement will be affected by them.

> ⚠ **KEY TERM**
>
> PHYSICAL STATUS MODIFIERS—Anesthesia modifiers that represent the physical condition of the patient.

The physical status modifiers are in accordance with the American Society of Anesthesiologist's (ASA) status categories. They represent the physical condition of the patient. For example, the P1 modifier represents a normal healthy patient and when added to an anesthesia code would indicate that the services rendered were typical. The P4 modifier indicates that the patient undergoing anesthesia has a life-threatening systemic disease. The administration of anesthesia is complicated by the patient's condition and may have required something like extra efforts, precautions, or more time than the normal healthy patient would have required.

> ⚠ **KEY TERM**
>
> QUALIFYING CIRCUMSTANCES—Risk factors or unusual circumstances related to anesthesia that can be further described with additional five-digit codes.

When anesthesia services are rendered to a patient with risk factors, under unusual circumstances, or in unusual conditions, CPT also has supplied the medical coder with five-digit codes that help to further describe the situation (Table 6–3). These codes are located in the Anesthesia Guidelines and in the Medicine section of the CPT. They only are to be used with an anesthesia CPT code and never by themselves. Not all third-party carriers will recognize the use of these qualifying circumstance codes and will not allow additional reimbursement. The medical coder should check with the carrier to see if these codes will be acknowledged.

■ SURGERY SECTION

The Surgery section is the largest section within CPT. It is divided into subsections that represent organ systems or specialties (Table 6–4). Each of these subsections is further divided into categories by anatomical site, generally sequenced from head to toe. Each category has subcategories that group

TABLE 6-2: Physical Status Modifiers

P1—A normal healthy patient.
P2—A patient with mild systemic disease.
P3—A patient with severe systemic disease.
P4—A patient with severe systemic disease that is a constant threat to life.
P5—A moribund patient who is not expected to survive without the operation.
P6—A declared brain-dead patient whose organs are being removed for donor purposes.

TABLE 6–3: Qualifying Circumstances Codes

99100—Anesthesia administered to a patient of extreme age, under one year or over 70 years of age.
99116—Anesthesia administered to a patient of extreme body hypothermia.
99135—Anesthesia administered to a patient with controlled hypotension.
99140—Anesthesia administered to a patient in a crisis situation where the risk of delay could be a threat to the patient's body part or to their life.

the type of procedures performed such as incision, excision, repair, revision/reconstruction, or laparoscopy.

The Surgery section of CPT contains codes for diagnostic and therapeutic surgical procedures. Diagnostic surgical procedures are procedures performed to determine or establish a patient's diagnosis. An example is code 45378, assigned for a flexible colonoscopy. A therapeutic surgery is considered a treatment for a condition or disease. An example is code 49505, assigned for inguinal hernia repair.

CPT instructions and guidelines are found within the categories and subcategories of the Surgery section. The medical coder must read these guidelines to fully understand how to properly assign codes. Taking the time to read and understand the CPT guidelines and notes will have the greatest impact on proper coding and reimbursement.

The medical coder will often code a surgical service from dictated operative report supplied by the physician. It is extremely important that the coder read through the report to find all of the elements included in a procedure to determine the correct CPT code to use. Often, the physician for whom the coder is working will provide similar services to his or her patients making it easy to determine the correct CPT code(s) to use. Whenever necessary, the coder should review any unfamiliar procedures or surgeries with the physician. The physician should provide precise information to ensure the correct CPT code(s) is/are used to represent the service(s) rendered.

Global Surgical Billing

Surgical procedure codes include not only the surgical procedure but also the administration of any necessary local anesthetic, materials such as drugs or sterile trays, one related E/M preoperative encounter for a history and physical, and any standard postoperative follow-up care. The physician receives a single fee for this "global" charge (also known as a "surgical package"). Any evaluation and management services or other medical services that are completely unrelated to the surgery performed may be coded and billed for separately and are not considered part of the global surgical charge.

TABLE 6–4: Surgery Subsections

Subsection	Code Range
General	10021–10022
Integumentary System	10000–19499
Musculoskeletal	20000–29999
Respiratory	30000–32999
Cardiovascular	33010–37799
Hemic and Lymphatic	38100–38794
Mediastinum and Diaphragm	39000–39599
Digestive	40490–49999
Urinary	50010–53899
Male/Female Genital	54000–59899
Endocrine	60000–60699
Nervous	61000–64999
Eye and Ocular	65091–68899
Auditory	69000–69979
Operating Microscope	69990

GLOBAL SURGERY BILLING—The single fee that includes all parts of a surgery, including anesthesia, instruments, and preoperative/postoperative care.

Follow-up care for therapeutic procedures includes the appropriate pre- and postoperative services. However, follow-up care for any diagnostic surgical procedure includes only the care for that procedure, with any conditions or complications requiring additional services coded and billed for separately. The physician must document the need for additional care during a postoperative period by using appropriate diagnostic coding to show the necessity. The medical coder may need to add a modifier to the procedure code explaining the reason for the additional service.

The most common postoperative/follow-up days for procedures are 0, 10, and 90 days. Medicare has a list of the designated follow-up days per procedure (see www.cms.hhs.gov), and the majority of other carriers have adopted the same system. A minor surgery, such as the suturing of a laceration, would have fewer follow-up days than a more major surgery, like a colon resection, which would include the full 90 days of postoperative care.

Surgical Materials and Medical Supplies

In general, any medical supplies and surgical materials that are used in conjunction with a surgical procedure are not charged for separately. For example, if a lesion was removed in the office, the procedure code and charge would include a sterile tray.

Multiple Procedures

Many procedure descriptions are written so the main procedure can be identified without having to list a separate code for each element performed in the same operative or investigative setting. Multiple procedure codes should be used only when two or more procedures performed are truly distinct procedures and not sharing inclusive elements, such as separate incisions for completely different services. An example of that would be a colonoscopy performed and at the same session, a mole was removed. Those are completely different procedures and would need to be coded as such. When **multiple procedures** are performed on the same day, separate codes are assigned to each procedure.

MULTIPLE PROCEDURES—Procedures that are separate and distinct from one another and are billed separately.

When a procedure that is usually part of a larger procedure has been performed separately, it should be reported as a separate procedure. For example, if a salpingo-oophorectomy is performed at the same time as a hysterectomy, one code would be assigned to include both procedures, for example, 58150, total abdominal hysterectomy with or without the removal tube(s) and/or ovary(s); or 58262, a vaginal hysterectomy with or without the removal tube(s) and/or ovary(s). If the procedure was done laparoscopically, code 58548. When a salpingo-oophorectomy is performed alone without a hysterectomy, it should be coded as is, 58720, salpingo-oophorectomy; or if done laparoscopically, 58661.

Add-on Codes

Add-on codes are designated in CPT by a plus sign (+) to the left of the five-digit code. The codes represent additional work performed with the primary procedure, but not separate from the primary procedure. Because of this, add-on codes are exempt from the guidelines for multiple procedures and must *never* be reported as a stand-alone code.

For example, add-on code 49568 (Mesh or other prosthetic implantation used for the repair of an incisional or ventral hernia) and procedure codes 49560, 49561, 49565, or 49566. The mesh prosthetic 49568, should be reported along with a code for the primary procedure, which is the hernia repair. CPT makes note of this after the code description, and separate charge and/or reimbursement should be given to the add-on code.

The entire list of add-on codes is located in Appendix D of the CPT.

Surgery Modifiers

Similar to E/M modifiers, the use of modifiers in surgery coding allows the medical coder to explain a specific circumstance involved in a procedure. Adding a modifier to a procedure code can affect reimbursement by justifying an additional service or an additional provider involved in a procedure.

For example, when a team of specialized surgeons or medical personnel is required to perform a complex surgery, CPT states that modifier 66 (Surgical Team) or modifier 62 (two surgeons working together on two distinct parts of the same surgery) be appended or added to the procedure code. Each team member bills separately for a share of the work and uses use modifier 66 in addition to the proper procedure codes. The use of this modifier explains to the insurance provider why more than one medical provider is billing for the same procedure on the same patient on the same day.

In some cases, the medical coder may need to use more than one modifier to describe a special circumstance surrounding a service. In that case, there is a primary modifier that should be used first; this is followed by any additional modifier(s), as needed. For example, if an assistant surgeon performs a bilateral total hip replacement surgery, he or she should append or just "add" modifier 80 (assistant surgeon) and modifier 50 (bilateral surgery) to the CPT code 27130 (for the hip replacement procedure).

A complete list of modifiers used within CPT can be found in Appendix A of CPT. A condensed list can be found on the inside front cover of CPT. Refer to Table 6–5 for a list of modifiers that generally pertain to the Surgery, Radiology, Pathology and Laboratory and/or Medicine sections of CPT.

TABLE 6–5: Other CPT Modifiers

Modifier	Definition
22 Increased Proc<None>edural Services	Service is greater than that usually required for the procedure.
23 Unusual Anesthesia	Procedure that usually requires no anesthesia must be done under general anesthesia.
26 Professional Component	When physician's part is reported separately from technical part of the service.
47 Anesthesia by Surgeon	Regional or general anesthesia provided by the surgeon (does not include local anesthesia).
50 Bilateral Procedure	Bilateral procedures performed at the same operative session.
51 Multiple Procedures	Multiple procedures, other than E/M services, performed at the same session by the same provider. Report the primary procedure as listed and add the 51 to the additional code.
52 Reduced Services	Procedure partially reduced or eliminated at the physician's discretion.
53 Discontinued Procedure	Physician elects to terminate procedure that was started but discontinued. Not used for elective cancellation or a procedure prior to patient's anesthesia induction and/or surgical preparation in the operating suite.
54 Surgical Care Only	One physician performs surgical procedure and another the pre- and/or postoperative care. Add 54 to the surgical code.
58 Staged or Related Procedure or Service by the Same Physician During the Postoperative Period	Used to indicate the service was (a) planned prospectively/stages, (b) more extensive than original procedure or (c) for therapy following a surgical procedure. Not used to report treatment of problem requiring return to operating room.
59 Distinct Procedural Service	Service is distinct or independent from other service performed on same day. Identifies procedures that normally may not be billed together.

Current Procedural Terminology © American Medical Association, All Rights Reserved.

TABLE 6–5:   Other CPT Modifiers—cont'd

Modifier	Definition
62 Two Surgeons	When two surgeons work together as co-surgeons performing distinct parts of a single reportable procedure, each adds 62 to the surgery code.
63 Procedure Performed on Infants less than 4 kg	Procedures performed on neonates or infants who weigh up to 4 kg may be more difficult and complicated than the same procedure performed on an older or larger patient.
66 Surgical Team	Highly complex procedures may require the simultaneous services of several physicians. Each physician adds 66 to surgery code.
76 Repeat Procedure by Same Physician	Procedure or service repeated subsequent to the original.
77 Repeat Procedure by Another Physician	Basic procedure performed by another physician had to be repeated.
78 Return to the Operating Room for a Related Procedure During the Postoperative Period	Another procedure was performed during the postoperative period of the original procedure that is related to the first one performed.
79 Unrelated Procedure or Service by the Physician During the Postoperative Period	Performance of a procedure during postoperative period was unrelated to the original procedure performed.
80 Assistant Surgeon	Use to identify surgical assistant services.
81 Minimum Assistant Surgeon	Use to identify minimal surgical assistant services.
82 Assistant Surgeon (when qualified resident surgeon is not available)	Use with the assistant's surgical code only when the assistant surgeon is not a qualified resident surgeon.
90 Reference (Outside) Laboratory	Laboratory procedures performed by a party other than the treating or reporting physician.
91 Repeat Clinical Diagnostic Laboratory Test	Use when the same laboratory procedure must be repeated on the same day to obtain subsequent test results. Not used if test must be repeated to confirm a result.
92 Alternative Laboratory Platform Testing	Laboratory procedure performed using a single use kit or disposable analytical chamber.
99 Multiple Modifiers	When more than one modifier must be used to completely explain a service. Add to the basic procedure with other applicable modifiers to describe the description of service.

SURGERY SUBSECTIONS

Coding a surgical or therapeutic procedure can be challenging. The medical coder must be able to understand the procedure that was performed and then identify the appropriate code to accurately describe that procedure. This next section will cover some of the specific details for various subsections within the surgery section.

Integumentary System

The Integumentary System section provides codes for services performed on any part of the body involving the skin and includes services performed on nails, glands, and hair (Table 6–6).

TABLE 6–6: Key Terminology for the Integumentary System

Term	Definition
Incision and Drainage	To cut into and remove fluids or discharge.
Excision	To take out or cut away.
Debridement	The removal of damaged tissue or foreign material from a wound.
Aspiration	To suck out fluid or discharge, no incision made.
Paring	To cut off or trim away lesions, such as corns or calluses.
Biopsy	Tissue sample for examination.
Destruction	The removal of benign, premalignant, or malignant tissue by means of laser or chemical treatment, cryosurgery, or electrosurgery.
Mohs micrographic surgery	A technique of microscopically controlled excision of skin cancers.
Needle Biopsy	Removal of tissue by means of a fine needle. May include ultrasound guidelines.
Acne vulgaris	Common acne
Seborrhea dermatitis	Acute/subacute inflammatory skin disease of unknown cause, beginning on the scalp.
Actinic keratosis	Premalignant lesions caused by excess to ultraviolet light.

It is critical that the medical coder understand the CPT definitions of medical terms used in the Integumentary System as well as the structure of skin to determine the appropriate code. The layers of skin (Fig. 6–2) or its depth can affect the code choice. A deeper incision would most likely require layered closure, which is more work than a single-layered closure and reimbursed accordingly.

Layers include the following:

■ Epidermis—the outer layer

■ Dermis—the inner layer containing nerve endings, hair follicles, sebaceous and sweat glands

■ Subcutaneous—the tissue just beneath the skin that connects the skin to muscle

■ Fascia—the membrane that covers and supports muscle

The medical coder may need to reference the medical record for procedure details such as site, length, depth, and the type of procedure performed.

Biopsy

Codes 11100–11101 are the codes for biopsies of the skin. These codes include the sample taken and a simple closure of the incision. Unless noted, these biopsy codes are not used with a surgical procedure in which a biopsy was done. The biopsy is included in the surgical code. Code 11100 is used for the first biopsy taken and 11001 is an add-on code used to account for each additional lesion that is biopsied.

Lesion Removal

Removing a lesion can be done in different ways, shaving, excising, cautery, laser, or chemical treatments. The Integumentary section is divided into groups of codes for the different types of removals. Codes 11200–11201 are used for removing skin tags, 11300–11313 are codes designated for the shaving of epidermal or dermal lesions, and codes 11400 through 11646 represent an excision of benign or malignant lesions, and each procedure code includes local anesthesia and the simple closure of the incision made to remove the lesion. If the incision is deep and requires a layered closure, repair codes,

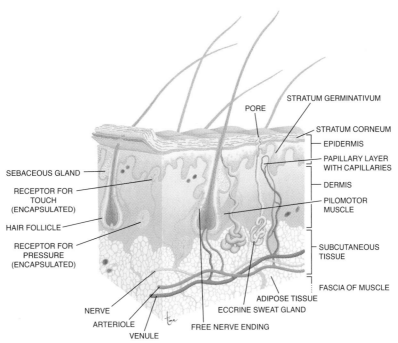

FIGURE 6-2: Layers of skin. *(From Taber's Cyclopedic Medical Dictionary, 21st ed. Philadelphia: FA Davis, 2009.)*

intermediate and complex, 12031–13160 may be used in addition to the removal code. These excision and repair codes must be chosen by length of incision and location of the lesion.

To determine the length of an incision/excision the diameter is measured. The physician should measure before the excision is made and determine the lesion length plus the narrowest margin needed to remove the lesion sufficiently.

Repairs

There is a range of codes in the Integumentary section designated for the repair or closure of a wound. This range of codes, 12001 through 13160, represents simple, intermediate, and complex closures and each indicates the length and the area of the body needing closure. The repair codes are used to designate the suturing of a wound as a result of an injury or made during the removal of a lesion. The intermediate or complex repairs codes are used to code for closures performed in layers. A simple repair includes repair of the epidermis, dermis, or subcutaneous tissue. Intermediate and complex repairs include the deeper layers of subcutaneous tissue, scar revisions, debridement, or traumatic lacerations that require more than just layered closure.

If there are multiple repairs made, the medical coder will need to add the lengths together that are done in the same area and choose a code that represents the total length repaired. Separate codes should be used for additional sites. For example, repairs made to the scalp, neck, axillae, external genitalia, trunk and/or extremities are grouped together into one set of codes and wounds of the face, ears, eyelids, nose, lips, and/or mucous membranes are grouped together in another set. Repairs made to the face would most likely be done as inconspicuously as possible to prevent unnecessary scarring, whereas a repair made to extremity or trunk would not need to be as intricate.

All repair codes include local anesthesia, sutures, staples, adhesive closures and incidental supplies. Metric lengths further classify both the removal of lesions codes and the repair codes. The medical coder may need to convert U.S. measurements dictated in a operative report into metric measurements (Table 6–7).

The medical coder should:

■ Remember that if the entire lesion is removed for the purpose of a biopsy, it should be coded as an excision and not just a sample for biopsy.

■ Distinguish all lesions excised as benign, premalignant, or malignant and code accordingly.

TABLE 6-7: Common Metric Conversions

1 millimeter (mm)	1/1000 or 0.001 meter
1 centimeter (cm)	1/100 or 0.01 meter
1 decimeter (dm)	1/10 or 0.1 meter
1 kilometer (km)	1000 meters
10 millimeters (mm)	1 centimeter (cm)
¼″ (inch)	0.635 centimeter (cm)
⅓″ (inch)	0.83 centimeter (cm)
½″ (inch)	1.27 centimeter (cm)
1″ (inch)	2.54 centimeter (cm)
1¼″ (inch)	3.175 centimeter (cm)
1⅓″ (inch)	3.386 centimeter
1½″ (inch)	3.81 centimeter (cm)
2″ (inch)	5.08 centimeter (cm)
3″ (inch)	7.62 centimeter (cm)
4″ (inch)	10.16 centimeter (cm)
5″ (inch)	12.7 centimeter (cm)

- Understand that the proper code for excision of lesions is determined by the anatomical area and the length of the excision.
- Be aware that an excision considered through the dermis includes local anesthesia and simple closure of the wound.
- Recognize that wound repairs are classified by simple, intermediate, and complex repair and by the anatomical area and the length of the repair.

Burns

The procedure codes found in the Integumentary System refer to the local treatment of the burn, which may provide the patient with some relief externally. The choice of codes is determined by the total percentage of body surface burned (Fig. 6–3). Procedure code 16000 is the only code designated for the treatment of a first-degree burn. Codes 16020–16030 include care for second- and third-degree burns that require dressings and debridement. These codes represent the total body area to be treated. The medical coder should choose a code that will represent the total combined body surface treated

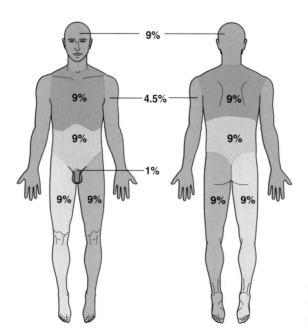

FIGURE 6–3: Rule of nines. (*From Taber's Cyclopedic Medical Dictionary, 21st ed. Philadelphia: FA Davis, 2009.*)

each visit rather than use separate codes for different body areas. Codes 16035 and 16036 represent treatment of eschar, which is the dead skin as a result of a chemical burn.

Skin Grafts and Tissue Grafts

The codes for skin grafts and tissue transfers are listed by the type of graft, the area of the body involved, and the size of the transfer or graft (Table 6–8). Grafts can come from the patient, a donor, or a nonhuman, such as a pig.

Tissue transfers are procedures in which a section of skin is moved from one area to the nearby defect. One edge of the skin flap is left connected to the donor site to keep the flap alive and to keep the area viable. The flap is then sutured in place. Tissue transfers may be referred to as V-plasty, W-plasty, Z-plasty, advancement, rotation, pedicle, sliding, or melolabial flaps, or by a Kutler procedure. These procedures are coded according to the size of the recipient site. Simple repair of the donor site is included in the tissue transfer.

Musculoskeletal System

The Musculoskeletal subsection is initially arranged by anatomical site, then further divided based on the types of service, such as incision, excision, introduction/removal, repairs, and fractures/dislocations. To ensure proper code selection, the medical coder must be mindful of the location of the provided service.

Included in this subsection are codes for the replantation of an amputated extremity, bone, cartilage, fascia and tendon grafts; incisions and excisions into bone, joints, muscle, and soft tissue for drainage; grafts or removal of abscesses, bones, tumors, or prosthetic devices, and the repair, revision, or reconstruction of bones, joints, or muscles.

Fracture treatment and dislocation codes are listed under each anatomical site and then further described as closed, open, or with/without manipulation. The medical coder must refer to the patient's medical record or operative report to determine the type of fracture being repaired (Fig. 6–4). Several types include the following:

- Closed—the site is not surgically opened for repair
- Open—the site is surgically opened
- With or without manipulation—when the fracture site is displaced and must be manually realigned or was not displaced and is already in proper position

Codes for fracture care include the examination and treatment and normal follow-up care as well as the application and removal of the first cast or a traction mechanism. Any replacement casts or a traction mechanism may be coded and billed for separately. The removal of any cast or traction mechanism is included in the application code unless removed by a different provider. For example, a patient fractures a bone while on vacation. A cast is applied in the emergency room there. A physician may bill for the removal of the cast after the patient arrives back home.

Cardiovascular System

Cardiovascular service codes will be found in three sections of CPT, the Surgery section, the Medicine section and the Radiological section. This section will address procedure codes from the surgical subsection only.

The Cardiovascular subsection is also arranged by anatomical site. Procedure codes for surgical services related to the heart, pericardium, and arteries (Figs. 6–5 and 6–6) and veins (Fig. 6–7) are

---

TABLE 6-8: Types of Skin Grafts

Type of Graft	Definition
Split	Part of the skin thickness
Autograft	Taken from one's own body
Xenograft	Taken from a pig
Full thickness	Equal amounts of epidermis and dermis layers
Allograft	Donor different from recipient
Pinch graft	Small autograft

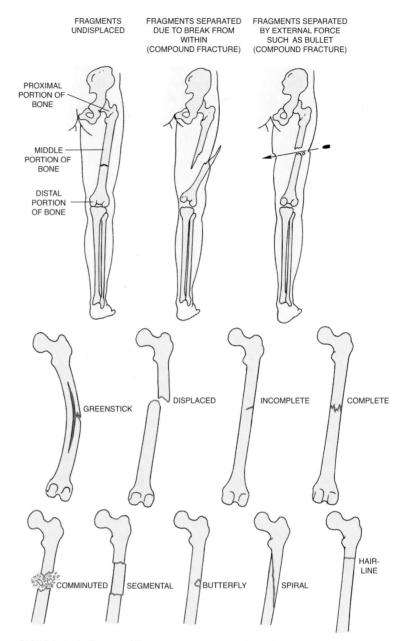

FRAGMENTS
UNDISPLACED

FRAGMENTS SEPARATED
DUE TO BREAK FROM
WITHIN
(COMPOUND FRACTURE)

FRAGMENTS SEPARATED
BY EXTERNAL FORCE
SUCH AS BULLET
(COMPOUND FRACTURE)

PROXIMAL
PORTION OF
BONE

MIDDLE
PORTION OF
BONE

DISTAL
PORTION
OF BONE

GREENSTICK   DISPLACED   INCOMPLETE   COMPLETE

COMMINUTED   SEGMENTAL   BUTTERFLY   SPIRAL   HAIR-LINE

FIGURE 6-4: Types of fractures. *(From Taber's Cyclopedic Medical Dictionary, 21st ed. Philadelphia: FA Davis, 2009.)*

found in this subsection as are codes for pacemaker implants and defibrillator procedures. Codes for heart and coronary vessel repair, pacemakers, and bypass procedures are located in this section. When coding a surgical procedure involving blood vessels, the medical coder must recognize the code difference between venous and arterial for proper code selection. Many codes have been designated for procedures involving just arteries or just veins.

Procedure codes for therapeutic services and diagnostic studies involving the heart and blood vessels, such as cardiographies, echocardiographies, diagnostic catheterizations, and vascular studies, are located in the Medicine section, under the Cardiovascular subsection. This will be addressed in the medicine section.

Digestive System

The Digestive System subsection is arranged in anatomical order of the digestive system, from lips and mouth to rectum and anus (Fig. 6–8). Accessory organs to the Digestive System, liver, pancreas, and gallbladder, are also included in this subsection.

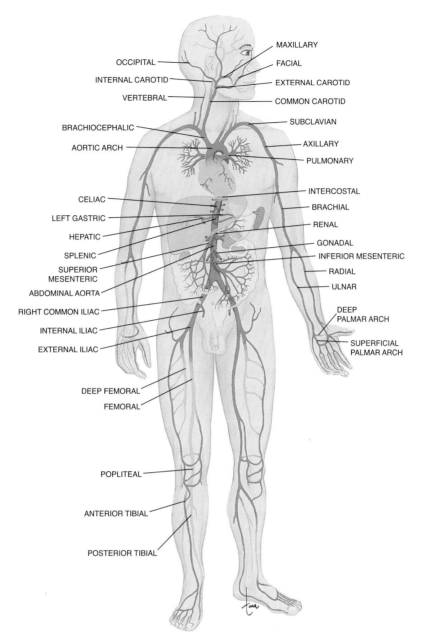

FIGURE 6–5: Arteries. (*From Taber's Cyclopedic Medical Dictionary, 21st ed. Philadelphia: FA Davis, 2009.*)

Within this section, it is important for the medical coder to recognize the procedures performed endoscopically versus incisionally. If a surgeon performs an exploratory laparotomy and then proceeds to excise or repair an abnormality found, a separate charge cannot be charged for the initial exploratory laparotomy. The medical coder may only code and bill for the surgical code to repair or remove the abnormality and not for the diagnostic component of the procedure. It should also be noted that any surgery performed incidental to the main abdominal surgery such as an appendectomy performed on a nondiseased appendix cannot be billed for separately. An incidental surgery such as the removal of a nondiseased appendix is not considered medically necessary and, therefore, should not be billed for.

The Digestive System subsection contains numerous procedures in which the patient would be consciously or moderately sedated. These codes are identified by the ⊙ symbol. This indicates that the sedation is a part of the service and is not billed for separately.

This subsection also contains the procedure codes representing hernia repairs. These repairs are listed individually by site, age of the patient, initial, or recurrent hernias, and whether or not the

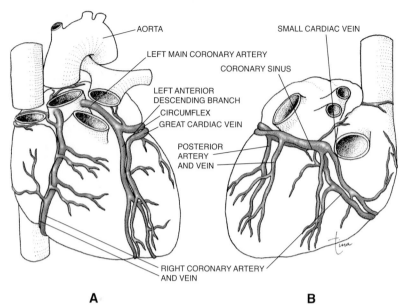

FIGURE 6–6: Coronary arteries. (*From Taber's Cyclopedic Medical Dictionary, 21st ed. Philadelphia: FA Davis, 2009.*)

hernia can be reduced, is incarcerated, or strangulated. All hernia repairs include a mesh implant used to strengthen the area except for the incisional or ventral hernia, in which the mesh implant is coded and billed separately. CPT makes note of this and identifies the proper procedure code for the implant.

Female Genital System

In addition to surgical procedures involving the vagina, uterus oviducts, and ovaries, the Female Genital subsection contains procedures involving maternity care and delivery (Fig. 6–9). Codes in this section include normal antepartum care, postpartum care, and delivery (either vaginal or cesarean section). The combination of services in these three areas are referred to as the "obstetrical package."

Any medical complications for pregnancy and delivery should be billed for separately. The medical coder may also bill separately for antepartum care, postpartum care, and/or delivery services if a patient's pregnancy is terminated or if the delivery is done by another physician in another practice.

Nervous System

This Nervous System subsection contains diagnostic and therapeutic procedures performed on the central, peripheral, and autonomic nervous systems. The codes in this subsection are divided by body system, specifically the brain, the spinal column, and type of nerve (Fig. 6–10).

Procedures involving the skull often require more than one surgeon to complete. These procedures are grouped together within the subsection as the following:

- Approach procedures—Those procedures necessary to gain access within the skull.

- Definitive procedures—The actual repair, biopsy, resection, or excision of lesion within the skull.

- Repair/reconstruction procedure—Procedure performed to repair or to close the entry made into the skull.

These procedures are generally performed by different surgeons and reported and reimbursed separately.

Diagnostic codes for the assessment of the nervous system such as sleep testing, electroencephalography (EEG), conduction and range-of-motion testing are included in the Medicine section, 95805–96125.

Eye and Ear Systems

Like the Cardiovascular and Neurological systems, the Eye subsection contains codes that are just for the surgical treatment of the eye. The medical coder must refer to the Medicine section for diagnostic

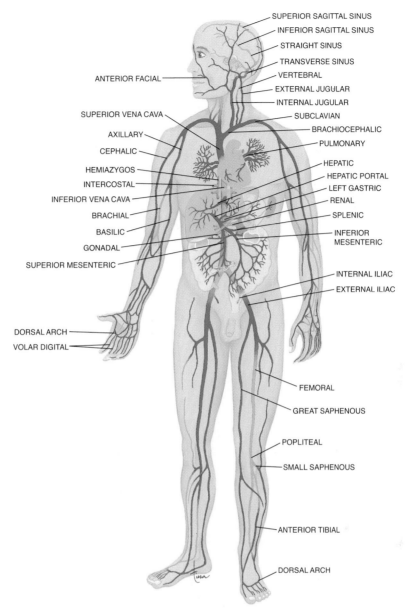

SUPERIOR SAGITTAL SINUS
INFERIOR SAGITTAL SINUS
STRAIGHT SINUS
TRANSVERSE SINUS
VERTEBRAL
EXTERNAL JUGULAR
INTERNAL JUGULAR
ANTERIOR FACIAL
SUBCLAVIAN
SUPERIOR VENA CAVA
BRACHIOCEPHALIC
AXILLARY
PULMONARY
CEPHALIC
HEPATIC
HEMIAZYGOS
HEPATIC PORTAL
INTERCOSTAL
LEFT GASTRIC
INFERIOR VENA CAVA
RENAL
BRACHIAL
SPLENIC
BASILIC
INFERIOR MESENTERIC
GONADAL
SUPERIOR MESENTERIC
INTERNAL ILIAC
EXTERNAL ILIAC
DORSAL ARCH
VOLAR DIGITAL
FEMORAL
GREAT SAPHENOUS
POPLITEAL
SMALL SAPHENOUS
ANTERIOR TIBIAL
DORSAL ARCH

FIGURE 6–7: Systemic veins. (*From Taber's Cyclopedic Medical Dictionary, 21st ed. Philadelphia: FA Davis, 2009.*)

and ophthalmological treatment procedures, such as evaluations or the prescription of corrective lenses, 92002–92499. Similarly, the Ear subsection contains the procedure codes for surgical treatment of the ear, and the procedure codes for any diagnostic services, such as audiometry, are contained in the Medicine section, 92502–92700.

RADIOLOGY SECTION

The Radiology section is arranged in four subsections.

- Diagnostic (includes computerized tomography [CT scans], magnetic resonance imaging [MRI], radiology interventional procedures)
- Ultrasound
- Oncology radiation
- Nuclear medicine (includes diagnostic and therapeutic services)

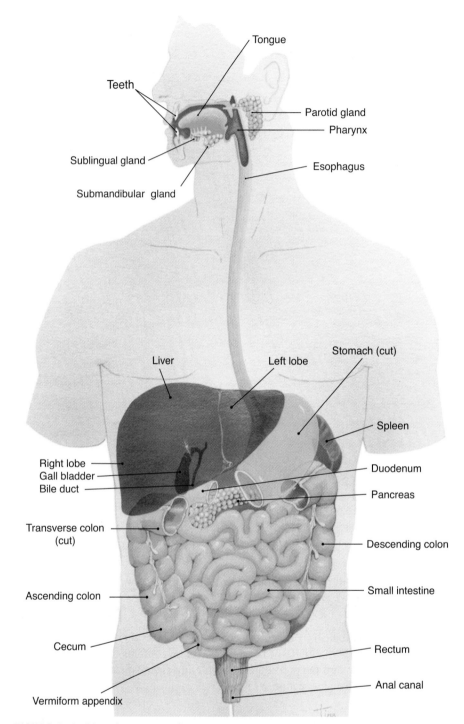

FIGURE 6–8: Digestive system. (*From Tamparo, CD, Lewis, MA . [2005]. Diseases of the Human Body, 4 ed. Philadelphia: FA Davis, page 203. Modified from Scanlon VC, Sanders T. [2003]. Essentials of Anatomy and Physiology, ed. 4. Philadelphia: FA Davis, page 357, with permission.*)

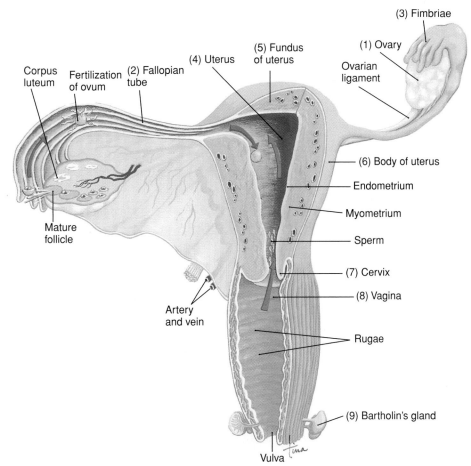

FIGURE 6-9: Female Genital System. (*From Tamparo, CD, Lewis, MA. [2005]. Diseases of the Human Body, 4 ed. Philadelphia: FA Davis, page 180. Modified from Scanlon VC, Sanders T. [2003]. Essentials of Anatomy and Physiology, ed. 4. Philadelphia: FA Davis, page 442, with permission.*)

As in the previous sections of CPT, codes are arranged anatomically from head to toe and by body system.

Radiology procedures can be placed into three components, depending on what service was rendered to the patient:

■ Technical component—The use of the machine, the film and processing, and a technologist to perform the test. Modifier TC is appended to the five-digit CPT procedure code to signify just that portion of the service was performed.

■ Professional component—The reading and the interpretation of the film/test by a physician. Modifier 26 is appended to the five-digit CPT code to signify just that portion of the service was performed.

■ Total procedure—This includes both technical and professional components performed by the same physician or facility. A five-digit CPT code is used without any modifier to signify the entire procedure was performed.

In all three situations, the medical coder must select the proper five-digit procedure code based on the anatomical site, type of procedure, and number of views performed on the patient. The applicable modifier can then be appended, if necessary.

Example: A chest x-ray, two views, frontal/PA or AP and lateral is coded 71020 if the film was taken, read, and interpreted in the same facility. 71020-TC if the same chest x-ray is taken in one facility and will be sent somewhere else to be read and interpreted. 71020-26 if the same x-ray was taken somewhere else and is now being billed for just the reading and interpretation of the films.

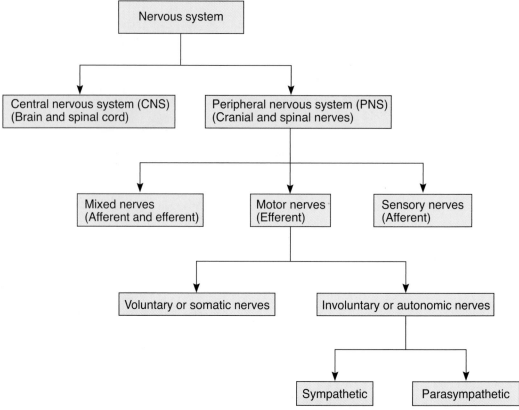

FIGURE 6-10: Subdivisions of the nervous system. *(From Tamparo, CD, Lewis, MA. [2005]. Diseases of the Human Body, 4 ed. Philadelphia: FA Davis, page 302. From Gylys BA, Wedding ME. [1999]. Medical Terminology: A Systems Approach, ed 4. Philadelphia: FA Davis page 296, with permission.)*

◼ PATHOLOGY/LABORATORY SECTION

The Pathology/Laboratory section of the CPT is divided into 14 subsections based on the type of tests performed such as chemistry, hematology, urinalysis, or surgical pathology. The medical coder must recognize the specimen and the method of examination. There are procedure codes to represent both manual and automated procedures.

Laboratory tests should be billed separately unless part of a panel test. In a panel test, more than one test is performed on a single blood specimen. For example, the code 80061 represents a lipid panel. The lipid panel must contain testing for cholesterol, triglycerides, and lipoprotein (high-density cholesterol [HDL]). These tests would not be billed for separately when performed as a panel test on one specimen.

Pathology and laboratory services are provided by a technologist under the supervision of a physician or by a pathologist. The majority of the codes represent the technical component of the test. If a pathologist renders an opinion of the results of a test, the test should be coded with the 26 modifier to indicate that a professional component also was provided.

Special Services, Procedures, and Reports
Codes 99000–99002 (handling and/or conveyance of specimen for transfer) are located in the Medicine section of the CPT.

Pathology and laboratory services include only the performed test and do not include specimen collection by means of venous or arterial puncture. There are codes in the Cardiovascular subsection under Vascular Injection Procedures designated for that type of specimen collection. The Medicine section also contains codes for the handling or transfer of specimens from a physician's office to a laboratory. For these codes, the medical coder must consult the third-party carrier for specific billing and payment procedures. Separate payment for these services is not always reimbursed.

Surgical Pathology

Surgical pathology codes represent the gross and microscopic examination of tissue specimens for pathological evaluation. The codes in the Surgical Pathology subsection are divided into six levels, based on the type of specimen and the level of work necessary for the pathologist to accurately examine the specimen.

88300 Level I: Specimens that do not normally need to be examined under a microscope.

88302 Level II: Specimens that are usually normal and have been removed for a reason other than disease (e.g., vas deferens for sterilization).

88304 Level III: Specimens that have a low probability of malignancy. These specimens are usually removed because of inflammation or disease.

88305 Level IV: Specimens that have a stronger possibility of being malignant.

88307 Level V: Specimens that have a strong possibility of being malignant and require more examination than the level IV.

88309 Level VI: Neoplastic specimens that require an extensive examination.

Levels 88302 through 88309 are specifically defined by the assigned specimens listed for each code by CPT. For example, an incidental appendix is listed under the 88302, level II surgical pathology and a brain biopsy is listed under 88307, level V surgical pathology.

■ MEDICINE SECTION

The Medicine section contains many subsections ranging from assessments to treatments. Besides the codes that have already been discussed in previous sections and subsections, the medical coder also will find codes for immunizations and vaccines, physical medicine, dialysis, psychiatry, and allergy testing.

As with any CPT code, the medical coder *must* read and understand the code description to select the proper code(s) for the rendered service(s). The code descriptions can direct the coder to use additional codes or indicate more appropriate codes for a given service. In addition, the instructional notes for each subsection provide the coder with valuable information on proper code assignment including what codes can be used together to provide the full reimbursement for the rendered services.

All of these CPT instructions are invaluable tools in accurate procedural coding. For example, the code description and instructions for Immunization Administration for Vaccines/Toxoids reads as follows: "Codes 90465-90474 must be reported in addition to the vaccine and toxoid code(s) 90476-90749. Report codes 90465-90486 only when the physician provides face-to-face counseling of the patient and family during the administration of a vaccine. For immunization administration of any vaccine that is not accompanied by face-to-face physician counseling to the patient/family, report codes 90471-90474."

These instructions tell the medical coder that there are separate codes for the administration of vaccines and toxoids. It names the codes that should be used for administration with face-to-face counseling provided by a physician and administration provided without a physician. Reimbursement would be significantly affected without the use of one of these administration codes because the medical coder would be billing for the vaccine or toxoid itself and not for the professional service of administering it.

■ CONCLUSION

Accurate procedural coding requires attention to detail and a strong background in anatomy, physiology, and medical terminology. A CPT code should never be assigned as "close enough." The CPT code used must represent the exact procedure performed. A code that is only "close enough" will either undercode or overcode the actual service provided. The reimbursement for any service is based on the procedure code used. If a code is close but does not include every detail performed, reimbursement will be inadequate. On the contrary, if the procedure code is close enough but includes a service(s) that was not performed, the provider will be reimbursed more than they should be. The use of the wrong procedure code can be considered fraud and abuse, which may result in penalties for the provider.

Great medical coders must be willing to keep up with the annual changes and updates applied to both diagnostic and procedural codes. A great coder is an invaluable ingredient to the success of any medical billing service.

RESOURCE LIST

Current Procedural Terminology 2009 (Standard Edition or Professional Edition), American Medical Association.

http://www.ama-assn.org

Principles of CPT Coding, American Medical Association.

http://www.ama-assn.org

Chapter Review Exercise

General CPT Coding

Assign codes to the following. Underline the main term in which you found the procedure code in the alphabetic index.

1. Intermediate repair of 3.5 cm laceration of the scalp _____

2. 50 minutes of insight oriented, outpatient group psychotherapy _____

3. Percutaneous scratch test, with allergenic extracts 90 tests _____

4. Treatment of a closed femoral shaft fracture, without manipulation _____

5. Cardiovascular treadmill stress test with physician supervision, interpretation and report

   _____

6. Measles, mumps, and rubella (MMR) immunization _____

7. Vaginal hysterectomy, for uterus 250 grams or less _____

8. Septoplasty _____

9. Complete external hemorrhoidectomy _____

10. 3-hour glucose tolerance test (GTT) _____

11. Definitive, bacterial, throat culture _____

12. Destruction of one benign skin lesion _____

13. Treatment of a closed radial and ulnar shaft fracture with manipulation

    _____

14. Routine venipuncture for collection of a specimen _____

15. Aspiration of accumulated fluid of the bursa, right hip _____

16. Chest x-ray, frontal and lateral _____

17. General Health Panel blood test _____

18. White blood count, automated _____

19. Anesthesia for a small intestinal endoscopy, 2 hours and 30 minutes _____

20. 12-lead electrocardiogram with interpretation and report _____

21. Wrist x-ray, two views _____

22. Closed treatment of a fractured wrist (carpal), excluding the scaphoid bone, without

    manipulation

    _____

23. Obstetric panel (blood tests, panel) _____

24. Routine obstetric care, vaginal delivery, episiotomy, and postpartum care

_____

25. Tubal ligation, postpartum, during same hospitalization _____

26. Diagnostic right heart catheterization _____

27. Coronary artery bypass, using three coronary arterial grafts _____

28. Screening mammography, bilateral _____

29. Surgical pathology, gross and microscopic examination of breast mastectomy with regional

lymph nodes _____

30. Radical mastectomy, including pectoral muscles, axillary and internal mammary lymph nodes

_____

ICD-9-CM and CPT Coding

Assign ICD-9 codes to the following:

31. Acute gastritis with hemorrhage   _____   _____

32. Menorrhagia in 12-year-old   _____   _____

33. Septic shock postoperative   _____   _____

34. Hemiplegia congenital   _____   _____

35. Papanicolaou smear as part of exam   _____

36. Corneal foreign body, right eye   ICD-9-CM: _____
    Removal foreign body, slit lamp, cornea   CPT: _____

37. Spondylolysis (lumbosacral region)   ICD-9-CM: _____
    Chiropractic manipulation of LS spine   CPT: _____

38. Bleeding duodenal ulcer   ICD-9-CM: _____
    Esophagogastroduodenoscopy (EGD)   CPT: _____

39. Bacterial meningitis (pneumococcal)   ICD-9-CM: _____
    Lumbar puncture   CPT: _____

40. Ingrown nail, right great toe with
    infection   ICD-9-CM: _____
    Avulsion of nail plate   CPT: _____

41. Insulin dependent diabetes mellitus
    with polyneuropathy   ICD-9-CM: _____
    EMGs of all four extremities   CPT: _____

42. Fibrocystic disease of the breast   ICD-9-CM: _____
    Bilateral mammograms   CPT: _____

43. Crohn's disease of colon   ICD-9-CM: _____
    Colonoscopy with biopsy   CPT: _____

Assign CPT codes to the following case studies.

44. A 35-year-old, established patient, sees the doctor for her annual physical. A Pap (Papan-icolaou) smear is taken and sent to an outside laboratory. The laboratory will bill patient for the Pap smear. Patient also has a furuncle on the right axilla at the time of the visit, which the doctor incises and drains (I&D).

CPT Code	Description of Service
_____	Periodic physical examination, established 35 y/o patient
_____	Collection & handling of the Pap smear
_____	I&D, furuncle, right axilla
_____	Sterile tray

45. A new patient is seen by the doctor for irregular vaginal bleeding. The doctor performs a detailed history and examination and finds cervical polyps. He performs a cauterization of polyps. The doctor takes a Pap smear and wet mount for bacterial fungi. The Pap smear is sent to an outside laboratory, which will bill the patient.

CPT Code	Description of Service
_____	Collection and handling of the Pap smear
_____	Wet mount smear for bacterial fungi
_____	Electro-cauterization of cervical polyps
_____	Initial detailed history and examination

46. An established patient, a young child, is admitted to the hospital for acute asthmatic bron-chitis. The doctor sees the patient after 11:00 p.m. and performs an initial, comprehensive history and physical with high complexity decision making. The doctor then remains with the child one additional hour to be sure the child is out of danger.

CPT Code	Description of Service
_____	Comprehensive Hx & Px, high complexity DM
_____	Services Performed after 11 p.m.
_____	Prolonged Services

47. A new patient is seen in the hospital. The doctor performs a comprehensive history and physical, including initiation of diagnostic and treatment programs, and prepares extensive hospital records. The doctor then performs a bronchoscopy with a single site, bronchial biopsy. The biopsy confirms her diagnosis, so the following day she performs a total right pneumonectomy.

CPT Code	Description of Service
_____	Comprehensive Hx & Px
_____	Bronchoscopy
_____	Right Total Pneumonectomy

48. Bill for the pneumonectomy on the patient in Question 47, performed by the assistant surgeon.

CPT Code	Description of Service
_____	Assist Right Total Pneumonectomy

49. A patient is sent to your office for a second opinion. The doctor performs a consultation requiring an expanded history and physical examination. He then returns the patient to the referring doctor for his recommended care.

CPT Code	Description of Service
_____	Consultation, expanded Hx & Px

Anesthesia Coding

Please code the anesthesia following procedures.

50. Anesthesia for an amniocentesis _____

51. Anesthesia administered for excision of a tumor of the humerus _____

52. Patient receiving anesthesia for a total hip replacement _____

53. General anesthesia for a simple repair of a 1.5 centimeter nose laceration _____

54. Anesthesia administered for a CAT scan of the kidney _____

Insurance

General Commercial Health Insurance Information

Chapter Outline

OBJECTIVES

- Describe insurance fundamentals
- Understand the difference between group and individual health insurance
- Recognize the difference between fee-for-service and managed care plans
- Gain knowledge of the different health insurance plans available
- Explain the various costs the patient can be responsible for
- Complete claim form accurately
- Be aware of the benefits of electronic claim filing
- Determine which insurance plan is primary for patients with more than one plan
- Clarify the order of benefits for stepchildren or children of separated or divorced parents
- Explain assignment of benefits

MEDICAL ASSISTING COMPETENCIES

ABHES

1i. conduct work within scope of education, training, and ability
2d. serve as liaison between Physician and others
2g. use appropriate medical terminology
2h. receive, organize, prioritize, and transmit information expediently
2j. use correct grammar, spelling and formatting techniques in written works
3b. prepare and maintain medical records
3e. locate resources and information for patients and employers
3v. perform diagnostic coding
3w. complete insurance claim forms
3x. use physician fee schedule
5b. document accurately
5c. use appropriate guidelines when releasing records or information
8b. implement current procedural terminology and ICD-9 coding
8c. analyze and use current third-party guidelines for reimbursement

CAAHEP

IV.P.3. Use medical terminology, pronouncing medical terms correctly, to communicate information, patient history, data and observations
VII.C.1. Identify types of insurance plans
VII.C.7. Describe how guidelines are used in processing an insurance claim
VII.P.3. Complete insurance claim forms
VIII.C.1. Describe how to use the most current procedural coding system
VIII.C.3. Describe how to use the most current diagnostic coding classification system
VIII.C.4. Describe how to use the most current HCPCS
VIII.P.1. Perform procedural coding
VIII.P.2. Perform diagnostic coding
VIII.A.1. Work with physician to achieve the maximum reimbursement

KEY TERMS

Benefits	Dependent	Major Medical Insurance
Birthday Rule	Electronic Data Interchange	Out-of-Pocket Expenses
CMS-1500		Policyholder
Coordination of Benefits	Fee-for-Service	Premium
Co-Insurance	Group Insurance	Prepaid Health Plan
Copayment	Individual Insurance	Subscriber
Deductible	Lifetime Maximum	

■ INTRODUCTION

Health insurance has been around since 1860 when a company in Massachusetts offered the first policy. According to the U.S. Census Bureau, the number of Americans currently with health insurance is more than 250 million. Health insurance, simply defined, is a contract between a person (the policyholder) and an insurance company or carrier to provide a monetary coverage for medical services incurred by the policyholder.

The **policyholder** or patient may be covered for his or her medical expenses by a commercial insurance company or by government sponsored programs such as Medicare, Medicaid, TRICARE/CHAMPUS/CHAMPVA, or Workers' Compensation.

! KEY TERM

POLICYHOLDER—An individual enrolled in a health insurance plan; also referred to as a subscriber.

■ INSURANCE FUNDAMENTALS

Medical insurance is a contract between an insurance company and a policyholder. No matter what they are called, the policyholder, member, recipient, subscriber, or insured is better known in the medical office as the patient.

A commercial insurance company is an organization that provides health-care benefits to people through (1) individual or private policies or (2) through group plans such as an employer or professional organization or prepaid health plan. Commercial insurance companies usually operate as *for-profit* organizations. Several well-known insurance companies are Aetna, Blue Cross Blue Shield, CIGNA, Prudential, Mutual of Omaha, Allied, Principal, or Farm Bureau.

! KEY TERMS

BENEFITS—Covered services available to an individual or group by a health insurance plan or government agency.

FEE-FOR-SERVICE—The traditional method of paying a health-care provider for services as they provided.

PREPAID HEALTH PLAN—A method of financing the cost of health care for a defined population in advance of receipt of services.

Types of Commercial Insurance

Insurance companies offer many types of plans or products. Each plan can offer various types of coverage to various groups of individuals or to a single individual. The types of health insurance are group health plans, individual plans, workers' compensation, and government health plans such as Medicare and Medicaid.

! KEY TERMS

DEPENDENT—The subscriber's spouse or children under a limiting age.

SUBSCRIBER—An individual enrolled in a health insurance plan; also referred to as a policyholder.

GROUP INSURANCE—A health insurance policy to a group of people who are part of the same company or organization (employees, members, etc.) and their dependents who are covered under a single contract.

Group Insurance

Group insurance can be offered to a group of employees or an organization's members and their dependents. Each employee or member would be given his or her own policy number or identification number and be responsible for his or her own premiums. A group policy usually provides better benefits and lower premiums than individual plans. The premiums are lower because the premiums are pooled from everyone in the group and the risk is spread among the entire group.

If a person leaves the employer or organization the group contract is terminated but the insured can continue the same or lesser coverage through provisions of **COBRA** and/or **HIPAA**. COBRA, an acronym for Consolidated Omnibus Budget Reconciliation Act of 1985 is a federal law that provides an employee working within a company of 20 or more employees, extension of their group health insurance for themselves and their dependents for up to 18 months after leaving the company. Many states go beyond this and require smaller groups and other federally exempted employers to also offer it. The employee must be offered the exact benefits they received immediately before they qualified for COBRA. The employee is responsible for the premiums of their policy. Premium amounts will vary depending on the group's coverage and rates. The premiums are, however, less than an individual plan would be.

HIPAA, the Health Insurance Portability and Accountability Act ,was created by the federal legislature to, among other things, protect workers and their families maintain health insurance if they change or lose their jobs. For more detailed information on HIPAA, see Chapter 3.

Individual Insurance

An individual policy is issued to an individual and his or her dependents. This type of policy typically has a higher premium and the benefits are less than those in a group plan. Unlike group insurance, an individual plan's premiums and coverage is based solely on the health and use of the individual and his or her dependents. The more claims and illness the individual incurs, the higher the premiums will be to cover those medical expenses.

❗ KEY TERM

INDIVIDUAL INSURANCE—An insurance plan issued directly to an individual and their dependents who are covered under a single contract.

Fee-for-Service versus Managed Care

Health insurance can be further classified into fee-for-service (traditional insurance) and managed care. The following are types of managed care plans:

- Health Maintenance Organization (HMO)
- Preferred Provider Organization (PPO)

Managed care plans are sold to both groups and individuals. A person's health care is managed by the insurance company. Approvals are needed for some services, including visits to specialist doctors, medical tests, or surgical procedures. In order for people to receive the highest level of coverage they must obtain services from the doctors, hospitals, labs, imaging centers, and other providers affiliated with their managed care plan.

Health Maintenance Organization

An HMO is a type of managed care. This type of coverage was designed to help keep people healthy by covering the cost of preventive care, such as medical checkups. The patient selects a primary care doctor, such as a family physician, from an HMO list. This doctor coordinates the patient's care and determines if referrals to specialist doctors are needed. Insured members pay a premium and a small fee, or copayment, to receive health-care services. The HMO has arrangements with caregivers and hospitals, and the copayment applies to those caregivers and facilities affiliated with the HMO. Although this type of coverage is more restrictive than fee-for-service coverage, the patient's out-of-pocket health-care costs are generally lower and more predictable. A person's out-of-pocket costs will be much higher if he or she receives care outside of the HMO unless prior approval from the HMO is received.

Preferred Provider Organization

A PPO combines the benefits of fee-for-service with the features of an HMO. If patients use health-care providers (e.g., doctors, hospitals) who are part of the PPO network, they will receive coverage for most of their bills after a deductible and copayment is met. Some PPOs require people to choose a primary care physician who will coordinate care and arrange referrals to specialists when needed. Other PPOs allow patients to choose specialists on their own. In addition, a PPO may offer less coverage for care given by doctors and other professionals not affiliated with the PPO. For more detailed information about managed care, see Chapter 10.

Government Health Plans

Medicare and Medicaid are two health plans offered by the U.S. government. They are available to individuals who meet a certain age, income, or disability criteria. TRICARE Standard, formerly called CHAMPUS, is the health plan for U.S. military personnel. These health plans are discussed in Chapters 8, 9, and 11.

Prepaid Health Plans

Better known as managed care organizations, prepaid health plans are contracts with a network of health-care providers. Services are performed for a predetermined fee that is paid on a monthly or yearly basis rather than for a fee-for-service. Details of plan features, coverage, and billing issues are included in Chapter 10.

Differences in Commercial Plans

Many commercial insurance companies offer a number of different plans. The medical coder cannot assume that every patient's coverage is the same, even when from the same carrier. For example, Blue Cross Blue Shield offers a number of different plans, Classic Blue, Blue Access, Blue Choice, Blue Advantage, to name a few. Each of these plans offer different benefits, coverage, and restrictions. The coder must know which plans their physician participates with and verify coverage for their patients.

■ PATIENT/POLICYHOLDER'S COSTS

The policy represents the benefits or coverage provided to the policyholder. The benefits or coverage defines the services that the insurance company will pay for when rendered to their policyholder, such as office and hospital services, emergency care or prescription drugs.

Whether or not the policyholder/patient's plan is an individual plan or a group plan, he or she is responsible for paying a **premium** to keep the policy enforced and to maintain health coverage. The premium is often part of an employee's company benefit and may be paid or subsidized by the patient's employer.

❗ KEY TERM

PREMIUM—The amount paid by an insured regularly (monthly/semi-monthly) to keep any health insurance policy.

In addition to the premium there may be other costs involved:

- A yearly deductible before the health insurance begins to contribute
- A per-visit copayment
- A percentage of health-care expenses, known as co-insurance.

In most cases, the insured is responsible for the deductible. A **deductible** is an amount that must be paid for covered medical services each calendar or fiscal year by the insured before the benefits of the insurance will begin. The deductible amount will vary depending on the policy anywhere from a $100 to $1000 or more dollars. The higher the deductible is, the lower the premium. A deductible will apply to each member of the plan. If the plan covers more than one family member, each family member will be responsible for meeting that annual deductible. Some plans offer a family deductible, which means all covered family members contribute to the deductible until it is satisfied. Once the deductible is met, the insurance company begins to pay benefits toward the rendered medical services for any covered family member. For example, if a plan has a $500.00 family deductible and each member has $100.00 individual deductible and five out of the six family members have met their $100.00

deductible, the family deductible kicks in and the sixth member does not need to qualify with additional $100.00 of expenses. The insurance company will begin paying for that sixth member's services automatically.

> **!** **KEY TERM**
>
> DEDUCTIBLE—An amount that must be paid for covered medical services each calendar year by the insured before the benefits of the insurance plan will begin.

Copayment is an amount that must be paid by the insured for any rendered services. The insured is usually responsible for the copayment at the time the service is rendered. For example, if an office visit copayment is $20.00 under the insurance plan, the patient would be expected to pay that amount at the appointment. Often, the patient's insurance identification card has the copayment amount(s) printed right on it. Not all patients will have a copayment in their coverage. Some plans have different copay amounts for different services and some plans may waive a copayment depending on the circumstance or type of service rendered (e.g., an accident or laboratory services). A medical coder may need to verify with the insurance company whether a copayment applies to a particular service rendered. If so, how much it is. The medical coder may need to verify with the person in charge of copayment collections, whether it was collected. When the third-party payer has paid the submitted charges and the patient has paid their copayment, there still may be co-insurance to collect.

> **!** **KEY TERM**
>
> COPAYMENT—The cost an insured person is expected to pay at the time a service is rendered, such as $20 per office visit.

Co-insurance is the amount or the balance that an insured person must pay for health-care services after the insurance company's payment. For example, if the insurance company pays 80% of the patient's $200.00 office visit, the patient's co-insurance would be the 20%, or $40.00. This co-insurance amount is the balance leftover after the patient's initial copayment at the time of service and any other write-offs that have been deducted.

> **!** **KEY TERM**
>
> CO-INSURANCE—A percentage of the cost of the service rendered that the person insured is responsible for.

Out-of-Pocket Expenses (OOPs)

Any medical expenses that are not covered by insurance are considered out-of-pocket expenses because they must be paid by the insured. These expenses include deductibles, co-insurance, and copayments. Medical insurance plans often have out-of-pocket limitations written into the plan that provide up to 100% payment of covered medical expenses after a certain amount of out-of-pocket expenses has been reached. For example, if an insured's policy stipulates a limit of $5000 for out-of–pocket expenses over the calendar year, either for the insured and/or any dependents, the insurance will pay 100% of the covered medical expenses incurred after the $5000 limit is reached.

Lifetime Maximum is a dollar amount that an insurance company will pay toward an illness or injury for each covered person while the policy is in effect. After that amount has been reached, there is no other coverage offered by that plan and the patient is responsible for all additional expenses.

> **!** **KEY TERMS**
>
> OUT-OF-POCKET EXPENSE—Any medical-care cost that must be paid by the person insured (coinsurance, co-payments, deductibles).
>
> LIFETIME MAXIMUM—The maximum dollar amount that an insurance company will pay toward care in the insured person's lifetime.

Flexible Spending

Flexible spending accounts are offered to many employees as a way of using non-taxable dollars to pay for medical expenses. The individual takes out a chosen dollar amount from his or her paycheck and deposits that money into a personal flexible spending account. This money has not been taxed yet and is set aside for any medical expenses occurred throughout the year. The account can be set up any way the employee wants, but is to be used only on medical expenses for themselves and/or family members. A patient may have a flexible spending credit card to be used when needed, or, if done manually, a patient may need a receipt or a copy of the superbill showing any expense(s) to be properly reimbursed.

LEVELS OF COVERAGE

There are various levels of coverage available in a group or individual plan:

- Basic health insurance
- Major Medical insurance
- Comprehensive insurance

KEY TERM

MAJOR MEDICAL INSURANCE—Insurance coverage for significant procedures or situations.

Basic health insurance may include the following:

- Hospital room and board and hospital care
- Hospital services and supplies such as x-rays and medicine
- Surgery, whether performed in or out of the hospital
- Doctor visits
- Prescription drugs

Major Medical insurance may include the following:

- Treatment for long-term, high-cost illnesses or injuries
- In-patient and outpatient expenses

Comprehensive insurance is a combination of basic insurance and major medical insurance. Premiums vary with the level of coverage. Major medical insurance, for example, can be very expensive.

COORDINATION OF BENEFITS

There may be times when patients (usually dependents) are covered under more than one policy. Information must be obtained from the patient to determine which insurance company is the primary one responsible for making the initial payment and which is the secondary to eliminate duplication or an overpayment for the services rendered.

KEY TERM

COORDINATION OF BENEFITS (COB)—The system that ensures insurance payments do not exceed 100% of a given charge when more than one insurance policy is in place.

Coordination of benefits (COB) refers to a method of limiting health insurance payments to no more than 100% of the actual charge. COB is written into the group policies to apply when a policyholder or designated dependents are covered by more than one health insurance policy. This coordination between plans prevents payments from each plan from exceeding the actual amount charged to the patient.

In the past, there had been long delays in the payment of these claims while the insurance companies involved decided who was the primary payer and who was the secondary payer. The medical coder will need to verify coverage of each patient and determine which plan is primary and which plan is secondary to properly submit the claims.

The Birthday Rule

In 1984, the National Association of Insurance Commissioners (NAIC) adopted the following coordination of benefits rule:

> The benefits of a plan covering a child as the dependent of a parent whose birthday occurs earlier in a calendar year will determine the primary insurance and pay before the benefits of a plan covering a child as the dependent of a parent whose birthday occurs later in the year. If both parents have the same birthday, the benefits of the plan that covered the parent longer are primary to those of the plan that covered the other parent for a shorter time.

! KEY TERM

BIRTHDAY RULE—A coordination of benefits rule that determines the order of benefits paid by parents of a dependent child if there is more than one insurance plan to consider.

"Birthday" means the month and the day, not the year of birth. If one of the plans does not have a **birthday rule** and the plans do not agree on the order of benefits, the plan without a birthday rule will be primary. Most states have adopted this rule, but the medical coder must inquire with the state insurance commissioner to determine if the birthday rule is applicable.

Separated or Divorced Parents

NAIC guidelines, regarding COB situations involving a child of divorced or separated parents, are as follows:

- If a divorce decree exists and the financial responsibility for the child's health care is placed on one of the parents, that parent's insurance plan is primary.
- If there is no divorce decree and/or financial responsibility has not been established, then the plan of the parent with custody is primary.
- If the parents share joint custody, the plan of the parent who claims the dependent for tax purposes is primary. If the parents claim the dependent in alternative years, the order of benefits also would alternate.

Parents Remarry

If parents remarry:

1. The plan of the parent with custody is primary.
2. The plan of the spouse of the parent with custody is secondary.
3. The plan of the parent without custody is tertiary.

Stepchild/Foster Child

If the child is a stepchild, custody of the child supersedes the birthday rule. For foster children covered under the foster parents' plans, the standard order of benefits applies.

■ ASSIGNMENT OF BENEFITS

An assignment of benefits takes place when the insured/patient has signed an agreement instructing their insurance company to pay the health-care provider directly for services rendered. The patient information form will include a statement for the patient to sign, which indicates the patient has given permission (Fig. 7–1). The information form is kept in the patient's medical record to document the authorization.

On the claim form the following area can be completed when a claim is submitted for payment (Fig. 7–2). Typically the words "signature on file" or the acronym "SOF" is entered on the signature line to instruct the insurance company to pay the doctor directly.

This signature on file refers to the patient's signature on the patient information sheet. The patients don't actually sign claim forms, instead they give their authorization when completing their patient information sheet. Patients would not typically ever see their claim forms. The patient receives a statement from his or her insurance company, either hard copy or electronic, indicating how a procedure was covered and paid for.

With Medicare, a provider who accepts assignment will receive reimbursement directly from Medicare *and* agrees to accept Medicare's approved reimbursement amount, as payment in full. This will be discussed in detail in Chapter 8.

■ THE CLAIM FORM

For many years there were several different claim forms and coding systems being used to communicate the diagnoses and procedures performed to third-party payers. There was no standardized form for physicians to report the services provided to their patients. In the 1980s, the AMA, CMS (known at the time as the Healthcare Finance Administration [HCFA]), and other organizations formed the Uniform Claim Form Task Force. They worked together to standardize and promote the use of a universal claim form. The HCFA-1500 claim form, now known as the CMS-1500 claim form (Fig. 7–3), was soon accepted nationwide by most insurance carriers as the standard claim form for submission of medical claims.

! KEY TERM

CMS-1500—The claim form used for submitting medical services for payment to an insurance organization.

Electronic Claim Filing

In the early 1980s, there was a push to move away from paper claims to claims sent via computer or telephone transmission. These claims became known as **Electronic Data Interchange (EDI)**, and that interchange was broadened to include prior authorizations and a variety of medical record information. The third-party carriers have also gone to Electronic Funds Transfers (EFT), which drastically cuts the payment time. Instead of processing and mailing a check to each provider, the payments are deposited into the provider's bank account and an online report is sent to the billing office. Based on the report, the medical coder applies insurance payments to the appropriate patient accounts for the paid services. Instead of waiting 2 to 4 weeks to receive payment or rejection of services, the medical coder receives weekly reports showing the total amount of money deposited and to whom it applies, for services processed in that group or batch of claims.

I hereby authorize payment of medical benefits billed to my insurance to John Smith, DO. I hereby accept responsibility for payment for any service(s) provided to me that is not covered by my insurance. I agree to pay all co-payments, coinsurance, and deductibles at the time the service is rendered.

_____   _____

Signature of Patient or Guardian   Date

FIGURE 7–1: Patient authorization for payment of medical benefits.

13. INSURED'S OR AUTHORIZED PERSON'S SIGNATURE I authorize payment of medical benefits to the undersigned physician or supplier for services described below.

SIGNED _____

FIGURE 7–2: Box 13 from CMS-1500 form.

1500

HEALTH INSURANCE CLAIM FORM

APPROVED BY NATIONAL UNIFORM CLAIM COMMITTEE 08/05

PICA | PICA

CARRIER

1. MEDICARE (Medicare #) | MEDICAID (Medicaid #) | TRICARE CHAMPUS (Sponsor's SSN) | CHAMPVA (Member ID#) | GROUP HEALTH PLAN (SSN or ID) | FECA BLK LUNG (SSN) | OTHER (ID)

1a. INSURED'S I.D. NUMBER (For Program in Item 1)

2. PATIENT'S NAME (Last Name, First Name, Middle Initial)

3. PATIENT'S BIRTH DATE MM DD YY SEX M F

4. INSURED'S NAME (Last Name, First Name, Middle Initial)

5. PATIENT'S ADDRESS (No., Street)

6. PATIENT RELATIONSHIP TO INSURED Self Spouse Child Other

7. INSURED'S ADDRESS (No., Street)

CITY STATE

8. PATIENT STATUS Single Married Other

CITY STATE

ZIP CODE TELEPHONE (Include Area Code) ( )

Employed Full-Time Student Part-Time Student

ZIP CODE TELEPHONE (Include Area Code) ( )

9. OTHER INSURED'S NAME (Last Name, First Name, Middle Initial)

10. IS PATIENT'S CONDITION RELATED TO:

11. INSURED'S POLICY GROUP OR FECA NUMBER

a. OTHER INSURED'S POLICY OR GROUP NUMBER

a. EMPLOYMENT? (Current or Previous) YES NO

a. INSURED'S DATE OF BIRTH MM DD YY SEX M F

b. OTHER INSURED'S DATE OF BIRTH MM DD YY SEX M F

b. AUTO ACCIDENT? YES NO PLACE (State)

b. EMPLOYER'S NAME OR SCHOOL NAME

c. EMPLOYER'S NAME OR SCHOOL NAME

c. OTHER ACCIDENT? YES NO

c. INSURANCE PLAN NAME OR PROGRAM NAME

d. INSURANCE PLAN NAME OR PROGRAM NAME

10d. RESERVED FOR LOCAL USE

d. IS THERE ANOTHER HEALTH BENEFIT PLAN? YES NO *If yes*, return to and complete item 9 a-d.

READ BACK OF FORM BEFORE COMPLETING & SIGNING THIS FORM.

12. PATIENT'S OR AUTHORIZED PERSON'S SIGNATURE I authorize the release of any medical or other information necessary to process this claim. I also request payment of government benefits either to myself or to the party who accepts assignment below.

SIGNED DATE

13. INSURED'S OR AUTHORIZED PERSON'S SIGNATURE I authorize payment of medical benefits to the undersigned physician or supplier for services described below.

SIGNED

PATIENT AND INSURED INFORMATION

14. DATE OF CURRENT: MM DD YY ILLNESS (First symptom) OR INJURY (Accident) OR PREGNANCY(LMP)

15. IF PATIENT HAS HAD SAME OR SIMILAR ILLNESS. GIVE FIRST DATE MM DD YY

16. DATES PATIENT UNABLE TO WORK IN CURRENT OCCUPATION FROM MM DD YY TO MM DD YY

17. NAME OF REFERRING PROVIDER OR OTHER SOURCE

17a.

17b. NPI

18. HOSPITALIZATION DATES RELATED TO CURRENT SERVICES FROM MM DD YY TO MM DD YY

19. RESERVED FOR LOCAL USE

20. OUTSIDE LAB? YES NO $ CHARGES

21. DIAGNOSIS OR NATURE OF ILLNESS OR INJURY (Relate Items 1, 2, 3 or 4 to Item 24E by Line)

1. ___ . ___

2. ___ . ___

3. ___ . ___

4. ___ . ___

22. MEDICAID RESUBMISSION CODE ORIGINAL REF. NO.

23. PRIOR AUTHORIZATION NUMBER

24. A. DATE(S) OF SERVICE From MM DD YY To MM DD YY	B. PLACE OF SERVICE	C. EMG	D. PROCEDURES, SERVICES, OR SUPPLIES (Explain Unusual Circumstances) CPT/HCPCS MODIFIER	E. DIAGNOSIS POINTER	F. $ CHARGES	G. DAYS OR UNITS	H. EPSDT Family Plan	I. ID. QUAL.	J. RENDERING PROVIDER ID. #
1								NPI	
2								NPI	
3								NPI	
4								NPI	
5								NPI	
6								NPI	

PHYSICIAN OR SUPPLIER INFORMATION

25. FEDERAL TAX I.D. NUMBER SSN EIN

26. PATIENT'S ACCOUNT NO.

27. ACCEPT ASSIGNMENT? (For govt. claims, see back) YES NO

28. TOTAL CHARGE $

29. AMOUNT PAID $

30. BALANCE DUE $

31. SIGNATURE OF PHYSICIAN OR SUPPLIER INCLUDING DEGREES OR CREDENTIALS (I certify that the statements on the reverse apply to this bill and are made a part thereof.)

SIGNED DATE

32. SERVICE FACILITY LOCATION INFORMATION

a. b.

33. BILLING PROVIDER INFO & PH # ( )

a. b.

NUCC Instruction Manual available at: www.nucc.org **PLEASE PRINT OR TYPE** APPROVED OMB-0938-0999 FORM CMS-1500 (08-05)

FIGURE 7–3. CMS-1500 form.

In the 1990s, the interest turned toward electronic claims submission and HIPAA regulations. The Uniform Claim Form Task Force was replaced by the National Uniform Claim Committee (NUCC). Their goal was to standardize the data used in the electronic claim submissions and remain consistent with the standard paper claim. The NUCC developed the NUCC Data Set (NUCC-DS), which is a set of standardized instructions for electronic claims. These instructions are consistent with the paper claim instructions. The claim completion instructions have been released by the NUCC and do not represent the requirements that every third-party payer demands, but rather a standard set of instructions to complete the CMS-1500 form. The medical coder must have an understanding of the requirements in each field of the claim form to determine if the form has been properly completed and ready to be sent to a third-party carrier. Upcoming chapters will address the data required by other carriers.

The NUCC is currently responsible for the maintenance of the claim form. The most recent version of the claim form is the CMS-1500 (08-05). The form was revised in 2007 to accommodate the **National Provider Identifier** (NPI), and the NUCC continues to study the type of data required by third-party payers. There are fields still labeled as "RESERVED FOR LOCAL USE," but the NUCC's ultimate goal is to standardize the claim form completion instructions to meet both public and private payers.

Completing the Claim Form

Completing the claim form properly is the key to expediting accurate payment for the services rendered to patients (Table 7–1 and Box 7–1). When a patient is seen for the first time, he or she completes a patient registration form. (See Fig. 1–1 for a sample patient registration or information form.) The patient demographics include name, address, phone number, place of employment, the responsible party for the bill, and the type of insurance coverage. The medical coder will use this information to complete the first half of the CMS-1500 claim form, items 1 through 13 (Fig. 7–4).

TABLE 7–1:   Information Needed to Complete the CMS-1500 Form

	Information Needed	Where the Information Will Be Found
Items 1–13 Patient and Insured Information		
Item 1: Type of Health Insurance	Check the box of the insurance company where the claim will be sent	Patient's insurance card and patient information sheet
Item 1a: Insured's ID Number	The ID number of person who holds the policy	Patient's insurance card and patient information sheet
Item 2: Patient's name (Last, First, Middle Initial)	The name of the patient who received the service	Patient information sheet
Item 3: Patient's Date of Birth	The patient's date of birth and gender, male or female	Patient information sheet
Item 4: Insured's Name (Last, First, Middle Initial)	The name of the person who holds the policy	Patient's Insurance Card & Patient information sheet
Item 5: Patient's Address	The patient's permanent address and phone number	Patient information sheet
Item 6: Patient's Relationship to Insured	Indicate how the patient is related to the insured	Patient information sheet
Item 7: Insured's Address	The insured's permanent mailing address	Patient information sheet
Item 8: Patient's Status	Indicate the patient's marital and employment status	Patient information sheet
Item 9: Other Insured's Name	The name of the person who holds another policy on the patient	Patient information sheet

Continued

TABLE 7–1: Information Needed to Complete the CMS-1500 Form—cont'd

	Information Needed	Where the Information Will Be Found
Items 1–13 Patient and Insured Information		
Item 9a: Other Insured's Policy or Group Number	The policy number of the insured in Box 9	Patient information sheet and Box 9 of claim
Item 9b: Other Insured's date of birth	The birth date and gender of the insured in Box 9	Patient information sheet and Box 9 of claim
Item 9c: Employer's name or School Name	The employer or school name of the insured in Box 9	Patient information sheet and Box 9 of claim
Item 9d: Insurance Plan Name or Program name	The name of the plan or program of the insured indicated in Box 9	Patient information sheet and Box 9 of claim
Item 10a: Is Patient's Condition Related To Employment?	Indicate yes or no if the condition of the patient's is related to an employment incident	Patient information sheet and/or the appointment schedule
Item 10b: Is Patient's Condition Related to Auto Accident?	Indicate yes or no if the condition of the patient's is related to an auto accident	Patient information sheet and/or the appointment schedule
Item 10c: Is Patient's Condition Related to Other Accident?	Indicate yes or no if the condition of the patient's is related to another type of accident	Patient information sheet and/or the appointment schedule
Item 10d: Reserved for Local Use	Any information required by the insurance company in Box 1	Insurance company information indicated in Box 1's policy manual
Item 11: Insured's Policy Group or FECA Number	The group ID number or the alphanumeric number (FECA) of the health, auto, or other insurance plan of the insured in Box 4	Patient information sheet and/or the ID card of the person indicated in Box 4
Item 11a: Insured's Date of Birth	The birth date and gender of the insured in Box 1a	Patient information sheet
Item 11b: Employer's Name or School Name	The employer or school name of the insured in Box 1a	Patient information sheet
Item 11c: Insurance Plan Name or Program Name	The name of the plan or program of the insured indicated in Box 1a	Patient information sheet
Item 11d: Is There Another Health Plan? *If yes, return to and complete 9 a–d*	If the patient is covered under another plan other than the one in Box 1	Patient Information Sheet and Boxes 9 a–d
Item 12: Patient's or Authorized Person's Signature	A signature on file authorizing a release of medical records or other information needed to process the claim	Patient information sheet
Item 13: Insured's or Authorized Signature	A signature on file authorizing payment for the services indicated on the claim, to be sent directly to the provider who appears in Boxes 31 and 32 of the claim	Patient information sheet

TABLE 7–1: Information Needed to Complete the CMS-1500 Form—cont'd

	Information Needed	Where the Information Will Be Found
Items 14–33 Patient and Insured Information		
Item 14: Date of Current Illness, Injury, Pregnancy	The first date of onset of illness, the actual date of the injury, or the LMP for pregnancy	Patient's medical record
Item 15: If Patient Has Had Same or Similar Illness	The first date the patient had the same or a similar illness	Patient's medical record
Item 16: Dates Patient Unable to Work in Current Occupation	The from and to dates that the patient is/was unable to work	Patient's medical record
Item 17: Name of Referring Provider or Other Source	Name of the referring, ordering, or supervising provider who referred, ordered, or supervised the service on the claim	Patient's medical record
Item 17a: Other ID #	Was used for the other ID # of the referring, ordering, or supervising provider listed in Box 17, who referred, ordered, or supervised the service on the claim	The referring, ordering, or supervising provider or directory containing the ID numbers
Item 17b: NPI #	HIPAA's National Provider Identifier (NPI) number of the referring, ordering, or supervising provider listed in Box 17	The referring, ordering, or supervising provider directory containing the ID numbers
Item 18: Hospitalization Dates Related to Current Illness	The admission and discharge dates of the inpatient stay related to the services listed on the claim	Patient's medical record
Item 19: Reserved for Local Use	The appropriate information requested by the payer the claim will be submitted to	The policy manual of the third-party payer indicated in Box 1
Item 20: Outside Lab? $ Charges	Yes or no; the service/s on the claim were purchased from an outside laboratory and the charged amount	Patient's medical record or log kept on file
Item 21: Diagnosis or Nature of Illness or Injury (relate items 1, 2, 3, or 4 to 24E by line)	The ICD-9-CM code representing the patient's diagnosis or condition. The reason for the services on the claim	Patient's medical record and current ICD-9-CM manual
Item 22: Medicaid Resubmission	The original reference number assigned by Medicaid to indicate a previously submitted claim	The instructions from the local and current Medicaid policy manual
Item 23: Prior Authorization Number	The number assigned by payer when a service has been approved/determined medically necessary	Patient's Medical Record or log kept on file
Item 24A: Date(s) of Service	The date service(s) where performed (mmddyyyy) (up to 6 services billed per claim)	Superbill
Item 24B: Place of Service	The location the service was rendered	Superbill
Item 24C: EMG	(Y) Yes or (N) No the service(s) was an emergency	Superbill
Item 24D: Procedures, Services, Supplies	The CPT/HCPCS code and modifier if needed, identifying the service	Superbill

Continued

TABLE 7–1:   Information Needed to Complete the CMS-1500 Form—cont'd

	Information Needed	Where the Information Will Be Found
Items 14–33 Patient and Insured Information		
Item 24E: Diagnosis Pointer	Indicates the line number from Box 21 that relates to the service(s) rendered	Superbill
Item 24F: $ Charges	Total billed amount for each service line	Log kept on file
Item 24G: Days or Units	The number of days indicated in the date span of Box 24A *or* the number of units or minutes the service was performed (1 visit = 1 unit)	Superbill
Item 24H: EPSDT Family Plan	If applicable, a Yes(Y)/No(N) indicating the service rendered was related to **E**arly **P**eriodic **S**creening, **D**iagnosis, and **T**reatment	The instructions from the local and current Medicaid or other third-party carrier's policy manual
Item 24I: ID Qualifier	Was used for the ID# of the provider of service if they do not have an NPI # (1C = Medicare)	The instructions from the local and current Medicaid or other third-party carrier's policy manual
Item 24J: Rendering Provider ID #	The ID number assigned to the provider of service indicated in Box 24D	The provider directory containing the ID numbers
Item 25: Federal Tax ID #	The tax ID or social security number of the provider of service	The provider of service's records
Item 26: Patient's Account No.	The identifying number assigned by the provider of service (if assigned)	Patient's medical record or file
Item 27: Accept Assignment	Yes or No box indicating if the provider of service accepts Medicare's payment	The provider of service's records
Item 28: Total Charge	The sum of all services entered in Box 24J	The superbill, a hospital report, or the patient's account
Item 29: Amount Paid	Amount patient or other payer paid toward the services in Box 24J	The superbill, a record of receipts, or statement from a third-party payer, or the patient's account
Item 30: Balance Due	Amount left after payment.	The superbill, a record of receipts or statement from a third-party payer, or the patient's account (this field does not exist on paperless claims)
Item 31: Signature of Physician or Supplier including Degrees or Credentials (I certify that the statements on the reverse apply to this bill and are made a part thereof)	The physician's or other health-care provider's signature or that of their representative Signature on File or SOF with the date the claim form was completed (6 or 8 digits MMDDYY or MMDDYYYY)	The provider or their representative's signature A signature is needed on any paper claim, but may be a stamped signature The signature and date field does not exist when billing paperless claims
Item 32: Service Facility Location Information Item 32a: NPI #	The name and address of facility where services were rendered The NPI number of the facility where the service took place	A provider directory or phone book The coder's place of employment The provider directory containing the ID numbers

TABLE 7–1: Information Needed to Complete the CMS-1500 Form—cont'd

Information Needed		Where the Information Will Be Found
Items 14–33 Patient and Insured Information		
Item 32b: Other ID #	Was used for the two-digit non-NPI number (see Fig. 7–6) followed by the NPI identification number of the facility where the service took place	The instructions from the third-party carrier's policy manual
Item 33: Billing Provider Info and Phone #	The name and address of the provider requesting payment for the service in Box 24	A provider directory or phone book, or the coder's place of employment
Item 33a: NPI #	The NPI number of the provider requesting payment for the service(s) in Box 24	The provider directory containing the ID numbers
Item 33b: Other ID #	Was used for the two-digit non-NPI number followed by the NPI identification number of the provider requesting payment for the service(s) in Box 24	The instructions from the third-party carrier's policy manual

---

BOX 7–1: General Claim Completion Tips

- Itemize all other services (laboratory and x-ray) from the office visit.
- Always include the date of birth and name of patient, the appropriate policy number, and name of the insured.
- Always complete Box 10 and use accurate diagnoses codes. They identify the accident or illness and can affect the percentage of reimbursement from the insurance company.
- Use of accurate CPT and ICD-9-CM codes will expedite the processing of your claims.
- Most commercial insurance companies will allow more than four diagnoses on the claim. Use more codes to show the severity or the full description of the patient's illness or injury, if needed.
- Up to six separate services may be billed on a claim form. The shaded area of each line item in 24 A through 24 J does not indicate space for two separate services/charges.
- The physician's Federal Tax ID number or given provider number must be included for processing claims. The physician's signature should be on the claim as well.
- Completed claim forms must be submitted to the appropriate third-party carriers'/insurance companies' address found on the back of most insurance ID cards. Manuals with third-party addresses also are available for purchase.
- The medical coder should rely on the information offered by a third-party carrier, either online or from manuals offered. Many carriers provide for either and the medical coder will find information pertinent to that carrier.
- The medical coder also may contact the local, state medical society. Each society provides information pertinent to the state in which the services were rendered.

Most offices will have a superbill or route slip (see Fig. 1–5 for a sample superbill) that will be used to document the following:

- **Date** of service
- **Service(s)** that were provided to the patient
- **Diagnoses** of the patient
- **Provider** of service to the patient
- **Location** the service was rendered

This information is used along with the patient's medical records to complete items 14 through 33 of the CMS-1500 (Fig. 7–5).

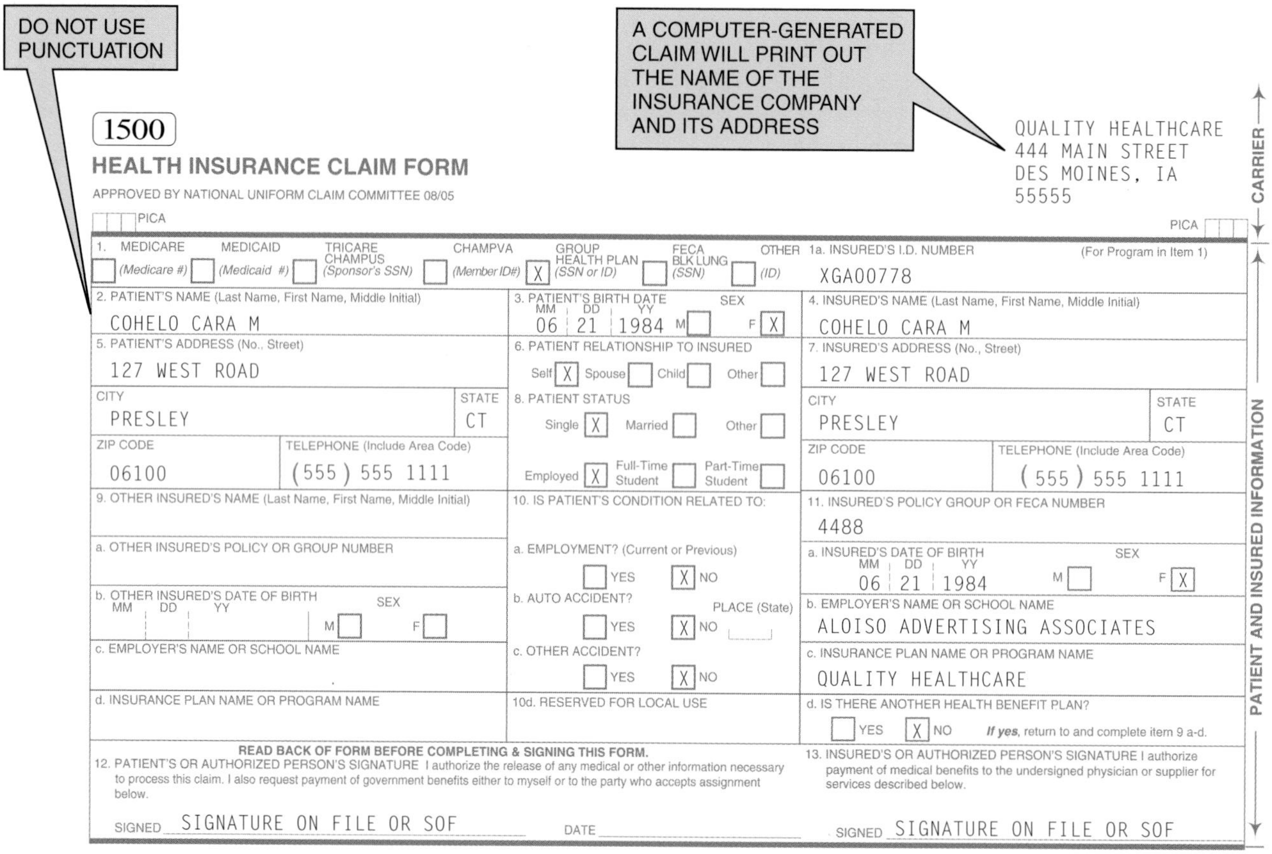

FIGURE 7–4: Top of completed CMS-1500 form.

A and B Boxes

During the implementation of the new identification numbers mandated by HIPAA, the carriers needed a way to identify or cross-reference each provider accurately. Before the implementation of new provider identification, a Provider Identification Number or PIN was assigned to providers by some carriers, such as Medicare, Medicaid, or Blue Cross Blue Shield. As the carriers were making provider number switches in their own systems, many carriers asked that the providers use their old provider identification numbers and their new NPIs to simplify the process. Boxes 17b, 32b, and 33b were used for this information. Identification number change was a huge transformation. The revised CMS-1500 claim form was designed with areas in which both new and old identification numbers could be included. The "B" boxes used the old provider number with a non-NPI two-digit number in front of it temporarily. Carriers assigned two-digit alphanumeric codes referred to as non-NPI number qualifiers, to be added to the health-care provider's identification number. The two-digit code identified what the old provider identification number had previously been used for.

For example, 1B was a Blue Shield identification number, 1D was a Medicaid identification number, and 1C was used by Medicare. Other two-digit numbers were created for the use of tax ID numbers, and commercial and managed care plans. After all providers and carriers were newly identified and systems were updated, the use of the "B" boxes was eliminated. The NPI numbers are used in boxes 17a, 32a and 33a. Box 24 "I" was used just like a "B" box and contained the non-NPI qualifier (Fig. 7–6).

Back of CMS-1500 Claim Form

On the back of the CMS-1500 claim form (Fig. 7–7), the medical coder will find certifications, authorizations, and validations for submitting the claim form. When signed, it becomes a legal document requesting money from the federal government or a third-party payer. The signatory on the front certifies that the information on the claim form is legitimate and accurate. If found to be false, the person of the signature may be prosecuted in a court of law. This alone is incentive for the medical coder to be accurate when coding and knowledgeable of current claim form completion rules and regulations.

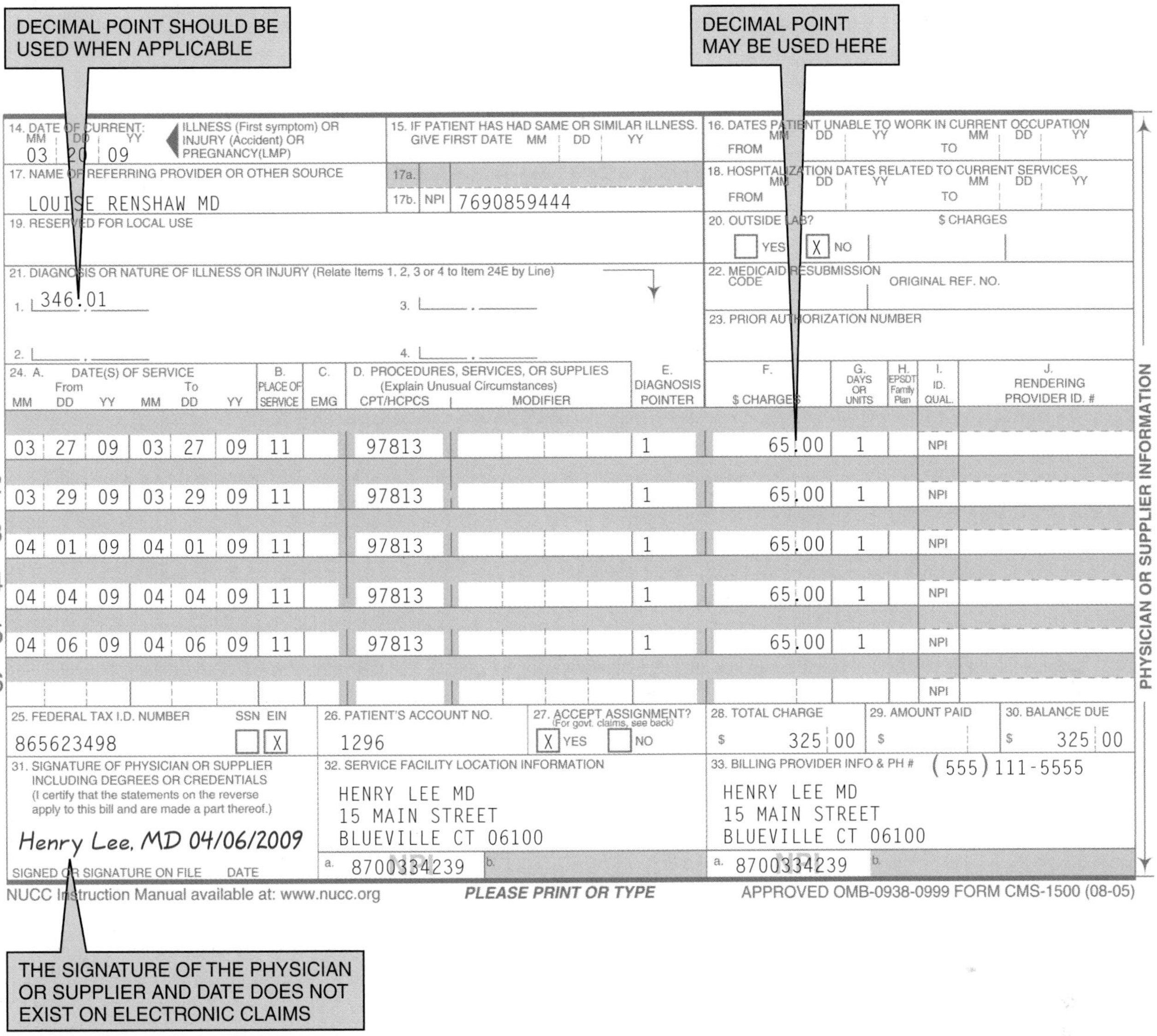

DECIMAL POINT SHOULD BE
USED WHEN APPLICABLE

DECIMAL POINT
MAY BE USED HERE

FIGURE 7-5: Bottom half of completed CMS-1500 form.

THE SIGNATURE OF THE PHYSICIAN
OR SUPPLIER AND DATE DOES NOT
EXIST ON ELECTRONIC CLAIMS

0B	State License Number
1A	Blue Cross Provider Number
1B	Blue Shield Provider Number
1C	Medicare Provider Number
1D	Medicaid Provider Number
1G	Provider UPIN Number
1H	CHAMPUS Identification Number
G2	Provider Plan Network Identification Number
LU	Location Number
N5	Provider Plan Network Identification Number
TJ	Federal Taxpayer's Identification Number
X4	Clinical Laboratory Improvement Amendment Number
X5	State Industrial Accident Provider Number
ZZ	Provider Taxonomy

FIGURE 7-6: Non-NPI qualifier list.

BECAUSE THIS FORM IS USED BY VARIOUS GOVERNMENT AND PRIVATE HEALTH PROGRAMS, SEE SEPARATE INSTRUCTIONS ISSUED BY APPLICABLE PROGRAMS.

NOTICE: Any person who knowingly files a statement of claim containing any misrepresentation or any false, incomplete or misleading information may be guilty of a criminal act punishable under law and may be subject to civil penalties.

REFERS TO GOVERNMENT PROGRAMS ONLY

MEDICARE AND CHAMPUS PAYMENTS: A patient's signature requests that payment be made and authorizes release of any information necessary to process the claim and certifies that the information provided in Blocks 1 through 12 is true, accurate and complete. In the case of a Medicare claim, the patient's signature authorizes any entity to release to Medicare medical and nonmedical information, including employment status, and whether the person has employer group health insurance, liability, no-fault, worker's compensation or other insurance which is responsible to pay for the services for which the Medicare claim is made. See 42 CFR 411.24(a). If item 9 is completed, the patient's signature authorizes release of the information to the health plan or agency shown. In Medicare assigned or CHAMPUS participation cases, the physician agrees to accept the charge determination of the Medicare carrier or CHAMPUS fiscal intermediary as the full charge, and the patient is responsible only for the deductible, coinsurance and noncovered services. Coinsurance and the deductible are based upon the charge determination of the Medicare carrier or CHAMPUS fiscal intermediary if this is less than the charge submitted. CHAMPUS is not a health insurance program but makes payment for health benefits provided through certain affiliations with the Uniformed Services. Information on the patient's sponsor should be provided in those items captioned in "Insured"; i.e., items 1a, 4, 6, 7, 9, and 11.

BLACK LUNG AND FECA CLAIMS

The provider agrees to accept the amount paid by the Government as payment in full. See Black Lung and FECA instructions regarding required procedure and diagnosis coding systems.

SIGNATURE OF PHYSICIAN OR SUPPLIER (MEDICARE, CHAMPUS, FECA AND BLACK LUNG)

I certify that the services shown on this form were medically indicated and necessary for the health of the patient and were personally furnished by me or were furnished incident to my professional service by my employee under my immediate personal supervision, except as otherwise expressly permitted by Medicare or CHAMPUS regulations.

For services to be considered as "incident" to a physician's professional service, 1) they must be rendered under the physician's immediate personal supervision by his/her employee, 2) they must be an integral, although incidental part of a covered physician's service, 3) they must be of kinds commonly furnished in physician's offices, and 4) the services of nonphysicians must be included on the physician's bills.

For CHAMPUS claims, I further certify that I (or any employee) who rendered services am not an active duty member of the Uniformed Services or a civilian employee of the United States Government or a contract employee of the United States Government, either civilian or military (refer to 5 USC 5536). For Black-Lung claims, I further certify that the services performed were for a Black Lung-related disorder.

No Part B Medicare benefits may be paid unless this form is received as required by existing law and regulations (42 CFR 424.32).

NOTICE: Any one who misrepresents or falsifies essential information to receive payment from Federal funds requested by this form may upon conviction be subject to fine and imprisonment under applicable Federal laws.

NOTICE TO PATIENT ABOUT THE COLLECTION AND USE OF MEDICARE, CHAMPUS, FECA, AND BLACK-LUNG INFORMATION
(PRIVACY ACT STATEMENT)

We are authorized by CMS, CHAMPUS and OWCP to ask you for information needed in the administration of the Medicare, CHAMPUS, FECA, and Black-Lung programs. Authority to collect information is in section 205(a), 1862, 1872 and 1874 of the Social Security Act as amended, 42 CFR 411.24(a) and 424.5(a) (6), and 44 USC 3101;41 CFR 101 et seq and 10 USC 1079 and 1086; 5 USC 8101 et seq; and 30 USC 901 et seq; 38 USC 613; E.O. 9397.

The information we obtain to complete claims under these programs is used to identify you and to determine your eligibility. It is also used to decide if the services and supplies you received are covered by these programs and to insure that proper payment is made.

The information may also be given to other providers of services, carriers, intermediaries, medical review boards, health plans, and other organizations or Federal agencies, for the effective administration of Federal provisions that require other third parties payers to pay primary to Federal program, and as otherwise necessary to administer these programs. For example, it may be necessary to disclose information about the benefits you have used to a hospital or doctor. Additional disclosures are made through routine uses for information contained in systems of records.

FOR MEDICARE CLAIMS: See the notice modifying system No. 09-70-0501, titled, 'Carrier Medicare Claims Record,' published in the Federal Register, Vol. 55 No. 177, page 37549, Wed. Sept. 12, 1990, or as updated and republished.

FOR OWCP CLAIMS: Department of Labor, Privacy Act of 1974, "Republication of Notice of Systems of Records," Federal Register Vol. 55 No. 40, Wed Feb. 28, 1990, See ESA-5, ESA-6, ESA-12, ESA-13, ESA-30, or as updated and republished.

FOR CHAMPUS CLAIMS: PRINCIPLE PURPOSE(S): To evaluate eligibility for medical care provided by civilian sources and to issue payment upon establishment of eligibility and determination that the services/supplies received are authorized by law.

ROUTINE USE(S): Information from claims and related documents may be given to the Dept. of Veterans Affairs, the Dept. of Health and Human Services and/or the Dept. of Transportation consistent with their statutory administrative responsibilities under CHAMPUS/CHAMPVA; to the Dept. of Justice for representation of the Secretary of Defense in civil actions; to the Internal Revenue Service, private collection agencies, and consumer reporting agencies in connection with recoupment claims; and to Congressional Offices in response to inquiries made at the request of the person to whom a record pertains. Appropriate disclosures may be made to other federal, state, local, foreign government agencies, private business entities, and individual providers of care, on matters relating to entitlement, claims adjudication, fraud, program abuse, utilization review, quality assurance, peer review, program integrity, third-party liability, coordination of benefits, and civil and criminal litigation related to the operation of CHAMPUS.

DISCLOSURES: Voluntary; however, failure to provide information will result in delay in payment or may result in denial of claim. With the one exception discussed below, there are no penalties under these programs for refusing to supply information. However, failure to furnish information regarding the medical services rendered or the amount charged would prevent payment of claims under these programs. Failure to furnish any other information, such as name or claim number, would delay payment of the claim. Failure to provide medical information under FECA could be deemed an obstruction.

It is mandatory that you tell us if you know that another party is responsible for paying for your treatment. Section 1128B of the Social Security Act and 31 USC 3801-3812 provide penalties for withholding this information.

You should be aware that P.L. 100-503, the "Computer Matching and Privacy Protection Act of 1988," permits the government to verify information by way of computer matches.

MEDICAID PAYMENTS (PROVIDER CERTIFICATION)

I hereby agree to keep such records as are necessary to disclose fully the extent of services provided to individuals under the State's Title XIX plan and to furnish information regarding any payments claimed for providing such services as the State Agency or Dept. of Health and Human Services may request.

I further agree to accept, as payment in full, the amount paid by the Medicaid program for those claims submitted for payment under that program, with the exception of authorized deductible, coinsurance, co-payment or similar cost-sharing charge.

SIGNATURE OF PHYSICIAN (OR SUPPLIER): I certify that the services listed above were medically indicated and necessary to the health of this patient and were personally furnished by me or my employee under my personal direction.

NOTICE: This is to certify that the foregoing information is true, accurate and complete. I understand that payment and satisfaction of this claim will be from Federal and State funds, and that any false claims, statements, or documents, or concealment of a material fact, may be prosecuted under applicable Federal or State laws.

According to the Paperwork Reduction Act of 1995, no persons are required to respond to a collection of information unless it displays a valid OMB control number. The valid OMB control number for this information collection is 0938-0999. The time required to complete this information collection is estimated to average 10 minutes per response, including the time to review instructions, search existing data resources, gather the data needed, and complete and review the information collection. If you have any comments concerning the accuracy of the time estimate(s) or suggestions for improving this form, please write to: CMS, Attn: PRA Reports Clearance Officer, 7500 Security Boulevard, Baltimore, Maryland 21244-1850. This address is for comments and/or suggestions only. DO NOT MAIL COMPLETED CLAIM FORMS TO THIS ADDRESS.

FIGURE 7–7: Back of the CMS-1500 form.

CONCLUSION

Accurate coding, claim form completion, and accounting are essential to the success and job gratification of any medical coder. It is a challenge to keep up with the ever-changing standards and codes. Joining or forming a network of and relationship with other coders and even third-party carrier representatives, provides the coder with a wealth of knowledge and the confidence to do the job right.

RESOURCE LIST

National Association of Insurances Commissioners (NAIC)
  www.naic.org

National Uniform Claim Committee
  www.nucc.org

Centers for Medicare & Medicaid
  www.cms.hhs.gov

Austrin, MS. (1999). *Managed Care Simplified: A Glossary of Terms.* Delmar Cengage Learning.

State of New Jersey
Medicaid Management Information Systems
  www.njmmis.com

State of California
Department of Health Care Service
  www.dhcs.ca.gov

New York State Department of Health
  www.health.state.ny.us

See the Davis*Plus* website for a full list of State Medical Societies.

Chapter Review Exercises

General Insurance

Complete the following questions.

1. The CMS-1500 claim form is designed to accommodate up to six different services. **True or False** (circle one)

2. A person can obtain health insurance in what three types of insurance policies?

   _____

   _____

   _____

3. The "Birthday Rule" is used to determine the order of benefits. **True or False** (circle one)

4. Always use the patient's social security number for identification when completing the claim form. **True or False** (circle one)

5. To the medical office, an individual is referred to as the patient. To third party insurance carrier that individual is known as the _____.

6. **Yes or No.** The state of _____ (insert your state here) has adopted the birthday rule.

Commercial Insurance Claim Completion

For the following exercises, you will fill out claims as if you were part of the insurance personnel for Dr. John Smith. You will find demographics, office fee schedule, and a blank CMS-1500 form in Appendix A. You will use this information along with Claim Completion scenarios to complete the claim form exercises.

7. Terri Jones

   Terri Jones is seen in Dr. Smith's office on April 3 of this year. She is covered under her husband's insurance that is through Aetna Life and Casualty. Her husband's name is Richard and he works for ABC Electric. His insurance I.D. number is 333-25-8888.

   Terri came to see Dr. Smith for headaches she has been suffering from. Dr. Smith performed an established patient, problem-focused exam, straightforward decision making office visit. He also took complete sinus x-rays.

   Terri's date of birth is 2-12-55. Her address is 730 West Grand, Anytown, USA 51111.

   Complete a CMS-1500 form using the information above, the appropriate patient registration information, superbill, and fee schedule in Appendix A.

8. John Doe

   John Doe is seen in the emergency room at Anytown Hospital on September 12, of this year.

   John was playing softball with his neighbors. He collided with another player and may have fractured his right arm.

   Dr. Smith performs an expanded problem-focused, low-complexity, emergency department visit and finds no fracture. The hospital will bill for the x-ray.

   Complete a CMS-1500 form using the information provided, the appropriate patient registration information, superbill, and fee schedule in Appendix A.

Medicare

Chapter Outline

VII. Remittance Advice

VIII. Conclusion

OBJECTIVES

- List the four different parts of Medicare coverage
- State the difference between Medicare Part A and B
- Name the annual deductible for Medicare Part B
- Identify who qualifies for Medicare coverage
- Explain the difference between a participating and a nonparticipating provider
- Give examples of Medicare covered and noncovered services
- State the reason behind the National Correct Coding Initiative implementation
- Be familiar with the Resource-Based Relative Value System (RBRVS)
- Demonstrate the completion of a claim form for Medicare
- Understand how Medicare coordinates benefits with other insurance coverage
- Become familiar with the Medicare remittance statement

MEDICAL ASSISTING COMPETENCIES

ABHES

  1i. conduct work within scope of education, training, and ability

  2d. serve as a liaison between Physician and others

  2g. use appropriate medical terminology

  2h. receive, organize, prioritize, and transmit information expediently

  3b. prepare and maintain medical records

  3e. locate resources and information for patients and employers

  3v. perform diagnostic coding

  3w. complete insurance forms

  3x. use physician fee schedule

  5a. determine the needs for documentation and reporting

  5b. document accurately

  5c. use appropriate guidelines when releasing records or information

  8b. implement current procedural terminology and ICD-9 coding

  8c. analyze and use current third-party guidelines for reimbursement

CAAHEP

  IV.P.3. Use medical terminology, pronouncing medical terms correctly, to communicate information, patient history, data and observations

  VII.C.1. Identify types of insurance plans

  VII.C.7. Describe guidelines for third-party claims

  VII.C.9. Describe guidelines for third-party claims

  VII.C.10. Discuss types of physician fee schedules

  VII.C.11. Describe the concept of RBRVS

  VII.P.2. Apply third-party guidelines

  VII.P.3. Complete insurance claim forms

  VIII.C.1. Describe how to use the most current procedural coding system

  VIII.C.3. Describe how to use the most current diagnostic coding classification system

  VIII.C.4. Describe how to use the most current HCPCS coding

  VIII.P.1. Perform procedural coding

  VIII.P.2. Perform diagnostic coding

  VIII.A.1. Work with physician to achieve the maximum reimbursement

KEY TERMS

Advanced Beneficiary Notice

American National Standards Institute (ANSI)

Coordination of Benefits Agreement (COBA)

Coordination of Benefits Contractor (COBC)

Crossover Claims

Established Provider Disclosure Report

Geographic Practice Cost Index (GPCI)

Local Coverage Determination (LCD)

Medicare Administrative Contractors (MACs)

Medicare Coverage Advisory Committee (MCAC)

Medicare Physician Fee Schedule

Medicare Summary Notice (MSN)

MediGap

Mutually Exclusive Edits

National Correct Coding Initiative (NCCI)

National Coverage Determination

Participating Agreement

Relative Value Unit (RVU)

Remittance Advice (RA)

Resource-Based Relative Value System (RBRVS)

■ INTRODUCTION

The Medicare program began in 1965 when the Social Security Act was signed into law by President Lyndon Johnson and became effective July 1, 1966. Originally designed as an insurance supplement for individuals 65 years old and older, Congress approved additional coverage for disabled persons under age 65 and people with end-stage renal disease (ESRD) in 1973.

In addition, individuals entitled to monthly disability benefits for 24 consecutive months under the Social Security or Railroad Retirement program qualify for Medicare eligibility. If a disabled employee is covered by an employee group health plan (EGHP) from an employer with 100 or more employees, that individual has primary coverage from his or her employer. Medicare is secondary unless that employee chooses to have Medicare as primary insurance. Patients with ESRD who require kidney dialysis or a kidney transplant may become Medicare eligible after a 3-month waiting period or after a 12-month waiting period if covered by an EGHP.

! KEY TERM

MEDICARE ADMINISTRATIVE CONTRACTORS (MACs)—A company appointed and created to process all Medicare claims for a designated jurisdiction.

All of this can be confusing for the patient, who is called the *"beneficiary"* under Medicare rules. Because of the stipulations for Medicare eligibility, the medical coder may need to determine which payer is considered the primary payer. It is critical that there is always current insurance information and copies of a patient's insurance cards in the patient's files when deciphering the order of benefits for each patient.

The Centers for Medicare & Medicaid Services (CMS) makes all the rules, regulations, and health-related policies governing the Medicare program. As required by section 911 of the Medicare Prescription Drug, Improvement, and Modernization Act (MMA) of 2003, CMS is in the process of replacing its current claims payment contractors (fiscal intermediaries and carriers) with new contract entities called Medicare Administrative Contractors (MACs). MACs were established to centralize and simplify the processing of all Medicare claims nationwide and each MAC will serve a designated jurisdiction. Table 8–1 lists the areas serviced in each jurisdiction.

TABLE 8–1:   MACs by Jurisdiction

Jurisdiction	States Included in Jurisdiction	Contractor
J1	American Samoa, California, Guam, Hawaii, Nevada, and Northern Mariana Islands	Palmetto GBA
J2	Alaska, Idaho, Oregon, and Washington	National Heritage Insurance Corp
J3	Arizona, Montana, North Dakota, South Dakota, Utah, and Wyoming	Noridian Administrative Services
J4	Colorado, New Mexico, Oklahoma, and Texas	TrailBlazer Enterprise
J5	Iowa, Kansas, Missouri, and Nebraska	Wisconsin Physicians Service Health Insurance
J6	Illinois, Minnesota, and Wisconsin	Noridian Administrative Services under protest, still pending
J7	Arkansas, Louisiana, and Mississippi	Pinnacle Business Solutions, Inc. under protest, still pending
J8	Indiana and Michigan	National Government Services under protest, still pending
J9	Florida, Puerto Rico, and U.S. Virgin Islands	First Coast Service Options, Inc.
J10	Alabama, Georgia, and Tennessee	Cahaba Government Benefit Government Administrator, LLC
J11	North Carolina, South Carolina, Virginia and West Virginia	Palmetto Government Benefit Government Administrator, LLC under protest, still pending
J12	Delaware, District of Columbia, Maryland, New Jersey, and Pennsylvania	Highmark Medicare Services, Inc.
J13	Connecticut and New York	National Government Services, Inc.
J14	Maine, Massachusetts, New Hampshire, Rhode Island, and Vermont	National Heritage Insurance Corp
J15	Kentucky and Ohio	Highmark Medicare Services under protest, still pending

MEDICARE COVERAGE AND ELIGIBILITY

Parts of Medicare

The Medicare program consists of four elements: A, B, C, and D. Part A, Hospital Insurance, and Part B, Medical Insurance, were established in the original legislation. Part A is financed through Social Security (FICA) tax paid by all workers and their employers and covers inpatient care, care in skilled nursing facilities, home health care, and hospice. Most individuals do not pay a monthly Part A premium because they or a spouse has 40 or more quarters of Medicare-covered employment (FICA). If the patient is entitled to benefits under Social Security or Railroad Retirement systems, there is no monthly premium for Medicare Part A.

Part B is offered to all individuals who are eligible for Part A. This coverage also can be purchased by most individuals age 65 and older who do not qualify for Part A coverage. The Part B premium is deducted from the beneficiary's Social Security check and is revised annually. Part B covers doctors' services, outpatient hospital services, diagnostic tests, durable medical equipment, ambulance services, and outpatient physical therapy. Part B also covers most of the vaccines that would be prescribed to a Medicare beneficiary such as pneumococcal, influenza, and hepatitis B, as well as other toxoids such as tetanus, when directly related to treatment.

Part C also known as Medicare Advantage Plans are alternative heath plans offered by private insurance companies. The insurance companies and their plans must be approved by Medicare and are considered part of the Medicare program. A Part C plan is a combination of Part A (for hospital) and Part B (for medical). Part C plans must offer all Part A and Medicare Part B benefits and at least all of the medically necessary services offered by the original Medicare plan. Most of the plans offer prescription drug coverage otherwise called Medicare Part D. A Medicare Advantage Plan can charge different copayments, coinsurance, and deductibles and also may offer extra benefits, such as vision, hearing, dental, and wellness programs. Most of these plans, like Health Maintenance Organiztions (HMOs) have a network of doctors. The patient's identification card will indicate what type of Medicare coverage they have. The medical coder must be sure to copy every patient's Medicare identification card and verify that the provider participates with the patient's plan. There are five different Part C advantage plans:

■ Preferred Provider Organization (PPO) Plans are types of managed care programs that offer health-care coverage at a fixed rate and typically from a network of participating providers.

■ Health Maintenance Organization (HMO) Plans are types of managed care programs that offer health-care coverage at a fixed rate and typically from a network of participating providers.

■ Private Fee for Service (PFFS) Plans are a traditional method of insurance in which the health-care provider is paid for each service rendered.

■ Medical Savings (MSA) Plans are options in which Medicare deposits an amount each year for the covered individual. The account acts like a bank account and the money deposited is used to cover health-care costs. A Medical Savings Plan has a high deductible. Any money left in the account at the end of the year is added to the next year's deposit.

■ Special Needs Plans (SNP) offer coverage for individuals who are chronically ill and living in institutions such as nursing homes or for individuals with other special needs.

Part D is Prescription Drug Coverage, and a copy of the patient's Part D drug plan identification card should be obtained and kept on file along with the patient's Medicare Health Insurance ID card. This section of Medicare coverage is intended to lower prescription drug costs for individuals and protect against higher costs in the future. Starting January 1, 2006, new Medicare prescription drug coverage was made available to everyone with Medicare. All Medicare beneficiaries are eligible for this coverage, although most are required to pay a monthly premium. Technically, Part D coverage is insurance, and private companies provide the coverage. Beneficiaries choose a specified drug plan and pay a monthly premium, as indicated by the rules of the insurance plan. Like other insurance, if a beneficiary decides not to enroll in a drug plan when he or she is first-eligible, he or she may pay a penalty when joining later.

Part D carriers and insurance plans will vary from state to state. Each carrier has a list of covered drugs and vaccines, called a formulary list. Certain vaccines that are not covered under Medicare Part B, will need to be submitted to the patient's Part D plan. Starting in 2008, CMS requires all Part D plans' formularies contain all commercially available vaccines, unless they are covered by Part B, to provide the beneficiaries with better access to preventive care.

Medicare Cards and Identification Numbers

Every person eligible for Medicare has a red, white, and blue card (Fig. 8–1) that indicates the coverage the beneficiary has and the effective dates of that coverage.

The cards may look slightly different depending on the specifics of the patient's Medicare coverage. For example, if the patient has joined a Medicare Part C health plan, he or she will use a card from that plan instead of the card shown in Figure 8–1.

The patient's ID number is called a Health Insurance Claim Number (HICN). It is usually nine numbers with a one- or two-letter suffix (Table 8–2). The health insurance claim number is usually the Social Security number of the person who has been employed and has paid into FICA. In the case of

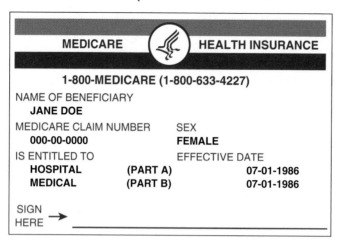

FIGURE 8–1: Sample Medicare card.

a married couple, the numbers may be the same if only one spouse had been employed and paid into FICA, but the letter suffix will be different. For example, if a man worked for a company and his wife did not work outside the home, the couple's Medicare ID cards would have his social security number on them. The husband's card would have an "A" suffix after his social security number to represent the wage earner. The wife's card would have her husband's social security number and a "B" suffix after the number to indicate she is the spouse of the wage earner. For the most part, the medical coder will see A, B, and D only. The suffixes mean that each patient has a unique number and card.

A patient with a six-digit HCIN indicates a Railroad Retiree. Some Railroad Retiree numbers begin with a one- or two-letter prefix followed by the Social Security number.

Coverage Determination

As discussed, Medicare covers items and services that are considered reasonable and necessary for the diagnosis or treatment of an illness or injury. On an as needed basis, national coverage determinations (NCDs) are made and can even allow for public participation. In some cases, CMS research will

TABLE 8–2:   Medicare ID Suffix Meanings

Suffix	Meaning
A	Wage earner (Retirement)
B	Wife of wage earner
C	Child
D	Widow (has been B, when spouse dies suffix becomes D)
E	Mother (widow)
F1	Parent or Legal Guardian
J1	Receiving special age 72 benefits
K1	Receiving wife's special age 72 benefits through her husband
M	No monthly Social Security benefits, but has enrolled for Part B only
T	No monthly Social Security benefits, but has enrolled for Part A and possibly Part B
W	Disabled widow or widower

include an outside technology review and/or consultation with the Medicare Coverage Advisory Committee (MCAC). The 120 appointed committee members are from various health care–related services, clinical and administrative medicine, biological and physical sciences, health-care management, and medical ethics. MCAC may be used to advise the Secretary of Health and Human Services on national coverage determinations.

❗ KEY TERMS

NATIONAL COVERAGE DETERMINATION—The process by which a procedure or services is determined to be covered by Medicare nationwide.

MEDICARE COVERAGE ADVISORY COMMITTEE (MCAC)—A group assigned to review or determine Medicare coverage policies.

In the absence of a national coverage policy, a service or supply may be covered at the discretion of the Medicare Administrative Contractors (MACs) based on a Local Coverage Determination (LCD), formerly referred to as Local Medical Review Policies (LMRPs). A decision to cover a certain service or supply not normally covered, but effects the beneficiaries residing in their jurisdiction can be made. That decision or exception to the rule is called a LCD and applies only to the beneficiaries residing in that particular jurisdiction.

❗ KEY TERM

LOCAL COVERAGE DETERMINATION (LCD)—The process by which a procedure or services is determined to be covered by Medicare in a particular jurisdiction. Formerly known as Local Medical Review Policies (LMRPs).

The national reviews, policies, and determinations can be found on the CMS website (www.cms.hhs.gov). The LCDs will only be found on a MAC website. It is extremely important for every medical coder to have knowledge of and/or be aware of policies and changes pertinent to their health-care specialty.

Medicare Covered Services

Medicare pays for most services, but some services may be considered not medically necessary and are not covered, such as cosmetic or experimental procedures. "Medical necessity" can be a difficult concept but it is very important that the medical coder understand it to help the patient. Only services or items needed for treatment or diagnosis of a condition are considered "medically necessary" under Medicare rules. Routine or preventive care is not always considered medically necessary and Medicare limits the coverage of those services. The following list shows *covered* preventive services and their limitations:

- Abdominal aortic aneurysm screening—one time screening
- Bone mass measurement—every 2 years
- Cardiovascular screenings—every 5 years
- Colorectal cancer screenings:
    - Fecal occult blood test—every year
    - Flexible sigmoidoscopy—every 4 years, then every 10 years unless high risk
    - Screening colonoscopy—every 10 years unless high risk
    - Barium enema—every 4 years unless high risk
- Diabetes screening—covered if patient has hypertension, high triglycerides/cholesterol levels, obesity, or history of high blood sugar
- Diabetes self-management training
- Flu shots, hepatitis B shots, pneumococcal shots
- Glaucoma tests

- Mammograms—every year
- Medical nutrition therapy services—if patient has diabetes or kidney disease
- Pap test and pelvic examinations—every 2 years, unless high risk, then every year
- Physical examination—one-time "Welcome to Medicare" physical examination and review of the patient's health, education and counseling about preventive care, including screenings, shots, referrals for other care if needed (must take place within first 6 months of Medicare eligibility)
- Prostate cancer screenings
- Smoking cessation counseling

Medicare Noncovered Services

Some of the services that **Medicare does not cover** include the following:

- Acupuncture
- Limited chiropractic services
- Cosmetic surgery
- Dental care
- Routine eye examinations and glasses except after cataract surgery
- Routine foot care
- Laboratory tests for screening purposes except the ones previously listed
- Orthopedic shoes
- Routine physical examinations
- Prescription drugs—covered under Medicare Part D only
- Shots to prevent illness except the ones previously listed
- Syringes or insulin in most cases—may be covered under Part D

A medical coder should always check the Medicare fee schedule to confirm whether or not the service is covered under Medicare rules. The CPT code/HCPCS codes will not be listed if the service is not covered by Medicare.

Advance Beneficiary Notice

A doctor who expects or suspects Medicare may not cover a procedure must notify the patient before rendering the service. The medical coder may be responsible for obtaining a signed **Advance Beneficiary Notice (ABN)** (Fig. 8–2) stating the patient is aware the service may not be covered by Medicare and that the patient will be held financially responsible for the expense. A claim may be submitted to Medicare in case the procedure will be considered a covered service, or the patient may need a denial from Medicare before supplemental insurance considers making a payment toward the service. If written notice is given before the service and the patient signs an agreement to pay for the service, he or she is held liable for the full charge.

! KEY TERM

ADVANCE BENEFICIARY NOTICE—A form created to alert a patient with Medicare when a procedure or service may not be covered by Medicare. When signed by the patient, it documents that the patient understands and accepts financial responsibility for the service rendered.

■ MEDICARE PROVIDERS

Participating Agreement

Under the Deficit Reduction Act of 1984 (DEFRA), a participating (par) physician program was established. A physician must decide whether or not to participate in the Medicare program. A par physician is one who voluntarily enters into an agreement to accept assignment for all services provided to Medicare patients. The agreement is valid for the 12-month period beginning January 1 of

(A) Notifier(s):
(B) Patient Name: **(C) Identification Number:**

ADVANCE BENEFICIARY NOTICE OF NONCOVERAGE (ABN)

<u>*NOTE:*</u> If Medicare doesn't pay for **(D)**_____ below, you may have to pay.

Medicare does not pay for everything, even some care that you or your health care provider have good reason to think you need. We expect Medicare may not pay for the **(D)**_____ below.

(D)_____	(E) Reason Medicare May Not Pay:	(F) Estimated Cost:

WHAT YOU NEED TO DO NOW:

- Read this notice, so you can make an informed decision about your care.
- Ask us any questions that you may have after you finish reading.
- Choose an option below about whether to receive the **(D)**_____ listed above.
    Note: If you choose Option 1 or 2, we may help you to use any other insurance that you might have, but Medicare cannot require us to do this.

(G) OPTIONS: **Check only one box. We cannot choose a box for you.**

☐ **OPTION 1.** I want the **(D)**_____ listed above. You may ask to be paid now, but I also want Medicare billed for an official decision on payment, which is sent to me on a Medicare Summary Notice (MSN). I understand that if Medicare doesn't pay, I am responsible for payment, but **I can appeal to Medicare** by following the directions on the MSN. If Medicare does pay, you will refund any payments I made to you, less co-pays or deductibles.

☐ **OPTION 2.** I want the **(D)**_____ listed above, but do not bill Medicare. You may ask to be paid now as I am responsible for payment. **I cannot appeal if Medicare is not billed.**

☐ **OPTION 3.** I don't want the **(D)**_____ listed above. I understand with this choice I am **not** responsible for payment, and **I cannot appeal to see if Medicare would pay.**

(H) Additional Information:

This notice gives our opinion, not an official Medicare decision. If you have other questions on this notice or Medicare billing, call **1-800-MEDICARE** (1-800-633-4227/**TTY**: 1-877-486-2048). Signing below means that you have received and understand this notice. You also receive a copy.

(I) Signature:	(J) Date

Form CMS-R-131 (03/08)   Form Approved OMB No. 0938-0566

FIGURE 8–2: Advance Beneficiary Notice.

a particular year. A provider may change his or her participating (par) status only during the November enrollment period every year. The agreement is renewed automatically unless before January 1 of any year the provider gives written notice that he or she wishes to terminate the agreement at the end of the current term. A new physician may file a par agreement with Medicare within 90 days after the participant is newly licensed to practice medicine or another health-care profession.

PARTICIPATING AGREEMENT—The agreement made by a health-care provider to accept Medicare's allowed amount as payment in full for any procedure or service billed.

A participating (par) doctor agreement applies to all services in all localities and under all names and identification numbers under which the physician does business. Under this agreement, the par physician cannot collect more than the applicable deductible and coinsurance for any covered service.

The par doctor receives more benefits from Medicare than a nonparticipating provider including the following:

■ All crossover/MediGap (secondary insurance) claims are sent automatically to the next insurance company.

■ Payment from Medicare will go directly to the physician.

■ 5% more payment.

The majority of all health-care providers participate in the Medicare program.

Assignment of Benefits Under Medicare

As discussed in Chapter 7, a provider who accepts assignment will be reimbursed directly from Medicare for covered services. The provider who accepts assignment also agrees to accept Medicare's approved amount as payment in full for rendered services. In most cases, Medicare will pay the provider 80% of the approved amount for a service. The patient is then responsible for the 20% left. Even though a patient may be responsible for a portion of that approved amount, it is advisable not to collect for covered services until the Medicare remittance notice is received showing the collectable amounts.

Under Medicare guidelines, the par doctor automatically accepts assignment. A non-par doctor must decide whether to accept assignment on each claim. Box 27 on the CMS-1500 must be checked yes or no to indicate whether or not the non-par doctor accepts assignment for the services included on each claim form. If the provider does not accept assignment, the Medicare payment goes directly to the patient.

MEDICARE PHYSICIAN FEE SCHEDULE (MPFS) or ESTABLISHED PROVIDER DISCLOSURE REPORT—A report generated and sent by Medicare to health-care providers listing the reimbursement amounts for every Medicare covered service.

Medicare provides the par or non-par doctor with a fee schedule indicating the reimbursement for all covered services. Figure 8–3 shows a copy of the **Medicare Physician Fee Schedule (MPFS)**, also known as the **Established Provider Disclosure Report**. This report is sent to all providers annually and is available on the Medicare carrier/contractor's website. The MPFS illustrates what the par doctor will be reimbursed for every covered service (HCPCS and CPT codes). It also illustrates what the non-par doctor may charge and will be reimbursed.

Nonparticipating physicians who do not accept assignment on a Medicare claim are limited in the amount they can charge a patient for a covered service. A non-par physician may charge, at most, 115% of the limiting charge amount for non-par physicians indicated on the MPFS (see Fig. 8–3). All Medicare carriers/contractors are required by CMS to monitor nonparticipating physicians for compliance with Medicare limiting charges. Physicians who knowingly, willfully, and repeatedly charge more than these amounts are subject to sanctions.

■ FEES AND COSTS RELATED TO MEDICARE SERVICES

The Resource-Based Relative Value System

Approved amounts for rendered services under Medicare Part B are based on a national fee schedule (see Fig. 8–3). This fee schedule is developed using the **Resource-Based Relative Value System**, or

2009 Medicare Physician's Fee Schedule—New Jersey Locality 01			
PROC CODE	PAR FEE	NON PAR FEE	LC
45380	$515.14	$489.38	$562.79
45380	$279.08	$265.13	$304.90
45381	$501.77	$476.68	$548.18
45381	$263.93	$250.73	$288.34
45382	$679.48	$645.51	$742.34
45382	$356.16	$388.35	$389.10
45383	$609.88	$579.39	$666.30
45383	$357.87	$339.98	$390.98
45384	$504.12	$478.91	$550.75
45384	$289.31	$274.84	$316.07
45385	$579.03	$550.08	$632.59
45385	$331.01	$314.46	$361.63
45386	$726.27	$689.96	$793.45
45386	$284.70	$270.41	$311.04
45387	$371.35	$352.78	$405.70
45391	$320.79	$304.75	$350.46
45392	$403.97	$383.77	$441.34
45395	$1,998.48	$1.898.56	$2,183.34
45397	$2,156.55	$2,048.72	$2,356.03
45400	$1,150.03	$1,092.53	$1,256.41
45402	$1,535.50	$1,458.73	$1,677.54
45500	$510.56	$485.03	$557.78
45505	$561.58	$533.50	$613.53
45520	$134.59	$127.86	$147.04
45520	$39.81	$37.82	$43.49
45540	$1,059.50	$1,006.53	$1,157.51
45541	$915.42	$869.65	$1,000.10
45550	$1,458.72	$1,385.78	$1,593.65
45560	$725.32	$689.05	$792.41
45562	$1,110.82	$1,055.28	$1,213.57
45563	$1,610.61	$1,530.08	$1,759.59
45800	$1,244.11	$1,181.90	$1,359.19
45805	$1,402.02	$1,331.92	$1,531.71
45820	$1,231.14	$1,169.58	$1,345.02
45825	$1,488.80	$1,414.36	$1,626.51
45900	$197.55	$187.67	$215.82
45905	$169.29	$160.83	$184.95
45910	$199.74	$189.75	$218.21
45915	$318.56	$302.63	$348.02
45915	$223.54	$212.17	$244.00
45990	$109.57	$104.09	$119.70
46020	$255.66	$242.88	$279.31
46020	$221.99	$210.89	$242.52

PAR FEE = the allowance for participating providers; NON PAR FEE = the allowance for nonparticipating providers. The amount is 95% of the participating provider. LC = limiting charge. The maximum amount that nonparticipating providers may bill their Medicare patients on nonassigned claims. The limiting charge is 115% of the nonparticipating allowance.

All Current Procedural Terminology (CPT) codes and descriptors are copyrighted 2008 by the American Medical Association.

FIGURE 8-3: 2009 Medicare Physician's Fee Schedule—New Jersey Locality 01.

RBRVS. RBRVS originated from a nationwide study performed by statisticians and researchers from Harvard University over a 3-year period between 1985 and 1988. Its purpose was to reveal the true cost of each procedure or service performed in a medical office or facility. The results of the study were submitted to Health Care Financing Administration (HCFA, now CMS) to be used as the Medicare payment system.

RESOURCE-BASED RELATIVE VALUE SYSTEM (RBRVS)—A nationwide system developed to establish the true cost of any given procedure, service, or supply.

Today, the majority of all third-party carriers use the national fee schedule that was created using RBRVS. This fee schedule is reviewed and updated by the Relative Value Update Committee (the RUC). Members of the RUC are appointed by national medical societies, the American Medical Association (AMA), the CPT Editorial Panel, and the American Osteopathic Association. The committee determines a value for each procedure code by using a formula (see Figs. 8–3 and 8–4) to assign a dollar value to each physician service. This formula is based on three elements:

1. The **Relative Value Unit (RVU)** (Fig. 8–5) derives from three factors:

   a. The physician work effort includes the physician's time, effort, skill, and judgment used to perform the service

   b. Practice expense or overhead (PE) includes expenses related to supplies, equipment, the cost of office lease or rent, and the salary of the physician's staff

   c. Malpractice premiums (MP) to cover the liability to perform each service

2. The **Geographic Practice Cost Index (GPCI)** reflects the practice locality (Fig. 8–6).

3. The **Conversion Factor (CF)** is a single national monetary number used to convert the RVUs and GPCIs into payment amounts.

RELATIVE VALUE UNIT (RVU)—Basic unit of value given to every procedure code to determine a dollar value for the procedure.

GEOGRAPHIC PRACTICE COST INDEX (GPCI)—Unit of measurement assigned to each procedure code to reflect the practice overhead by the practice locality.

All three factors are updated regularly by the RUC. The conversion factor is updated every year to adjust fees for inflation and changes in medical practice. The RVUs are updated every 5 years, and the GPCIs are updated every 3 years. Because of these frequent updates, a health-care provider receives a new fee schedule for the upcoming calendar year in November.

Calculating Fees Using RBRVS

The 2010 CF is $36.0846 for all procedures. The annual conversion factor dictates the reimbursement of every medical service provided each year. The RVUs, GPCIs, and the Conversion Factor are converted into payments using the formula in Figure 8–4. This formula is performed on every CPT and HCPCS code and the results are published as the Medicare Fee Schedule or Provider Disclosure Report (see Fig. 8–3).

```
Work RVU _____      X Work GPCI _____        = _____
Expense RVU _____     X Expense GPCI _____       = _____
Malpractice RVU _____    X Malpractice GPCI _____      = _____
                                                    Total = _____

                                                         X  $36.0846
                                                         = _____
```

FIGURE 8–4: Medicare's conversion factor formula.

2009 National Physician Fee Schedule Relative Value File
CPT codes and descriptions only are copyright 2008 American Medical Association. All Rights Reserved. Applicable FARS/DFARS Apply.
Dental codes (D codes) are copyright 2002 American Dental Association. All Rights Reserved.

RELEASED 11/1/2008

HCPCS	Mod	Description	Transitioned non-FAC PE RVU	Transitioned non-FAC NA indicator	Fully implemented non-FAC PE RVU	Fully implemented facility PE RVU	MP RVU	GLOB days	Conv factor
47420....	....	Incision of bile duct	8.87	NA	8.88	8.88	2.63	090	36.0666
47425....	....	Incision of bile duct	8.92	NA	8.93	8.93	2.62	090	36.0666
47460....	....	Incise bile duct sphincter	9.16	NA	9.39	9.39	2.21	090	36.0666
47480....	....	Incision of gallbladder	6.61	NA	6.83	6.83	1.42	090	36.0666
47490....	....	Incision of gallbladder	5.59	NA	5.58	5.58	0.43	090	36.0666
47500....	....	Injection for liver x-rays	0.75	NA	0.79	0.79	0.12	000	36.0666
47505....	....	Injection for liver x-rays	0.29	NA	0.31	0.31	0.04	000	36.0666
47510....	....	Insert catheter, bile duct	4.94	NA	4.90	4.90	0.46	090	36.0666
47511....	....	Insert bile duct drain	5.40	NA	5.49	5.49	0.62	090	36.0666
47525....	....	Change bile duct catheter	13.84		13.38	1.29	0.33	010	36.0666
47530....	....	Revise/reinsert bile tube	31.45		30.57	3.68	0.37	090	36.0666
47550....	....	Bile duct endoscopy add-on	0.90	NA	0.85	0.85	0.40	ZZZ	36.0666
47552....	....	Biliary endoscopy thru skin	2.67	NA	2.76	2.76	0.42	000	36.0666
47553....	....	Biliary endoscopy thru skin	2.39	NA	2.50	2.50	0.37	000	36.0666
47554....	....	Biliary endoscopy thru skin	3.46	NA	3.49	3.49	0.96	000	36.0666
47555....	....	Biliary endoscopy thru skin	2.92	NA	3.06	3.06	0.45	000	36.0666
47556....	....	Biliary endoscopy thru skin	3.30	NA	3.46	3.46	0.50	000	36.0666
47560....	....	Laparoscopy w/cholangio	1.45	NA	1.37	1.37	0.65	000	36.0666
47561....	....	Laparo w/cholangio/biopsy	1.73	NA	1.66	1.66	0.66	000	36.0666
47562....	....	Laparoscopic cholecystectomy	5.32	NA	5.42	5.42	1.46	090	36.0666
47563....	....	Laparo cholecystectomy/graph	5.26	NA	5.24	5.24	1.58	090	36.0666
47564....	....	Laparo cholecystectomy/explr	5.72	NA	5.63	5.63	1.89	090	36.0666
47570....	....	Laparo cholecystoenterostomy	5.26	NA	5.21	5.21	1.65	090	36.0666
47579....	....	Laparoscope proc, biliary	0.00		0.00	0.00	0.00	YYY	36.0666
47600....	....	Removal of gallbladder	7.14	NA	7.46	7.46	1.80	090	36.0666
47605....	....	Removal of gallbladder	6.58	NA	6.60	6.60	1.95	090	36.0666
47610....	....	Removal of gallbladder	7.98	NA	7.98	7.98	2.49	090	36.0666
47612....	....	Removal of gallbladder	8.01	NA	8.04	8.04	2.48	090	36.0666
47620....	....	Removal of gallbladder	8.61	NA	8.61	8.61	2.74	090	36.0666
47630....	....	Remove bile duct stone	5.02	NA	5.05	5.05	0.65	090	36.0666
47700....	....	Exploration of bile ducts	7.62	NA	7.67	7.67	2.07	090	36.0666
47701....	....	Bile duct revision	12.60	NA	12.93	12.93	3.68	090	36.0666
47711....	....	Excision of bile duct tumor	10.04	NA	10.05	10.05	3.05	090	36.0666
47712....	....	Excision of bile duct tumor	12.24	NA	12.14	12.14	3.93	090	36.0666
47715....	....	Excision of bile duct cyst	8.73	NA	8.81	8.81	2.49	090	36.0666
47720....	....	Fuse gallbladder and bowel	7.87	NA	7.98	7.98	2.11	090	36.0666

FIGURE 8-5: Relative Value Units by procedure code.

Costs for Patients

Both Part A and Part B require deductible and coinsurance amounts to be paid by the beneficiary or the supplemental insurance the beneficiary may carry. The patient's costs for Part B services will vary depending on the type of plan, original Medicare or a Medicare Advantage plan they choose.

Deductibles and Coinsurance for Part A

Part A deductibles change every year. In 2010, the Part A deductible is $1100 per benefit period. Medicare will pay all charges for covered hospital services during the first 60 days of a benefit period except for the deductible.

A *benefit period* begins the first day the patient goes into the hospital or skilled nursing facility (SNF) and ends when the patient has not received inpatient hospital or SNF care for 60 days in row. If the patient goes into the hospital or SNF after one benefit period has ended, a new benefit period begins and the patient will have to pay the deductible again. There is no limit to the number of benefit periods a patient can have.

For the 61st through the 90th day of an inpatient stay, Part A pays for all covered services except for the coinsurance of $275.00 a day. The patient or his or her supplemental insurance is responsible for the coinsurance.

Under Part A, the patient also has 60 lifetime reserve days for inpatient hospital care. Those days may be used whenever the patient needs more than 90 days of inpatient hospital stay in a benefit period. When a reserve day is used, Part A pays for all covered services except for the coinsurance of $550.00 a day. Again, the coinsurance is the patient's or his or her supplemental insurance's responsibility.

2009 Geographic Practice Cost Indices (GPCIs) by State and Medicare Locality***

Contractor	Locality	Locality name	Work** GPCI	PE GPCI	MP GPCI
00510......	00	Alabama	1.000	0.853	0.496
00831......	01	Alaska	1.500	1.090	0.646
03102......	00	Arizona	1.000	0.957	0.822
00520......	13	Arkansas	1.000	0.846	0.446
01192......	26	Anaheim/Santa Ana, CA	1.034	1.269	0.811
01192......	18	Los Angeles, CA	1.041	1.225	0.804
01102......	03	Marin/Napa/Solano, CA	1.034	1.265	0.432
01102......	07	Oakland/Berkeley, CA	1.053	1.286	0.425
01102......	05	San Francisco, CA	1.059	1.441	0.414
01102......	06	San Mateo, CA	1.072	1.433	0.394
01102......	09	Santa Clara, CA	1.083	1.294	0.377
01192......	17	Ventura, CA	1.027	1.265	0.766
01102......	99	Rest of California*	1.007	1.058	0.549
01192......	99	Rest of California*	1.007	1.058	0.549
04102......	01	Colorado	1.000	0.992	0.641
13102......	00	Connecticut	1.038	1.185	0.980
12202......	01	DC + MD/VA Suburbs	1.047	1.218	1.032
12102......	01	Delaware	1.011	1.046	0.678
00590......	03	Fort Lauderdale, FL	1.000	1.018	2.250
00590......	04	Miami, FL	1.000	1.069	3.167
00590......	99	Rest of Florida	1.000	0.939	1.724
00511......	01	Atlanta, GA	1.009	1.014	0.836
00511......	99	Rest of Georgia	1.000	0.883	0.829
01202......	01	Hawaii/Guam	1.000	1.161	0.665
05130......	00	Idaho	1.000	0.883	0.546
00952......	16	Chicago, IL	1.025	1.080	1.940
00952......	12	East St. Louis, IL	1.000	0.919	1.793
00952......	15	Suburban Chicago, IL	1.017	1.068	1.629
00952......	99	Rest of Illinois	1.000	0.880	1.219
00630......	00	Indiana	1.000	0.918	0.599
05102......	00	Iowa	1.000	0.870	0.434
05202......	00	Kansas	1.000	0.882	0.557
00660......	00	Kentucky	1.000	0.860	0.652
00528......	01	New Orleans, LA	1.000	1.044	0.956
00528......	99	Rest of Louisiana	1.000	0.878	0.892
31142......	03	Southern Maine	1.000	1.025	0.492
31142......	99	Rest of Maine	1.000	0.893	0.492
12302......	01	Baltimore/Surr. Cntys, MD	1.012	1.057	1.086
12302......	99	Rest of Maryland	1.000	0.982	0.874
31143......	01	Metropolitan Boston	1.029	1.291	0.764
31143......	99	Rest of Massachusetts	1.007	1.106	0.764
00953......	01	Detroit, MI	1.036	1.040	1.906

*Indicates multiple contractors.
**2009 work GPCI reflects the 1.000 floor (1.500 floor in Alaska).
***2009 GPCIs are the second year of the update transition and reflect the fully implemented updated GPCIs.

FIGURE 8–6: The 2008 Geographic Practice Cost Indices by state and Medicare.

If a patient receives SNF care, he or she pays $0 for the first 20 days of each benefit period, $137.50 per day for days 21 through 100 days, and the patient is responsible for every day after day 100 in a benefit period. After being used, the reserve days are not renewed.

Deductibles and Coinsurance for Part B

The Part B annual deductible in 2010 is $155.00. After the patient meets the deductible, Part B generally pays 80% of the Medicare-approved amount for covered services the patient receives the rest of the year. The patient or his or her supplemental insurance is responsible for the other 20%.

Medicare Benefits Payable in Full

Medicare provides benefits for certain Part B procedures at 100% rather than the standard 80/20 copayment. Those procedures covered include the following:

1. *Influenza, pneumococcal, and hepatitis B vaccinations.* These vaccinations also are not subject to the annual deductible.

2. *Clinical laboratory charges* are paid on a separate fee schedule. Deductibles and coinsurance do not apply these services.

3. *Used durable medical equipment (DME),* if the deductible has already been met for DME. To be eligible for 100% payment, the DME must be billed at least 25% lower than the Medicare allowance for the new item and the DME must be warranted.

MEDICARE CLAIMS

Part of the Health Insurance Portabliltiy and Accountability Act (HIPAA) legislation was designed to "simplify" claim form completion by establishing one set of guidelines for claim completion that would apply to every third-party payer. Although close, not every payer requires the same information on the claim form. Table 8–3 instructs the medical coder, box by box, what is required for Medicare. These completion instructions change and the medical coder can verify the current completion instructions with Medicare at: http://www.cms.hhs.gov/manuals/downloads/clm104c26.pdf.

National Correct Coding Initiative

CMS developed the **National Correct Coding Initiative (NCCI)** to promote correct coding methods nationwide and to prevent improper payment when incorrect code combinations are used. Whenever a single code exists that describes the service rendered, multiple codes should not be used. CMS developed its coding policies based on CPT coding guidelines and a review of standard medical and surgical practices. CMS updates and publishes the coding policies in the National Correct Coding Initiative Coding Policy Manual annually.

The Medicare carriers use the Coding Policy Manual to explain the rationale for NCCI edits. The NCCI contains two edit tables. Both tables include pairs of codes that should not be billed together.

KEY TERM

NATIONAL CORRECT CODING INITIATIVE (NCCI)—The Medicare program designed to prevent improper coding procedures, which result in incorrect Medicare payments.

The Column One/Column Two Correct Coding Edits Table

The codes in column 1 are called comprehensive codes and are considered to be the main procedure performed. Column 2 codes are called component codes (Table 8–4). They are considered to be an integral part of the column 1 codes. The component code in most cases, should not be reported when a comprehensive code is billed. The column 1, comprehensive codes have a much higher value and will receive a higher reimbursement than the column 2 component codes.

If the two codes of a code pair edit are billed together for the same date of service without an appropriate modifier, just the column 1 code is paid. Payment of both codes may be considered only if documentation warrants. Code 26011 is the code for the complicated drainage of an abscessed finger. Services performed to carry out the drainage procedure such as an application of a cast, a bladder catheter, nerve blocks, or the use of an operating microscope should not be billed for separately; they are included with the procedure code 26011.

KEY TERM

MUTUALLY EXCLUSIVE EDITS—Edits placed on pairs of codes (procedures) that cannot reasonably be performed together based on their definitions or their anatomy.

The Mutually Exclusive Edits Table

The **Mutually Exclusive Edits** Table (Table 8–5) indicates the procedures or services with the higher value codes in column 2. They are the nonpayable procedure or service when reported with the column 1 code. The mutually exclusive edit table contains pairs of codes (procedures) that cannot reasonably be performed together based on their definitions or their anatomy. For example, 40650 is a full thickness (layered) repair of only the vermilion (external) portion of the lip. The 40650 series of codes can

TABLE 8–3:   Claim Form Completion Guidelines for Medicare

Items	Information Needed	Where the Information Will Be Found
Items 1–13 Patient and Insured Information		
Item 1 Type of Health Insurance	Check the Medicare box where the claim will be sent	Patient's Medicare card and patient information sheet
Item 1a Insured's ID Number	The patient's Medicare health insurance claim number (HICN)	Patient's Medicare card and patient information sheet
Item 2 Patient's name (Last, First, Middle Initial)	The name of the patient who received the service	Superbill and patient information sheet
Item 3 Patient's Date of Birth	The patient's date of birth MM/DD/CCYY and gender, male or female	Patient information sheet
Item 4 Insured's Name (Last, First, Middle Initial)	If Medicare is primary, leave blank; if there is insurance primary to Medicare, list name of insured or Same	Patient's insurance card and patient information sheet
Item 5 Patient's Address	The patient's mailing address and phone number	Patient information sheet
Item 6 Patient's Relationship to Insured	If Medicare is primary, leave blank or in- dicate how the patient is related to the insured in Box 4	Patient information sheet
Item 7 Insured's Address	Insurance primary to Medicare, insured's address and phone number; complete only when items 4, 6, and 11 are com- pleted; enter same if address is same as patient	Patient information sheet
Item 8 Patient's Status	Indicate the patient's marital and employment status	Patient information sheet
Item 9 Other Insured's Name	If no MediGap benefits are assigned, leave blank **or** enter the last name, first name, and middle initial of the enrollee in a MediGap policy if it is different from Box 2 Otherwise, enter the word SAME	Patient information sheet **Note:** Only participating providers are to complete 9, and 9a–9d and only if the patient wants to assign benefits to the participating provider Do not list other supplemental coverage in Items 9, 9a–9d at the time the claim is filed with Medicare. Other supplemen- tal claims are sent automatically to the supplemental insurer **IF** the insurer con- tracts with the Medicare carrier If there is no contract, patient must file his or her own claim
Item 9a Other Insured's Policy or Group Number	The MediGap policy or group number of the insured in Box 9	Patient information sheet and Box 9 of claim
Item 9b Other Insured's date of birth	The date of birth MM/DD/CCYY and gender of the insured in Box 9	Patient information sheet and Box 9 of claim

TABLE 8–3: Claim Form Completion Guidelines for Medicare—cont'd

Items	Information Needed	Where the Information Will Be Found
Item 9c Employer's Name or School Name	If a MediGap payer ID is listed in 9d, leave blank; otherwise, enter the MediGap payer's address of the insured in Box 9	Patient information sheet or MediGap identification card
Item 9d Insurance Plan Name or Program name	Enter the MediGap payer ID number; if there is no number, enter the name of MediGap insurance program	Patient information sheet or Medigap identification card
Item 10a Is Patient's Condition Related to Employment?	Indicate yes or no if the condition of the patient is related to an employment incident	Patient information sheet and/or the appointment schedule
Item 10b Is Patient's Condition Related to Auto Accident?	Indicate yes or no if the condition of the patient is related to an auto accident	Patient information sheet and/or the appointment schedule
Item 10c Is Patient's Condition Related to Other Accident?	Indicate yes or no if the condition of the patient is related to another type of accident	Patient information sheet and/or the appointment schedule
Item 10d Reserved for Local Use	Leave blank; not required by Medicare	
Item 11 Insured's Policy Group or FECA Number	The group ID number or the alphanumeric number (FECA) of the health, auto, or other insurance plan of the insured in Box 4; if there is no insurance primary to Medicare, enter the word "NONE," anything else is unacceptable	Patient information sheet and/or the ID card of the person indicated in Box 4
Item 11a Insured's Date of Birth and Sex	The birth date and gender of the insured in Box 11 MM/DD/CCYY	Patient information sheet
Item 11b Employer's Name or School Name	The employer or school name of the insured in Box 1a	Patient information sheet
Item 11c Insurance Plan Name or Program Name	This box must be completed if a policy number is in 11 The ID number or name of the plan or program of the insured indicated in Box 11	Patient information sheet
Item 11d Is There Another Health Plan? *If yes, return to and complete 9a–d*	Leave blank; not required by Medicare	
Item 12 Patient's or Authorized Person's Signature	A signature on file authorizing a release of medical records or other information needed to process the claim	Patient information sheet
Item 13 Insured's or Authorized Signature	A signature on file authorizing payment for the services indicated on the claim, to be sent directly to the provider who appears in Boxes 31 and 32 of the claim	Patient information sheet

Continued

TABLE 8–3:   Claim Form Completion Guidelines for Medicare—cont'd

Items	Information Needed	Where the Information Will Be Found
Items 14–33 Patient and Insured Information		
Item 14 Date of Current Illness, Injury, Pregnancy	The first date of onset of illness, the actual date of the injury, or the LMP for pregnancy **or** date of treatment initiation or x-ray taken for chiropractic care	Patient medical record
Item 15 If Patient Has Had Same or Similar Illness	Leave blank; not required by Medicare	
Item 16 Dates Patient Unable to Work in Current Occupation	The from and to dates that the patient is/was unable to work	Patient's medical record
Item 17 Name of Referring Provider or Other Source	Name of the referring or ordering provider who referred or ordered the service on the claim	The patient or the referring or ordering provider
Item 17a Other ID #	Leave blank, no longer required by Medicare	
Item 17b NPI #	The National Provider Identifier (NPI) number of the referring or ordering provider listed in Box 17	The referring or ordering provider or directory containing the ID numbers
Item 18 Hospitalization Dates Related to Current Illness	The admission and discharge dates of the inpatient stay related to the services listed on the claim	Patient's medical record
Item 19 Reserved for Local Use	Multiple uses; specifically for a physician's office: • Date and NPI of attending physician when a patient is receiving foot care • A concise description of an unlisted procedure code • All applicable modifiers when a 99 modifier I entered in 24D • "Patient refuse to assign benefits" if applicable • Assumed or relinquished date for a global surgery claim when physicians share postoperative care	Patient's medical record or the referring or ordering provider or directory containing the ID numbers or patient information sheet **Note:** Electronic claims can hold up to 80 characters in Box 19 for a concise statement If needed information does not fit in Box 19 on a paper form, an attachment must be submitted with the claim
Item 20 Outside Lab? $ Charges	Yes or No The service/s on the claim were purchased from an outside laboratory and the charged amount If "yes" is checked here, Box 32 must contain the name and NPI of the laboratory	Patient's medical record, log kept on file, or provider or directory containing the ID numbers
Item 21 Diagnosis or Nature of Illness or Injury (relate items 1, 2, 3, or 4 to 24E by line)	The ICD-9-CM code representing the patient's diagnosis or condition; the reason for the services on the claim; up to eight diagnosis codes may be entered	Patient's medical record and current ICD-9-CM manual

TABLE 8–3: Claim Form Completion Guidelines for Medicare—cont'd

Items	Information Needed	Where the Information Will Be Found
Item 22 Medicaid Resubmission	Leave blank **Note:** Required by Medicare	
Item 23 Prior Authorization Number	Not applicable with physician's services	
Item 24A Date(s) of Service	The date the service was performed (mmddyy) or (mmddyyyy) (up to six services billed per claim)	Superbill
Item 24B Place of Service	The location the service was rendered	Superbill
Item 24C EMG	Leave blank; not required by Medicare	
Item 24D Procedures, Services, Supplies	The CPT/HCPCS code and modifier(s) if needed, identifying the service	Superbill
Item 24E Diagnosis Pointer	Enter the primary reference # of the line number from Box 21 (1, 2, 3, or 4) that relates to the service(s) rendered. **Only** one reference number per line item	Superbill
Item 24F $ Charges	The charged amount for each service line Do not use $ signs, decimals, dashes, commas, or lines (e.g., 2400)	Superbill or log kept on file
Item 24G Days or Units	The number of days indicated in the date span of 24A **or** the number units or minutes the service was performed (1 visit = 1 unit)	Superbill
Item 24H EPSDT Family Plan	Leave blank; not required by Medicare	
Item 24I ID Qualifier	Enter the qualifier "1C" in shaded area when a physician's NPI is in 24J	The instructions from the local and current Medicaid or other third-party carrier's policy manual
Item 24J Rendering Provider ID #	The individual NPI of the rendering provider of service indicated in 24D **who is:** • An incorporated, solo provider with an individual NPI and a group NPI # • A provider working in a group practice or clinic	The provider directory containing the ID numbers
Item 25 Federal Tax ID Number	The tax ID or Social Security number of the provider of service and mark an X in the appropriate box; do not use hyphens or spaces	The provider of service's records
Item 26 Patient's Account No.	The identifying number assigned by the provider of service (if assigned)	Patient's medical record or file

Continued

TABLE 8-3: Claim Form Completion Guidelines for Medicare—cont'd

Items	Information Needed	Where the Information Will Be Found
Item 27 Accept Assignment	Yes or No box indicating if the provider of service accepts Medicare's payment	The provider of service's records
Item 28 Total Charge	The sum of all services entered in 24F. Do not use $ signs, decimals, dashes, commas, or lines. (e.g., 2400)	The superbill, a hospital report or the patient's account
Item 29 Amount Paid	Total amount patient paid only, toward the services in 24F Do not use $ signs, decimals, dashes, commas, or lines (e.g., 2400)	The superbill, a record of receipts, or the patient's account
Item 30 Balance Due	Leave blank; not required by Medicare	The superbill, a record of receipts, or statement from a third-party payer or the patient's account (this field does not exist on paperless claims)
Item 31 Signature of Physician or Supplier Including Degrees or Credentials (I certify that the statements on the reverse apply to this bill and are made a part thereof)	The physician's signature or a representative of and the date the claim form was completed using (six or eight digits MMDDYY or MMDDYYYY) A signature stamp or computer-generated stamp is also acceptable	The provider or their representative's signature A signature is needed on any paper claim, but may be a stamped signature; the signature and date field does not exist when billing paperless claims
Item 32 Service Facility Location Information	The name and address of facility where services were rendered	A provider directory or phone book; the coder's place of employment
Item 32a NPI #	The NPI number of the facility where the service took place of the facility where the service took place	The provider directory containing the ID numbers
Item 32b Other ID #	No longer required by Medicare	
Item 33 Billing Provider Info & Ph #	The name, address, and telephone number of the provider requesting payment for the service in 24	A provider directory or phone book, or the coder's place of employment
Item 33a NPI #	The NPI number of the solo or group practice requesting payment for the service(s) in 24	The provider directory containing the ID numbers
Item 33b Other ID #	No longer required by Medicare	

be used for cosmetic repair and the 13150 series of codes are usually used for repairing different lengths of lip wounds. The 13150 series of codes can include débridement, removing of foreign material left in the wound, even stents or special suturing in preparation for reconstruction procedures. The medical coder must choose the code that represents exactly or comes closest to the procedure performed and would use one code or the other, but not both codes at the same time.

The last column of each table lists one of the following:

■ **0, modifier not allowed.** No matter the circumstances, a modifier will not be accepted with the codes that would allow both codes to be considered for payment.

TABLE 8–4:   The Column One/Column Two Correct Coding Edits Table

Column 1	Column 2	* = In existence prior to 1996	Effective Date	Deletion Date * = no data	Modifier 0 = not allowed 1 = allowed 9 = not applicable
26011	29086		20021001		1
26011	36000		20021001		1
26011	51701		20071001		1
26011	62318		20021001		1
26011	64450		20021001	*	1
26011	64470		20021001	*	1
26011	64475		20021001	*	1
26011	69990		20000605	*	0

■ **1, modifier allowed.** A modifier could be attached to document the need to bill both codes. The documentation would be reviewed and medical necessity would be considered.

■ **9, a modifier is not applicable to the procedure.** Means just that, this is a code that a modifier would not even be appropriate or considered for payment with the code listed.

Modifiers and Medicare

As demonstrated in the edit tables, Medicare uses modifiers just as any other insurance carrier/third-party payer would to demonstrate specific circumstances that apply to the procedure being billed. One of Medicare's most common claim submission errors is "Procedure code is inconsistent with modifier" or "Modifier is missing."

Important modifiers for Medicare billing:

■ **Modifier TC**—Technical Component appears frequently on the Medicare Fee Schedule. The modifier indicates the part of the procedure that includes the use of equipment, facilities, or supplies. When used with a CPT code, reimbursement will be made just for that portion of the service.

■ **Modifier 26**—Professional Component also appears often in the Medicare Fee Schedule. This modifier indicates the other portion of the TC modifier. It is the charge for physician's (example, radiologist or pathologist) portion of the service. When used with a CPT code, reimbursement will be made just for that portion of the service.

■ **Modifier 59**—Distinct Procedural Service is an important NCCI modifier. When NCCI edits allow, the 59 modifier can be used to demonstrate that the services billed together were performed on different anatomical sites or performed during different sessions and therefore payable as two separate procedures.

TABLE 8–5:   The Mutually Exclusive Edits Table

Column 1	Column 2	* = In existence prior to 1996	Effective Date	Deletion Date * = no data	Modifier 0 = not allowed 1 = allowed 9 = not applicable
40650	13150		19960101	*	1
40650	13151		19960101	*	1
40650	13152		19960101	*	1
40650	40652		19960101	*	1

■ **Modifier 78**—Return to the Operating Room for a Related Procedure (during the Postoperative Period) (Table 8–6). An operating room (OR), is defined here as a place of service equipped and staffed for the sole purpose of performing procedure, such as a cardiac catheterization suite, endoscopy suite, or laser suite). It does not include a patient's room, minor treatment room, recovery room, or an intensive care unit, unless the patient's condition is so critical, that there is not enough time to transport to the operating room. If the subsequent service is performed within the 90-day global period, was *unrelated* to the original procedure, *modifier 79* (rather than 78) is the appropriate modifier to be reported.

■ **Modifier 79**—Unrelated Procedure or Service by the Same Physician during Postoperative Period (Table 8–7). This modifier is used when the procedures billed are not the same operations or treatment for complications of a procedure performed. Modifier 79 is valid on any procedure code representing a different procedure being performed within 90 days postoperatively of a major procedure that has a 90-day postoperative period listed with the procedure on the physician fee schedule.

HCPCS and Medicare

Chapters 5 and 6 introduced information regarding Category 1, procedure codes. Category 1 codes consist of two levels, Level 1 is the CPT codes and Level 2 codes are commonly referred to as HCPCS (Healthcare Common Procedure Coding System) codes. These codes are used to report supplies, materials, injections, and certain services and procedures not found in the CPT manual itself. Medicare, Medicaid, and private insurers use HCPCS codes. Medicare developed certain HCPCS codes for certain preventative and disease screening procedures. For example the HCPCS code G0105 represents colorectal cancer screening; colonoscopy on individual at high risk or code G0202 direct digital image diagnostic mammography. Medicare instructs the medical coder to replace the appropriate CPT code with a designated HCPCS code for certain preventive/screening services. They should be used only for patients who are having a "well" physical or test performed. If a patient goes in for a screening procedure and an abnormality is discovered, the medical code should always use the appropriate CPT code. The use of these screening HCPCS codes should only be used to report a screening. The medical coder will find an annually updated list of these codes on the Medicare website: http://www.cms.hhs.gov/MLNProducts/downloads/MPS_QuickReferenceChart_1.pdf.

There are also designated HCPCS codes for the following:

■ The initial physical provided to every new Medicare enrollee

■ Medical nutrition therapy

■ Screening Pap smears

■ Screening pelvic examinations

■ Ultrasound screening for abdominal aortic aneurysms

■ Diabetes self management training

■ Bone mass measurements

■ Prostate cancer screenings

■ Glaucoma screenings

■ Administration of influenza, pneumococcal, and hepatitis B vaccines

---

TABLE 8–6: Examples of Using Modifier 78

Date of Service	Treatment	CPT/Modifier
08/30/2008	Coronary arteries bypass	33514
08/30/2008	Explore chest wall	35820 78
09/15/2008	Partial removal of pancreas	48140
09/15/2008	Drain abdominal abscess	49020 78

TABLE 8–7: Examples of Using Modifier 79

Date of Service	Treatment	CPT/Modifier
07/25/2008	Removal of cataract right eye (90 day post-op)	66984 RT
07/25/2008	Removal of cataract left eye (90 day post-op)	66984 79 LT
10/01/2008	Excision, abdominal wall tumor	22900
10/15/2008	Ankle fracture	27814 79

National Provider Identification (NPIs) for Referring/Ordering Physicians

A *referring* physician is one who refers the patient to another physician for services. An *ordering* physician orders a test for a patient. The health-care facility receiving the patient is responsible for obtaining the NPI from the referring/ordering physician. It may be obtained at the time of referral/order or through the NPI national registry at https://nppes.cms.hhs.gov/NPPES/NPIRegistryHome.do.

The referring/ordering physician's name and NPI must be entered in boxes 17 and 17b of the CMS-1500 claim form. The NPI replaced Medicare's unique provider identification numbers (now referred to as legacy numbers). During the transition period of the new number system, providers placed their Medicare number in box 17a. Now box 17a should no longer be used.

Claim Submission

Medicare claims can be submitted electronically or on paper. All claims are sent to the MAC responsible for each jurisdiction. A MAC provides free software for any provider who chooses to submit their own claims directly to Medicare. The MAC also accepts claims from **health-care clearinghouses** that they participate with. Each MAC will provide a current list of those clearinghouses to the medical provider on their websites.

Clearinghouses and the MAC software have all been developed using standard versions or formats that produce the information found on the paper CMS-1500. Each version must be able to "talk" to the clearinghouse or third-party carrier to transfer the information. The version or format used by a health-care provider depends on the software responsible for generating the electronic claims.

! **KEY TERMS**

AMERICAN NATIONAL STANDARDS INSTITUTE (ANSI)—National standard guidelines for the completion and submission of all claims for services, supplies, equipment, and health care.

■ MEDICARE AND OTHER PAYERS

Medicare and Medicaid

Medicaid is a joint federal and state program that helps pay medical expenses for qualifying individuals. Medicare refers to these individuals as "dual eligibles." Some states refer to these patients as Medi-Medi. Regardless, the title, the medical coder just needs to know how to file claims to these organizations. In these cases, Medicare is considered the primary coverage. Most health-care costs (deductibles and coinsurance) will be covered by the combination of Medicare and Medicaid. After Medicare has made a payment, a claim will be filed automatically with Medicaid. The medical coder does not need to provide Medicaid information on the claim form. Medicare contracts with Medicaid and will know the patient also has Medicaid coverage. (See Chapter 9 for additional Medicaid information.)

Medicare and Military Benefits (TRICARE)

TRICARE is the health-care program for active-duty service members, retirees, and their families. A patient may be covered under a TRICARE for Life (TFL) plan that provides coverage for

Medicare-entitled uniformed service retirees, their eligible family members and survivors, and even certain former spouses. Medicare is considered the primary insurance and should be billed first for Medicare-covered services. TRICARE is considered secondary for any of the services that also are a TRICARE benefit. If Medicare does not cover a service provided to a patient, TRICARE should be billed. The patient will be responsible for the TRICARE deductible and their share of the cost. (See Chapter 11 for additional TRICARE information.)

Medicare as the Secondary Payer

Medicare is secondary to other insurance when:

1. The individual, 65 or over, is still employed, and has chosen to maintain the employer's benefits.
2. The spouse, any age, of a Medicare beneficiary is an employee of a company with 20 or more employees and has family coverage.
3. Automobile medical, no fault, or any third-party liability exists for an illness or an injury.
4. ESRD (end-stage renal disease) patients are in their first year of treatment and have an employee group health plan.
5. Black Lung liability exists.
6. Worker's Compensation applies.
7. Veteran's Administration (VA), Public Health Service (PHS), or any other federal agency benefits exist.

In all of these cases, file claims directly to the other insurance company first. After the primary payer's statement that shows their payment is received, file the claim to Medicare with a copy of the primary payer's statement. Medicare will then consider the claim for any secondary benefits.

! KEY TERMS

COORDINATION OF BENEFITS AGREEMENT (COBA)—An agreement made between CMS and any Medicare supplemental insurance carrier for the purpose of automated coinsurance payments.

COORDINATION OF BENEFITS CONTRACTOR (COBC)—The agency responsible for the processing of all supplemental (MediGap) insurance claim-based crossover claims.

MEDIGAP—A supplemental insurance policy that will pay for medical services/supplies after Medicare pays (co-insurance).

MediGap/Crossover

! KEY TERM

CROSSOVER CLAIMS—Claim form payment information transferred from Medicare to a third-party carrier for the additional reimbursement after Medicare's payment.

MediGap is a supplemental insurance policy that can be purchased to help pay for medical services/supplies after Medicare pays. The balance is the patient's responsibility and is referred to as the co-insurance. Not long ago, a second claim had to be sent to the MediGap company after the Medicare payment was made. In most cases, a copy of the Remittance Advice (RA) or often referred to as the Explanation of Medicare Benefits (EOMB) also had to accompany the claim form to document what Medicare had paid and what balance was to be considered by the MediGap carrier. Since the RAs usually contain the payment information on several patients, their names had to be hidden to protect their privacy. Only the information for the MediGap insured could be revealed. There was no way to insure confidentiality and this was not HIPAA compliant.

CMS developed the Coordination of Benefits Agreement (COBA), which standardized the way that Medicare claims information was exchanged. COBAs permit other health insurance organizations (also known as trading partners) to send Medicare beneficiaries eligibility information and receive Medicare paid claims data for processing supplemental insurance, from a national crossover contractor, called the Coordination of Benefits Contractor (COBC). Third party carriers/trading partners may enter into an agreement with the COBC so all of the information needed for consideration of payment is automatically sent to them. This is commonly referred to as an automatic "cross over" and means that boxes 9, 9a–9d could be left blank because Medicare already knows by the patient's Medicare ID number where to send the claim next for more payment. It should be noted that including this information in boxes 9, 9a–9d will not hinder payment or the automatic crossover process.

Providers should reference a weekly updated listing of the newly assigned COBA MediGap claim-based IDs for Medicare billing purposes at the CMS website. All third party carriers that participate in the COBA crossover process will be found at: http://www.cms.hhs.gov/COBAgreement/Downloads/Contacts.pdf.

If a company has not signed a COBA, notification will be sent to the provider's office indicating the crossover could not be performed. A copy of the original claim and a copy of the Medicare RA showing payment must then be submitted to the MediGap carrier for their consideration.

REMITTANCE ADVICE

After a Medicare Part B claim is processed, the provider is notified of payment, adjustment, or denial by a statement called a **Remittance Advice (RA)**. The RA is generated and sent either electronically or in hard copy. An Electronic Remittance Advice (ERA) is shown in Figure 8–7. A paper, or Standard Remittance Advice (SRA), is shown in Figures 8–8 and 8–9. The RA will display the claims that have been received and processed.

> **KEY TERM**
>
> REMITTANCE ADVICE (RA)—A statement sent from Medicare to providers, indicating the reimbursement, denial, or pending charges submitted.

The medical coder will use the RA to post payments and adjustments to patient accounts and identify any problems with original claim. Medicare has developed software called Medicare Remit Easy Print (MREP) to view, search, and print remittance information. The software is free of charge to all providers. The MREP can generate reports that will show paid, adjusted, and denied claims and reason for payment amount or denial. With that information, the medical coder can resubmit corrected claims and post payments to patient accounts for paid claims. Additional software is available that will automatically post the proper payment to the proper account using account numbers.

The format of an RA varies (see Figs. 8–8 and 8–9), depending on the software used. However, the following basic information will always be the same:

- Patient's name
- Date of service
- Place of service
- Amount billed
- Amount applied to the deductible
- Amount applied to co-insurance
- Total amount paid for procedure performed

If the payment is going to a participating provider, remember the provider has agreed to accept Medicare's approved amount as payment in full and adjustments will have to be made. See Table 8–8 for some examples.

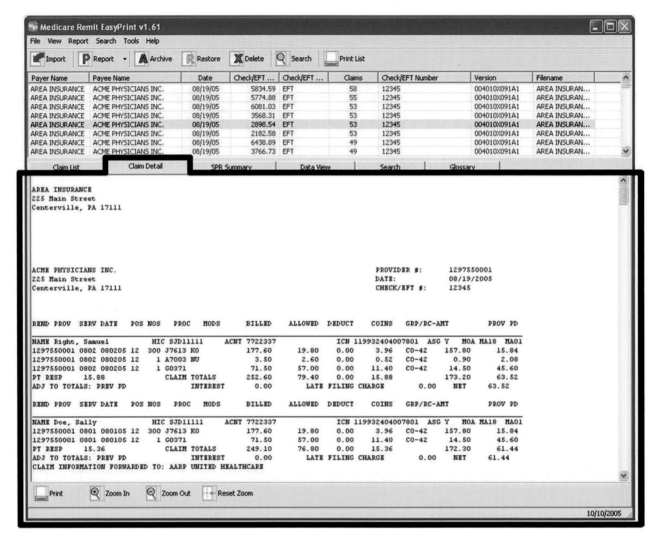

FIGURE 8–7: Electronic remittance advice.

More information on the remittance advice can be found at: *http://www.cms.hhs.gov/MLNProducts/ downloads/RA_Guide_Full_03-22-06.pdf.*

About every 3 months, the patient/Medicare beneficiary will receive a Medicare Summary Notice (MSN) (Fig. 8–10) showing the charges and payments for any Medicare-covered services they have had during that time. Medicare encourages all beneficiaries to review the MSNs. If they disagree with a charge or payment they are instructed to file an appeal. The MSN explains the step-by-step process in which the appeal can be filed.

! KEY TERM

MEDICARE SUMMARY NOTICE (MSN)—A statement sent to the Medicare beneficiary that shows the charges and the payments made for services rendered to the beneficiary during the previous months.

```
EXAMPLE MEDICARE CARRIER
1000 SOMEPLACE LANE
FAIRFAX, VA 22033-0000                          MEDICARE
1-877-555-1234                                  REMITTANCE
                                                NOTICE
1
EXAMPLE MEDICARE PROVIDER                       PROVIDER #:999999
200 DOCTORS DRIVE                               PAGE #:  1 OF 2
SUITE 200                                       DATE:  01/28/03
SOMEWHERE, NJ   16666-0200                      CHECK/EFT #:  000234569
****************************************************************************************
*                                                                                    *
*            WELCOME TO THE MEDICARE PART B STANDARD PAPER REMITTANCE                 *
*                                                                                    *
*                                                                                    *
*                                                                                    *
*                                                                                    *
```

```
PERF PROV   SERV DATE  POS NOS  PROC   MODS   BILLED   ALLOWED   DEDUCT    COINS    GRP/RC    AMT    PROV PD
NAME FISCHER, BENNY       HIC 9999999999 ACNT  FISC6123133-01    ICN 0202199306840    ASG Y           MOA MA01
123456ABC  0225 022502 11  1  99213          66.00    49.83     0.34     9.97    PR-96   16.17       39.52
PT RESP   10.31                 CLAIM TOTALS  66.00    49.83     0.34     9.97            16.17
                                                                                   NET   39.52

NAME FISCHER, BENNY       HIC 9999999999 ACNT  FISC6123133-01    ICN 0202199306850    ASG Y      MOA MA01 MA07
123456ABC  0117 011702 11  1  99213          66.00    49.83     0.00     9.97    PR-96   16.17       39.86
PT RESP    9.97                 CLAIM TOTALS  66.00    49.83     0.00     9.97            16.17       39.86
CLAIM INFORMATION FORWARDED TO:  NEW JERSEY MEDICAID                                NET   39.86

NAME HURT, I. M.          HIC 9999999999 ACNT  HURT5-329          ICN 0202199306860    ASG Y           MOA MA01
123456ABC  0117 011702 11  1  90659          25.00     3.32     0.00     0.00    CO-42   21.68        3.32
123456ABC  0117 011702 11  1  G0008          10.00     4.46     0.00     0.00    CO-42    5.54        4.46
PT RESP    0.00                 CLAIM TOTALS  35.00     7.78     0.00     0.00            27.22        7.78
                                                                                   NET    7.78

NAME MARLOWE, PHILIP      HIC 9999999999 ACNT  MARLO861-316       ICN 0202199306870    ASG Y      MOA MA01 MA07
123456ABC  0209 020902 11  1  99213          66.00    49.83     0.00     9.97    PR-96   16.17       39.86
PT RESP    9.97                 CLAIM TOTALS  66.00    49.83     0.00     9.97            16.17       39.86
ADJ TO TOTALS:  PREV PD  10.00    INT  0.00         LATE FILING CHARGE  0.00
CLAIM INFORMATION FORWARDED TO:  NEW JERSEY MEDICAID                                NET   29.86
NAME RAP, JACK            HIC 9999999999 ACNT  RAP33-721          ICN 0202199306880    ASG Y      MOA MA01 MA07
123456ABC  0314 031402 11  1  99213          66.00    49.83     0.00     9.97    PR-96   16.17       39.86
123456ABC  0314 031402 11  1  82962          10.00     4.37     0.00     0.00    CO-42    5.63        4.37
123456ABC  0314 031402 11  1  94760          12.00     0.00     0.00     0.00    CO-B15  12.00        0.00
REM: M80
PT RESP    9.97                 CLAIM TOTALS  88.00    54.20     0.00     9.97            33.80       44.23
                                                                                   NET   44.23
```

```
TOTALS:   # of    BILLED   ALLOWED   DEDUCT    COINS    TOTAL     PROV PD       PROV      CHECK
          CLAIMS    AMT       AMT      AMT       AMT     RC AMT      AMT       ADJ AMT      AMT
3            5    321.00   211.47    0.34     39.88    109.53    161.25       31.25     130.00
     PROVIDER ADJ DETAILS:        PLB REASON CODE       FCN         HIC       AMOUNT
                                        50                                    15.44
                                        FB        0202199306770   9999999999    5.81
```

FIGURE 8-8: Paper remittance advice (example 1).

1 EXAMPLE MEDICARE CARRIER
PROVIDER #: 999999
CHECK/EFT: 00234569   01/28/2003

GOODHEALTH GROUP PRACTICE
PAGE 2 OF 2

MEDICARE
REMITTANCE
NOTICE

SUMMARY OF UNASSIGNED CLAIMS

PERF PROV	SERV DATE POS NOS PROC	MODS	BILLED	ALLOWED	DEDUCT	COINS	GRP/RC	AMT	PROV PD

2
NAME FINE, R. U.   HIC 9999999999 ACNT FINE7-002   ICN 0202199000150 ASG N   MOA MA28
123456ABC 0526 052602 11 1 99214   60.47   52.58   0.00   10.52 CO-42 0.00   7.89
PT RESP   60.47   CLAIM TOTALS   60.47   52.58   0.00   10.52   0.00
ADJ TO TOTALS: PREV PD   0.00. INT   0.00 LATE FILING CHARGE   0.00

NAME LAWN, MOE D.   HIC 9999999999 ACNT LAWN4-667   ICN 0202199140370 ASG N   MOA MA28
123456ABC 0222 022202 11 1 99214   60.47   52.58   0.00   10.52 CO-42 0.00   7.89
PT RESP   60.47   CLAIM TOTALS   60.47   52.58   0.00   10.52   0.00
ADJ TO TOTALS: PREV PD   0.00 INT   0.00 LATE FILING CHARGE   0.00

GROUP CODES:
PR   Patient Responsibility
CO   Contractual Obligation
OA   Other Adjustment

GLOSSARY: Group, Reason, MOA, Remark and Adjustment Codes
CO   Contractual Obligation. Amount for which the provider is financially liable. The patient may
          not be billed for this amount.
PR   Patient Responsibility. Amount that may be billed to a patient or another payer.
42   Charges exceed our fee schedule or maximum allowable amount.
96   Noncovered charge(s)
B15   Claim/service denied/reduced because this procedure/service is not paid separately.
          Charges exceed our fee schedule or maximum allowable amount.
M80   We cannot pay for this when performed during the same session as another approved procedure for
          this beneficiary.
3
MA01   (Initial Part B determination, carrier or intermediary) If you do not agree with what we
          approved for these services, you may appeal our decision. To make sure that we are fair to you,
          we require another individual that did not process your initial claim to conduct the review.
          However, in order to be eligible for a review, you must write to us within 6 months of the date
          of this notice, unless you have a good reason for being late. (An institutional provider, e.g.,
          hospital, SNF, HHA may appeal only if the claim involves a medical necessity denial, a SNF
          recertified bed denial, or a home health denial because the patient was not homebound or was not
          in need of intermittent skilled nursing services, and either the patient or the provider is
          liable under 1879 of the Social Security Act, and the patient chooses not to appeal.) NOTE: If
          you are a member of the telephone review demonstration, or if telephone reviews are expanded,
          add the following to the end of the description for MA01. If you meet the criteria for a
          telephone review, you may phone to request a telephone review.
MA07   The claim information has also been forwarded to Medicaid for review.
MA28   Receipt of this notice by a physician who did not accept assignment is for information only and
          does not make the physician a party to the determination. No additional rights to appeal this
          decision, above those rights already provided for by regulation/instruction, are conferred by
          receipt of this notice.
50   Late Filing Reduction
FB   Forwarding Balance

FIGURE 8–9: Paper remittance advice (example 2).

TABLE 8–8: Medicare Payment Examples

	Medicare Deductible Met	Medicare Deductible Not Yet Met
Billed Amount	$100.00	$100.00
Medicare Allowed Amount	$ 80.00	$80.00
Deductible	$0.00	$20.00
Balance	$80.00	$60.00
Medicare Pays 80% of Allowed Amount	$64.00 (80% of 80)	$48.00 (80% of $60.00)
Co-insurance owed from patient or their supplemental insurance	**$16.00**	**$32.00** ($20 deductible plus the 20% of $60)

	Page 1 of 2
Medicare Summary Notice	July 1, 2006

BENEFICIARY NAME
STREET ADDRESS
CITY, STATE ZIP CODE

BE INFORMED: Beware of telemarketers offering free or discounted Medicare items or services.

CUSTOMER SERVICE INFORMATION

Your Medicare Number: 111-11-1111A

If you have questions, write or call:
   Medicare (#12345)
   555 Medicare Blvd., Suite 200
   Medicare Building
   Medicare, US XXXXX–XXXX

Call: 1-800-MEDICARE (1-800-633-4227)
Ask for Doctor Services
TTY for Hearing Impaired: 1-877-486-2048

This is a summary of claims processed from 05/10/2006 through 08/10/2006.

PART B MEDICAL INSURANCE – ASSIGNED CLAIMS

Dates of Service	Services Provided	Amount Charged	Medicare Approved	Medicare Paid Provider	You May Be Billed	See Notes Section
Claim Number: 12435-84956-84556						a
Paul Jones, M.D., 123 West Street, Jacksonville, FL 33231-0024						
Referred by: Scott Wilson, M.D.						
04/19/06	1 Influenza immunization (90724)	$5.00	$3.88	$3.88	$0.00	b
04/19/06	1 Admin. flu vac (G0008)	5.00	3.43	3.43	0.00	b
	Claim Total	**$10.00**	**$7.31**	**$7.31**	**$0.00**	
Claim Number: 12435-84956-84557						a
ABC Ambulance, P.O. Box 2149, Jacksonville, FL 33231						
04/25/06	1 Ambulance, base rate (A0020)	$289.00	$249.78	$199.82	$49.96	
04/25/06	1 Ambulance, per mile (A0021)	21.00	16.96	13.57	3.39	
	Claim Total	**$310.00**	**$266.74**	**$213.39**	**$53.35**	

PART B MEDICAL INSURANCE - UNASSIGNED CLAIMS

Dates of Service	Services Provided	Amount Charged	Medicare Approved	Medicare Paid You	You May Be Billed	See Notes Section
Claim Number: 12435-84956-84558						a
William Newman, M.D., 362 North Street Jacksonville, FL 33231–0024						
03/10/06	1 Office/Outpatient Visit, ES (99213)	$47.00	$33.93	$27.15	$39.02	c

THIS IS NOT A BILL– Keep this notice for your records.

FIGURE 8–10: Beneficiary's Medicare Summary Notice.

Your Medicare Number: 111-11-1111A

Notes Section:

a This information is being sent to your private insurer. They will review it to see if additional benefits can be paid. Send any questions regarding your supplemental benefits to them.

b This service is paid at 100% of the Medicare approved amount.

c Your doctor did not accept assignment for this service. Under Federal law, your doctor cannot charge more than $39.02. If you have already paid more than this amount, you are entitled to a refund from the provider.

Deductible Information:

You have met the Part B deductible for 2006.

General Information:

You have the right to make a request in writing for an itemized statement which details each Medicare item or service which you have received from your physician, hospital, or any other health supplier or health professional. Please contact them directly, in writing, if you would like an itemized statement.

Compare the services you receive with those that appear on your Medicare Summary Notice. If you have questions, call your doctor or provider. If you feel further investigation is needed due to possible fraud and abuse, call the phone number in the Customer Service Information Box.

Appeals Information – Part B

If you disagree with any claims decisions on this notice, your appeal must be received by **November 1, 2006**. Follow the instructions below:

1) Circle the item(s) you disagree with and explain why you disagree.

2) Send this notice, or a copy, to the address in the "Customer Service Information" box on Page 1. (You may also send any additional information you may have about your appeal.)

3) Sign here _____ Phone number _____

Revised 08/06

FIGURE 8–10: cont'd

IMPORTANT INFORMATION ABOUT YOUR MEDICARE PART B MEDICAL INSURANCE BENEFITS

For more information about services covered by Medicare, please see your Medicare Handbook.

MEDICARE PART B MEDICAL INSURANCE: Medicare Part B helps pay for doctors' services, diagnostic tests, ambulance services, durable medical equipment, and other health care services. Medicare Part A Hospital Insurance helps pay for inpatient hospital care, inpatient care in a skilled nursing facility following a hospital stay, home health care and hospice care. You will be sent a separate notice if you received Part A services or any outpatient facility services.

MEDICARE ASSIGNMENT: Medicare Part B claims may be **assigned** or **unassigned**. Providers who accept **assignment** agree to accept the Medicare approved amount as total payment for covered services. Medicare pays its share of the approved amount directly to the provider. You may be billed for unmet portions of the annual deductible and the coinsurance. You may contact us at the address or telephone number in the Customer Service Information box on the front of this notice for a list of **participating providers** who always accept assignment. You may save money by choosing a participating provider.

Doctors who submit **unassigned** claims have not agreed to accept Medicare's approved amount as payment in full. Generally, Medicare pays you 80% of the approved amount after subtracting any part of the annual deductible you have not met. A doctor who does not accept assignment may charge you up to 115% of the Medicare approved amount. This is known as the Limiting Charge. Some states have additional payment limits. The NOTES section on the front of this notice will tell you if a doctor has exceeded the Limiting Charge and the correct amount to pay your doctor under the law.

YOUR RESPONSIBILITY: The amount in the **You May Be Billed** column is your share of cost for the services shown on this notice. You are responsible for:

- **annual deductible:** taken from the first Medicare Part B approved charges each calendar year,

- **coinsurance:** 20% of the Medicare approved amount, after the deductible has been met for the year,

- the amount billed, up to the **limiting charge**, for unassigned claims, and

- charges for services/supplies that are **not covered** by Medicare. You may not have to pay for certain denied services. If so, a NOTE on the front will tell you.

If you have supplemental insurance, it may help you pay these amounts. If you use this notice to claim supplemental benefits from another insurance company, make a copy for your records.

WHEN OTHER INSURANCE PAYS FIRST: All Medicare payments are made on the condition that you will pay Medicare back if benefits could be paid by insurance that is primary to Medicare. Types of insurance that should pay before Medicare include employer group health plans, no-fault insurance, automobile medical insurance, liability insurance and workers' compensation. Notify us right away if you have filed or could file a claim with insurance that is primary to Medicare.

YOUR RIGHT TO APPEAL: If you disagree with what Medicare approved for these services, you may appeal the decision. You must file your appeal within **120 days of the date you receive this notice.** Unless you show us otherwise, we assume you received this notice 5 days after the date of this notice. Follow the appeal instructions on the front of the last page of the notice. If you want **help with your appeal,** a friend or someone else can help you. Also, groups such as legal aid services may provide free assistance. To contact us for the names and telephone numbers of groups in your area, please see our Customer Service Information box on the front of this notice.

HELP STOP MEDICARE FRAUD: Fraud is a false representation by a person or business to get Medicare payments: Some examples of fraud include:

- offers of goods or money in exchange for your Medicare Number,

- telephone or door-to-door offers for free medical services or items, and

- claims for Medicare services/items you did not receive.

If you think a person or business is involved in fraud, you should call Medicare at the Customer Service telephone number on the front of this notice.

INSURANCE COUNSELING AND ASSISTANCE: Insurance Counseling and Assistance programs are located in every State. These programs have volunteer counselors who can give you free assistance with Medicare questions, including enrollment, entitlement, Medigap, and premium issues. If you would like to know how to get in touch with your local Insurance Counseling and Assistance Program Counselor, please call us at the number shown in the Customer Service Information box on the front of this notice.

Centers for Medicare & Medicaid Services

FIGURE 8–10: cont'd

■ CONCLUSION

As with commercial insurance claims, Medicare claims require accurate coding and attention to detail. Medicare guidelines change on a regular basis, making it difficult to determine proper fees and billing procedures. A medical coder needs to carefully review patient information, coding regulations, and updated fee schedules to ensure proper procedures are always followed.

RESOURCES LIST

MAC Jurisdictions

WPS

    http://www.wpsmedicare.com

    http://www.wpsic.com

Modifier 59 and the Office of Inspector General, in *The Coding Edge*, American Academy of Professional Coders, March 2007

By Barbar J. Cobuzzi, MBA, CPC, CPC-H, CPC-P, CHCC

CRN Healthcare Solutions

Medicare 101 by Robert B. Helms

    http://www.aei.org/speech/19437

Medicare Learning Network

    http://cms.hhs.gov/medlearn/

Medicare Online Manual System

    http://cms.hhs.gov/manuals

    http://cms.hhs.gov/medlearn/MediGap COBA IDs

    http://www.cms.hhs.gov/COBAgreement/Downloads/Medigap Claim-based COBA IDs for Billing Purpose.pdf

MEDPAC Medicare Payment Advisory Commission

601 New Jersey Ave., NW

Washington, DC 20001

    www.medpac.gov

Noridian

    https://www.noridianmedicare.com/p-medb/

Physician Information Resource for Medicare

    http://cms.hhs.gov/physicians/default.asp

For Railroad Retirees claims:

Palmetto Government Benefit Administrators

Railroad Medicare Services

PO Box 10066

Augusta, GA 30999-001

Chapter Review Exercises

Please answer the following questions.

1. What is the annual deductible for Medicare Part B? _____

2. What does the letter "B" stand for in a patient's Medicare number?

   _____

3. Who qualifies for Medicare?

   _____

   _____

   _____

4. What is Medicare Part A coverage?

   _____

5. What is Medicare Part B Coverage?

   _____

6. Is there a monthly premium for Medicare Part A? _____

7. How is Medicare Part A financed? _____

8. Every patient will have their own Medicare ID number.   **True or False** (circle one)

9. The patient's ID number is referred to as _____.

10. As of 2007, what is the health-care provider's ID number called?

    _____

11. What does the acronym COBA stand for?

    _____

12. Medicare is always the primary payer.   **True or False**. (circle one)

13. What does it mean to accept assignment with Medicare?

    _____

14. A physician must notify their patients if the service rendered may not be determined medically necessary.   **True or False** (circle one)

15. Who is liable if Medicare determines a service is not medically necessary?

    _____

16. After the patient's deductible is met, what percentage of payment is made by Medicare?

_____ Who is responsible for the other percent? _____

17. Where does the patient's Medicare ID number go on the claim form?

_____

18. On a Medicare claim, who's name appears in box 4? _____

19. What box does the NPI number of the billing provider belong on a Medicare claim?

_____

Medicare Claim Completion

For the following exercises, you will fill out claims as if you were part of the insurance personnel for Dr. John Smith. You will find demographics, office fee schedule, and a blank CMS-1500 form in Appendix A. You will use this information along with Claim Completion scenarios to complete the claim forms exercises.

20. Adeline Johnson saw Dr. Smith as a new patient in your office, on March 10 of this year. She was seen for a bunion. Dr. Smith performs an expanded problem-focused history/exam, straightforward decision making office visit and schedules Adeline for a bunionectomy at the Anytown Hospital for March 15th. On March 15th, Dr. Smith performed a Bunion repair, without a sesamoidectomy, simple exostectomy. Adeline was treated and released as an outpatient.

    Dr. Smith participates in the Medicare program. Adeline signed an authorization and assignment of benefits form when she was first seen on March 10th.

    Complete a CMS-1500 form using the information above and the appropriate information from Appendix A.

21. Dr. Welby has asked Dr. Smith to see a patient that he suspects has pneumonia. Mary Smith was seen in the office and diagnosed with viral pneumonia on October 10, of this year. Dr. Smith performed an expanded problem focused consult and a chest x-ray. He prescribed an antibiotic and bed rest. He sent a letter to Dr. Welby explaining his findings and treatment.

    Complete a CMS-1500 form using the information above and the appropriate information from Appendix A.

Medicaid

Chapter Outline

OBJECTIVES

- List the criteria for Medicaid eligibility
- Recognize the Medicaid programs available
- Understand Medicaid funding
- Explain why programs differ from state to state
- Identify Medicaid's covered and noncovered services
- Demonstrate completion of a CMS-1500 claim form for a patient with Medicaid

MEDICAL ASSISTING COMPETENCIES
ABHES

1i. conduct work within scope of education, training, and ability
2d. serve as a liaison between Physician and others
2g. use appropriate medical terminology
2h. receive, organize, prioritize, and transmit information expediently
3b. prepare and maintain medical records
3e. locate resources and information for patients and employers
3v. perform diagnostic coding
3w. complete insurance forms
3x. use physician fee schedule
5a. determine the needs for documentation and reporting
5b. document accurately
5c. use appropriate guidelines when releasing records or information
8b. implement current procedural terminology and ICD-9 coding
8c. analyze and use current third-party guidelines for reimbursement

CAAHEP

IV.P.3. Use medical terminology, pronouncing medical terms correctly, to communicate information, patient history, data, and observations
VII.C.1. Identify types of insurance plans
VII.C.7. Describe guidelines for third-party claims
VII.C.9. Describe guidelines for third-party claims
VII.C.10. Discuss types of physician fee schedules
VII.C.11. Describe the concept of RBRVS
VII.P.2. Apply third party guidelines
VII.P.3. Complete insurance claim forms
VIII.C.1. Describe how to use the most current procedural coding system
VIII.C.3. Describe how to use the most current diagnostic coding classification system
VIII.C.4. Describe how to use the most current HCPCS coding
VIII.P.1. Perform procedural coding
VIII.P.2. Perform diagnostic coding
VIII.A.1. Work with physician to achieve the maximum reimbursement

KEY TERMS

Beneficiary	Medically Needy	Recipient
Dual Eligibles	Presumptive Eligibility	Resident Alien
Fiscal Agent	Qualified Provider	Spenddown

■ INTRODUCTION

Medicaid is health-care coverage for individuals and families with low incomes. Unlike Medicare, Medicaid is funded jointly by state and federal government and managed by each individual state. Each state designs its own policies on eligibility and health-care coverage within federal guidelines.

States may choose their own name for the program. Examples include "Medi-Cal" in California, "MassHealth" in Massachusetts, and "TennCare" in Tennessee. Added programs such as State Children's Health Insurance Program (SCHIP) may also be available to provide health-care coverage for children and minors. Even though participation is voluntary, every state currently provides Medicaid programs. Some states have subcontracted with private health insurance companies to administer the programs, while other states pay heath-care providers directly.

■ MEDICAID COVERAGE

Under Medicaid guidelines, states have the flexibility to design their own benefits, subject to federal minimum requirements. However, states must provide a minimum set of benefits for certain groups. Services that states must offer include the following:

- Hospital care (inpatient and outpatient)
- Nursing home care
- Physician services
- Laboratory and x-ray services
- Immunizations and other early and periodic screening, diagnostic, and treatment (EPSDT) services for children
- Family planning services
- Federally qualified health center (FQHC) and rural health clinic (RHC) services
- Nurse midwife and nurse practitioner services

States also may cover additional types of services and receive matching federal funds for the costs of those benefits. Additional services may include the following:

- Prescription drugs
- Institutional care for individuals with mental retardation
- Home- and community-based care for the frail elderly, including case management
- Personal care and other community-based services for individuals with disabilities
- Dental care
- Vision care for adults

Coverage Policies

In most cases, Medicaid follows Medicare coverage policies. However, Medicaid covers a wider range of health-care services than Medicare and there are some services that are only covered by Medicaid, such as early and periodic screening, diagnosis, and treatment (EPSDT), elective sterilization procedures, or vision and dental care. This difference in coverage is because the Medicaid population varies widely in age, whereas the Medicare population is made up mostly of elderly adults.

Eligibility and Qualifications

Limited income and resources are the main qualifications for Medicaid eligibility. States provide up to half of the funding for the Medicaid program and the federal government funds the rest. In some states, counties also contribute funds.

Similar to Medicare, CMS establishes the rules and regulations for Medicaid coverage, and the Department of Human Services in every state determines eligibility. The eligibility rules differ significantly from state to state because of this, although all states must follow the same basic federal guidelines. Anyone seeking Medicaid is required to prove that he or she is a United States citizen or **resident alien**.

> **! KEY TERM**
>
> RESIDENT ALIEN—One who has temporary or permanent residence in a foreign country.

Eligibility requirements include the following:

- Families who meet states' Aid to Families with Dependent Children (AFDC).
- Pregnant women and children under age 6 years whose family income is at or below 133% of the federal poverty level.
- Children ages 6 to 19 years with family income up to 100% of the federal poverty level.
- Caretakers (relatives or legal guardians who take care of children under age 18 years (or 19 if still in high school).
- Supplemental Security Income (SSI) recipients (or, in certain states, aged, blind, and disabled people who meet requirements that are more restrictive than those of the SSI program).
- Individuals and couples who are living in medical institutions and who have monthly income up to 300% of the SSI income standard (federal benefit rate).

> **! KEY TERM**
>
> BENEFICIARY OR RECIPIENT—A patient covered under the Medicaid program.

A patient covered under the Medicaid program is referred to as a **recipient** or **beneficiary**. Recipient eligibility is determined on a monthly basis. Each family member is assigned a number that represents his or her eligibility, and identification cards are issued with the recipient's name and ID number. Some states may also include the recipient's date of birth, the Medicaid program the recipient is enrolled in, or other third-party insurance that is in addition to Medicaid coverage. Identification cards are issued and mailed to the recipient, either monthly or annually. The monthly cards will indicate the current recipient eligibility. Annual cards cannot show monthly eligibility so the medical coder should always verify eligibility if an annual card is provided. Most states have an automated eligibility verification system that allows a quick check by keying the ID number over the telephone.

The medical coder also can verify eligibility with the state organization administering the Medicaid program. That organization is referred to as a **fiscal agent**. Each state determines who will be the fiscal agent: a third-party administrator such as an insurance company or the state Department of Human Services will manage it.

MEDICAID PROGRAMS AND OTHER PAYERS

Many states provide several extra programs along with Medicaid coverage. Some focus on eligibility, while others focus on coverage. The medical coder needs to be familiar with the programs offered in his or her state to properly submit insurance claims. To help educate medical staff, fiscal agents supply a provider manual, specific to each type of health-care setting, such as physician offices or hospitals. The manual contains information on the state's specific rules concerning eligibility, general policies, covered services, noncovered services, claim completion, explanation of benefits, and state and federal contacts. The manual is intended to provide information to all providers of medical and health services participating in the program.

> **! KEY TERMS**
>
> QUALIFIED PROVIDER—A provider designated by the state Department of Human Services to determine presumptive eligibility after meeting certain guidelines.
>
> PRESUMPTIVE ELIGIBILITY—A limited period of time for which a categorically needy pregnant woman is determined eligible for Medicaid assistance. Its purpose is to encourage pregnant women to receive adequate prenatal care in the earlier months of their pregnancy, and to ensure qualified providers of payment for the prenatal care.

Presumptive Eligibility

The Presumptive Eligibility Program was created to make it easier for pregnant women to obtain medical care while they are waiting for formal Medicaid eligibility determination from the Department of Health and Human Services. For **presumptive eligibility**, a **qualified provider** "presumes" that the pregnant person will be eligible for Medicaid based on her family income. The program also grants Medicaid coverage during the Medicaid application process to pay for the cost of ambulatory medical care for a set number of days. Coverage may continue from that date of the presumptive eligibility determination or until a decision is made on the application. Under the program, "Ambulatory prenatal care" means all Medicaid-covered services except inpatient hospital care and charges associated with the delivery of the baby.

State Children's Health Insurance Program (SCHIP)

The majority of states offer a program to provide health insurance to children. The program was designed to cover uninsured children in families with incomes that are modest but too high to qualify for Medicaid. The program receives matching funds from the federal government to provide this coverage. Each state determines the design and name of its program, eligibility, benefits, levels of reimbursement, and administrative and operating procedures.

Early and Periodic Screening, Diagnosis, and Treatment (EPSDT)

EPSDT is the early periodic screening, diagnosis, and treatment program for children who are enrolled in Medicaid. The program was designed for children to receive quality health care beginning at birth and continuing throughout childhood and adolescence to ensure the identification, diagnosis, and treatment of medical conditions as early as possible. Children are screened for health and developmental problems according to standards set by the American Academy of Pediatrics. Covered services include health history, developmental assessment, physical examinations, immunizations, laboratory tests, health education, dental examinations, and vision and hearing screenings.

The focus of the program is to ensure that eligible children ages birth through 20 years receive preventive health and oral health-care services. Each state is able to administer its own program, and some states may offer more services than others. In addition, the EPSDT program is referred to differently in each state; for example, Iowa's program is called Care for Kids, whereas the California program is known as Child Health and Disability Prevention (CHDP).

! KEY TERM

MEDICALLY NEEDY—Persons who are eligible for Medicaid and whose income, minus total medical bills, is below state income limits for the Medicaid program.

Medically Needy Program

Every state has the option of extending Medicaid coverage to certain patients who do not qualify for Medicaid, but have extenuating circumstances. Under different standards, these individuals may qualify for the medically needy program.

The **medically needy** program provides medical coverage to people who are pregnant, under 21 years of age, caretaker relatives, aged, blind, or disabled, and those who would qualify for other Medicaid programs except:

■ They have slightly too much income or resources.

■ They have substantially higher incomes but have unusually high medical expenses.

The medically needy income level is based on family size, and potentially eligible patients must meet the necessary income requirements of the program to receive Medicaid benefits. Medically needy recipients are entitled to receive all the basic services covered by Medicaid, and the state decides what additional health-care coverage to make available to the medically needy recipients.

! KEY TERM

SPENDDOWN—A process that allows patients to reduce excess income through medical expenses to qualify for the medically needy program.

People who meet all eligibility factors for the medically needy program except for income are allowed to reduce their excess income through incurred medical expenses. This process is called **spenddown**. To qualify for the medically needy spenddown program, a patient must verify their outstanding medical expenses. The fees for these outstanding medical services may be used to "spend down" the patient's income. Simply put, a patient must show what their monthly income would be if every outstanding medical bill was paid. Those expenses would significantly take away from the patient's actual monthly income, allowing them to financially qualify for Medicaid coverage. Any service that was used to meet their spenddown obligation, before their Medicaid eligibility, will not be paid by Medicaid, and remains the patient's financial obligation. The amount used for the spenddown will be listed on the Remittance Statement. Recipients are notified which of their medical expenses were used to meet their spenddown and remain their personal obligation.

Medicaid and Managed Care

Medicaid also provides a managed health-care option that assigns or offers certain Medicaid recipients a specified primary care physician. The program was developed for the following reasons:

- Contain Medicaid costs
- Ensure appropriate utilization of services
- Enhance quality and continuity of care

Well over half of the nation's Medicaid recipients receive their benefits from managed care plans. The majority of the managed care plans are either Risk-based or Fee-for-Service Primary Care Case Management (PCCM). In a risk-based plan, the managed care company is paid a fixed monthly amount per Medicaid enrollee. In a PCCM plan, a provider, usually a primary care provider, is responsible for the care received and is paid for each covered service rendered. It is the responsibility of the primary care physician to make referrals to any needed specialist.

Physicians, rural health clinics, and federally qualified health centers are eligible to become patient managers. An agreement in addition to the regular Medicaid agreement is required for the provider and managed services are listed on the recipient's Medical Assistance Eligibility Card. Services that are not authorized by the patient manager are not payable.

The medical coder's role is to verify the patient's plan and type of coverage before service are rendered, whenever possible. The coder or front desk personnel should always ask to see a patient identification card to verify this information and know where claims should be submitted for reimbursement. (Information provided by the Kaiser Commission on Medicaid and the Uninsured, Publication number 206803, Publish date 12/2001. More information on managed care can be found in Chapter 10.)

Medicare/Medicaid Dual Eligibles

Dual eligibles are individuals who are entitled to Medicare Part A and/or Part B and are also eligible for some form of Medicaid benefit as a result of certain circumstances. People with Medicare who have limited income and resources may get help paying for their out-of-pocket medical expenses from their state Medicaid program. There are various benefits to "dual eligibles" who are entitled to Medicare and are eligible for some type of Medicaid benefit. These benefits can also be called "Medicare Savings Programs" (MSP).

> **KEY TERM**
>
> DUAL ELIGIBLES—Individuals who are entitled to a Medicaid benefit along with Medicare Part A or Part B.

For people who are eligible for full Medicaid coverage, the Medicaid program supplements Medicare coverage by providing services and supplies that are available under their states Medicaid program. Services that are covered by both programs are first paid by Medicare and then Medicaid pays the balance, up to the state's payment limit. Medicaid uses the same fee schedule as Medicare, so no additional payment is needed in many cases. However, Medicaid can assist with a patient's Medicare deductible and also cover additional services (e.g., nursing facility care beyond the current limited days covered by Medicare, eyeglasses, and hearing aids).

MEDICAID PROVIDERS

Medicaid Patient Administration

Every health-care provider has the option of providing care to Medicaid patients. Unlike Medicare, a provider must enroll with each state in order to provide Medicaid services. The state Department of Human Services will direct any provider to the local fiscal agent for all provider enrollment procedures. If the provider decides to participate in the Medicaid program, care must be rendered to any Medicaid recipient. As with Medicare, the provider must accept the Medicaid allowances as payment in full for all covered services.

For Medicaid claims, the physician must agree to the following statements and conditions listed on the back of the CMS-1500 claim form (Fig. 9–1).

Medicaid Payments

Providers who participate in a Medicaid program must abide by all of the state and federal guidelines. Each state chooses its timely filing limits and the state's Medicaid manual will define the time limit regulations currently in effect. If a claim form is not submitted on time, the claim will be denied. Generally, the only exceptions are retroactive eligibility or delay due to third party insurance filing, but it is up to each state to determine the procedure for accepting an old claim. The medical coder may need to work directly with the state Department of Human Services for reimbursement.

With every claim submitted the health-care provider agrees to abide by the rules and regulations of Medicaid. The provider verifies that the services and charges being submitted are true. The claim form becomes a signed legal document.

FEES AND COSTS RELATED TO MEDICAID SERVICES

Reimbursement Guidelines

Medicaid reimbursement rates are determined by each state. The payment policies for global surgery, multiple surgeries, and other related policies are similar to Medicare. Each state provides its participating health-care providers with this information. Most can be found on their individual websites (a list is included on the Davis*Plus* website). As discussed earlier in this chapter, physicians and other providers who choose to participate in Medicaid must accept the amounts that Medicaid pays as payment in full; besides collecting the copayment, the provider must agree to accept the Medicaid payment and cannot balance bill the patient.

Medicaid is the payer of last resort for any service covered by the program. If another insurance plan has not paid the full charge for a service, Medicaid may be billed. However, if the third-party payment is equal to or more than the Medicaid allowance, Medicaid will make no payment. Providers must consider the claim paid in full and cannot bill the recipient.

I hereby agree to keep such records as are necessary to disclose fully the extent of services provided to individuals under the State's XIX plan and to furnish information regarding any payments claimed for providing such services as the State Agency of Dept. of Health and Human Services may request.
I further agree to accept, as payment in full, the amount paid by the Medicaid program for those claims submitted for payment under that program, with the exception of authorized deductible, coinsurance, copayment or similar cost-sharing charge.
SIGNATURE OF PHYSICIAN (OR SUPPLIER): _____
I certify that the services listed above were medically indicated and necessary to the health of the patient and were personally furnished by me or my employee under my personal supervision.
NOTICE: This is to certify that the foregoing information is true, accurate and complete. I understand that payment and satisfaction of the claim will be from Federal and State funds, and that any false claims, statements, or documents, or concealment of a material fact, may be prosecuted under applicable Federal or State laws.

FIGURE 9–1: Legal statement from the back of the CMS-1500 form.

Copayment

A copayment is a charge that must be paid by the patient when a provided service is covered under Medicaid. States may require a small copayment on most nonemergency services, including for prescription drugs. Copayments may **NOT** be charges for the following individuals or types of services:

- Children under 18 years of age
- Pregnant women for any services relating to pregnancy or any other medical condition that may complicate the pregnancy
- Terminally ill patients receiving hospice care
- Inpatients in hospitals, nursing facilities, intermediate care facility (ICF), or Mental Retardation Institute with a minimal income
- Emergency services
- Family planning services and supplies

The medical coder may be responsible for the collection of the copayment at the time of service. However, if the beneficiary is unable to pay their copayment, the provider may not deny care or services to the beneficiary.

MEDICAID CLAIMS

Medicaid also follows Medicare guidelines for claim form completion, although the medical coder should always refer to the state Medicaid manual for the required claim completion specifications. As with other insurance claims, electronic claim filing is preferable to paper claims because it offers improved efficiency for both Medicaid and the provider. If the medical coder *must* submit a paper claim, the back of the claim form must be included with every submission. As previously discussed, the claim form also must be signed because it is considered a legal document.

Claim Submission

Table 9-1 instructs the medical coder what is typically required to complete a Medicaid claim (Fig. 9–2). Keep in mind each state may have a requirement that should be followed, and the state agency provider manual should always be consulted.

REMITTANCE ADVICE

When Medicaid processes claims, a statement is issued to the provider showing claims paid, denied, or in process. The statement can be referred to as a remittance advice (Fig. 9–3), remittance statement, or explanation of benefits. If claims are paid, a check will be included with the remittance statement. All payments are sent directly to the health-care provider and are never sent to the recipient. This means Box 13 on the CMS-1500 claim form does not need to be completed.

Figure 9–3 is a sample remittance statement. This remittance statement is used by the state of Iowa. Every state will use its own remittance format. Basic information always present includes the following:

- Date of service
- Name of patient/Medicaid recipient
- Procedure code representing the service(s) rendered
- Charge for each service
- Total charge for each claim
- Status of each claim as paid, denied, or pending
- Remittance statement most generally will give an explanation for the denial
- Total amount of the check sent to the provider

TABLE 9–1: Medicaid Claim Form Completion Guidelines

	Information Needed	Where the Information Will Be Found
Items 1–13 Patient and Insured Information		
Item 1 Type of Health Insurance	Check the Medicaid box where the claim will be sent	Patient's Medicaid card and patient information sheet
Item 1a Insured's ID Number	The Patient's Medicaid identification number	Patient's Medicaid card and patient information sheet
Item 2 Patient's name (Last, First, Middle Initial)	The name of the patient who received the service	Superbill and patient information sheet
Item 3 Patient's Date of Birth	The patient's date of birth MM/DD/CCYY and gender, male or female Optional in some states	Patient information sheet Check with local agency for requirements
Item 4 Insured's Name (Last, First, Middle Initial)	For Medicaid purposes this will always be the same as the patient Optional in some states	Patient's insurance card and patient information sheet Check with local agency for requirements
Item 5 Patient's Address	The patient's mailing address and phone number Optional in some states	Patient information sheet Check with local agency for requirements
Item 6 Patient's Relationship to Insured	For Medicaid purposes this will always be the same as the patient Optional in some states	Patient information sheet Check with local agency for requirements
Item 7 Insured's Address	For Medicaid purposes this will always be the same as the patient Optional in some states	Patient information sheet
Item 8 Patient's Status	Indicate the patient's marital and employment status Optional in some states	Patient information sheet
Item 9 Other Insured's Name	If no benefits exist, leave blank **or** Enter the last name, first name, and middle initial of the policy holder If patient's insurance, enter the word SAME	Patient information sheet
Item 9a Other Insured's Policy or Group Number	If no benefits exist, leave blank **or** Enter the identification number of the insured in Box 9	Patient information sheet, insurance ID card
Item 9b Other Insured's Date of Birth	If no benefits exist, leave blank **or** Enter the date of birth MM/DD/CCYY and gender of the insured in Box 9	Patient information sheet
Item 9c Employer's Name or School Name	If no other benefits exist leave blank, otherwise list address of the insurance company	Patient information sheet or insurance identification card
Item 9d Insurance Plan Name or Program name	Enter the name of insurance for insured in Box 9 If 11d is marked "Yes," Boxes 9, 9a–9d must be completed	Patient information sheet or insurance identification card

Continued

TABLE 9–1:   Medicaid Claim Form Completion Guidelines—cont'd

Information Needed		Where the Information Will Be Found

Items 1–13 Patient and Insured Information

Item 10a Is Patient's Condition Related To Employment?	Indicate yes or no if the condition of the patient is related to an employment incident	Patient information sheet and/or the appointment schedule
Item 10b Is Patient's Condition Related To Auto Accident?	Indicate yes or no if the condition of the patient is related to an auto accident	Patient information sheet and/or the appointment schedule
Item 10c Is Patient's Condition Related To Other Accident?	Indicate yes or no if the condition of the patient is related to another type of accident	Patient information sheet and/or the appointment schedule
Item 10d Reserved For Local Use	Optional, may not be required in some states	Check with local agency for requirements
Item 11 Insured's Policy Group or FECA Number	The group ID number or the alphanumeric number (FECA) of the health, auto, or other insurance plan of the insured in Box 4 If there is no insurance primary to Medicaid, enter the word "NONE"	Patient information sheet and/or the ID card of the person indicated in Box 4. May be optional, check with local agency for requirements
Item 11a Insured's Date of Birth and Sex	Optional in some states The birth date and gender of the insured in Box 11 MM/DD/CCYY For Medicaid purposes this will always be the same as the patient	Patient information sheet Check with local agency for requirements
Item 11b Employer's Name or School Name	Optional in some states The employer or school name of the insured in Box 1a For Medicaid purposes this will always be the same as the patient	Patient information sheet Check with local agency for requirements
Item 11c Insurance Plan Name or Program Name	Optional in some states This box must be completed if a policy number is in 11 The ID number or name of the plan or program of the insured indicated in Box 11 For Medicaid purposes, this will always be the same as the patient	Patient information sheet Check with local agency for requirements
Item 11d Is There Another Health Plan? *If yes, return to and complete 9a–d*	Optional in some states Required if the patient has other insurance Mark "Yes," then Boxes 9a–9d must be completed If there is no other insurance mark "NO" If there has been a denial from another insurance, some states require that both boxes be checked	Patient information sheet Check with local agency for requirements
Item 12 Patient's or Authorized Person's Signature	Optional in some states Authorization may have been given at the start of eligibility If required, a signature on file authorizing a release of medical records or other information is needed to process the claim	Patient information sheet Check with local agency for requirements

TABLE 9–1:   Medicaid Claim Form Completion Guidelines—cont'd

	Information Needed	Where the Information Will Be Found

Items 1–13 Patient and Insured Information

Item 13 Insured's or Authorized Signature	Authorization is optional in some states For Medicaid purposes payment will always be sent directly to the provider who appears in Boxes 31 and 33 of the claim	Patient information sheet Check with local agency for requirements

Items 14–33 Encounter and Provider Information

Item 14 Date of Current Illness, Injury, Pregnancy	Situational in some states Can be used for the first date of onset of illness, the actual date of the injury, or the LMP for pregnancy **or** date of treatment initiation or x-ray taken for chiropractic care	Patient's medical record Check with local agency for requirements
Item 15 If Patient Has Had Same or Similar Illness	Situational in some states, may be required for chiropractors to enter patient's current date of x-ray	Check with local agency for requirements
Item 16 Dates Patient Unable to Work in Current Occupation	Optional in some states The from and to dates that the patient is/was unable to work	Patient's medical record Check with local agency for requirements
Item 17 Name of Referring Provider or Other Source	Situational—Name of the referring provider who referred patient	The patient or the referring or ordering provider
Item 17a Other ID #	Optional—ID number of provider in Box 17 or leave blank if no longer required by Medicaid	Check with local agency for requirements
Item 17b NPI #	The National Provider Identifier (NPI) number of the referring provider listed in Box 17	Directly from the referring or ordering provider or directory containing the ID numbers
Item 18 Hospitalization Dates Related to Current Illness	Situational in some states The admission and discharge dates of the inpatient stay related to the services listed on the claim	Patient's medical record Check with local agency for requirements
Item 19 Reserved for Local Use	Optional in some states Multiple uses Check with local Medicaid agency for their instruction	Patient's medical record or the referring or ordering provider or directory containing the ID numbers or patient information sheet
		Note Electronic claims can hold up to 80 characters in Box 19 for a concise statement. If needed information does not fit in 19 on a paper form, an attachment must be submitted with the claim.

Continued

TABLE 9–1: Medicaid Claim Form Completion Guidelines—cont'd

	Information Needed	Where the Information Will Be Found

Items 14–33 Encounter and Provider Information

	Information Needed	Where the Information Will Be Found
Item 20 Outside Lab? $ Charges	Optional in some states Yes or No the service/s on the claim were purchased from an outside laboratory and the charged amount If "yes" is checked here, Box 32 must contain the name and NPI of the laboratory	Patient's medical record, log kept on file, or provider or directory containing the ID numbers Check with local agency for requirements
Item 21 Diagnosis or Nature of Illness or Injury (relate items 1, 2, 3, or 4 to 24E by line)	The ICD-9-CM code(s) representing the patient's diagnosis or condition in order of importance Some states allow up to eight diagnosis codes be entered	The reason for the services on the claim found in patient's medical record and diagnosis codes found in current ICD-9-CM manual Check with local agency for requirements
Item 22 Medicaid Resubmission	Optional in some states Leave blank if not required by state agency	Check with local agency for requirements
Item 23 Prior Authorization Number	Situational in some states Used to show Medicaid has approved a service before it was rendered to a patient	Patient's medical records Check with local agency for requirements
Item 24 A Date(s) of Service	The date the service was performed (mmddyy) or (mmddyyyy) (up to six services billed per claim)	Superbill Check with local agency for 6- or 8-digit date requirements
Item 24 B Place of Service	The two-digit location code that represents where the service was rendered	Superbill for place of service Place of service codes can be found in front of CPT
Item 24 C EMG	Optional—This represents emergency services in some states	Super bill or patient's medical records Check with the local agency
Item 24 D Procedures, Services, Supplies	The CPT/HCPCS code and modifier(s) if needed, identifying the service	Superbill for services rendered CPT and HCPCS manuals for codes
Item 24 E Diagnosis Pointer	May be optional Check with local agency for requirements Enter the primary reference # of the line number from Box 21 (1, 2, 3, or 4) that relates to the service(s) rendered	Superbill for diagnoses and Box 21 of claim Check with local agency, some states limit one reference number per line item
Item 24 F $ Charges	The charged amount for each service line	Superbill or log/spreadsheet kept on file Check with local agency, some states do not use $ signs, decimals, dashes, commas, or lines (e.g., 2400)
Item 24 G Days or Units	The number of days indicated in the date span of 24A **or** the number units or minutes the service was performed (1 visit = 1 unit, 1 minute = 1 unit)	Superbill and patient's medical record

TABLE 9–1:   Medicaid Claim Form Completion Guidelines—cont'd

	Information Needed	Where the Information Will Be Found
Items 14–33 Encounter and Provider Information		
Item 24 H EPSDT Family Plan	Optional—Some states use this area to indicate the type of service given For example, an "F" to indicate services were family planning related, "E" to indicate a health-check service that does not require any follow-up service, or an "R" to indicate a health-check service that does require a follow up service	Check with local agency
Item 24 I ID Qualifier	Optional—Some states request a non-NPI number be placed here if something other than the provider's NPI is used in Box 24J For example, the qualifier "1D" in the shaded area to indicate a provider number other than the physician's NPI is in 24J	The instructions from the local and current Medicaid or other third-party carrier's policy manual
Item 24 J Rendering Provider ID #	Required by some states For example, used to indicate the individual NPI of the provider rendering the service indicated in 24D **who is:** • An incorporated, solo provider with an individual NPI and a group NPI # • A provider working in a group practice or clinic	The provider directory containing the ID numbers Check with local agency for requirements, some states do not allow multiple providers in a practice billing on the same claim
Item 25 Federal Tax ID Number	Optional—Some states require the tax ID or Social Security number of the provider of service and mark an X in the appropriate box	The provider of service's records Check with local agency for requirements
Item 26 Patient's Account No.	Optional—If office assigns patient ID numbers, enter the identifying account number for the patient in Box 2 The account number may then be indicated on the remittance statement	Patient's medical record or file
Item 27 Accept Assignment	Not required—For Medicaid purposes payment will always be sent to the provider All providers accept Medicaid's allowance as payment in full	The provider of service's records
Item 28 Total Charge	The sum of all services entered in 24F	The superbill, a hospital report, or the patient's account Check with local agency for requirements, some states do not use $ signs, decimals, dashes, commas, or lines (e.g., 2400)

Continued

TABLE 9–1: Medicaid Claim Form Completion Guidelines—cont'd

	Information Needed	Where the Information Will Be Found
Items 14–33 Encounter and Provider Information		
Item 29 Amount Paid	Situational—Total amount patient paid only, toward the services in 24F	The superbill, a record of receipts, or the patient 's account Check with local agency for requirements, some states do not use $ signs, decimals, dashes, commas, or lines (e.g., 2400) Some states may require additional information in Boxes 10d or 19 regarding the payment amount shown
Item 30 Balance Due	Situational—Enter the difference between Box 28 and Box 29 to indicate total balance amount due	The superbill, a record of receipts, or statement from a third-party payer, or the patient's account Check with local agency and software provider for requirements This field may not exist on paperless claims
Item 31 Signature of Physician or Supplier Including Degrees or Credentials (I certify that the statements on the reverse apply to this bill and are made a part thereof)	The physician's signature or a representative of and the date the claim form was completed Some states for use of 6- or 8-digit MMDDYY or MMDDYYYY format In some states, a signature stamp or computerized generated stamp is also acceptable	Check with local agency and software provider for requirements The signature and date field may not exist when billing paperless claims
Item 32 Service Facility Location Information	The name and address of facility where services were rendered	If different from Box 33, a provider directory or phone book may contain the facility address
Item 32a NPI #	The NPI number of the facility where the service took place.	The provider directory containing the ID numbers
Item 32b Other ID #	Situational—The non-NPI number identifying the provider number in Box 32a, if other than an NPI	Check with local agency, may no longer be required
Item 33 Billing Provider Info & Ph #	The name, address, and telephone number of the provider requesting payment for the service in 24 The phone number may be optional in some states	A provider directory or phone book, or the coder's place of employment
Item 33a NPI #	The NPI number of the solo or group practice requesting payment for the service(s) in 24	Check the local agency for requirements for this box The provider directory containing the ID numbers
Item 33b Other ID #	Situational—The non-NPI number identifying the provider number in Box 33a, if other than an NPI	Check with local agency, may no longer be required

1500

HEALTH INSURANCE CLAIM FORM

APPROVED BY NATIONAL UNIFORM CLAIM COMMITTEE 08/05

| | | | PICA | | | | | | PICA | | |

1. MEDICARE MEDICAID TRICARE CHAMPUS CHAMPVA GROUP HEALTH PLAN FECA BLK LUNG OTHER	1a. INSURED'S I.D. NUMBER (For Program in Item 1)
☐ (Medicare #) ☒ (Medicaid #) ☐ (Sponsor's SSN) ☐ (Member ID#) ☐ (SSN or ID) ☐ (SSN) ☐ (ID)	1234567A

2. PATIENT'S NAME (Last Name, First Name, Middle Initial)	3. PATIENT'S BIRTH DATE SEX	4. INSURED'S NAME (Last Name, First Name, Middle Initial)
GARDNER NANCY	01 10 1980 M ☐ F ☒	GARDNER NANCY

5. PATIENT'S ADDRESS (No., Street)	6. PATIENT RELATIONSHIP TO INSURED	7. INSURED'S ADDRESS (No., Street)
123 MAIN STREET	Self ☒ Spouse ☐ Child ☐ Other ☐	123 MAIN STREET

CITY	STATE	8. PATIENT STATUS	CITY	STATE
ANYTOWN	MA	Single ☐ Married ☒ Other ☐	ANYTOWN	MA

ZIP CODE	TELEPHONE (Include Area Code)		ZIP CODE	TELEPHONE (Include Area Code)
55595	(555) 111-5555	Employed ☐ Full-Time Student ☐ Part-Time Student ☐	55595	(555) 111-5555

9. OTHER INSURED'S NAME (Last Name, First Name, Middle Initial)	10. IS PATIENT'S CONDITION RELATED TO:	11. INSURED'S POLICY GROUP OR FECA NUMBER
OPTIONAL		OPTIONAL

a. OTHER INSURED'S POLICY OR GROUP NUMBER	a. EMPLOYMENT? (Current or Previous) ☐ YES ☒ NO	a. INSURED'S DATE OF BIRTH MM DD YY SEX M ☐ F ☐
b. OTHER INSURED'S DATE OF BIRTH MM DD YY SEX M ☐ F ☐	b. AUTO ACCIDENT? PLACE (State) ☐ YES ☒ NO	b. EMPLOYER'S NAME OR SCHOOL NAME
c. EMPLOYER'S NAME OR SCHOOL NAME	c. OTHER ACCIDENT? ☐ YES ☒ NO	c. INSURANCE PLAN NAME OR PROGRAM NAME
d. INSURANCE PLAN NAME OR PROGRAM NAME	10d. RESERVED FOR LOCAL USE	d. IS THERE ANOTHER HEALTH BENEFIT PLAN? ☐ YES ☐ NO If yes, return to and complete item 9 a-d.

READ BACK OF FORM BEFORE COMPLETING & SIGNING THIS FORM.

12. PATIENT'S OR AUTHORIZED PERSON'S SIGNATURE I authorize the release of any medical or other information necessary to process this claim. I also request payment of government benefits either to myself or to the party who accepts assignment below.

SIGNED OPTIONAL SIGNATURE ON FILE (SOF)   DATE _____

13. INSURED'S OR AUTHORIZED PERSON'S SIGNATURE I authorize payment of medical benefits to the undersigned physician or supplier for services described below.

SIGNED OPTIONAL SIGNATURE ON FILE (SOF)

14. DATE OF CURRENT: ILLNESS (First symptom) OR INJURY (Accident) OR PREGNANCY(LMP) MM DD YY	15. IF PATIENT HAS HAD SAME OR SIMILAR ILLNESS. GIVE FIRST DATE MM DD YY	16. DATES PATIENT UNABLE TO WORK IN CURRENT OCCUPATION MM DD YY FROM TO MM DD YY
17. NAME OF REFERRING PROVIDER OR OTHER SOURCE	17a. ___ 17b. NPI	18. HOSPITALIZATION DATES RELATED TO CURRENT SERVICES MM DD YY FROM TO MM DD YY
19. RESERVED FOR LOCAL USE		20. OUTSIDE LAB? ☐ YES ☐ NO $ CHARGES

21. DIAGNOSIS OR NATURE OF ILLNESS OR INJURY (Relate Items 1, 2, 3 or 4 to Item 24E by Line)	22. MEDICAID RESUBMISSION CODE ORIGINAL REF. NO.
1. 784.0 3. ⌞___	
2. ⌞___ 4. ⌞___	23. PRIOR AUTHORIZATION NUMBER

24. A. DATE(S) OF SERVICE From To MM DD YY MM DD YY	B. PLACE OF SERVICE	C. EMG	D. PROCEDURES, SERVICES, OR SUPPLIES (Explain Unusual Circumstances) CPT/HCPCS MODIFIER	E. DIAGNOSIS POINTER	F. $ CHARGES	G. DAYS OR UNITS	H. EPSDT Family Plan	I. ID. QUAL.	J. RENDERING PROVIDER ID. #
									OPTIONAL PER STATE AGENCY
1 04 19 09 04 19 09	11		99212	1	90 00	1		NPI	1234567890
2								NPI	
3								NPI	
4								NPI	
5								NPI	
6								NPI	

25. FEDERAL TAX I.D. NUMBER SSN EIN	26. PATIENT'S ACCOUNT NO.	27. ACCEPT ASSIGNMENT? (For govt. claims, see back)	28. TOTAL CHARGE	29. AMOUNT PAID	30. BALANCE DUE
OPTIONAL ☐ ☐	12456 (OPTIONAL)	☐ YES ☐ NO	$ 90 00	$	$ 90 00

31. SIGNATURE OF PHYSICIAN OR SUPPLIER INCLUDING DEGREES OR CREDENTIALS (I certify that the statements on the reverse apply to this bill and are made a part thereof.) *Joe Smith MD* 09/30/09 SIGNED DATE	32. SERVICE FACILITY LOCATION INFORMATION OPTIONAL PER STATE AGENCY a. NPI b.	33. BILLING PROVIDER INFO & PH # ( ) OPTIONAL JOE SMITH MD 555 COLUMBIA PRAIRIE CITY MA 55502 a. 1234567890 b.

FIGURE 9-2: Completed CMS-1500 form for patient with Medicaid.

MEDICAID MANAGEMENT INFORMATION SYSTEM Run date 06/12/97

(1.) **(2.)** **REMITTANCE ADVICE** **(4.)** **(5.)**

To: R.A. No.: 0000006 **(3.)** Date paid: 05/19/97 Provider Number: Page: 1

**** Patient name ****	Recip ID /	Trans-control-number /		Billed	Other	Paid by	Copay	Med rcd num /	S EOB EOB
Last First MI	Line	SVC-date Proc/mods	Units	amt.	sources	MCaid	amt.	Perf. prov.	

* **(6.)** Claim type: HCFA 1500 * **(7.)** Claim status: Paid

Original claims:

(8.)	**(9.)**	**(10.)**		**(11.)**	**(12.)**	**(13.)**	**(14.)**	**(15.)**	**(16.)**
		4–96331–00–053–0038–00		38.00	0.00	16.06	0.00	8606006088	900 000
	(17.) 01 **(18.)** 10/3 **(19.)** 99212 **(20.)** 1	**(21.)** 38.00 **(22.)** 0.00 **(23.)** 16.06 **(24.)** 0.00 **(25.)**							000 000
		4–96348–00–018–0060–00		50.00	0.00	35.26	0.00	8606006088	000 000
	01	11/15/96 J1055	1	41.00	0.00	33.18	0.00		F 000 000
	02	11/15/96 9C782	1	9.00	0.00	2.08	0.00	**(26.)**	F 000 000

(27.)

Remittance totals

Paid original claims:	Number of claims	2	------------	88.00	51.32
Paid adjustment claims:	Number of claims	0	------------	0.00	0.00
Denied original claims:	Number of claims	0	------------	0.00	0.00
Denied adjustment claims:	Number of claims	0	------------	0.00	0.00
Pended claims (in process):	Number of claims	0	------------	0.00	0.00
Amount of check:	--				51.32

---- The following is a description of the explanation of benefit (EOB) codes that appear above:

(28.) 900 The claim is in suspense. Do not resubmit the claim.

Medicaid Remittance Advice Field Descriptions	
Field #	**Field Description**
1	Billing provider's name as specified on the Medicaid Provider Enrollment Application
2	Remittance Advice number
3	Date claim paid
4	Billing provider's Medicaid (Title XIX) number
5	Remittance Advice page number
6	Type of claim used to bill Medicaid
7	Status of following claims: • Paid - claims for which reimbursement is being made • Denied - claims for which no reimbursement is being made • Suspended - claims in process. These claims have not yet been paid or denied
8	Recipient's last and first name
9	Recipient's Medicaid (Title XIX) number
10	Transaction control number assigned to each claim by the fiscal agent. Use this number when making claim inquiries
11	Total charges submitted by provider
12	Total amount applied to this claim from other resources, i.e., other insurance or spenddown
13	Total amount of Medicaid reimbursement as allowed for this claim
14	Total amount of recipient copayment deducted from this claim
15	Medical record number as assigned by provider; 10 characters are possible
16	Explanation of benefits code for information purposes or to explain why a claim denied
17	Line item number

FIGURE 9–3: Medicaid remittance statement sample.

	Medicaid Remittance Advice Field Descriptions *(continued)*
Field #	Field Description
18	The first date of service for the billed procedure
19	The procedure code for the rendered service
20	The number of units of rendered service
21	Charge submitted by provider for the line item
22	Amount applied to this line item from other resouces, i.e., other insurance, spenddown
23	Amount of Medicaid reimbursement as allowed for this line item
24	Amount of recipient copayment for this line item
25	Treating provider's Medicaid (Title XIX) number
26	Allowed charge source code: **B** = Billed charge **F** = Fee schedule **M** = Manually priced **N** = Provider charge rate **P** = Group therapy **Q** = EPSDT total screen over 17 years **R** = EPSDT total screen over 18 years **S** = EPSDT partial screen over 17 years **T** = EPSDT partial screen over 18 years **U** = Gynecology fee **V** = Obstetrics fee **W** = Child fee
27	Remittance totals (found at the end of the Remittance Advice): • Number of paid original claims, the amount billed by the provider and the amount allowed and reimbursed by Medicaid • Number of paid adjusted claims, amount billed by provider and amount allowed and reimbursed by Medicaid • Number of denied original claims and amount billed by provider • Number of denied adjusted claims and amount billed by provider • Number of pended claims (in process) and amount billed by provider • Amount of check
28	Description of individual explanation of benefits codes

FIGURE 9–3: cont'd

■ CONCLUSION

Medicaid is funded jointly by state and federal governments and managed by each individual state. Each state designs its own policies within federal guidelines to provide health-care coverage for individuals and families with low incomes. To comply with policy and receive maximum coverage for services rendered, the medical coder must be familiar with the guidelines of his or her state's Medicaid agency. To accomplish this, the medical coder should take advantage of provider education programs offered and the agency's online policy resources. Equally important is verifying the patient's current eligibility status at each visit.

RESOURCE LIST

Centers for Medicare and Medicaid Services (CMS)
http://www.cms.hhs.gov

Iowa Department of Human Services
www.dhs.state.ia.us

Iowa Medicaid Enterprise
www.ime.state.ia.us

The Kaiser Commission on Medicaid and Uninsured
www.kff.org/medicaid/2236-index.cfm

The Kaiser Family Foundation – State Health Facts
http://www.statehealthfacts.org/profile.jsp

National Association of State Medicaid Directors
www.nasmd.org/links/state_medicaid_links.asp

South Carolina Department of Health and Human Services
www.dhhs.state.sc.us/dhhsnew/index.asp

Chapter Review Exercises

General Medicaid

Please answer the following questions.

1. Name five services that states must offer their Medicaid recipients:

   _____

   _____

   _____

2. Name five services states may choose to offer in addition to the mandatory service:

   _____

   _____

   _____

   _____

   _____

3. Medicaid is a public assistance medical care program administered by states and financed jointly through _____ and _____ funds.

4. Medicaid recipient eligibility may be verified using:
   a. An automated verification system
   b. The Department of Health and Human Services
   c. The recipient's ID card
   d. The Office of Inspector General

5. Medicaid is health-care coverage for: individuals and families with

   _____.

6. Every health-care provider has the option of providing care to Medicaid patients.   **True or False** (circle one)

7. Every state designs its own Medicaid eligibility and health-care coverage policies.   **True or False** (circle one)

8. Anyone seeking Medicaid is now required to prove that he or she is:

   _____ or _____.

9. People who meet all eligibility factors for the program except for income are allowed to reduce their excess income through incurred medical expenses through a process known as.

10. Medicaid covers a wider range of health-care services than Medicare.   **True or False** (circle one)

For the following exercises, you will fill out claims as if you were part of the insurance personnel for Dr. John Smith. You will find demographics, office fee schedule, and a blank CMS-1500 form in Appendix A. You will use this information along with Claim Completion scenarios to complete the claim forms exercises at the end of Chapters 7, 8, and 9.

11. Jane Smith

    On May 1 of this year, Jane Smith, an established patient, comes into Dr. Smith's office suffering from sinus headaches. Dr. Smith performs an expanded problem focused examination. Sinus x-rays were taken. With low complexity decision making, Dr. Smith determines that Jane is suffering from a sinus infection and prescribes Amoxicillin 500 mg taken twice a day.

    Complete a CMS-1500 form using this information, the appropriate patient registration information, superbill, and fee schedule that appear in Appendix A.

12. Lynn White

    Dr. Jones has asked Dr. Smith to see a patient with possible heart problems. Dr. Smith performs a detailed, low complexity consultation and a complete M-Mode, 2D echocardiography on Lynn White in the office.

    Dr. Smith diagnoses Lynn with mitral valve prolapse.

    Complete a CMS-1500 form using this information; the appropriate patient registration information, superbill, and fee schedule appear in Appendix A.

Managed Care Plans

Chapter Outline

OBJECTIVES

- Recognize the difference between an HMO and a PPO
- List the three major types of managed care
- Define the role of a primary care physician
- Explain the difference between gatekeeper and open access styles of managed care
- Describe a copayment and its significance
- Define precertification
- Define prior authorization
- Educate a patient regarding their managed care responsibilities

MEDICAL ASSISTING COMPETENCIES
ABHES

1i. conduct work within scope of education, training, and ability

2d. serve as a liaison between Physician and others

2g. use appropriate medical terminology

2h. receive, organize, prioritize, and transmit information expediently

3e. locate resources and information for patients and employers

3t. apply managed care policies and procedures

3u. obtain managed care referrals and pre-certification

5a. determine the needs for documentation and reporting

5b. document accurately

5c. use appropriate guidelines when releasing records or information

CAAHEP

IV.P.3. Use medical terminology, pronouncing medical terms correctly, to communicate information, patient history, data and observations

VII.C.2. Identify models of managed care

VII.C.4. Describe procedures for implementing both managed care and insurance plans

VII.C.6. Discuss referral process for patients in a managed care program

VII.P.1. Apply both managed care policies and procedures

VII.P.4. Obtain pre-certification, including documentation

VII.P.5. Obtain prior-authorization, including documentation

VII.P.6. Verify eligibility for managed care services

VIII.A.1. Work with physician to achieve the maximum reimbursement

---

KEY TERMS

Capitation	Point of Service (POS)	Preferred Provider
Health Maintenance	Pre-admission certification	Organizations (PPO)
Organizations (HMO)	Pre-certification	Primary Care Physician
Network		Prior authorization

■ HISTORY OF MANAGED CARE

In 1973, Congress passed the Health Maintenance Organization Act, which promoted the rapid growth of **Health Maintenance Organizations (HMOs)**, the first form of managed care. Ronald Reagan was the first political leader who worked to reform health care from a not-for-profit business into a for-profit business driven by the insurance industry.

The goals of managed health care are to make certain of the following:

■ Health-care providers provide high-quality care in a method that manages or controls costs.

■ The care provided is medically necessary and appropriate for the patient's condition.

■ Care is rendered by the most appropriate health-care provider.

■ Care is rendered in the most appropriate and least restrictive environment.

The National Library of Medicine states that managed care was created to "reduce unnecessary health care costs through a variety of mechanisms:

■ Incentives for physicians and patients to select less costly forms of care

■ Programs for reviewing the medical necessity of specific services

■ Increased beneficiary cost sharing

■ Controls on inpatient admissions and lengths of stay

■ The establishment of cost sharing incentives for outpatient surgery

■ Selective contracting with health care providers

■ Intensive management of high-cost health care services"*

*Source: http://www.qualitymeasures.ahrq.gov/resources/glossary.aspx
The National Quality Measures Clearinghouse™ (NQMC))

In the late 1980s, managed care plans helped hold down rising medical costs by reducing unnecessary hospitalizations, influencing providers to discount their rates, and prompting the health-care industry to become more proficient and competitive. The managed care system grew quickly, as did criticism from consumers. Since health care was "managed" by for-profit organizations, money-saving efforts were perceived as profit-boosting and unrelated to quality health care. However, reports show that even with an increase to managed care premiums, out-of-pocket expenses have decreased by 25% since managed care plans were implemented.

Today, managed care organizations are common in the United States. According to America's Health Insurance Plans, a trade association, 90% of insured Americans are currently enrolled in some form of managed care. However, despite a large number of users, managed care has not been successful at maintaining rising health-care costs.

MANAGED CARE METHODS

A panel or "**network**," of health-care providers is the most common method of managed care delivery. A network is simply a selected group of providers that have been contracted to deliver a full range of health-care services. Patients must select from this network of health-care providers and are frequently offered preventive care incentives and rewards for efficiently using health care. Other common methods include a formal utilization review board and similar quality control programs. The utilization review board reviews the appropriateness and outcomes of care in order to monitor the amount of services providers give and the quality of care received by the patients.

> **! KEY TERM**
>
> NETWORK—A group of doctors, hospitals, pharmacies, and other health-care providers who contract to provide health services to members of a health plan.

TYPES OF MANAGED CARE PROGRAMS

There are different types of managed care products in the market today. The three major types of managed care plan include:

- **Health Maintenance Organizations (HMOs)**
- **Preferred Provider Organizations (PPOs)**
- **Point of Service (POS)**

There are two styles of managed care:

1. **Gatekeeper**—The patient must identify a **primary care physician**. Only the primary care physician can refer the patient to another provider, usually a specialist.
2. **Open Access**—The patient chooses a physician from a list of participating providers.

> **! KEY TERM**
>
> PRIMARY CARE PHYSICIAN—A physician, usually a family, general practice, OB-GYN, pediatrician, or internal medicine specialist, who is responsible for coordinating the total health care of members within a managed care program.

Health Maintenance Organizations (HMOs)

Health Maintenance Organizations (HMOs) are the most popular of all the managed care plans. A wide range of health-care providers, surgical centers, and hospitals enter contracts with HMO companies, and the providers agree to offer quality health care at a discount rate to receive more patients from the HMO network. HMO members must choose a **primary care physician (PCP)** who provides care and authorizes specialist services, if added care is required. There are several different types of HMOs offered today. The most common types include:

1. **Staff Model**—Health-care providers are salaried and have offices within an HMO facility. These health-care providers see only the patients insured through an HMO.

2. **Individual Practice Association or Independent Practice Association (IPA)**—A health plan contracts with a group of health-care providers to provide health-care coverage for their members. The participating providers treat the members of the managed care plan as well as non-IPA patients.

3. **Group Model**—The HMO contracts with a single multi-specialty provider group that agrees to devote a fixed percentage of time just to the HMO members.

4. **Network Model**—Similar to the Group HMO, the Network contracts medical services from two or more medical groups for their members.

HMOs are the most restrictive type of managed care because of the limited choice of providers. However, when HMOs were first introduced, many traditional insurance plans did not cover preventive medicine, such as immunizations and well physicals. HMOs offer these preventative services with the intention of maintaining each member's health. That's how the name "health maintenance" was decided.

Preferred Provider Organizations (PPOs)

A Preferred Provider Organization (PPO) provides health-care coverage through a panel of health-care providers who have agreed to provide services to patients at discount rates. Unlike HMOs, there is no primary care physician involved in a PPO contract. Patients can go to any physician, but will pay less for services if they see a participating physician. For visits to participating physicians, the patient is usually responsible for small co-payments. For visits to nonparticipating physicians, the patient is usually responsible for meeting a deductible, then paying 20% of the allowed charge. In some cases, payment is made directly to the physician. However, specifics of the PPO are spelled out in the contract with the provider and can vary, depending on the PPO.

! **KEY TERM**

PREFERRED PROVIDER ORGANIZATIONS (PPOs)—A health-care program in which members are encouraged to use medical providers who have contracted with the program to provide medical care at a fixed rate. Members do not have to choose a primary care provider and are rewarded for using those providers by paying less out of their own pockets.

PPOs are thought to be less restrictive than HMO plans because of the choice of providers available. However, PPO plans can require more "out of pocket" expenses from their insureds. The medical coder must find out what each plan offers and what is expected from each patient.

Point of Service (POS)

Point of Service (POS) managed care combines the provider choice benefits of a PPO with premiums of an HMO. The POS is becoming the most popular form of managed care, because this type of plan gives the insured greater freedom in choosing a provider.

Under a POS plan, the insured can choose any physician (in- or out-of-network) and is not required to choose a primary care physician. When an insured chooses to stay within the provider network, the costs are significantly less than out-of-network services. There is usually no deductible or coinsurance and a lower copay. If a patient chooses an out-of-network provider, there is usually a deductible in addition to a higher copay.

! **KEY TERM**

POINT OF SERVICE (POS)—The most popular form of managed care that combines the low cost of HMOs with the greater health-care choices of PPO plans. Members are encouraged to choose a primary care physician within the network of providers, but have the choice of other physicians and hospital facilities as well.

MANAGED CARE PAYMENT SYSTEMS

There are two types of payment systems:

1. **Fee-for-Service**—Usually 90% of the charge, if no maximum, applies to that procedure. Payments are compared to the relative value system and are made directly to the contracting physician.
2. **Capitation**—Capitation funds are determined by the number of members signed up with a physician. The physician receives a check for the same amount whether or not they have seen the patient.

❗ KEY TERM

CAPITATION—A payment method for health-care services in which the provider is paid a fixed rate per month for every patient enrolled under their care rather than a payment for every service provided to each of the patients.

Most services over a certain dollar amount must have prior authorization, such as diagnostic tests and surgeries. Services not covered by an HMO can be billed to the patient, but the patient should be notified in advance whenever possible.

Information specific to the bookkeeping for capitation payments is addressed in Chapter 13.

Copayments

Under plan guidelines, the proper copayments should be collected from the patient at the time of service. The patient has agreed with their plan to pay for all copayments at the time of service and may also be responsible for a certain percentage of the fees. Collection at the time of service is more cost-effective than billing the patient after services are rendered. Postage and the costs to generate a patient statement only deducts from the value of the service. Depending on office procedures, a 20-dollar copayment may not even cover the overhead cost of generating a bill.

The importance of making a copy of the patient's insurance card must be repeated here. The insurance card may provide information about the appropriate copayment collection amount to be received. Often a managed care plan will call for different copayment amounts depending on either the type of care or the place of service. For example, $20.00 is a common copayment in conjunction with an office visit. But the patient may be expected to pay more if the services are rendered in the emergency room, inpatient hospital service, or in an outpatient surgical center. Or a copayment may be waived entirely for certain services provided, such as influenza shots, or screening services such as a mammogram, an annual Pap smear, or a colonoscopy. When the medical coder has this necessary information, the copayment can be collected at the time of service, thus saving the cost of generating a statement or surprising the patient with an unexpected bill.

Monitoring Managed Care Payments

Managed care contracts are periodically renewed. To benefit from and maintain proper reimbursement, the physician must contract with the plans that abide by their contract agreements. Every managed care group that the physician participates in should cover the costs of treating their insureds and be worth the efforts to do so. The medical coder may be asked to provide reimbursement information from the contracted managed care carriers to determine whether or not it is beneficial for a provider to continue an agreement with a program. The original intention of managed care programs was to provide quality care at a lower cost in return for the receipt of more patients.

Figure 10–1 shows a completed CMS-1500 claim form for a patient with a managed care insurance plan.

MANAGED CARE AND MEDICARE/MEDICAID

In 1984, the Department of Health and Human Services gave Medicare beneficiaries and Medicaid recipients the right to enroll in an HMO or PPO to receive all of their medical benefits. All services provided to a beneficiary are then submitted directly to the managed care company and not to

1500

HEALTH INSURANCE CLAIM FORM

APPROVED BY NATIONAL UNIFORM CLAIM COMMITTEE 08/05

PICA | PICA

CARRIER

1. MEDICARE (Medicare #) [ ] MEDICAID (Medicaid #) [ ] TRICARE CHAMPUS (Sponsor's SSN) [ ] CHAMPVA (Member ID#) [ ] GROUP HEALTH PLAN (SSN or ID) [X] FECA BLK LUNG (SSN) [ ] OTHER (ID) [ ]

1a. INSURED'S I.D. NUMBER (For Program in Item 1): AL090822

2. PATIENT'S NAME (Last Name, First Name, Middle Initial): LYNDE GEORGE

3. PATIENT'S BIRTH DATE MM DD YY: 11 03 1985 SEX M [X] F [ ]

4. INSURED'S NAME (Last Name, First Name, Middle Initial): LYNDE GEORGE

5. PATIENT'S ADDRESS (No., Street): 4111 SPRINGDALE DRIVE

6. PATIENT RELATIONSHIP TO INSURED: Self [X] Spouse [ ] Child [ ] Other [ ]

7. INSURED'S ADDRESS (No., Street): 4111 SPRINGDALE DRIVE

CITY: MONROE STATE: NE

8. PATIENT STATUS: Single [ ] Married [X] Other [ ]

CITY: MONROE STATE: NE

ZIP CODE: 33331 TELEPHONE (Include Area Code): (555) 777-8888

Employed [X] Full-Time Student [ ] Part-Time Student [ ]

ZIP CODE: 33331 TELEPHONE (Include Area Code): (555) 777-8888

9. OTHER INSURED'S NAME (Last Name, First Name, Middle Initial)

10. IS PATIENT'S CONDITION RELATED TO:

11. INSURED'S POLICY GROUP OR FECA NUMBER: XX123

a. OTHER INSURED'S POLICY OR GROUP NUMBER

a. EMPLOYMENT? (Current or Previous) [ ] YES [X] NO

a. INSURED'S DATE OF BIRTH MM DD YY: 11 03 1985 SEX M [X] F [ ]

b. OTHER INSURED'S DATE OF BIRTH MM DD YY SEX M [ ] F [ ]

b. AUTO ACCIDENT? [ ] YES [X] NO PLACE (State)

b. EMPLOYER'S NAME OR SCHOOL NAME: OK FINANCE

c. EMPLOYER'S NAME OR SCHOOL NAME

c. OTHER ACCIDENT? [ ] YES [X] NO

c. INSURANCE PLAN NAME OR PROGRAM NAME: MANAGE HEALTH CORPORATION

d. INSURANCE PLAN NAME OR PROGRAM NAME

10d. RESERVED FOR LOCAL USE

d. IS THERE ANOTHER HEALTH BENEFIT PLAN? [ ] YES [X] NO *If yes,* return to and complete item 9 a-d.

READ BACK OF FORM BEFORE COMPLETING & SIGNING THIS FORM.

12. PATIENT'S OR AUTHORIZED PERSON'S SIGNATURE I authorize the release of any medical or other information necessary to process this claim. I also request payment of government benefits either to myself or to the party who accepts assignment below.

SIGNED SIGNATURE ON FILE (SOF) DATE

13. INSURED'S OR AUTHORIZED PERSON'S SIGNATURE I authorize payment of medical benefits to the undersigned physician or supplier for services described below.

SIGNED SIGNATURE ON FILE (SOF)

PATIENT AND INSURED INFORMATION

14. DATE OF CURRENT: MM DD YY ILLNESS (First symptom) OR INJURY (Accident) OR PREGNANCY(LMP)

15. IF PATIENT HAS HAD SAME OR SIMILAR ILLNESS. GIVE FIRST DATE MM DD YY

16. DATES PATIENT UNABLE TO WORK IN CURRENT OCCUPATION FROM MM DD YY TO MM DD YY

17. NAME OF REFERRING PROVIDER OR OTHER SOURCE

17a.

17b. NPI

18. HOSPITALIZATION DATES RELATED TO CURRENT SERVICES FROM MM DD YY TO MM DD YY

19. RESERVED FOR LOCAL USE

20. OUTSIDE LAB? [ ] YES [ ] NO $ CHARGES

21. DIAGNOSIS OR NATURE OF ILLNESS OR INJURY (Relate Items 1, 2, 3 or 4 to Item 24E by Line)

1. 574.20

2.

3.

4.

22. MEDICAID RESUBMISSION CODE ORIGINAL REF. NO.

23. PRIOR AUTHORIZATION NUMBER

24. A. DATE(S) OF SERVICE From MM	DD	YY	To MM	DD	YY	B. PLACE OF SERVICE	C. EMG	D. PROCEDURES, SERVICES, OR SUPPLIES (Explain Unusual Circumstances) CPT/HCPCS	MODIFIER	E. DIAGNOSIS POINTER	F. $ CHARGES	G. DAYS OR UNITS	H. EPSDT Family Plan	I. ID. QUAL.	J. RENDERING PROVIDER ID. #
1 08	25	09	08	25	09	22		47563		1	1995.00	1		NPI	
2														NPI	
3														NPI	
4														NPI	
5														NPI	
6														NPI	

25. FEDERAL TAX I.D. NUMBER: 881112424 SSN [ ] EIN [X]

26. PATIENT'S ACCOUNT NO.: LY485

27. ACCEPT ASSIGNMENT? (For govt. claims, see back) [X] YES [ ] NO

28. TOTAL CHARGE: $ 1995 00

29. AMOUNT PAID: $

30. BALANCE DUE: $ 1995 00

31. SIGNATURE OF PHYSICIAN OR SUPPLIER INCLUDING DEGREES OR CREDENTIALS (I certify that the statements on the reverse apply to this bill and are made a part thereof.)

Joe Smith MD 08/30/09

SIGNED DATE

32. SERVICE FACILITY LOCATION INFORMATION

JOE SMITH MD
555 COLUMBIA
PRAIRIE CITY MA 55502

a. 1234567890 b.

33. BILLING PROVIDER INFO & PH # ( ) OPTIONAL

JOE SMITH MD
555 COLUMBIA
PRAIRIE CITY MA 55502

a. 1234567890 b.

PHYSICIAN OR SUPPLIER INFORMATION

NUCC Instruction Manual available at: www.nucc.org PLEASE PRINT OR TYPE APPROVED OMB-0938-0999 FORM CMS-1500 (08-05)

FIGURE 10–1: Completed CMS-1500 form for patient with a managed care insurance plan.

Medicare or the state Medicaid agency. The patient will be issued an identification card from the private carrier rather than from Medicare. Medicaid recipients are still issued a Medicaid ID card. In some states, the identification card will be printed to indicate the Medicaid patient is covered under a managed care contract. Other states use the same ID card for all recipients and it is the responsibility of the physician's office, typically the medical coder, to contact the state's eligibility department to obtain each patient's type of available coverage. The physician's office will receive all reimbursement from the private managed care carrier rather than from Medicare or from Medicaid. The Centers for Medicare and Medicaid (CMS) reimburse the managed care carriers directly for the beneficiaries and recipients who use the option by a fee-for-service or capitation method. Each third-party carrier must produce a financial statement indicating the number of members they have and the cost of their medical care.

As explained in Chapter 8, Medicare beneficiaries pay the managed care carrier a monthly premium that covers the cost of patient's deductibles and coinsurance. The beneficiaries do not need a supplemental plan. Some carriers provide services that are not covered by Medicare, such as routine physicals, prescriptions, or eyeglasses. Medicaid recipients generally do not pay premiums for this coverage.

The primary message to beneficiaries is that change is not mandatory; if they are happy with the way they receive health care, they do not need to change to a new plan. It is important that beneficiaries learn as much as possible about the choices so they can select the appropriate plan. The medical coder can help patients with this decision by referring them to the State Health Insurance Information Program (SHIIP), which serves as an information source. SHIIP provides information to Medicare beneficiaries regarding Medicare benefits, supplemental plans, long-term care policies, and can find assistance from other programs as needed. Patients can find their local SHIIP services by either calling Medicare at 1-800-MEDICARE (1-800-633-4227) or by visiting the Medicare website, www.medicare.gov. Under Search Tools on the website, the patient must select "Compare Health Plans" and then "Medigap Policies in Your Area."

SCHEDULING PATIENTS WITH MANAGED CARE COVERAGE

When patients make appointments, it is important to ask what type of insurance they have, especially those with a managed care plan. A physician will not be enrolled in every managed care plan offered, and the patient must be informed immediately if the provider does not participate in the patient's plan. If the patient still requests to see the physician, the patient should be informed of what the out-of-pocket expenses will be. Some plans will pay only for services rendered to the patient by "in-network" providers. Other plans allow the patient to see a health-care provider who is out-of-network, but a deductible may apply or reimbursement may be less, increasing the patient's liability. To protect the patient from unnecessary expenses and safeguard proper reimbursement, the medical coder must keep a current list of the managed care plans in which the provider is enrolled.

❗ KEY TERMS

PRIOR AUTHORIZATION—Advance notice given to and approved by the third-party carrier before a patient's treatment or service is rendered.

PRE-CERTIFICATION—A method of evaluating the appropriateness of a medical service such as a hospitalization or a surgery before the service is rendered. Also referred to as pre-admission certification.

Often, a managed care program will require a **prior authorization** or pre-approval of certain services before reimbursement is made. The medical coder may find keeping a list of plans the doctor is NOT enrolled in just as helpful. These lists can serve as a valuable reference when making appointments or completing paperwork.

◼ LEGAL RESPONSIBILITIES

Managed care has had various influences on the insurance industry. Cost containment versus freedom of choice will be debated and reviewed for years to come. Lawsuits have been aimed at the restrictions HMOs impose, citing necessary care that has been prevented, jeopardizing the health of patients. The HMO controls the financial aspect of health care and the health-care provider controls the medical aspect, so it comes down to finding blame with the managed health care's administrative actions or the provider's actions. Since the 1980s, HMO benefits administered through private employer health plans have been protected by federal law from malpractice under the Employment Retirement Income Security Act (ERISA) of 1974.

◼ MANAGED CARE CONTRACTS

Before the physician signs a contract and agrees to the requirements of a managed care plan, the specifics of the contract must be reviewed and understood. The medical coder may be asked to evaluate the covered services, the reimbursement and the referral stipulations in addition to the number of patients the physician can expect to receive. The existing patient base also should be monitored. If the practice is losing patients to another facility because it is not contracted with a managed care program, the medical coder may be asked to explore the possibility of joining that program.

Every managed care contract should be reviewed for the following:

- ◼ Reimbursement Schedule—The reimbursement should be comparable to what is customary in the area for the specialty of the physician.
- ◼ Indemnity Plan—The physician agrees to cover any losses to the managed care carrier, which may include the carrier's legal costs.
- ◼ Risk Pool—A pool of funds set aside as a reserve to cover overutilization. The pool is usually based on the number of insureds, their geographic location and/or reimbursement per individual insured. Some capitation plans will disperse this to the providers at the end of the contract year. Other plans may continue to add to the pool.
- ◼ Clean Claim—A claim with no errors, all information, codes, etc., are correct. A clean claim is one that does not require extra documentation of special circumstances.
- ◼ Policies and Procedures—Additional rules, regulations, and miscellaneous information. For example, the time frame in which reimbursement is received, the definition of a clean claim or overutilization, who the utilization review board is made up of, the appeal rights of the physician, what managerial duties the carrier is providing. A copy should be kept by the physician's office in case of any discrepancies.
- ◼ Termination Clause—Information on how either the physician or the managed care plan can terminate their agreement.

◼ CONCLUSION

In review, the medical coder should always reference the guidelines and stipulations in each of the managed care plans in which the physician is enrolled. It is imperative that the medical coder know what managed care plans the physician participates in. Monitoring payments and the procedures necessary to file the claims must be evaluated when renewing any contract. Workshops are often offered so that the medical coder can remain current on the policies of managed care plans and discuss common problems with other workshop attendees.

RESOURCE LIST

American Heart Association

www.americanheart.org

Austrin, MS. (1999). *Managed Health Care Simplified: A Glossary of Terms.* Delmar Centrage Learning.

Medicare & You 2010: Available at http://www.medicare.gov/Publications/Pubs/pdf/10050.pdf

National Library of Medicine: www.nlm.nih.gov

The National Quality Measures Clearinghouse™ (NQMC)

http://www.qualitymeasures.ahrq.gov/resources/glossary.aspx

The Southern Medical Association

http://www.sma.org/residents/managedcare.cfm

Chapter Review Exercises

Please complete the following questions.

1. Who is credited for initiating health-care reform? _____

2. When was the HMO act passed by congress? _____

3. Name the four most common types of HMOs today.

    _____

    _____

    _____

    _____

4. The method of evaluating the appropriateness of a medical service such as a hospitalization or a surgery before the service is rendered is called:

    _____

5. PPOs generally do not include copayments. **True or False** (circle one)

6. Managed care has been successful in controlling health-care costs. **True or False** (circle one)

7. What percent of Americans are now enrolled in some kind of managed care?

    _____

8. The most common method of the delivery of managed care today is through a

    _____ of providers.

9. Federal law protects some HMOs from _____.

10. What role does a gatekeeper play in managed care?

    _____

TRICARE and CHAMPVA

Chapter Outline

OBJECTIVES

- Understand who qualifies for TRICARE and CHAMPVA
- Describe the kinds of providers
- Name the three TRICARE programs and understand their differences
- Recognize the difference between Transitional Survivors and Survivors
- Identify who may file a claim
- Explain the TRICARE regions
- Locate where to submit claims

MEDICAL ASSISTING COMPETENCIES
ABHES

1i. conduct work within scope of education, training, and ability
2d. serve as a liaison between Physician and others

2g. use appropriate medical terminology

2h. receive, organize, prioritize, and transmit information expediently

3e. locate resources and information for patients and employers

3v. perform diagnostic coding

3w. complete insurance claim forms

5a. determine the needs for documentation and reporting

5b. document accurately

5c. use appropriate guidelines when releasing records or information

8c. analyze and use current third-party guidelines for reimbursement

CAAHEP

IV.P.3. Use medical terminology, pronouncing medical terms correctly, to communicate information, patient history, data and observations

VII.P.2. Apply third-party guidelines

VII.P.3. Complete insurance claim form

VII.P.4. Obtain pre-certification, including documentation

VII.P.5. Obtain prior-authorization, including documentation

VIII.A.1. Work with physician to achieve the maximum reimbursement

IX.A.3. Recognize the importance of local, state, and federal legislation and regulations in the practice setting

---

KEY TERMS

Catastrophic Cap	Managed Care Support Contractor (MCSC)	Non-Network Provider
CHAMPUS		Sponsor
CHAMPVA	Military Treatment Facility (MTF)	Survivors
Civilian	Network Provider	Transitional Survivors
Cost Share		TRICARE

◼ INTRODUCTION TO TRICARE

In 1966, Congress created the Civilian Health and Medical Program of the Uniformed Services (**CHAMPUS**) to provide benefits for dependents of military personnel. CHAMPUS covered only the dependents, while uniformed personnel received care from the military and Veterans Administration hospitals. The uniformed services include the U.S. Army, U.S. Navy, U.S. Air Force, U.S. Marine Corps, U.S. Coast Guard, the Commissioned Corps of the U.S. Public Health Service, and the Commissioned Corps of the National Oceanic and Atmospheric Administration.

❗ KEY TERMS

CHAMPUS—The previous health coverage for dependents of active duty military personnel and veterans. It was replaced by TRICARE in 1994.

TRICARE—The program that provides health benefits for active duty military personnel and their dependents.

TRICARE replaced the standard coverage of CHAMPUS in 1994 and continues to provide health care to active duty, activated guard and reserves, retired members of the uniformed services, their families, and survivors. TRICARE offers health care through networks of **civilian** health-care providers to provide quality health care in addition to the health care from the Army, Navy, and Air Force.

TRICARE is managed jointly by the TRICARE Management Activity (TMA) and the TRICARE Regional Offices. It is available worldwide and is divided into six separate TRICARE regions:

1. TRICARE North
2. TRICARE South
3. TRICARE West
4. TRICARE Europe
5. TRICARE Pacific
6. TRICARE Latin America and Canada

TMA has partnered with civilian **managed care support contractors (MCSCs)** in the North, South, and West regions to assist TRICARE regional directors and **military treatment facility (MTF)** commanders in operating an integrated health-care delivery system.

‼ KEY TERM

MILITARY TREATMENT FACILITY (MTF)—A facility operated by the military that provides health care to eligible TRICARE beneficiaries.

TRICARE Authorized Providers

A provider must be authorized by TRICARE. An authorized provider must either be licensed by the state or accredited national organization or meet other standards of the medical community. TRICARE contractors must verify a provider's authorized status before they can pay for any services rendered by the provider. TRICARE will not pay for services rendered by an unauthorized provider.

There are two types of authorized providers:

1. **Network Providers** have signed an agreement with TRICARE to provide care and file claims for TRICARE beneficiaries. These providers can only bill the beneficiary for the applicable deductible, copayment, or **cost share**.

‼ KEY TERMS

NETWORK PROVIDER—Any provider that has agreed to care for and file claims for TRICARE beneficiaries. They may only bill for applicable costs, per TRICARE guidelines.

COST SHARE—The 25% of TRICARE allowable amount.

---

2. **Non-Network Providers** do not have a signed agreement with TRICARE. There are two types of non-network providers:

   ■ **Participating**—Providers that have agreed to file claims for TRICARE beneficiaries, to accept payment directly from TRICARE, and to always accept the TRICARE allowable amount as payment in full for their services. They may participate on a claim-by-claim basis.

   ■ **Nonparticipating**—Providers that have not agreed to file claims or accept TRICARE allowable amounts. These providers have the right to charge the beneficiaries 15% above TRICARE's allowed amount.

‼ KEY TERM

NON-NETWORK PROVIDER—Any provider that has not signed an agreement with TRICARE. A non-network provider can be participating or nonparticipating.

TRICARE Program Options

TRICARE has three main health-care options, Standard, Extra, and Prime. This three-prong (or "tri") organization is how the name TRICARE was determined.

TRICARE *Standard* is a fee-for-service option in which the beneficiary may receive health care from any TRICARE-authorized provider for covered services. Beneficiaries contribute to a cost share for every service they receive. After the annual deductible, the TRICARE beneficiary's cost share is 20% of the allowed charges. Standard beneficiaries are able to seek most services without obtaining a referral or authorization. TRICARE Standard is available for all eligible beneficiaries, except active-duty service members, and dependent parents and parents-in-law.

TRICARE Extra is a preferred-provider type option, available to all TRICARE-eligible Standard beneficiaries (except active-duty service members). After the annual deductible, the TRICARE Extra cost share paid by the beneficiary is 15% of the allowed charge. Beneficiaries select civilian physicians and specialists from a list of providers in the Managed Care Support Contractors (MCSC) network. The provider files the beneficiary's claim forms with TRICARE. Beneficiaries can still receive care from a military treatment facility (MTF), but on a space-available basis only.

KEY TERMS

CIVILIAN—A non-military citizen.

MANAGED CARE SUPPORT CONTRACTORS (MCSC)—Approved civilian providers that TRICARE beneficiaries may select for health care

All active-duty service members are eligible for TRICARE *Prime*. The MTFs and a preferred provider network are the principal sources of health care. The beneficiary has no annual deductible or cost share. Beneficiaries should contact their Primary Care Managers (PCMs) or the regional contractor when seeking care from a provider other than their PCM or if they are admitted to a facility after an emergency room visit. Service members should check with their managed care support contractor and the Military Medical Support Office (MMSO) when traveling, to get authorization for urgent care. There is also a Point of Service (POS) option under TRICARE Prime that allows enrollees the freedom to seek and receive nonemergency health-care services from any TRICARE authorized civilian provider, in or out of the TRICARE network, without requesting a referral from their Primary Care Manager (PCM). The POS claims have an outpatient deductible ($300 individual and $600 family), 50% cost-shares for outpatient and inpatient claims, and excess charges up 15% over the allowed amount.

TRICARE Eligibility

TRICARE Standard is available to all TRICARE-eligible beneficiaries, except active-duty service members, and dependent parents and parents-in-law.

TRICARE Extra is available to all TRICARE-eligible Standard beneficiaries.

TRICARE Prime (where available) is offered to active-duty service members and their families, retirees, retiree family members, and eligible **survivors** who are not eligible for Medicare. Certain Reserve component members, and Medal of Honor recipients, along with their families, also may be eligible.

KEY TERM

SPONSOR—A member of the military or a civilian employee with dependents.

TRICARE Cost Share

Standard and Extra beneficiaries are responsible for annual deductibles and cost shares. Prime beneficiaries are responsible for copays and point of service charges. All programs have a **catastrophic cap**, which is the maximum amount (per fiscal year) that a beneficiary pays for TRICARE-covered services or supplies.

! KEY TERM

CATASTROPHIC CAP—The maximum amount (per fiscal year) that a beneficiary pays for TRICARE-covered services or supplies.

Survivors and Transitional Survivors

Eligible family members whose **sponsor** died while on active duty are called survivors and **transitional survivors**. Family members are categorized as Transitional Survivors for 3 years from the date of death of their sponsor. After 3 years, the surviving spouse converts to survivor status and TRICARE benefits continue at the retiree payment rate.

! KEY TERMS

TRANSITIONAL SURVIVOR—Eligible family member of a deceased TRICARE sponsor who receive the same active-duty coverage (for the same rate). This is a 3-year status, unless there are other circumstances that change TRICARE eligibility of the survivor.

SURVIVOR—Eligible family member of a deceased TRICARE sponsor who receives retiree coverage at the retiree payment rate.

Survivors and transitional survivors status for children typically ends at age 21 years (or 23 if enrolled in a full-time course of study at secondary school or an institution of higher education). If they join the military or marry, they are no longer eligible for benefits.

Incapacitated children retain their transitional survivor status until 3 years from the sponsor's date of death, or their 21st birthday, or 23rd birthday if enrolled in a full-time course of study at a secondary school or an institution of higher education. They are then reclassified as survivors and are covered as a retired family member, unless they lose TRICARE eligibility.

After the death of their sponsor, any survivor or transitional survivor can continue TRICARE coverage for 30 or more consecutive days and are automatically eligible for TRICARE Standard/Extra. They may enroll in TRICARE Prime or TRICARE Overseas Program (TOP) Prime if they wish. Transitional survivors pay active-duty family member (ADFM) payment rates, whereas survivors pay at the retiree payment rates.

◼ ADDITIONAL TRICARE INFORMATION

- ◼ If a patient has private health insurance in addition to TRICARE benefits, TRICARE pays only after all other plans that are not designated as TRICARE supplements (e.g., Medicaid).
- ◼ When there is other primary coverage involved, TRICARE will only pay for covered services up to the plan's approved amount, as if no other coverage was available. For example, if the primary insurance allows and pays more than TRICARE normally allows on a particular procedure, TRICARE will not make an additional payment.
- ◼ When TRICARE was implemented, the TRICARE Enabling Statute [Title 10, United States Code, Section 1079(h)(1)] gave the Secretary of Defense the authority to set the reimbursement rates for health-care services provided to TRICARE beneficiaries. Those rates are set in accordance with the same reimbursement rules that apply to payments for similar services under Medicare.
- ◼ A TRICARE beneficiary may submit their own claims, but 97% of all health-care providers submit the claims on their patient's behalf.

Noncovered Services
- ◼ Acupuncture
- ◼ Artificial insemination
- ◼ Birth control (non-prescription)

■ Bone marrow transplants for ovarian cancer

■ Chiropractic care

■ Comfort items

■ Experimental procedures

■ Foot care

■ Laser/Lasik surgery

■ Learning disability treatment

■ Naturopaths

■ Nonsurgical treatment for obesity

■ Smoking cessation service of supplies

■ CHAMPVA

The Civilian Health and Medical Program of the Veterans Affairs (**CHAMPVA**) was created in 1973 as the health benefits program for dependents of permanently and totally disabled veterans, survivors of veterans who died from service-connected conditions, or who, at the time of death, were rated permanently and totally disabled from a service-connected condition. Under CHAMPVA, the Veterans Administration (VA) shares the cost of covered medical services and supplies with eligible beneficiaries.

> **! KEY TERM**
>
> CHAMPVA—The program that provides health benefits for dependents of disabled veterans.

From 1973 through 1986, VA medical centers processed all CHAMPVA applications and determined if applicants were eligible for the program. In June 1986, the Veterans Health Administration (VHA) established the CHAMPVA Center in Denver, Colorado, and transferred the responsibility of determining beneficiary eligibility to the CHAMPVA Center.

By 1994, the CHAMPVA Center was processing all claims, all beneficiary eligibility determinations, and payments for beneficiaries residing in the United States and its territories. The center assumed responsibility for all foreign CHAMPVA claims processing and payments in 1996 and was officially renamed the Health Administration Center (HAC).

CHAMPVA Coverage and Cost Share

CHAMPVA is a fee-for-service program and is similar to TRICARE Standard coverage. It provides reimbursement for most medical expenses, including inpatient services, outpatient service, well-child examinations and immunizations, cancer screenings, mental health services, prescription medication, skilled nursing care, ambulance services, and durable medical equipment (DME). There is also a very limited adjunct dental benefit that requires preauthorization.

In most cases, CHAMPVA payments are equivalent to Medicare/TRICARE allowable amounts. The allowable amounts can be viewed online at http://www.tricare.osd.mil/cmac. Some services, like maternity and delivery services, require the patient pay a "cost share." The beneficiary cost share (after the annual deductible) is currently 25% of the allowable amount under CHAMPVA. The medical coder may be responsible for collecting the cost share from the patient, unless the patient has other health insurance.

If the beneficiary has other health insurance, CHAMPVA pays either 75% of the allowable amount (after deductible) or the remainder of the charges, whichever is less. In both cases, the beneficiary will normally not have a cost share. By law, CHAMPVA is always the secondary payer, except in cases with Medicaid, State Victims of Crime Compensation, and CHAMPVA supplemental policies. For example, if a beneficiary enrolled in both Medicare Part A (hospitalization insurance) and Medicare Part B (outpatient insurance) and is also eligible for CHAMPVA, CHAMPVA is the secondary payer to Medicare, any Medicare supplemental plans, and Medicare HMO plans.

CHAMPVA Deductible

Each beneficiary is responsible for the first $50 of covered services received during a calendar year. In the case of families, there is a $100 family deductible per calendar year, which can be paid by any combination of family members. After the entire family deductible has been met during a calendar year, the deductible is considered met for every family member throughout the rest of the calendar year.

Provider Contracts

CHAMPVA does contract providers, but health-care providers must be properly licensed in their practicing state to receive payment from CHAMPVA. If submitting a CHAMPVA claim, a provider must accept the CHAMPVA allowable charges and cannot bill the beneficiary for any remaining charges. The only exceptions are the following:

- If the beneficiary is notified (prior to any services being rendered) that a provider does not accept CHAMPVA. The beneficiary must then pay the entire billed amount and file the claim to CHAMPVA.

- If the beneficiary is responsible for payment of services and supplies that are not covered under CHAMPVA.

■ TRICARE AND CHAMPVA CLAIM FORM COMPLETION GUIDELINES

CMS-1500 claim form completion guidelines for TRICARE and CHAMPVA do not differ from the standard guidelines of the National Uniform Claim Committee (NUCC). Paper claims are accepted, but providers are encouraged to file claims electronically. As with other insurance carriers, electronic claims are paid faster than paper claims; TRICARE and CHAMPVA normally pay 95% of the claims within 30 days of receipt, whereas the average turnaround time for paper claims is 50 days.

General TRICARE Claim Completion Information

- Submit a separate claim form for each beneficiary or patient.

- Claims should be filed within 90 days from the service date and must be filed no later than 1 year from the date of service.

- TRICARE follows the NUCC claim form completion guidelines. See Figure 11–1 for a sample TRICARE claim and refer to Chapter 7 for the specific guidelines.

Claim Submission for CHAMPVA

CHAMPVA only requests that the **national provider identifiers** (NPIs) for the rendering, referring, and prescribing health-care provider be included on all paper submissions along with any tax identification numbers.

All paper claim forms for CHAMPVA-covered patients should be filed through the VA Health Administration Center. The address for paper claims is listed at the end of the chapter.

As of October 2003, HAC began accepting HIPAA compliant electronic claims. However, CHAMPVA claims must be sent electronically to Emdeon Business Services (www.emdeon.com), the **clearinghouse** for CHAMPVA. As with other types of claim filing, the patient is always listed as the subscriber when completing a CMS claim form. When completing a CHAMPVA claim, the name and member ID must be submitted just as it appears on the patient's HAC identification card.

Providers may use Emedeon to verify all the status of electronically submitted claims and to verify patient eligibility. The Electronic Remittance Advice (ERA) also is available through Emedeon. To take advantage of this service, the medical coder must verify that an ERA provider setup form has been completed and sent to Emedeon. The ERA form can be found at http://www.emdeon.com/ClaimsAdministration/payers_ecommerce.php. The medical coder also can contact the clearinghouse used by the office to be sure the CHAMPVA payer IDs have been added to their software system.

FIGURE 11–1: Completed CMS-1500 from for patient with a TRICARE or CHAMPVA plan.

Claim Submission for TRICARE

TRICARE claims are submitted to the appropriate regional claims processor (Table 11-1). For example, if a beneficiary lives in the North region, his or her claims are submitted to Palmetto Government Benefits Administrators (PGBA). If the beneficiary lives in the South region, his or her claims are sent to Humana Military Healthcare Services, Inc. (HMHS). The status of claims for these two regional centers can be reviewed online at www.myTRICARE.com.

If a beneficiary lives in the West region, lives overseas, or is a TRICARE For Life (TFL) beneficiary, his or her claims are submitted to Wisconsin Physicians Service (WPS). The status of claims for this regional center can be reviewed online at www.tricare4u.com.

To facilitate electronic claim filing and electronic remittance statements, the medical coder may need to set up **electronic data interchange** (EDI) with the TRICARE regional service providers. Each center has its own guidelines and information and should be contacted as follows:

West region:
WPS/West Region Claims, 1-888-874-9378,
www.triwest.com/Provider Connection/YourEDIConnection or
www.wpsic.com/edi/edi_home.shtml

North region:
PGBA, LLC, 1-877-EDI-CLAIM (1-877-334-2524),
  https://www.hnfs.net/provider/claims/Electronic+Filing+Options.htm

TABLE 11–1: Regional Claim Filing Office Jurisdictions

TRICARE North Region	TRICARE South Region	TRICARE West Region
North Regional Claims	**Humana Military Healthcare**	**TRIWEST**
PGBA, LLC	**Services, Inc.**	**WPS/West Region Claims**
P.O. Box 870140	**Claims Department**	**P.O. Box 77028**
Surfside Beach, SC 29587-9740	**P.O. Box 7031**	**Madison, WI 53707-1028**
1-887-874-2273	**Camden, SC 29020-7031**	**1-888-874-9378**
	1-800-403-3950	
www.healthnetfederalservices.com	www.humana-military.com	www.triwest.com
Connecticut	Alabama	Alaska
District of Columbia	Arkansas	Arizona
Illinois	Florida	California
Indiana	Georgia	Colorado
Iowa (partial)	Louisiana	Hawaii
Kentucky	Mississippi	Idaho
Maine	Oklahoma	Iowa (partial)
Maryland	South Carolina	Kansas
Massachusetts	Tennessee	Minnesota
Michigan	Texas (partial)	Missouri (partial)
Missouri (partial)		Montana
New Hampshire		Nebraska
New Jersey		Nevada
New York		New Mexico
North Carolina		North Dakota
Ohio		Oregon
Pennsylvania		South Dakota
Rhode Island		Texas (El Paso and
Tennessee (partial)		Ft. Bliss only)
Vermont		Utah
Virginia		Washington
Wisconsin		Wyoming

South region:
Humana Military
Electronic Claims Filing Assistance
1-800-325-5920, option 2
www.myTRICARE.com or www.humana-military.com

Beneficiaries also will receive an Explanation of Benefits (EOB) after the claim has been submitted and processed. The EOB details what services were rendered and how payment was allocated.

Claims, whether submitted electronically or via paper, should be filed within a reasonable amount of time of the date service, in general, within 60 days. A regional service provider may grant exceptions from these filing deadlines if there is documentation available to support the request.

Most importantly, always file a TRICARE or CHAMPVA claim secondary to any other third-party coverage.

■ CONCLUSION

TRICARE and CHAMPVA have made great strides toward keeping up with the present technology. The military health system must comply with the requirements of HIPAA, both as a provider of health care—through their Military Treatment Facilities—and as the TRICARE health plan—through contracted network health-care services. Whenever a question arises, the regional service should be contacted. Answers can be found by phone, by mail, and through the Internet.

RESOURCE LIST
VA Health Administration Center CHAMPVA
P.O. Box 65023
Denver, CO 80206-9023
Phone: 1-800-733-8387 Monday–Friday 8:05 a.m.–7:30 p.m. Eastern Time
FAX: 1-303-331-7804
  http://www.va.gov/hac
  (click on the CHAMPVA link)

CHAMPVA paper claims can be mailed to:
VA Health Administration Center
CHAMPVA
P.O. Box 65024
Denver, CO 80206-9024

TRICARE Management Activity
Skyline 5, Suite 810,
5111 Leesburg Pike, Falls Church, VA 22041-3206
  http://www.tricare.mil

Health Net Federal Services, Inc.
c/o PGBA, LLC/TRICARE Claims
P.O. Box 870140
Surfside Beach, SC 29587-9740
  https://www.hnfs.net/common/companyInfo/contact_us_main.htm

PGBA South Region Claims Department
P.O. Box 7031
Camden, SC 29020-7031
  http://hmd.humana-military.com/South/phonenumbers.asp

West Region Claims
P.O. Box 77028
Madison, WI 53707-1028
  http://www.triwest.com/beneficiary/frames.aspx?page=http://www.triwest.com/unauth/content/triwest/
    contact.asp

Chapter Review Exercises

1. What does CHAMPVA stand for? _____

2. What is the time limit for filing claims to TRICARE? _____

3. Is there a deductible requirement for CHAMPVA? _____

4. Do members of CHAMPVA have a copay? _____

5. What is the CHAMPVA allowable amount based on? _____

6. What is the maximum percent CHAMPVA will pay toward an allowable service?

_____

7. What portion of the bill is the CHAMPVA member required to pay?

_____

8. Does the physician have to accept CHAMPVA's payment as payment in full?

_____

9. What identification number identifies the physician on the claim forms submitted

to CHAMPVA? _____

10. What identification number identifies the physician on the claim form submitted to

TRICARE? _____

11. Does TRICARE have managed care plans? _____

12. If a patient has other insurance besides TRICARE, which payer do you submit to first?

_____

13. A TRICARE nonparticipating provider must accept assignment.   **True or False** (circle one)

14. When a nonparticipating provider files a claim, where is the TRICARE payment sent?

_____

15. What does TRICARE pay when the patient has other insurance?

_____

16. A Medicare patient may also have TRICARE coverage.   **True or False** (circle one)

17. What did TRICARE replace? _____

Workers' Compensation

Chapter Outline

OBJECTIVES

- Define the reason for Workers' Compensation
- Know who qualifies for Workers' Compensation
- Recognize the importance of accurate recordkeeping
- Practice the proper authorization skills
- Gain knowledge of the patient's choice of care
- State patient's rights
- State patient's benefits
- Able to locate the local state Department of Disability

- Define the difference between temporary and permanent disability benefits
- Recognize the health-care providers' responsibilities
- Gain the skills needed when billing for Workers' Compensation benefits

MEDICAL ASSISTING COMPETENCIES
ABHES

- 1i. conduct work within scope of education, training, and ability
- 2d. serve as a liaison between Physician and others
- 2g. use appropriate medical terminology
- 2h. receive, organize, prioritize, and transmit information expediently
- 3e. locate resources and information for patients and employers
- 3v. perform diagnostic coding
- 3w. complete insurance claim forms
- 5a. determine the needs for documentation and reporting
- 5b. document accurately
- 5c. use appropriate guidelines when releasing records or information
- 8c. analyze and use current third-party guidelines for reimbursement

CAAHEP

- IV.P.3. Use medical terminology, pronouncing medical terms correctly, to communicate information, patient history, data, and observations
- VII.P.2. Apply third-party guidelines
- VII.P.3. Complete insurance claim form
- VII.P.4. Obtain pre certification, including documentation
- VII.P.5. Obtain prior authorization, including documentation
- VIII.A.1. Work with physician to achieve the maximum reimbursement
- IX.A.3. Recognize the importance of local, state and federal legislation and regulations in the practice setting
- IX.P.1. Respond to issues of confidentiality
- IX.P.3. Apply HIPAA rules in regard to privacy/release of information
- IX.P.7. Document accurately in the patient record

KEY TERMS		
Death Benefits	Permanent Disability	Temporary Disability

■ INTRODUCTION

Workers' Compensation is designed to protect employees with any work-related illness or injury. This is a separate medical and disability reimbursement program unrelated to a patient's health-care benefits. Through a Workers' Compensation plan, employees are provided with a fixed monetary amount that helps compensate for a work-related illness, injury, disability, or death. The first laws mandating compensation for workers were developed in the early 1900s and federal law now requires each state to have a Workers' Compensation program.

The programs are managed at the state level and coverage may differ slightly from state to state. However, all states are required by federal law to provide the basic coverage of medical bills and lost wages. The most common differences between states is the waiting period for payment and how much of the wages are replaced.

A minority of states do not require workers' compensation coverage by employers with fewer than a designated number of employees. Usually, employers of four or more employees are legally required to furnish Workers' Compensation to their employees. Some employers are exempt from providing workers' compensation benefits at all including the following:

1. Domestic and casual employees, such as repairmen, groundskeepers, and maintenance workers, working in a private household. Any minimum salary requirements will vary from state to state.
2. Agricultural employees who have earned less than a certain state-determined amount. These individuals may include the spouse of a sole proprietor employer or partner engaged in agriculture and his or her parents, brothers, sisters, children, stepchildren, and spouses.
3. The president, vice president, secretary, and treasurer of a corporation and their spouses, and the parents, brothers, sisters, children, stepchildren and the spouses of either officers.
4. Police officers and firefighters who are entitled to benefits under any fire-fighter's or police officer's disability and/or pension fund established by each state.
5. Real estate salespersons.
6. Employees who are entitled to benefits under another method of liability or compensation, such as firefighters, police officers, emergency medical technicians, or other public service employees.

GENERAL COVERAGE UNDER WORKERS' COMPENSATION

Most employees who have a work-related injury, are under an employment contract made in the state, or the place of employment is primarily in the state, are covered under workers' compensation for any job-related injury. Employers may purchase workers' compensation insurance from a private insurance company or a state-run workers' compensation insurance fund, if available. Some states also permit certain employers to self-insure for such claims.

Work-related Illnesses and Injuries

A work-related illness is defined as any disorder, illness, or condition that occurs or is related to the work environment. This can include injuries that occur during a job-related activity, whether in or out of the office. A work-related illness is considered to be an abnormal condition or disease that developes as a result of exposure to elements associated with employment. This includes any acute or chronic illness or disease that has been caused by ingestion, inhalation, direct contact, or absorption of a substance. Disease and hearing losses are considered to be health impairments if they result from on-the-job exposure. Any pre-existing conditions are not covered under Workers' Compensation unless they have been aggravated or worsened.

WORKERS' COMPENSATION LAWS

Worker's Compensation is regulated by state and federal laws. Federal laws apply only to coal miners, maritime/nautical workers, and federal government employees. State laws apply to private employers and their employees and to any state government employee not covered under federal law.

State Workers' Compensation

State laws apply to all other qualifying private employers and their employees. The federal law mandates that states set up workers' compensation laws that cover the following issues:

- Medical claims with no disability
- Temporary disability
- Vocational rehabilitation
- Permanent disability
- Death of a worker

Report of Illness or Injury

If an employee becomes ill or is injured as a result of work, he or she has a time limit to report the incident to their employer. The employer must then file the first report of illness or injury (Fig. 12–1)

Form 122

For your protection Connecticut Law requires notice that worker's compensation fraud is a crime. Please see next page for the full fraud statement

WORKER'S COMPENSATION EMPLOYER'S FIRST REPORT OF INJURY OR ILLNESS
STATE OF CONNECTICUT - THE LABOR COMMISSION - DIVISION OF INDUSTRIAL ACCIDENTS
HARTFORD, CT 06555

GENERAL

EMPLOYER (Name & Address Incl. Zip)
Barry Manufacturing
2589 Industrial Drive
Presley, CT 06001

CARRIER/ADMINISTRATOR CLAIM NUMBER | OSHA CASE/FILE # | REPORT PURPOSE CODE

JURISDICTION | JURISDICTION CLAIM NUMBER

INSURED REPORT NUMBER
87TYM5673472

EMPLOYER'S LOCATION ADDRESS (IF DIFFERENT)
Same

LOCATION #
Same

SIC CODE | EMPLOYER FEIN

PHONE #
860-123-3876

CARRIER / CLAIMS ADMIN

CARRIER (NAME, ADDRESS & PHONE #)
Worker Compensation Fund
P.O. Box 1195
Presley, CT 06001
Telephone: 1-800-123-4786

POLICY PERIOD
TO 12/31/10

CLAIMS ADMINISTRATOR (NAME, ADDRESS & PHONE #)

CHECK IF APPROPRIATE
SELF INSURANCE

CARRIER FEIN | POLICY/SELF-INSURED NUMBER | ADMINISTRATOR FEIN

AGENT NAME & CODE NUMBER
Baldwin Insurance Agency, Code #96360

EMPLOYEE

NAME (LAST, FIRST, MIDDLE)
Hansen, Craig, William

DATE OF BIRTH
12/30/71

SOCIAL SECURITY NUMBER
000-00-0000

DATE HIRED
01/14/98

STATE OF HIRE
active

ADDRESS (INCL ZIP)
42 Wilshire Ave.
Blueville, CT 06100

SEX
X MALE
FEMALE
UNKNOWN

MARITAL STATUS
UNMARRIED SINGLE/DIVORCED
X MARRIED
SEPARATED
UNKNOWN

OCCUPATION/JOB TITLE
machinist

EMPLOYMENT STATUS
active

PHONE
860-543-2100

OF DEPENDENTS
3

NCCI CLASS CODE

WAGE

RATE
$680.00
PER: X WEEK | DAY | MONTH | OTHER:

OF DAYS WORKED/WEEK
5

FULL PAY FOR DAY OF INJURY? X YES   NO
DID SALARY CONTINUE?   YES X NO

OCCURRENCE

TIME EMPLOYEE BEGAN WORK X AM 8:00 PM

DATE OF INJURY/ILLNESS
09/15/08

TIME OF OCCURRENCE
4:22   AM X PM

LAST WORK DATE
09/15/08

DATE EMPLOYER NOTIFIED
09/15/08

DATE DISABILITY BEGAN
09/15/08

CONTACT NAME/PHONE NUMBER
Henry Watanabee
860-555-7400 ext 43

TYPE OF INJURY/ILLNESS
lower back sprained

PART OF BODY AFFECTED
Lower back

DID INJURY/ILLNESS EXPOSURE OCCUR ON EMPLOYER'S PREMISES?
X YES   NO

TYPE OF INJURY/ILLNESS CODE

PART OF BODY AFFECTED CODE

DEPARTMENT OR LOCATION WHERE ACCIDENT OR ILLNESS EXPOSURE OCCURRED
Loading dock

ALL EQUIPMENT, MATERIALS, OR CHEMICALS EMPLOYEE WAS USING WHEN ACCIDENT OR ILLNESS EXPOSURE OCCURRED
dolly

SPECIFIC ACTIVITY THE EMPLOYEE WAS ENGAGED IN WHEN THE ACCIDENT OR ILLNESS EXPOSURE OCCURRED
unloading boxes from truck

WORK PROCESS THE EMPLOYEE WAS ENGAGED IN WHEN ACCIDENT OR ILLNESS EXPOSURE OCCURRED
shipping

HOW INJURY OR ILLNESS/ABNORMAL HEALTH CONDITION OCCURRED, DESCRIBE THE SEQUENCE OF EVENTS AND INCLUDE ANY OBJECTS OR SUBSTANCES THAT DIRECTLY INJURED THE EMPLOYEE OR MADE THE EMPLOYEE ILL
slipped on water on loading dock while carrying heavy box

CAUSE OF INJURY CODE

DATE RETURN(ED) TO WORK
10/22/08

IF FATAL, GIVE DATE OF DEATH

WERE SAFEGUARDS OR SAFETY EQUIPMENT PROVIDED? X YES   NO
WERE THEY USED? X YES   NO

TREATMENT

PHYSICIAN/HEALTH CARE PROVIDER (NAME & ADDRESS)
Robert Greer, MD
15 Main Street
Blueville, CT 06100

860-555-3212

HOSPITAL (NAME & ADDRESS)
Hartell Memorial
773 Carson Street
Blueville, CT 06100

INITIAL TREATMENT
NO MEDICAL TREATMENT
MINOR: BY EMPLOYER
MINOR CLINIC/HOSP
X EMERGENCY CARE
HOSPITALIZED >24 HRS
FUTURE MAJOR MEDICAL/ LOST TIME ANTICIPATED

OTHER

WITNESS (NAME & PHONE #)
Sarah Kramer   860-555-7868

DATE ADMINISTRATOR NOTIFIED
09/16/08

DATE PREPARED
09/16/08

PREPARER'S NAME & TITLE
Rebecca Stavola, Legal Counsel

PHONE NUMBER
860-555-7400 ext 62

SEE NEXT PAGE FOR IMPORTANT INFORMATION

White: Labor Commission   Yellow: W.C. Insurance Carrier   Pink: Employee   Goldenrod: Employer's File

FIGURE 12–1: First report of injury for a Workers' Compensation insurance claim.

with the state's Workers' Compensation Commissioner within an appointed time frame after notification. Any employee filing a Workers' Compensation Claim usually must also complete a Workers' Compensation Information Release Authorization (Fig. 12–2). In most states, the injury must then be reported to the workers' compensation insurance provider within 90 days of the occurrence.

Although each state's forms will vary by design, the same type of information will be obtained by the employee and the employer to initially report the occurrence of an illness or injury.

Choice of Medical Care

As part of Workers' Compensation insurance, the employer provides medical care reasonably suited to treat the employee's injury, and has the right to choose medical care. If the employee is dissatisfied with the care, the employee should discuss the problem with the employer or insurance carrier. In certain situations, the employee may wish to request alternate care. If the employer or insurance

---

AUTHORIZATION TO RELEASE INFORMATION
REGARDING CLAIMANTS SEEKING WORKERS' COMPENSATION BENEFITS

Name of Patient: _____ Date of Birth: _____

SECTION I. AUTHORIZATION FOR RELEASE OF INFORMATION AND FOR REDISCLOSURE

I authorize _____
to disclose and deliver to _____
the following information related to me: Any and all information EXCEPT substance abuse (drug or alcohol), mental health, and AIDS-related information, unless specifically authorized to be released in Section II of this form. NOTE: If the information includes mental health treatment, substance abuse treatment or HIV-related information it will not be released unless the undersigned patient agrees to the release on the reverse side of this form. I understand the information is being disclosed and may be used only for legal and/or litigation purposes relating to claims and/or suit against _____.
I understand that this Authorization may be used to obtain information from health care providers, schools, former and current employers, providers of vocational rehabilitation services, the Social Security Administration, and the Iowa Department of Workforce Development. I understand that I have a right to inspect the disclosed information at any time. This Authorization is effective until the conclusion of a contested case on the claim. I understand that I may revoke this Authorization, except to the extent that action has already been taken in reliance upon it, by giving written notice to the health care provider or record keeper. I also understand that if I revoke, the revocation will take effect on the day it is received in writing by the entity from whom disclosure is sought.
I understand that if the person or entity that receives the information requested is not covered by the federal privacy regulations or is not an individual or entity who has signed an agreement with such a person or entity, the information described above may be redisclosed and will no longer be protected by the regulations.
Iowa and Federal law provide that I have a right to prohibit redisclosure of confidential medical information and further disclosure may not be had without my express written authorization, except as indicated below. I understand that the Recipient of this Authorization, WITHOUT FURTHER AUTHORIZATION, may redisclose this information to:

Parties and their legal counsel, insurers, experts, potential experts, but only after they have been advised of their obligations under the law and this authorization, including the prohibition against redisclosure of this information; Agents, employees, or representatives of the parties, but only after they are involved in conducting the prosecution or defense of the case, and only after they have been advised of their obligations under the law and this authorization, including the prohibition against redisclosure of this information; Administrative agency and court officials hearing the claim, and their support staff.

I SPECIFICALLY AUTHORIZE AND CONSENT TO ANY SAID DISCLOSURE AND REDISCLOSURE DESCRIBED ABOVE.

_____   _____

Claimant or Legal Representative   Date

_____

Printed Name and Relationship of Claimant's Legal Representative

FIGURE 12–2: Release authorization for Workers' Compensation insurance claim.

SECTION II. SPECIFIC AUTHORIZATION FOR RELEASE OF INFORMATION PROTECTED BY STATE OR FEDERAL LAW CONCERNING MENTAL HEALTH, SUBSTANCE ABUSE TREATMENT, OR AIDS-RELATED INFORMATION

I acknowledge that information to be released may include material that is protected by Federal and/or State law applicable to substance abuse, mental health, and/or AIDS-related information. I SPECIFICALLY AUTHORIZE the release of confidential information relating to: [Place "YES" or "NO" in ALL applicable boxes:]

____ Substance Abuse (Drug or Alcohol) information from all health care providers and facilities and any other person or entity in possession of records concerning me.

____ Mental Health information from all health care providers and facilities and any other person or entity in possession of records concerning me.

____ HIV or AIDS-related information, diagnosis, and test results from all health care providers and facilities and any other person or entity in possession of records concerning me.

Furthermore, I SPECIFICALLY AUTHORIZE disclosure and redisclosure of this confidential information to all of the persons referred to in the REDISCLOSURE Section I.

In order for the above information to be released, you must sign here AND at the end of Section I.

_____   _____
Signature of Claimant or Legal Representative   Date

_____
Street Address/ City/ State/ Zip Code

_____
Printed Name and Relationship of Claimant's Legal Representative

Federal and/or State law specifically require that any disclosure or REDISCLOSURE of substance abuse, alcohol or drug, mental health, or AIDS-related information must be accompanied by the following written statement:

This information has been disclosed to you from records protected by Federal confidentiality rules (42 CFR Part 2). The Federal rules prohibit you from making any further disclosure of this information unless further disclosure is expressly permitted by the written consent of the person to whom it pertains or as otherwise permitted by 42 CFR Part 2. A general authorization for the release of medical or other information is NOT sufficient for this purpose. The Federal rules restrict any use of the information to criminally investigate or prosecute any alcohol or drug abuse patient.

FIGURE 12–2: cont'd

carrier does not allow alternate care, the employee may apply to the industrial commissioner for alternate medical care.

Some state Workers' Compensation Divisions use a medical provider network for the examination and treatment of work-related illness and injury. The medical provider network is made up of healthcare providers from various specialties who have agreed to provide care to any individual who has filed a work-related illness and injury report. The patient does have a right to another examination by a doctor of his or her choice for a second opinion, at the employer's expense.

Independent Medical Examinations

Medical examinations may be performed by an independent medical examiner to provide unbiased findings or diagnoses. An independent examination may be necessary to assist in the evaluation of physical problems and a diagnosis and prognosis of the ill or injured worker. An independent examination may help to determine what activity the employee may or may not be capable of compared to what they were able to do in the past.

Benefits Provided

All states allow for "full coverage" under Workers' Compensation benefits. This means there is no statutory limitation on either the cost or time for medical care. Most states allow for coverage by the private insurance industry. Three states, North Dakota, Puerto Rico, and Wyoming, have an exclusive fund wherein the state is the insurance carrier. Three states Ohio, Washington, and West Virginia also permit self-insurance (by the employer) along with the state funded plan. The rest of the country offers a combination of worker's compensation plans, self-insurance, private insurance, and/or combinations of each. The medical coder will want to check with their local division of Worker's Compensation.

Medical Benefits

The law provides for the payment of all reasonable and necessary medical care incurred to treat the injury. This includes reasonably necessary transportation expenses. Mileage for use of a private auto is reimbursed at a rate determined by each state.

Disability Benefits

The weekly amount of disability benefit is determined by the following:

- Employee's average gross weekly earnings
- Number of exemptions
- Marital status

Disability benefits include the following:

- Temporary Total Disability (TTD)—Employees with an injury that last more than 3 calendar days qualifies for TTD. They receive 80% of their weekly spendable earnings. Benefits begin on the day four of disability and end when the employee returns to work or is medically capable of returning.
- Temporary Partial Disability (TPD)—Employees who are recuperating from an injury and able to return to work performing a lesser-paying job because of their temporary partial disability, qualify for TPD. They receive a percentage of the difference between their average weekly earnings and the weekly earnings of the lesser-paying job. Each state determines the waiting period before benefits begin.

> **! KEY TERM**
>
> TEMPORARY DISABILITY—A limitation caused by injury that requires time away from work but will eventually heal and allow the employee to return to work.

- Healing Period (HP)—Employees recuperating from an injury that produces a permanent impairment qualify for HP. They receive a percentage of their weekly spendable earnings. Each state determines the waiting period before benefits begin after the injury.
- Permanent Partial Disability (PPD)—Employees who are permanently disabled from a work-related injury but capable of gainful employment qualify for PPD. They receive a percentage of their weekly spendable earnings. Benefits begin after the HP benefits terminate.
- Permanent Total Disability (PTD)—Employees who are permanently disabled from a work-related injury and incapable of gainful employment qualify for PTD. They receive a percentage of their weekly spendable earnings. Benefits begin on the date of injury and are payable as long as the employee remains permanently disabled.

> **! KEY TERM**
>
> PERMANENT DISABILITY—A limitation caused by an injury that will never heal. An employee may be unable to return to work depending on the nature of the limitation.

- **Death Benefits**—The dependents of the employee who died from a work-related injury qualify for Death Benefits. They receive a percentage of the deceased employees' weekly spendable earnings. Benefits begin on the date of death and are payable to the surviving spouse for life or until re-marriage.

Total weekly compensation for any employee is not to exceed 80 of the employee's weekly spendable earnings. The law defines "spendable earnings" as that amount remaining after payroll taxes are deducted from gross weekly earnings. The weekly compensation benefit amount is usually based upon a 7-day calendar week.

Types of Permanent Partial Disabilities (PPDs)

Each state determines the length of time benefits are payable for the loss of body parts. An example can be found in Table 12–1.

Federal Workers' Compensation

The United States Department of Labor's Office of Workers' Compensation Programs (OWCP) administers four major disability compensation programs under four federal acts:

1. The Federal Employees' Compensation Act (FECA) covers federal employees, employees of the U.S. Postal Service, civilian employees of the Department of Defense, members of the Peace Corps, and employees of American Embassies.

2. The Longshore and Harbor Workers' Compensation Act (LHWCA) covers longshoremen, harbor workers, and other maritime (marine) workers. Others covered under the LHWCA are employees working to extract the natural resources on the outer continental shelf, overseas defense contractors, and employees at post exchanges on military bases.

3. The Federal Black Lung Benefits Act (FBLBA) covers miners' pulmonary diseases, specifically pneumoconiosis (black lung disease), acquired from working in the nation's coal mines.

4. The Energy Employees Occupational Illness Compensation Program Act (EEOIC) covers the employees of the U.S. Department of Energy's (DOE) nuclear weapons agencies.

These programs serve only these specific employee groups who may become ill or injured as a result of their work. This coverage may not apply to individuals employed by state or local government agencies. The employer should contact their state department of Workers' Compensation for direction (Box 12–1).

TABLE 12–1: Benefits Period for Loss of Body Parts

Values of Scheduled Body Parts	Weeks
Loss of thumb	60
Loss of first finger	35
Loss of second finger	30
Loss of third finger	25
Loss of fourth finger	20
Loss of hand	190
Loss of arm	250
Loss of great toe	40
Loss of any other toe	15
Loss of foot	150
Loss of leg	220
Loss of eye	140
Loss of hearing in one ear	50
Loss of hearing in both ears	175
Permanent disfigurement, face or head	150

BOX 12–1: Federal Workers' Compensation Provider Tips

The Federal Employees' Compensation Act (FECA) Only
- Authorization is needed for surgery, physical therapy, occupational therapy, and some durable medical equipment, office visits and consultations, laboratory work, inpatient hospital services, x-rays (including MRIs and CT scans), emergency services including surgery. If pre-authorization is needed to treat a Department of Labor (DOL) employee, the medical coder should contact the website or phone number listed earlier.

The Federal Black Lung Benefits Act FBLBA Only
- Physician services rendered in the treatment of a miner's pulmonary disease are reimbursable under the following categories: office visits, hospital visits, procedures at an outpatient clinic, home visits, pulmonary consultations, immunizations for flu and pneumonia, radiology for the diagnosis and/or treatment of a pulmonary disease, pulmonary therapy, and prescriptions for and administration of drugs on the lists of drugs and laboratory tests covered by the Department of Labor program. When care is rendered for an acute condition causing hospitalization, emergency room, or ambulatory care services, the acute condition must be indicated on the billing form before reimbursement can be considered.
- Some services, specifically home nursing services, pulmonary rehabilitation, and durable medical equipment, require prior authorization in the form of a certificate of medical necessity.

Obtaining Medical Information

An employer filing a claim for Workers' Compensation benefits agrees to release all pertinent information concerning an employee's physical or mental condition and waives any rights for the release of the information; a patient signature authorizing the release of information is not needed. In most states, the law requires that information should be available when requested by any participant involved in the case.

Under the law, the Workers' Compensation carrier can review *only* the patient's medical records related to the work-related illness or injury. This means if an established patient is seen by a provider for a work-related illness or injury, a separate file and ledger card *must* be used.

Health-Care Providers' Responsibilities

The physician must file a First Report of Injury (see Fig. 12–1 for sample). The form contains information regarding the date, time, and place of the injury or illness. The physician must document the patient's complaint, the findings/diagnoses, and plan of treatment. Each state has time limits for reporting work-related injuries, disabilities, and deaths.

Health-care providers may be asked to provide a medical testimony concerning the diagnosis, treatment, and prognosis of the injured worker. Testimony may be given either in court or through the use of a deposition. Usually, depositions are taken in workers' compensation cases and are read by the judge hearing the case. Health-care providers may be called to appear before the judge. Preparation with attorneys or their representatives before the testimony may be necessary. Health-care providers may charge for the testimony given either by deposition or court appearance. In some cases, the fees are already set or the health-care provider may be able to charge their own fee for their time.

The injured patient will be examined by the physician to determine the extent of the injury, the diagnosis, and the prognosis. The physician must document what the patient's limitations are compared to what the patient was able to perform before the injury. This information will be shared with other medical professionals, with the attorneys, the judge, and the patient.

It may be necessary for the medical-care provider to write medical reports for a Workers' Compensation case. The reports not only will be read by other medical-care providers experienced in the field but also nonmedical-care people, including the injured worker, attorneys, and judges. The medical coder should be sure the documentation is complete with dates, signatures, and necessary reports.

Medical Records for a Workers' Compensation case should be kept separate from the patient's private medical records. The authorization to release private medical records is different from the authorization to release Workers' Compensation records. A covered entity may not use or disclose protected health information without proper authorization. The major purpose of the Privacy Rule under HIPAA is to limit the circumstances in which an individual's protected health information may be used or disclosed.

WORKERS' COMPENSATION BILLING INFORMATION

The medical coder will need to obtain the name and address of the workers' compensation carrier at the time of the patient's visit. As previously stated, this is a separate medical and disability reimbursement program unrelated to a patient's health-care benefits. Any service rendered to the patient related to the patient's work-related illness or injury should be sent to the Workers' Compensation carrier.

Providers are required to accept payment in full from Workers' Compensation. The patient should not be billed for any remaining balance. If the payment does not seem satisfactory to the provider, the matter should be taken up with the Workers' Compensation carrier.

The CMS-1500 claim form should be used for billing and be sent to the appropriate Workers' Compensation carrier, not the patient's private insurance carrier. The previous claim completion guidelines should be followed. See Figure 12–3 for a completed CMS-1500 for a Workers' Compensation patient.

Electronic Data Interchange (EDI)

Most states mandate the First Report of Injury (FROI) and Subsequent Reports of Injury (SROI) be filed electronically. After an injury, an employer gathers the information and forms and gives it to their Workers' Compensation insurer or claim administrator who in turn stores the data in their computer system. All claims and information related to the injury are forwarded on to the state Division of Workers' Compensation electronically.

The Electronic Data Interchange (EDI) Support Unit assists providers who have questions about electronic bill submission. The EDI Support Unit is available to all providers Monday through Friday from 8:00 a.m. to 8:00 p.m. Eastern Standard Time at 800-987-6717. EDI Support will:

- Provide information on available services.
- Assist in enrolling users for electronic bill submission and report retrieval.
- Process test transmissions.
- Provide technical assistance on transmission difficulties.

Federal Workers' Compensation Billing Information

To be paid for treating federal employees covered by the FECA, a provider must enroll as a participating provider. The medical coder can enroll the provider as a Department of Labor provider with ACS EDI Gateway, Inc.

> ACS Enrollment Department
>
> P.O. Box 14600
>
> Tallahassee, FL 32317-4600
>
> Providers can also sign up online at the website owcp.dol.acs-inc.com, or call (850) 558-1818.

For federal Workers' Compensation claims, the standard CMS-1500 is used and should be submitted to:

> U.S. Department of Labor
>
> DFEC Central Mailroom
>
> P.O. Box 8300
>
> London, KY 40742-8300

Claims may also be sent electronically.

Federal Worker's Compensation Fee Schedule

The OWCP fee schedule applies to FECA, EEOIC, and LHWCA, and the FBLBA reimbursement rates follow a different customized fee schedule. The OWCP fee schedule follows the Centers for Medicare and Medicaid Services' relative value units (RVU). The OWCP creates its own conversion factors based on program-specific data, national billing data from other federal programs, state Workers' Compensation programs, and data from the U.S. Department of Labor's Bureau of Labor and

1500

HEALTH INSURANCE CLAIM FORM

APPROVED BY NATIONAL UNIFORM CLAIM COMMITTEE 08/05

PICA

	PICA

1. MEDICARE (Medicare #) **MEDICAID** (Medicaid #) **TRICARE CHAMPUS** (Sponsor's SSN) **CHAMPVA** (Member ID#) **GROUP HEALTH PLAN** (SSN or ID) **FECA BLK LUNG** (SSN) **OTHER** [X] (ID)

1a. INSURED'S I.D. NUMBER   (For Program in Item 1)
411WK99

2. PATIENT'S NAME (Last Name, First Name, Middle Initial)
CASSELL ROBERT

3. PATIENT'S BIRTH DATE MM 02 DD 04 YY 1978 **SEX** M [X] F [ ]

4. INSURED'S NAME (Last Name, First Name, Middle Initial)
BRUBAKER PRINTING

5. PATIENT'S ADDRESS (No., Street)
12997 EVENINGSIDE DRIVE

6. PATIENT RELATIONSHIP TO INSURED Self [ ] Spouse [ ] Child [ ] Other [X]

7. INSURED'S ADDRESS (No., Street)
4242 N 13TH STREET

CITY AIRLANE   **STATE** MA

8. PATIENT STATUS Single [ ] Married [X] Other [ ]

CITY PRAIRIE CITY   **STATE** MA

ZIP CODE 55610   **TELEPHONE (Include Area Code)** (555) 181-6262

Employed [X] Full-Time Student [ ] Part-Time Student [ ]

ZIP CODE 55510   **TELEPHONE (Include Area Code)** (555) 960-9600

9. OTHER INSURED'S NAME (Last Name, First Name, Middle Initial)
LEAVE BLANK

10. IS PATIENT'S CONDITION RELATED TO:

11. INSURED'S POLICY GROUP OR FECA NUMBER
LEAVE BLANK

a. OTHER INSURED'S POLICY OR GROUP NUMBER

a. EMPLOYMENT? (Current or Previous) [X] YES [ ] NO

a. INSURED'S DATE OF BIRTH MM DD YY   **SEX** M [ ] F [ ]

b. OTHER INSURED'S DATE OF BIRTH MM DD YY   **SEX** M [ ] F [ ]

b. AUTO ACCIDENT? [ ] YES [X] NO   **PLACE (State)**

b. EMPLOYER'S NAME OR SCHOOL NAME

c. EMPLOYER'S NAME OR SCHOOL NAME

c. OTHER ACCIDENT? [ ] YES [X] NO

c. INSURANCE PLAN NAME OR PROGRAM NAME

d. INSURANCE PLAN NAME OR PROGRAM NAME

10d. RESERVED FOR LOCAL USE

d. IS THERE ANOTHER HEALTH BENEFIT PLAN? [ ] YES [ ] NO   **If yes**, return to and complete item 9 a-d.

READ BACK OF FORM BEFORE COMPLETING & SIGNING THIS FORM.
12. PATIENT'S OR AUTHORIZED PERSON'S SIGNATURE I authorize the release of any medical or other information necessary to process this claim. I also request payment of government benefits either to myself or to the party who accepts assignment below.

SIGNED SIGNATURE ON FILE (SOF)   DATE

13. INSURED'S OR AUTHORIZED PERSON'S SIGNATURE I authorize payment of medical benefits to the undersigned physician or supplier for services described below.

SIGNED SIGNATURE ON FILE (SOF)

14. DATE OF CURRENT: MM 06 DD 06 YY 2009 ILLNESS (First symptom) OR INJURY (Accident) OR PREGNANCY(LMP)

15. IF PATIENT HAS HAD SAME OR SIMILAR ILLNESS. GIVE FIRST DATE MM DD YY

16. DATES PATIENT UNABLE TO WORK IN CURRENT OCCUPATION FROM MM 06 DD 07 YY 2009 TO MM 08 DD 10 YY 2009

17. NAME OF REFERRING PROVIDER OR OTHER SOURCE   17a.   17b. NPI

18. HOSPITALIZATION DATES RELATED TO CURRENT SERVICES FROM MM DD YY TO MM DD YY

19. RESERVED FOR LOCAL USE

20. OUTSIDE LAB? [ ] YES [ ] NO   **$ CHARGES**

21. DIAGNOSIS OR NATURE OF ILLNESS OR INJURY (Relate Items 1, 2, 3 or 4 to Item 24E by Line)
1. 839.20
2. E919.80
3.
4.

22. MEDICAID RESUBMISSION CODE   **ORIGINAL REF. NO.**

23. PRIOR AUTHORIZATION NUMBER

24. A. DATE(S) OF SERVICE						B. PLACE OF SERVICE	C. EMG	D. PROCEDURES, SERVICES, OR SUPPLIES (Explain Unusual Circumstances)		E. DIAGNOSIS POINTER	F. $ CHARGES	G. DAYS OR UNITS	H. EPSDT Family Plan	I. ID. QUAL.	J. RENDERING PROVIDER ID. #
	From			To				CPT/HCPCS	MODIFIER						
MM	DD	YY	MM	DD	YY										
06	10	09	06	10	09	21		63005		12	2635.00	1		NPI	
														NPI	
														NPI	
														NPI	
														NPI	
														NPI	

25. FEDERAL TAX I.D. NUMBER SSN [ ] EIN [ ]

26. PATIENT'S ACCOUNT NO.

27. ACCEPT ASSIGNMENT? (For govt. claims, see back) [ ] YES [ ] NO

28. TOTAL CHARGE $ 2635 00

29. AMOUNT PAID $

30. BALANCE DUE $ 2635 00

31. SIGNATURE OF PHYSICIAN OR SUPPLIER INCLUDING DEGREES OR CREDENTIALS (I certify that the statements on the reverse apply to this bill and are made a part thereof.)
Joe Smith MD 08/12/09
SIGNED   DATE

32. SERVICE FACILITY LOCATION INFORMATION
MCNEAL COUNTY HOSPITAL
1800 COLUMBIA
PRAIRIE CITY MA 55502
a. 6987654321   b.

33. BILLING PROVIDER INFO & PH # ( ) OPTIONAL
JOE SMITH MD
555 COLUMBIA
PRAIRIE CITY MA 55502
a. 1234567890   b.

NUCC Instruction Manual available at: www.nucc.org   **PLEASE PRINT OR TYPE**   APPROVED OMB-0938-0999 FORM CMS-1500 (08-05)

Along the right margin: CARRIER — PATIENT AND INSURED INFORMATION — PHYSICIAN OR SUPPLIER INFORMATION

FIGURE 12-3: Completed CMS-1500 form for a patient with a Workers' Compensation claim.

Statistics consumer price index. The OWCP medical fee schedule is available at the Department of Labor website at: http://www.dol.gov/esa/regs/feeschedule/fee.htm.

The patient may not be billed for any balance that remains after payment has been made. If a provider does not agree with the payment decision, a request for reconsideration may be made within 30 days. Sufficient documentation must accompany the appeal to illustrate that the claim warrants additional reimbursement, such as an indication of an incorrect CPT code or evidence showing the difficulty of the procedure.

■ HANDLING DISPUTES

The majority of disputes in Workers' Compensation claims are resolved among the employee, employer, and insurance carrier. The employee should be advised of the reasons for the decisions made, and the evidence that supports those decisions. If the dispute is not resolved, a contested case may be brought before the Workers' Compensation commissioner. It is usually advisable (though not required) to have legal representation when filing a contested case. However, before contacting an attorney or filing a contested case, the employee is encouraged to contact a compliance administrator in the Workers' Compensation commissioner's office to discuss any other options.

The Workers' Compensation commissioner is the head of the Division of Workers' Compensation, which is part of the state Workforce Development. The commissioner has the responsibility of administering, regulating, and enforcing the Workers' Compensation laws. Though the Workers' Compensation commissioner's office cannot represent the interests of any party, the agency provides information regarding the provisions of the Workers' Compensation Law, the rights of the parties, and the procedures that the parties can follow to resolve disputes.

■ CONCLUSION

Worker's Compensation claims like any other claim form must be completed accurately. The patient's medical record must justify the reason for any service rendered. The medical coder should learn the rules and regulations specific to their state for compliance and best possible reimbursement. All documentation with the patient, their employer, the Workers' Compensation carrier or any other related source must be recorded in the patient's medical or financial record to provide the documentation needed for the final outcome—accurate reimbursement.

RESOURCE LIST
For individual state contacts and guidelines:
WorkersCompensation.com/stateregs.php
For general information:
    justia.com/injury/workers-compensation
    ssa.gov/policy/docs

OWCP website
    http://www.dol.gov/esa/regs/compliance/owcp/CBPOutreach.htm

U.S. Dept of Labor
    www.dol.gov/dol/topic/workcomp/index/htm

Chapter Review Exercises

1. What is Workers' Compensation?

_____

2. What types of injuries are covered?

_____

3. Who is eligible for Workers' Compensation?

_____

4. Who chooses the Medical Care? _____

5. How are disputes handled? _____

6. Who oversees disputes? _____

7. Who pays the benefits? _____

8. What two types of benefits does the law provide? _____

9. Who gets the payment from death benefits? _____

10. On average, how long does an employee have to report a claim?

_____

11. How is medical information obtained? _____

12. How many weeks do you receive Workers' Compensation benefits for loss of a thumb?

_____

13. How many weeks do you receive Workers' Compensation benefits for loss of a leg?

_____

14. How many weeks do you receive Workers' Compensation benefits for loss of hearing?

Insurance Payments, Patient Billing, and Follow-Up Procedures

Chapter Outline

OBJECTIVES

- Describe the billing process for a manual office
- Describe the billing process for a computerized office
- Set up collection procedures
- Identify the billing cycle
- Recognize the importance of claim follow-up

MEDICAL ASSISTING COMPETENCIES

ABHES

 1i. conduct work within scope of education, training, and ability
 2d. serve as liaison between Physician and others
 2g. use appropriate medical terminology
 2h. receive, organize, prioritize, and transmit information expediently
 2j. use correct grammar, spelling, and formatting techniques in written works
 3b. prepare and maintain medical records
 3e. locate resources and information for patients and employers
 3x. use physician fee schedule
 5a. determine needs for documentation and reporting
 5b. document accurately
 5c. use appropriate guidelines when releasing records or information
 8a. use manual and computerized bookkeeping systems
 8c. analyze and use current third-party guidelines for reimbursement
 8d. manage accounts payable and receivable

CAAHEP

 IV.P.3. Use medical terminology, pronouncing medical terms correctly, to communicate information, patient history, data and observations
 VI.C.1. Explain basic bookkeeping computations
 VI.C.6. Differentiate between accounts payable and accounts receivable
 VI.C.9. Explain both billing and payment options
 VI.C.10. Identify procedure for preparing patient accounts
 VI.C.11. Discuss procedures for collecting outstanding accounts
 VI.C.12. Describe the impact of both the Fair Debt Collection Act and the Federal Truth in Lending Act of 1968 as they apply to collections
 VI.C.13. Discuss types of adjustments that may be made to a patient's account
 VI.P.2. Perform accounts receivable procedures, including:
 a. Post entries on a day sheet
 b. Perform billing procedures
 c. Perform collection procedures
 d. Post adjustments
 e. Process a credit balance
 f. Process refunds
 g. Post non-sufficient fund (NSF) checks
 h. Post collection agency payments
 VI.P.3. Utilize computerized office billing procedures
 VIII.A.1. Work with physician to achieve the maximum reimbursement
 IX.P.1. Respond to issues of confidentiality
 IX.A.1. Demonstrate sensitivity to patients' rights
 IX.A.2. Demonstrate awareness of the consequences of not working within the legal scope of practice

---

KEY TERMS

Accounts Receivable	Ledger	Pegboard system
Cash Flow	Ledger Card	Reimbursement
Day Sheet	Once Write	Revenue
Guarantor	Payments	

INTRODUCTION

Previous chapters have explained how patient demographics, medical records, coding, and claim completion are all parts of the billing cycle in the medical office. These are the main components in the claim cycle and **reimbursement** is the fundamental goal. The term "reimbursement" means receiving payment for services rendered to the patients, and "**payments**" or "**cash flow**" is the **revenue** for the medical office. These payments are used for the operating expenses required to provide services to patients, including salaries, employee benefits, and utilities. Accuracy in coding, billing, and accounting is mandatory to optimize reimbursement and bring revenue into the medical practice.

KEY TERMS

PAYMENTS OR CASH FLOW—Money or revenue received and spent within a business.

REIMBURSEMENT—The receipt of payment in exchange for the medical services provided to a patient.

REVENUE—The earnings or source of income.

THE BUSINESS OFFICE

As previously discussed, the business office of a medical practice can operate manually (on paper) or can be automated by computers, and filing claims and receiving payments can be performed either way. Most offices rely on computers to electronically manage the financial side of the practice. A few offices still prefer to run their business manually. Either method will record the services rendered and the reimbursement received for those services.

THE MANUAL ACCOUNTING PROCESS

Patient Accounts

The front office keeps track of charges, payments, and outstanding balances, called account receivables. When using manual or paper accounting, the patient's records of service and payments are kept on paper files commonly referred to as **ledgers** or **ledger cards** (Fig. 13–1). The medical coder or other front office personnel use the patient's superbill or route slip to record the services and charges related to each patient encounter onto a daily log or spreadsheet, often referred to as a **day sheet** (Fig. 13–2). This spreadsheet system is called a **pegboard system** or a "**once write.**" It is made with carbonless paper that can be positioned so that an entry is made once on the top document, which is usually the patient's receipt. As the receipt is completed, the entry will show up on the ledger card and on the daily log beneath. The system has proven to be a time and error saver, because only one entry is needed.

Each day, the patient encounters are recorded onto the day sheet, along with any charges, payments, or adjustments made toward those services. The charges, payments, and adjustments are totaled daily, and a running balance is kept, similar to a checkbook. The end-of-day totals are carried over to the next day, then to the next month, and, eventually, the next year, in a continuous cycle.

Patient name	Description	Charges	Payments	New Balance	Old Balance
Joe Smith	OV, X-ray	150.00	15.00	155.00	20.00
Mike Connors	OV, UA, X-ray	180.00	10.00	340.00	170.00
Maria Sanchez	New Pt OV	210.00	15.00	195.00	0.00
Insurance payment Tina Sawyer	---------	0.00	415.00	0.00	415.00
TOTALS		540.00	455.00	690.00	605.00

THE AMOUNTS RECEIVABLE, OR AMOUNT OF MONEY OWED TO THE PRACTICE, WENT FROM $605.00 TO $690.00

FIGURE 13–1: Entering charges and payments on a day sheet.

KEY TERMS

ACCOUNTS RECEIVABLE—The amount of money owed for services already rendered.

DAY SHEET—Daily log or spreadsheet of the financial activity in the office.

LEDGER OR LEDGER CARD—Forms that list the patient's record of service and payments.

PEGBOARD SYSTEM (ONCE-WRITE)—Accounting system that requires only one entry. Information is carried through carbonless paper onto the ledger card, day sheet, and receipt.

Each office has a routine or schedule for filing insurance claims, billing patients, and following up on any outstanding charges. Usually, patients are billed on a monthly basis. However, insurance claims should be filed often to maintain a steady cash flow for the office. Claims can be generated and submitted as often as the office prefers—weekly, daily, or after each service is rendered. The medical services noted on each ledger card are recorded again on paper claim forms and then mailed to the appropriate third-party payer. Very few medical offices type the information onto the claim form; most offices have medical software that takes the place of typewriters and enters the information onto the claim form. When a medical computer program is used with a manual system, it will generate paper claims for the services rendered to every patient during a certain timeframe. For example, the medical coder could generate a claim for every patient service rendered from the start of business on Monday morning through closing time on Friday. Software is designed to place the name and address of the insurance company on the top right hand corner of the claim. The medical coder collates all of the claim forms generated by insurance company and mails them. Claims going to the same payer can be sent out in the same envelope.

Paper claims need to be kept in a manner that makes them accessible and easy to track, so they are usually printed on carbonless paper. The top claim is mailed to the insurance company, and the second copy is retained in a pending file in the office. Claims copies are best kept alphabetized by patient name and date of service and/or by insurance carrier. The pending claims are removed as payments are received, and the medical code should follow up on the remaining claims with phone calls and inquiries to the third-party payers for processing status. Claims can be refiled as needed, either by generating another claim or making a photocopy. Every time a claim form is generated and sent out to an insurance company, the medical coder must mark the patient's ledger card to indicate which charges have been sent out for processing and when they were sent.

Keeping Track of Claims

Using a tracking system keeps the **accounts receivable** lower and gives the office a chance to resubmit claims that did not get paid. Third-party carriers usually have time limits for accepting claims and will not pay claims past their set time limit. If a claim is not submitted on time, the charges are not the patient's responsibility, the fees for those services must be written off and are never collected from the patient. The responsibility of timely filing falls on the shoulders of the medical coder.

Andrew Stevenson
167 Main Street, Colbrush, CT
860-123-0932

Date	Procedure	Charge	Payment	Balance
	Balance brought forward			170.00
03/06/2008	office surgery	650.00	25.00	795.00

Hannah Martin
36 Gratuity Way, Blueville, CT
860-555-9778

Date	Procedure	Charge	Payment	Balance
	Balance brought forward			0.00
03/08/2008	ECG	105.00	0.00	105.00

Jenna Collins
14 Wayside Drive, Blueville, CT
860-555-9778

Date	Procedure	Charge	Payment	Balance
	Balance brought forward			150.00
03/08/2008	OV-exp. xray, LBP, PT, Acu	404.00	15.00	539.00

John Rivera
83 Pinecrest Road, Blueville, CT
860-555-7695

Date	Procedure	Charge	Payment	Balance
	Balance brought forward			50.00
03/08/2008	PE, stress test	153.00	15.00	188.00

Barry Chen
762 Elm Street, Blueville, CT
860-555-6823

Date	Procedure	Charge	Payment	Balance
	Balance brought forward			100.00
03/07/2008	office surgery	410.00	25.00	485.00

Gary Travini
11 Appleton Drive, Blueville, CT
860-555-7833

Date	Procedure	Charge	Payment	Balance
	Balance brought forward			0.00
10/20/2007	office surgery	404.00	20.00	384.00
11/22/2007	OV, UA, stress test	185.20	20.00	549.00
12/01/2007	check returned NSF	20.00		569.00
12/13/2007	patient check		69.00	500.00
01/05/2008	patient billed			
02/05/2008	patient billed			
03/05/2008	patient billed final notice to collect			
04/01/2008	account sent to ACME collections			500.00

FIGURE 13-2: Sample ledgers/ledger cards for balancing.

Inquiries should be made with the third-party payer on any claims that have not been processed within 6 weeks. All phone calls and written inquiries should be documented to provide a history of the pending claim's process. This demonstrates the efforts taken to receive payment and may be needed if a complaint has to be filed with the insurance carrier or the state insurance commissioner's office.

Insurance Payments

The majority of payments the medical coder handles come from insurance companies, Medicare, and Medicaid. Some payments also come in from patients for their deductibles, copayments, and coinsurance balances not covered by insurance.

In some medical offices, a medical coder may be responsible for accepting and recording all payments. It is common practice for a third-party payer to send one check to pay for several patients' services. A statement referred to as a Remittance Advice (RA) or Explanation of Benefits (EOB) will accompany the payment and will list every patient, every charge, adjustment, or denial the third-party payer has just processed.

Payments, adjustments, or denials must be documented on each patient's ledger or account. Payments are recorded and subtracted from the patient's balance, and a notation must always be made explaining which service was paid. This makes it easy to spot services not yet paid and can serve as a prompt to inquire or resubmit those charges. If the patient has a secondary insurance carrier, another claim should be generated showing what the primary insurance company has already paid toward the services. Often, the coder will make a copy of the RA, attach it to a new paper claim, and send that claim on to the secondary insurance for consideration of the balance. The resubmission should also be documented on the ledger.

Insurance Denials

When a claim is denied, the denial reason will be stated on the EOB. If an error was made, the coder will need to take action to correct and resubmit the claim for payment. If additional information is requested to consider payment, it can be included with a new claim form and sent back to the insurance company for payment consideration. As with insurance submissions and payments, these actions need to be recorded on the patient's ledger card.

If a denial was made because the service was not covered under the patient's plan or the patient was not covered under that insurance when the service took place, the balance will become the patient's responsibility. That information is documented, and a bill sent to the patient. The insurance companies usually inform their insureds when a claim has been paid or denied; most offices will have written policies in place and will inform their patients that such balances will be considered their financial responsibility.

Billing the Patient Manually

Every ledger card with a balance is copied and then sent to the patient or the **guarantor**, who is the person responsible for payment. Ledgers with credit balances are collected and refunds are issued. As payments come in, the ledger is pulled, and the payment is posted with a brief explanation regarding the date of payment, what service the payment was made toward, and form of payment, (e.g., insurance payment, cash, check and check number). If a balance remains, the process starts all over in the next billing cycle.

Without the computer, paper recordkeeping, billing, coding, and collections is more time-consuming. A medical coder working in an office that operates manually, must be a very accurate and thorough bookkeeper to maintain a profitable and compliant billing cycle.

■ COMPUTERS IN THE MEDICAL OFFICE

Most offices today consider the computer to be a most effective way to manage their practice. Practice management software can take care of billing, filing claims, making appointments, and other recordkeeping tasks.

In Chapter 1, the advantages of a computerized office were listed as the following:

■ Better management control and more current information at the office's disposal
■ Efficiency

- Accounts receivable more accurately monitored
- Collections can improve
- Use of electronic claims (paperless claims) transmission

Other advantages of a computerized office are that insurance payments can be made automatically and EOBs can also be received electronically.

In the medical office, a computer can be used to keep track of patient demographics and financial information. All payments made to the office by the insurance companies and patients are recorded in the computer, along with all of the information about the services rendered on each patient's account. Payments can be applied directly to the related charges.

The following are just a few of the statistics that can be kept track of with computerized reports:

- Generation of revenue
- Services rendered
- Geographical area the office is serving
- Bad debt collections

The computerized claim form generation and submission can save time. The office staff inputs the service and diagnosis for each patient encounter, and the computer completes and submits the claim forms, tracks claims for reimbursement, and generates claims for any secondary insurance and submits or resubmits as needed.

Regulating Electronic Data Interchange

As discussed in Chapter 3, the administrative simplification provision of HIPAA directed the health-care industry to standardize the automatic transfer of data between providers and third-party payers referred to as **electronic data interchange** (EDI). Before HIPAA, each third-party payer had a separate set of standards and requirements, and computer software systems had to be programmed to meet each carrier's criteria to be compatible. In addition, some third-party payers were not compatible with all software programs. The administrative simplification of HIPAA set the standards for the exchange of data so that health-care providers would be able to submit electronic claims to any or all third-party carriers.

Electronic or Paperless Claims Submission

There are two different ways that insurance claims can be transmitted electronically: the carrier-direct method and the **clearinghouse** method. The carrier-direct method is a software program that transmits claims from the health-care provider directly to a specific carrier through a modem. Many carrier-direct systems are free of charge to the provider, but the direct system can only transmit to specific carriers.

Several different companies provide the clearinghouse method and their networks accept claims from providers nationwide. A clearinghouse network receives and sorts electronic claims and then transmits them to the various third-party carriers. The health-care provider deals with only one software system that can communicate with numerous third-party insurers. Clearinghouses also are called third-party administrators (TPA) and are designed to receive electronic claims from any provider.

The clearinghouse will perform edits on the claims to catch any errors. The claims will either be forwarded on to the proper insurance carrier or returned to the provider with an explanation of the error. Once corrected, the claim can be resent to the clearinghouse and if no errors are found, the corrected claim can be forwarded to the insurance company for payment. Some clearinghouses will even turn electronically submitted claims into paper and transmit them to third-party insurers who do not do business electronically.

There is a fee for using a clearinghouse. It may be a one-time sign-up fee, a monthly fee, or per-claim fee. In most cases, the user fee will be minimal compared with the cost of paper, toner, postage, and the coder's time.

To file a claim electronically, the medical coder enters the date of service, diagnosis and procedure codes into individual patient accounts that have been set up with the patient's current demographics. The computer completes an electronic image gathering all of the data entered on each patient and transmits the data to a clearinghouse or appropriate third-party carrier.

Keeping Track of Electronic Claims

The medical coder can generate reports to list outstanding claims and age them so that they can follow-up on claims that have been pending longer. Many of the carrier-direct software programs also can be used to track outstanding claims, paid or denied claims, or to verify patient eligibility. These are important features and makes tracking those claims much easier.

Electronic Insurance Payments

Insurance payments can be received electronically and deposited directly into the provider's account. The Remittance Advice (RA) or Explanation of Benefits (EOB) (Fig 13–3) is also sent electronically. As with a paper statement, the electronic statement will have all of the information needed to apply proper payments, adjustments, or payment denials to the appropriate patient accounts. Some software also will post this information directly into the patient account, and automatically deduct the payment amounts from the account. The computer program will also generate a bill or statement that is printed off and sent to the patient, showing all of the monthly activity on an account. Other software programs will generate a statement so the medical coder can post the results into each patient account.

An example of carrier-direct software is the program the Centers for Medicare and Medicaid (CMS) developed known as Medicare Remit Easy Read (MREP). This software sends remittance

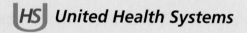

HS *United Health Systems*

United Health Systems
283 Commerce Park Drive
PO Box 6978
Blueville, CT 06100

Claims 1-800-555-1212

EXPLANATION OF BENEFITS – THIS IS NOT A BILL

Patient name: Steven E. Muzinski
United Health Systems ID# XGA00658   Group # 4388
Provider: Hector Rodriguez, MD   NPI # 12244559988

Patient name	DOS	CPT	Charge	Paid	Allowed	Code	Pt res
Muzinski, Steven E.	04/23/09	99215	95.00	80.00	90.00		10.00

Reason code

To file an appeal of a denial of a claim, send explanation to:

UHS, Inc., Claims Department
283 Commerce Park Drive
PO Box 6978
Blueville, CT 06100

FIGURE 13–3: Examples of Explanation of Benefits (EOBs) forms.

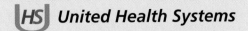

United Health Systems

United Health Systems
283 Commerce Park Drive
PO Box 6978
Blueville, CT 06100

Claims 1-800-555-1212

EXPLANATION OF BENEFITS – THIS IS NOT A BILL

Patient name: Cara Cohelo
United Health Systems ID# XGA00778   Group # 4488
Provider: Henry Lee, MD   NPI # 8700334239

Patient name	DOS	CPT	Charge	Paid	Allowed	Code	Pt res
Cohelo, Cara	03/27/09	97813	65.00	0.00	0.00	A12	65.00
Cohelo, Cara	03/29/09	97813	65.00	0.00	0.00	A12	65.00
Cohelo, Cara	04/01/09	97813	65.00	0.00	0.00	A12	65.00
Cohelo, Cara	04/04/09	97813	65.00	0.00	0.00	A12	65.00
Cohelo, Cara	04/06/09	97813	65.00	0.00	0.00	A12	65.00

Reason code

A12 – further documentation needed to process claim

To file an appeal of a denial of a claim, send explanation to:

UHS, Inc., Claims Department
283 Commerce Park Drive
PO Box 6978
Blueville, CT 06100

FIGURE 13–3: cont'd

advices to participating providers, and is available free of charge. The MREP format is nearly identical to their Standard Paper Remittance Advice (SPR) but provides much more information than was ever available on paper. The software will generate reports to show adjusted and denied claims as well as the paid ones. It will show which claims went toward the patient's deductible and allows the medical coder the ability to search for submitted claims by the beneficiary's last name, account number, health insurance claim number (HICN), date of service, and more.

The electronic Medicare EOBs will supply the patient's name, date of service, the CPT codes for services rendered, a payment amount, or reason for denial. Remark codes are used to provide specific information about payment amounts and reasons for denials or adjustments. The remark codes give the medical coder information on how to proceed. Remark codes used by Medicare for example:

M76–Missing/incomplete/invalid diagnosis or condition

M77– Missing/incomplete/invalid place of service

M78–Missing/incomplete/invalid charge

N13–Payment based on professional/technical component modifier(s)

N22–This procedure code was added/changed because it more accurately describes the service rendered.

Billing the Patient Electronically

Practice management software can automatically determine the patient's balance after every entry, payment, or charge is recorded. At scheduled intervals, usually monthly, a program is activated and paper statements are generated for every account with a balance due, so they can be sent out to patients. The program usually keeps track of age of the balance in 30-day increments. There are different kinds of statements available. There are the standard statements that look similar to a patient ledger card and convert mailers that can automatically print the statement inside an envelope that converts itself into a return envelope.

■ REIMBURSEMENT FOR SERVICES RENDERED

No matter how a medical business office operates, the main goal remains the same: optimal reimbursement for services rendered. All contracts with third-party carriers should be monitored to ensure proper reimbursement is received. Contracts with managed care plans may be set up to include a guaranteed dollar amount for each service. Regardless of the contract specifics, it is up to the medical coder to pay attention to the reimbursement, to be sure the correct amount has been received.

By tracking this information, a medical office can make better decisions about patient care, financial practices, and the internal revenue cycle. A computer system can easily pull important data from patient records and provide reports to the office staff of important statistics (Box 13–1).

■ COLLECTIONS

Most patients pay their bills after receiving a monthly statement. If a patient understands and agrees to the office policies on patient responsibilities, there is less chance of a patient ignoring a balance. In Chapter 1, the Patient Information Form (see Fig. 1–1) was discussed. When patients sign the document, they are agreeing to release their medical information for the purpose of filing claims with their insurance provider, allowing the insurance payment to be sent directly to the provider's office, and assuming responsibility for any charges not covered by their insurance, or any remaining balance.

Many offices have office pamphlets made to welcome a patient to the practice, with general information about the office and explaining the financial policy. It is not unethical or abnormal to have a patient sign a copy of the office financial policy when completing or updating the patient information form. The patient's signature on the patient information form indicates an understanding of the patient's financial responsibilities.

The medical office should have a means of aging a patient balance. The aging process can begin from the date of service or the date the insurance payment(s) is received. The balance can then be billed to the patient. Many offices will send statements to patients that indicate the total charge for the services rendered and that an insurance claim has been filed. The patient should not be deemed "late" while waiting on the insurance to reimburse the provider. There are too many variables that are out of the patient's hands while the claim waits for insurance to make a payment. The following are some examples:

■ How long it takes the office to initially file a claim with the patient's insurance company.

■ How the office files the claim, on paper or electronically.

■ How accurate the claim was completed: correct patient information, correct place of service, ICD-9-CM and CPT codes, correct provider information, such as the NPI and or tax ID number.

BOX 13–1: Advantages to a Computerized Office

■ Better management control and more current information at the office's disposal
■ Increased efficiency
■ More accurately monitored accounts receivable
■ Improved collection techniques
■ Electronic claim submission (paperless claim)

An account should be considered current if it has been less than 30 days since the initial insurance payment was received and the first bill was sent. Typically, a balance is aged in 30-day increments. Accounts are considered past due from 30 to 60 days and then from 60 to 90 days. Anything past 90 days usually requires a more assertive process.

Collection Calls and Communication Rules

If the medical coder does have to collect an old debt, documentation and follow-up is the key. Every attempt and contact with the patient should be documented. The patient can be contacted by phone or addressed if he or she comes into the office during the collection period.

Whenever the patient is contacted by phone, it should be done in a professional and courteous manner. The Fair Debt Collection Act prohibits all debt collectors from communicating by phone before 8 a.m. or after 9 p.m. Harassment and harsh language are also prohibited. For more information regarding the Fair Debt Collection Act, visit their website at: http://www.fair-debt-collection. com/statue-limitations.html.

Following the office policy, the medical coder may need to set up a payment plan with a patient. A schedule of regular payments can be created to allow a patient the opportunity to make payment toward their balance over a determined length of time. The plan will explain the arrangement agreed upon and should be signed by the patient. If the patient agrees to a payment schedule, the medical coder must follow-up. The collection process is only as good as the collector. If the patient was told he or she would be contacted again in a set amount of time, then the medical coder must make every attempt to do so.

If the arranged payments become late again or do not come in at all, the patient may be banned from future care from the office. In most cases, the medical provider does have the right to suspend or discontinue care of a patient due to nonpayment of their bill; as long as the patient is not currently being seen for or immediately following a major medical occurrence and patient is considered stable. It is advisable that the office consults with their state medical society for specific rules in their state. Consult the national website at: http://www.ama-assn.org/ama/pub/category/7630.html. This website provides a list of medical societies in each state.

Collection Agencies

Many physician offices rely on the help of a collection agency for outstanding patient accounts. After the medical coder has made a reasonable attempt to collect an outstanding debt, the account can be turned over to a collection agency. The patient's account should be flagged so that no additional statements are sent to the patient from the physician's office. The collection agency should be notified if a payment is sent to the physician's office after the account as been turned over. Phone calls about the account should be referred to the collection agency and not handled in the office.

A collection agency will generally charge the provider's office a percentage of the amount recovered. However, there are time limits for collecting a debt and this limit is referred to as statute of limitations. The statutes differ from state to state and the medical coder must be aware of the limitations imposed in his or her state. The statue of limitations for every state can be found at: http://www.fair-debt-collection.com/statue-limitations.html.

Uncollectible Write-offs

An office policy should be in place that tells the coder when to give up on a debt that seems uncollectible. The office spends money to send out statements and pay the salary of the medical coder doing collecting. A balance should be substantial enough to make the extra collection process beneficial to the practice, otherwise the collection process will cost the provider more than what the debt is worth.

When it has been decided the debt will never be collected, the amount is written off of the accounts receivable. The documentation that has been accumulated on the debt collection process should be filed with the patient's records and the patient's account should be flagged to prevent a repeat of the situation.

■ BILLING SERVICES

Some offices use a billing agency to do the insurance filing, record the payments, and even send the statements out to the patients. The billing service takes the place of the medical coder in the office. Many medical coders also work for billing services.

The medical practice can contract with the billing service that outlines what work will be done for the practice and a rate the billing services charges for those services. Most billing services conduct business electronically, are efficient, and always available. The billing service will have a HIPAA-compliant process that secures the privacy of patient with every transaction. A medical office will have periods during employee vacations and sick times when the work cannot be done. A billing service can offer continuous work helping the accounts receivable and creating a steady cash flow.

■ TRACKING CLAIMS

When a payment from a third-party carrier is not received in a reasonable amount of time, the medical coder must take immediate action with the third-party carrier. If the claim was originally submitted within the appropriate time limit, a copy of the original claim indicating the date first filed (see Box 31 on the claim) should be provided. If a copy of the original claim is resent and appears on a new explanation of benefits as a duplicate of a paid claim, additional work will be needed. The medical coder will have to contact the carrier and ask that the actual amount and date of payment be provided. If payment is confirmed, the medical coder will need to research the practice records. Going back over the original EOB and verifying that each payment was posted to the correct patient account is necessary to determine where that payment was posted.

Outstanding or Denied Claims

An estimated 30% to 40% of all pending or denied claims are never investigated or appealed. It costs the medical practice money whenever medical claims are denied. The coder should always compare the amounts paid with the contracted or customary amounts to ensure proper payment has been received.

When claim payments are suspended, also known as pending, cash flow is affected. A medical coder should develop a way to follow up on all claims that are denied, pending, or lost. Reviewing the explanation of benefits is the first place to start working on denied claims. Any errors in claims can be corrected or updated. Errors may occur in the main information of the computer system. For example, a miscoded diagnosis code that was added to the computer maintenance file will cause an error every time the code is used. An error in a patient's identification would have the same effect. The insurance carrier will not be able to match an insured with the ID number used and every time a claim is submitted it will not be paid.

The coder can work to resolve outstanding claims by using a simple aging file. The medical office should have guidelines that direct the medical coder about how to proceed. For example, each insurance carrier will be contacted after a certain period of time to inquire the status of a claim that has been submitted. Claims should be resubmitted accordingly.

If a claim is underpaid or denied, the medical coder must first make sure of the following:

■ All information is correct—patient demographics, codes, dates of service.

■ The claim documentation supports the coding.

When an appeal is called for, the medical coder should provide the insurance carrier with precise information including the following:

■ Explain the reason for the appeal, claim was underpaid or denied.

■ Explain the coding and include documentation to support the coding.

■ Any information regarding coverage for the service rendered.

■ Contact information, in case the carrier has additional questions.

■ The state medical society can be contacted when appropriate and provide assistance.

OVERPAYMENTS

Sometimes overpayments are made and can result in a credit balance on a patient's account. After verifying the date of service, procedure and diagnosis codes, and contracted payment, the medical coder may need to issue a refund.

If the refund is going to the patient, a brief explanation should accompany the check. The medical coder may wish to include information regarding the date of service, the service, and reason for the overpayment. For example, the insurance company may decide to pay more than the covered amount anticipated and a portion of the patient's copayment may need to be refunded.

If a refund is owed to a third-party carrier, a medical coder should provide a brief explanation and a copy of the EOB. A copy of the original claim form may also be necessary to show where the overpayment was made. The patient's identification number and the provider's identification number, NPI, and tax ID should also be included.

INSURANCE COMMISSIONER

Every state has an Insurance Commissioner's Office where insurance issues can be reported. The insurance commissioner's office monitors the third-party payer's compliance with the insurance laws, investigates problems as a neutral party, and resolves insurance conflicts when appropriate. For example, the medical coder could ask for assistance regarding unusual delays in reimbursement or improper denials of submitted claims. The National Association of Insurance Commissioners website has a list of state offices: http://www.naic.org/state_web_map.htm. It is the best source for information on insurance companies' issues.

THE REIMBURSEMENT PROCESS

Claims submitted electronically contained fewer errors and omissions than those on paper. These claims also mean less handling, clerical work, postage, and sorting for the insurance personnel. Electronically submitted claims improve the cash flow of the office because payment of electronic claims can be expected in 2 weeks or less, whereas payment for a paper claim can take from 4 to 6 weeks to receive.

Regardless of a manual or electronically generated front office, the medical coder will follow the same course of reimbursement.

1. A current demographic record must be obtained and maintained.
2. A copy of the patient's insurance card, front and back, must be taken.
3. If the patient does not have insurance, a payment plan should be put into place.
4. After the patient has had services rendered, every superbill or route slip generated must be accounted for and completed with a diagnosis and procedure to document the patient's encounter.
5. Every diagnosis and procedure must be coded properly.
6. Every patient encounter must be applied to the patient's account.
7. A claim form, paper or electronic, must be generated and sent to the appropriate insurance carriers.
8. Any necessary follow-ups must be done to ensure payment is made.
9. If appropriate, file secondary claims with the patient's secondary insurance.
10. An explanation of benefits (EOB) and a form of reimbursement must be received.
11. The medical coder must review each EOB and make the necessary transaction on each patient account that is affected by each EOB.
12. The medical coder must carefully review the payments and compare them to the services rendered.
13. Each payment must be posted to the correct patient's account and any adjustments made.

■ CONCLUSION

The responsibility of every medical coder is to produce accurate claims in return for accurate reimbursement. An accurate payment will rely on several factors including the following:

- Correct date of service.
- Correct procedure and diagnosis codes.
- Correct payment based on the contract or fee schedule of each third-party carrier.

Although this textbook is a valuable resource for any medical coder, ongoing training and continuing education will be necessary to keep up with the ever-changing rules, regulations, and code updates. The coding profession is very challenging because of those ongoing changes but is also very worthwhile. There is a sense of accomplishment that goes along with every payment received. A great medical coder will never know all of the answers but will know where to find the answers. With attention to detail, good organizational skills, and determination, the medical coding career can be very rewarding.

RESOURCE LIST

Aetna
http://www.aetna.com

The Coding Edge, American Academy of Professional Coders, June 2004, February 2008, and February 2009
Fair Debt Collections
http://www.fair-debt-collection.com/statue-limitations.html

State Insurance Commissioners
http://www.naic.org/state_web_map.htm

State Medical Societies listed by the American Medical Association
http://www.ama-assn.org/ama/pub/category/7630.html.

Chapter Review Exercises

Please complete the following questions.

1. What is the name the paper daily log system? _____

2. Claims can be submitted in two formats:

   _____ and _____

3. Claims too old to be considered by a third party carrier become the patient's responsibility.
   True or False (circle one)

4. The paper record that keeps track of a patient's service, charges, and payments is known as a

   _____.

5. The statement that accompanies an insurance payment is known as an Explanation of

   Benefits or a _____.

6. Prior to _____, each third party payer had

   their own set of standards and requirements for electronic billing.

7. Electronic claims are generally paid in _____.

8. It is unethical for a medical office to use financial policies. **True or False** (circle one)

9. Account balances are usually aged in _____ day time

   increments.

10. It is unethical for a physician to dismiss a patient from their practice because of an
    outstanding account. **True or False** (circle one)

Accounts receivable—The amount of money owed for services already rendered.

Acute versus chronic conditions—An acute condition strikes quickly with severe symptoms and runs a short course. A chronic condition progresses slowly with little change in symptoms.

Add-on codes—Five-digit codes that represent additional work that was performed with the primary procedure. These are indicated in the CPT by a plus sign (+).

Administrative disclosure—The release of patient information, such as name, sex, address, date of service, type of service, name of health-care provider, and facility location for the sake of reimbursement for services rendered.

Advance beneficiary notice—A form created to alert a patient with Medicare when a procedure or service may not be covered by Medicare. When signed by the patient, it documents that the patient understands and accepts financial responsibility for the service rendered.

Adverse effects of drugs—Any unwanted side effect or reaction to a drug taken properly.

American Medical Association (AMA)—The largest medical organization in the United States, which represent physicians from every specialty. The association helps doctors work together on important professional and public health issues. The AMA is also responsible for maintaining the Current Procedural Terminology (CPT).

American National Standards Institute (ANSI)—National standard guidelines for the completion and submission of all claims for services, supplies, equipment, and health care.

Assessment—The patient evaluation provided by the physician.

Assignment of benefits—An agreement signed by the patient directing his or her insurance company to pay the physician or health-care provider directly for any covered service provided.

Audit—To examine patient records, accounts, and claims for accuracy and verification.

Authorization—1. A patient grants the medical provider permission to release medical records to a third party or grants the third-party carrier permission to pay the insurance company directly. 2. Issued by a third-party carrier after determining that a service is medically necessary.

Beneficiary or recipient—A patient covered under the Medicaid program.

Benefits—Covered services available to an individual or group by a health insurance plan or government agency.

Birthday rule—A coordination of benefits rule that determines the order of benefits paid by parents of a dependent child if there is more than one insurance plan to consider.

Capitation—A payment method for health-care services in which the provider is paid a fixed rate per month for every patient enrolled under their care rather than a payment for every service provided to each of the patients.

Catastrophic cap—The maximum amount (per fiscal year) that a beneficiary pays for TRICARE-covered services or supplies.

Category(s)—A three-digit code used to represent a particular disease or condition is termed a category.

Centers for Medicare and Medicaid Services (CMS)—The federal agency that manages Medicare, Medicaid, and Children's Health Insurance Program.

Certification and authorization—Process that determines whether or not a service is medically necessary and/or covered under a patient's health-care plan

CHAMPUS—The previous health coverage for dependents of active duty military personnel and veterans. It was replaced by TRICARE in 1994.

CHAMPVA—The program that provides health benefits for dependents of disabled veterans.

Chief complaint—A patient's reason for seeking medical care.

Civilian—A non-military citizen.

Classifications—Groups or types of neoplasms.

CMS-1500—The claim form used for submitting medical services for payment to an insurance organization.

Code set—Any set of codes used for coding data such as medical diagnoses or medical procedure codes.

Codes—A collection of 3-, 4- and 5-digit numbers that convert the verbal description of diseases or conditions into a numerical system.

Coding manuals—Guidebooks containing the alpha/numerical codes used to represent medical procedures, services, and patient diagnoses.

Co-insurance—A percentage of the cost of the service rendered that the person insured is responsible for.

Compliance—To accept and work within the rules and regulations of HIPAA.

Comprehensive—A complete history and review of systems along with a report on the patient's current illness or condition.

Concurrent diagnosis—A condition that is present at the same time as the primary diagnosis.

Confidentiality—To protect and keep secret personal and medical information of patients revealed during the course of treatment.

Conscious sedation—A partial or total loss of sensation without total loss of consciousness.

Consent—To give or obtain permission.

Consultation—An examination requested by the primary physician to obtain another opinion regarding a patient's condition.

Contributing factors—Other conditions or situations the patient has that may affect the treatment and outcome or the quality of health.

Coordination of benefits (COB)—The system that ensures insurance payments do not exceed 100% of a given charge when more than one insurance policy is in place.

Coordination of benefits contractor (COBC)—The agency responsible for the processing of all supplemental (MediGap) insurance claim-based crossover claims.

Coordination of benefits—Process of managing benefits when an individual is covered under more than one health-insurance plan.

Coordination of care—The steps taken by the physician to provide care that will harmonize with the patient's existing health care.

Copayment—The cost an insured person is expected to pay at the time a service is rendered, such as $20 per office visit.

Cost share—The 25% of TRICARE allowable amount.

Counseling—The advice and direction the physician provides to his or her patient.

Covered entity—Refers to an organization, in this case a health-care provider, a health-care clearinghouse, or a health plan. For purposes of the HIPAA Privacy Rule, health-care providers include hospitals, physicians, and other caregivers, and researchers who provide health-care and receive, access, or generate individually identifiable health-care information.

Crossover claims—Claim form payment information transferred from Medicare to a third-party carrier for the additional reimbursement after Medicare's payment.

Current Procedural Terminology (CPT)—A manual containing the 5-digit numerical codes used to report medical services and procedures.

Day sheet—Daily log or spreadsheet of the financial activity in the office.

Death benefits—Percentage of earnings paid out to dependents after the death of an employee from a work-related injury.

Deductible—An amount that must be paid for covered medical services each calendar year by the insured before the benefits of the insurance plan will begin.

Department of Health and Human Services (HHS)—The principal government agency designed to protect the health of all Americans and provide essential human services.

Dependent—The subscriber's spouse or children under a limiting age.

Detailed—A more extensive review of systems along with a report on the patient's current illness or condition.

Diagnosis, diagnoses (plural)—The cause, disease, or condition a person is identified with.

Disclaimer—A measurement taken to protect the sender. The notice explains the intentions of the fax sent and relieves the sender of any responsibility for the condition of the information sent.

Disclosure—Release of protected health information from one entity to another.

Disease—A condition marked by subjective complaints, a specific history, and clinical signs, symptoms, and laboratory or radiographic findings. (Source: Taber's Cyclopedic Medical Dictionary, 21st ed. FA Davis Company, 2009.)

Documentation guidelines (DG)—The rules and instructions created to regulate and standardize the coding of the Evaluation and Management services.

Domiciliary care facility—A home that provides care to persons who need help in assisted living as a result of their physical or mental conditions.

Dual eligibles—Individuals who are entitled to a Medicaid benefit along with Medicare Part A or Part B.

E codes (E800–E999)—Alpha-numeric ICD-9-CM codes used to indicate external circumstances responsible for injuries or conditions.

Electronic data interchange—The exchange of claims and other health-care related information by means of computers.

Electronic data transmission—The transfer or exchange of data using computers.

Electronic file interchange (EFI)—The process in which a provider can fill out one application for a National Provider Identifier (NPI) through one organization, called an Electronic File Interchange Organization (EFIO) and that organization will grant the provider an NPI and then submit the NPI to Medicare, Medicaid, and all health-care insurance organizations.

Electronic medical record—Also known as electronic health record (EHR), is the electronic version of a patient's medical history and demographics.

Electronic protected health information (EPHI)—Any protected health information (PHI), which is generated, maintained, sent, and received electronically.

Employer identification number (EIN)—The EIN is also known as a Federal Tax Identification Number and is used to identify a business entity. Most businesses need an EIN.

Encounter forms (also known as Route Slips or Superbills)—A preprinted list of commonly performed procedures, their fees, and the most common diagnoses of the patients seen in an office.

Evaluation and management services—The medical encounter provided to a patient by a physician. This section of the CPT manual contains codes assigned to describe the examination, history, and medical decision making portion of a patient encounter.

Examination—To look over or inspect a patient's body and systems to determine the presence or the absence of disease.

Expanded problem focused—A report on the patient's current illness or condition along with more information about the affected system.

Fee-for-service—The traditional method of paying a health-care provider for services as they are provided.

Fiscal agent—An association contracted to provide a system for processing data, claim processing, and the administrative duties for Medicare or Medicaid.

Formulary—A list of drugs available for routine use at a health-care facility. (Source: Taber's Cyclopedic Medical Dictionary, 21st ed. FA Davis Company, 2009.)

Geographic practice cost index (GPCI)—Unit of measurement assigned to each procedure code to reflect the practice overhead by the practice locality.

Global surgery billing—The single fee that includes all parts of a surgery, including anesthesia, instruments, and preoperative/postoperative care.

Group insurance—A health insurance policy to a group of people who are part of the same company or organization (employees, members, etc.) and their dependents who are covered under a single contract.

Guarantor—The individual responsible for the payment of the medical bill.

Health-care clearinghouse—An entity that standardizes health information data into a standardized billing format.

Healthcare Common Procedure Coding System (HCPCS)—Alphanumeric codes used to represent special services, medical supplies, and certain drug items.

Health-care provider—Any individual or business entity that furnishes health-care services, or bills for and is paid for those services.

High complexity—Decision making that includes extensive information and a high risk.

History—A synopsis of the patient's pertinent medical, social, and family events and conditions.

ICD-9-CM—*The International Classification of Diseases, 9th Revision, Clinical Modification (ICD-9-CM) is a coding system used by health-care providers to represent diagnoses, collect data, and communicate with third-party carriers.*

History of present illness—A chronological sequence of events defining the patient's current illness.

Identifiers—Number used in the administration of health care to identify health-care providers, health plans, employers, and individuals (patients).

Insurance card—Identification issued to an insured person by his or her insurance company and used to verify or provide information concerning the insured's medical coverage.

Insurance identification number—The number that appears on the health plan identification card and used in all claims, communications, and inquiries.

Insurance manuals—Guidebooks maintained by an insurance company containing the coverage, billing, and claims processing regulations followed by that company.

Intelligence-free—Identifiers that do not carry specific identifying information such as the state or medical specialty of the medical practice.

Judicial or statutory disclosure—The release of mental health information when ordered by a court of law.

Key components—The main elements, history, examination, and medical decision making completed during the evaluation of a patient.

Late effect—A remaining condition left after an acute phase of an illness or injury has ended.

Ledger or ledger card—Forms that list the patient's record of service and payments.

Level of care—The coding process a physician uses to report the extent of evaluation and management care provided to each patient.

Levels of risk—The danger of a patient's existing condition, the danger of any diagnostic tests performed, and the chance a patient takes on the treatment options the physician recommends after examination.

Lifetime maximum—The maximum dollar amount that an insurance company will pay toward care in the insured person's lifetime.

Local coverage determination (LCD)—The process by which a procedure or services is determined to be covered by Medicare in a particular jurisdiction. Formerly known as Local Medical Review Policies (LMRPs).

Low complexity—Decision making that includes limited information and a low risk.

Major medical insurance—Insurance coverage for significant procedures or situations.

Managed care support contractors (MCSC)—Approved civilian providers that TRICARE beneficiaries may select for health care.

Management options—The options for treatment after an examination is completed and a diagnosis is determined.

Manifestations—The demonstration of the presence of a sign, symptom, or alteration, especially one that is associated with a disease process. (Source: Taber's Cyclopedic Medical Dictionary, 21st ed. FA Davis Company, 2009.)

Medical decision making—The evaluation of medical data the physician reviews to arrive at a diagnosis and/or treatment.

Medically needy—Persons who are eligible for Medicaid and whose income, minus total medical bills, is below state income limits for the Medicaid program.

Medicare administrative contractors (MACs)—A company appointed and created to process all Medicare claims for a designated jurisdiction.

Medicare coverage advisory committee (MCAC)—A group assigned to review or determine Medicare coverage policies.

Medicare physician fee schedule (MPFS) or Established provider disclosure report—A report generated and sent by Medicare to health-care providers listing the reimbursement amounts for every Medicare covered service.

Medicare summary notice (MSN)—A statement sent to the Medicare beneficiary that shows the charges and the payments made for services rendered to the beneficiary during the previous months.

Medigap—A supplemental insurance policy that will pay for medical services/supplies after Medicare pays (co-insurance).

Metastasis—1. Movement of bacteria or body cells (especially cancer cells) from one part of the body to another. 2. Change in location of a disease or its manifestations or transfer from one organ or part to another not directly connected. The usual application is to the manifestation of a malignancy as a secondary growth arising from the primary growth in a new location. The malignant cells may spread through the lymphatic circulation, the bloodstream, or avenues such as the cerebrospinal fluid. (Source: Taber's Cyclopedic Dictionary, 21st ed. FA Davis, 2009.)

Military treatment facility (MTF)—A facility operated by the military that provides health care to eligible TRICARE beneficiaries.

Moderate complexity—Decision making that includes several diagnoses or treatments along with a moderate risk.

Modifier—A two-digit numeric or alphanumeric code that can be added to a five-digit procedure code to describe a circumstance that has occurred and alters the code in some way. Example: modifier 50 added to a code explains that the procedure was performed bilaterally. Procedure code 19303-50 represents a bilateral mastectomy was performed.

Morphology—The form and structure of a neoplasm.

Mortality—The cause of death.

Multiple procedures—Procedures that are separate and distinct from one another and are billed separately.

Mutually exclusive edits—Edits placed on pairs of codes (procedures) that cannot reasonably be performed together based on their definitions or their anatomy.

National Correct Coding Initiative (NCCI)—The Centers for Medicare and Medicaid developed the National Correct Coding Initiative (NCCI) to promote national accurate coding practices and to manage improper coding leading to the improper payment in Part B claims.

National coverage determination—The process by which a procedure or services is determined to be covered by Medicare nationwide.

National provider identifier (NPI)—The NPI is a unique identification number for covered health-care providers. The NPIs must be used in the administrative and financial transactions adopted under HIPAA. The NPI is a 10-digit number, intelligence-free numeric identifier. The numbers do not carry other information about health-care providers, such as the state in which they live or their medical specialty.

Nature of presenting problem—The degree of severity of the reason for the medical encounter if the patient's condition is left untreated.

NEC—Not Elsewhere Classified—This abbreviation appears after a subterm in Volume 1. If a code has an NEC designation, it means that ICD-9-CM does not provide a more specific code for this diagnosis, even though the diagnostic statement in the medical record may be more specific. The code may be classified as "other."

Neoplasm—An abnormal development of tissue as in a tumor or growth.

Network—A group of doctors, hospitals, pharmacies, and other health-care providers who contract to provide health services to members of a health plan.

Network provider—Any provider that has agreed to care for and file claims for TRICARE beneficiaries. They may only bill for applicable costs, per TRICARE guidelines.

New and established patients—The status of frequency of the relationship between the patient and the physician.

New/emerging technology—Any up-and-coming medical knowledge and/or equipment.

Nonessential modifiers—Supplementary words added to a diagnosis that do not change the code assignment.

Non-network provider—Any provider that has not signed an agreement with TRICARE. A non-network provider can be participating or nonparticipating.

NOS—Not Otherwise Specified—This abbreviation appears next to code descriptions in Volume 1 and indicates the code is unspecified or generic. The coder should use a NOS code when the diagnosis from the patient's medical record does not give any definite information or specifics for an exact code to be used.

Office and outpatient services—Evaluation and management services performed in a physician's office, outpatient or other ambulatory facility.

Office of Inspector General—The Office of the Inspector General (OIG) conducts independent investigations, audits, inspections, and special reviews of United States Department of Justice programs to detect fraud, abuse, and misconduct, and to promote efficiency within the Medicare program.

Out-of-pocket expense—Any medical-care cost that must be paid by the person insured (coinsurance, co-payments, deductibles).

Participating agreement—The agreement made by a health-care provider to accept Medicare's allowed amount as payment in full for any procedure or service billed.

Patient demographics—Personal and financial information (e.g., address, date of birth, or insurance coverage) obtained from the patient and kept on file for the billing and processing of claims.

Patient ledger—An individual financial document of the patient's services, charges, balance, and payments.

Payments or cash flow—Money or revenue received and spent within a business.

Pegboard system (once-write)—Accounting system that requires only one entry. Information is carried through carbonless paper onto the ledger card, day sheet, and receipt.

Performance measures—The collection of medical data used to evaluate the quality of care a patient receives.

Permanent disability—A limitation caused by an injury that will never heal. An employee may be unable to return to work depending on the nature of the limitation.

Personal, family, social history—A review of the patient's closely related family's medical events and illnesses, as well as their own and their medications, surgeries, and life routines.

Physical status modifiers—Anesthesia modifiers that represent the physical condition of the patient.

Point of service—The most popular form of managed care that combines the low cost of HMOs with the greater health-care choices of PPO plans. Members are encouraged to choose a primary care physician within the network of providers, but have the choice of other physicians and hospital facilities as well.

Poisoning of a drug—A toxic reaction to a drug taken improperly.

Policyholder—An individual enrolled in a health insurance plan; also referred to as a subscriber.

Pre-certification—A method of evaluating the appropriateness of a medical service such as a hospitalization or a surgery before the service is rendered. Also referred to as pre-admission certification.

Preferred provider organization (PPO)—A health-care program in which members are encouraged to use medical providers who have contracted with the program to provide medical care at a fixed rate. Members do not have to choose a primary care provider and are rewarded for using those providers by paying less out of their own pockets.

Premium—The amount paid by an insured regularly (monthly/semi-monthly) to keep any health insurance policy.

Prepaid health plan—A method of financing the cost of health care for a defined population in advance of receipt of services.

Presumptive eligibility—A limited period of time for which a categorically needy pregnant woman is determined eligible for Medicaid assistance. Its purpose is to encourage pregnant women to receive adequate prenatal care in the earlier months of their pregnancy, and to ensure qualified providers of payment for the prenatal care.

Preventive medicine services—The routine examination or check-up provided to a patient with no current medical complaint or illness.

Primary care physician—A physician, usually a family, general practice, OB-GYN, pediatrician, or internal medicine specialist, who is responsible for coordinating the total health care of members within a managed care program.

Primary diagnosis—A diagnosis or condition in an outpatient setting that indicates the reason the patient was seen. This is always coded first.

Principal diagnosis—A diagnosis determined in an inpatient setting after diagnostic testing or procedures determine the reason for hospitalization.

Prior authorization—Advance notice given to and approved by the third-party carrier before a patient's treatment or service is rendered.

Privacy officer—Person who is responsible for implementing and adhering to HIPAA policies and procedures and the handling privacy complaints.

Problem focused—A brief report on the patient's current illness or condition.

Problem oriented medical record (POMR)—A process of documenting patient health status information in a problem-solving system.

Procedures—The provision of care or treatment provided to a patient by medical personnel.

Protected health information (PHI)—Any information that identifies an individual. The information includes past, present, and future physical and mental health information and payment for health care.

Puerperium—The 6 weeks following childbirth.

Qualified provider—A provider designated by the state Department of Human Services to determine presumptive eligibility after meeting certain guidelines.

Qualifying circumstances—Risk factors or unusual circumstances related to anesthesia that can be further described with additional five-digit codes.

Reimbursement—The receipt of payment in exchange for the medical services provided to a patient.

Relative value unit (RVU)—Basic unit of value given to every procedure code to determine a dollar value for the procedure.

Remittance advice (RA)—A statement sent from Medicare to providers, indicating the reimbursement, denial, or pending charges submitted. A form issued from a third-party carrier indicating any claims processed for a health-care provider.

Resident alien—One who has temporary or permanent residence in a foreign country.

Resource-based relative value system (RBRVS)—A nationwide system developed to establish the true cost of any given procedure, service, or supply.

Revenue—The earnings or source of income.

Review of systems (ROS)—A series of questions asked of the patient and used to provide for an inventory of body systems.

Sanctions—Penalties imposed by the courts. Sanctions are usually monetary fines imposed for violating rules of procedure.

Secondary diagnosis—A diagnosis used in addition to the main, primary diagnosis.

SOAP notes—A process of documenting patient health status information in a patient's chart.

Spenddown—A process that allows patients to reduce excess income through medical expenses to qualify for the medically needy program.

Sponsor—A member of the military or a civilian employee with dependents.

Straightforward—Decision making that included minimal information and very low risk.

Subcategories—Most three-digit categories have been expanded to 4- or 5-digit codes that provide more specific information regarding the disease or condition. The fourth digit of an ICD-9-CM code is called a subcategory.

Subclassification—A fifth digit added on to a 4-digit ICD-9-CM code is called a sub-classification. The fifth digit provides even greater details regarding the condition.

Subscriber—An individual enrolled in a health insurance plan; also referred to as a policyholder.

Supervision and interpretation—To oversee and evaluate a diagnostic procedure.

Survivor—Eligible family member of a deceased TRICARE sponsor who receives retiree coverage at the retiree payment rate.

Tabular—A list of diagnosis codes arranged in a numerical sequence.

Temporary disability—A limitation caused by injury that requires time away from work but will eventually heal and allow the employee to return to work.

Third-party carrier—An organization that pays or insures health or medical expenses.

Time—Average amount of time typically spent with a patient.

Transitional survivor—Eligible family member of a deceased TRICARE sponsor who receive the same active-duty coverage (for the same rate). This is a 3-year status, unless there are other circumstances that change TRICARE eligibility of the survivor.

TRICARE—The program that provides health benefits for active duty military personnel and their dependents.

Uncertain behavior—The specimen showed signs of both malignancy and benign cells. The tumor may be changing and additional studies would be necessary to decide the tumor type.

V codes—Diagnosis codes that begin with the letter V and represent a circumstance other than diseases or injuries as a diagnosis or problem.

Voluntary disclosure—The patient's free choice and authorization to release mental health information.

Office and Patient Demographics for Claim Completion Exercises

The content in Appendix A should be used to complete the Claim Completion Exercises in Chapters 7, 8, and 9. For these exercises, you will fill out the claim forms as if you were the medical coder for John Smith, DO. You will find the office demographics, office fee schedule, patient forms, superbills, and blank CMS-1500s that coincide with the Claim Completion Exercises at the end of each of those chapters.

Some procedure codes are given and you will need to look up others in the current CPT. All dates of services should be the current year (or XXXX), and the patient's age can be calculated based on the patient's birth date.

Office Demographics

Physician:	John Smith, D.O.
Address:	1234 Main Street
	Anytown, Iowa 52222
Phone Number:	515-555-1111
Tax ID Number:	44-1235656
NPI Number	1234567890

Hospital Affiliation:	Anytown Hospital
	600 Elm Street
	Anytown, IA 52221
NPI	5554443331

Referring Physicians:	George Welby, D.O.
	NPI Number 0987654321
	Dr. Jones
	NPI Number 45612309876

Fee Schedule for:
John Smith, D.O.
1234 Main Street
Anytown, Iowa 52222

OFFICE VISITS

NEW PATIENT		ESTABLISHED PATIENT		EMERGENCY DEPT.	
99201	$75.00	99211	$70.00	99281	$175.00
99202	$100.00	99212	$90.00	99282	$200.00
99203	$125.00	99213	$120.00	99283	$225.00
99204	$150.00	99214	$145.00	99284	$250.00

OFFICE CONSULTATIONS		PHYSICALS New Patient		PHYSICALS Established Patient	
99241	$110.00	99381	$75.00	99391	$70.00
99242	$130.00	99382	$85.00	99392	$80.00
99243	$150.00	99383	$95.00	99393	$90.00
99244	$175.00	99384	$105.00	99394	$100.00
99245	$195.00	99385	$115.00	99395	$110.00
		99386	$125.00	99396	$120.00
		99387	$150.00	99397	$140.00

OTHER SERVICES

LABORATORY		RADIOLOGY	
81000	$45.00	71020	$80.00
85018	$40.00	73590	$55.00
85014	$45.00	73500	$80.00
85048	$55.00	70220	$105.00
85031	$70.00	72100	$80.00
99000	$10.00	70260	$135.00

SURGERY		IMMUNIZATIONS/INJECTIONS	
Occlusion Oviducts	$1250.00	DPT	$105.00
Bunionectomy	$750.00	OPV	$90.00
Lesion Removal (1st)	$125.00	MMR	$125.00
Lesion Removal (2nd–14th)	$15.00/lesion	Tetanus	$90.00
15 or more Lesions	$325.00	Morphine	$90.00
Administration	$12.00		

DIAGNOSTIC SERVICES

EKG	$130.00
M/Mode, 2D Echo	$875.00

CHAPTER 7, CHAPTER REVIEW EXERCISE 7

Patient Information Form

Please complete information in the spaces provided. Be sure to complete and sign the statement at the bottom of this form.

Patient		
Last Name	First Name	M.I.
Jones	Terri	A.

Home Address			
Street	City	State	Zip
730 West Grand	Anytown	IA	51111

Phone Numbers & E-mail			
Home	Work	Cell	E-mail
515-222-3333	None	515-333-2222	jones@mail.com

Identity Information	
Social Security Number	Date of Birth
555-11-4444	2-12-55

Primary Insurance	
Company Name	Phone Number
Aetna Life & Casualty	212-655-4545
Billing Address	
1212 Cedar Street, Anytown, Iowa	
Name of Insured	Relation to Patient
Richard Jones	Husband
Insured's ID Number	Group Number
333-25-8888	X456

Secondary Insurance	
Company Name	Phone Number
None	
Billing Address	
Name of Insured	Relation to Patient
Insured's ID Number	Group Number

Emergency Information		
Emergency Contact Name	Relation	Phone
Mary Crown	Mother	233-1111

I authorize the release of any medical or other information necessary to process this claim.
I hereby authorize payment of medical benefits billed to my insurance to John Smith, DO. I hereby accept
responsibility for payment for any service(s) provided to me that is not covered by my insurance. I agree
to pay all co-payments, coinsurance, and deductibles at the time the service is rendered.

Terri Jones   12/22/XXXX

Signature of Patient or Guardian   Date

Date of service: 4-3-XXXX	

Patient name: Terri Jones	Insurance: Aetna Life
	Subscriber name: Richard
Address: 730 Grand Anytown, IA 51111	Group #: X456 · Previous balance: 0.00
	Copay: 0.00 · Today's charges: 195.00
Phone: 222-3333	Account #: · Today's payment: 0.00 · Check#
DOB: 2-12-55 · Age: 47 · Sex: F	Physician name: Smith · Balance due: 195.00

Office visit		New	Est
	Minimal		99211
X	Problem focused	99201	99212
	Expanded problem focused	99202	99213
	Detailed	99203	99214
	Comprehensive	99204	99215
	Comprehensive (new patient)	99205	
	Significant, separate service	–25	–25

Well visit	New	Est
< 1 y	99381	99391
1–4 y	99382	99392
5–11 y	99383	99393
12–17 y	99384	99394
18–39 y	99385	99395
40–64 y	99386	99396
65 y +	99387	99397

Medicare preventive services	
Pap	Q0091
Pelvic & breast	G0101
Prostate/PSA	G0103
Tobacco counseling/3–10 min	G0375
Tobacco counseling/>10 min	G0376
Welcome to Medicare exam	G0344
ECG w/Welcome to Medicare exam	G0366
Flexible sigmoidoscopy	G0104
Hemocult, guaiac	G0107
Flu shot	G0008
Pneumonia shot	G0009

Consultation/preop clearance	
Expanded problem focused	99242
Detailed	99243
Comprehensive/mod complexity	99244
Comprehensive/high complexity	99245

Other services	
After posted hours	99050
Evening/weekend appointment	99051
Home health certification	G0180
Home health recertification	G0179
Post-op follow-up	99024
Prolonged/30–74 min	99354
Special reports/forms	99080
Disability/Workers comp	99455

Radiology	
X Complete Sinus X-ray	

X Diagnoses	
1 Headache	
2	
3	
4	

Next office visit

Recheck	Prev	PRN	_____ D W M Y

Instructions:

Referral

To:

Instructions:

Physician signature

X _____

Office procedures	
Anoscopy	46600
Audiometry	92551
Cerumen removal	69210
Colposcopy	57452
Colposcopy w/biopsy	57455
ECG, w/interpretation	93000
ECG, rhythm strip	93040
Endometrial biopsy	58100
Flexible sigmoidoscopy	45330
Flexible sigmoidoscopy w/biopsy	45331
Fracture care, cast/splint	29____
Site: _____	
Nebulizer	94640
Nebulizer demo	94664
Spirometry	94010
Spirometry, pre and post	94060
Tympanometry	92567
Vasectomy	55250

Skin procedures		Units
Burn care, initial	16000	
Foreign body, skin, simple	10120	
Foreign body, skin, complex	10121	
I&D, abscess	10060	
I&D, hematoma/seroma	10140	
Laceration repair, simple	120___	
Site: _____ Size: ____		
Laceration repair, layered	120___	
Site: _____ Size: ____		
Lesion, biopsy, one	11100	
Lesion, biopsy, each add'l	11101	
Lesion, excision, benign	114___	
Site: _____ Size: ____		
Lesion, excision, malignant	116___	
Site: _____ Size: ____		
Lesion, paring/cutting, one	11055	
Lesion, paring/cutting, 2–4	11056	
Lesion, shave	113___	
Site: _____ Size: ____		
Nail removal, partial	11730	
Nail removal, w/matrix	11750	
Skin tag, 1–15	11200	
Wart, flat, 1–14	17110	
Wart, plantar, single	17000	
Wart, plantar, each add'l	17003	

Medications		Units
Ampicillin, up to 500 mg	J0290	
B-12, up to 1,000 mcg	J3420	
Epinephrine, up to 1 ml	J0170	
Kenalog, 10 mg	J3301	
Lidocaine, 10 mg	J2001	
Normal saline, 1000 cc	J7030	
Phenergan, up to 50 mg	J2550	
Progesterone, 150 mg	J1055	
Rocephin, 250 mg	J0696	
Testosterone, 200 mg	J1080	
Tigan, up to 200 mg	J3250	
Toradol, 15 mg	J1885	

Miscellaneous services

Laboratory	
Venipuncture	36415
Blood glucose, monitoring device	82962
Blood glucose, visual dipstick	82948
CBC, w/ auto differential	85025
CBC, w/o auto differential	85027
Cholesterol	82465
Hemocult, guaiac	82270
Hemocult, immunoassay	82274
Hemoglobin A1C	85018
Lipid panel	80061
Liver panel	80076
KOH prep (skin, hair, nails)	87220
Metabolic panel, basic	80048
Metabolic panel, comprehensive	80053
Mononucleosis	86308
Pregnancy, blood	84703
Pregnancy, urine	81025
Renal panel	80069
Sedimentation rate	85651
Strep, rapid	86403
Strep culture	87081
Strep A	87880
TB	86580
UA, complete, non-automated	81000
UA, w/o micro, non-automated	81002
UA, w/o micro, non-automated	81003
Urine colony count	87086
Urine culture, presumptive	87088
Wet mount/KOH	87210

Vaccines	
DT, <7 y	90702
DTP	90701
DtaP, <7 y	90700
Flu, 6–35 months	90657
Flu, 3 y +	90658
Hep A, adult	90632
Hep A, ped/adol, 2 dose	90633
Hep B, adult	90746
Hep B, ped/adol 3 dose	90744
Hep B-Hib	90748
Hib, 4 dose	90645
HPV	90649
IPV	90713
MMR	90707
Pneumonia, >2 y	90732
Pneumonia conjugate, <5 y	90669
Td, >7 y	90718
Varicella	90716

Immunizations & Injections		Units
Allergen, one	95115	
Allergen, multiple	95117	
Imm admin, one	90471	
Imm admin, each add'l	90472	
Imm admin, intranasal, one	90473	
Imm admin, intranasal, each add'l	90474	
Injection, joint, small	20600	
Injection, joint, intermediate	20605	
Injection, joint, major	20610	
Injection, ther/proph/diag	90772	
Injection, trigger point	20552	

Supplies

Infectious and Parasitic Diseases
053.9	Herpes zoster, NOS
054.9	Herpetic disease, uncomplicated
075	Mononucleosis
034.0	Strep throat
079.99	Viral infection, unspec.
078.10	Warts, all sites

Neoplasms
Benign Neoplasms
239.2	Skin, soft tissue neoplasm, inspec.
216.9	Skin, unspec.

Endocrine, Nutritional and Metabolic Disorders
Endocrine
250.01	Diabetes I, uncomplicated
250.91	Diabetes I, w/unspec. complications
250.00	Diabetes II/unspec., w/o complications, not uncontrolled
250.90	Diabetes II, w/unspec. complications
242.90	Hyperthyroidism, NOS
244.9	Hypothyroidism, inspec.

Metabolic/Other
274.9	Gout, unspec.
272.0	Hypercholesterolemia
272.2	Hyperlipidemia, mixed
272.1	Hypertriglyceridemia
278.01	Obesity, morbid
278.00	Obesity, NOS
278.02	Overweight

Blood Diseases
285.9	Anemia, other, unspec.

Mental Disorders
300.00	Anxiety state, unspec.
314.00	Attention deficit, w/o hyperactivity
290.0	Dementia, senile, NOS
311	Depression, NOS

Nervous System and Sense Organ Disorders
Nervous System Diseases
354.0	Carpal tunnel
345.90	Epilepsy, unspec., w/o status
346.90	Migraine, unspec., not intractable

Eye Diseases
372.30	Conjunctivitis, unspec.
368.10	Visual disturbance, unspec.

Ear Diseases
380.4	Cerumen impaction
389.9	Hearing loss, unspec.
380.10	Otitis externa, unspec.
382.00	Otitis media, acute

Circulatory System
Arrythmias
427.31	Atrial fibrillation

Cardiac
413.9	Angina pectoris, NOS
428.0	Heart failure, congestive, unspec.
414.9	Ischemic heart disease, chronic, unspec.
424.1	Valvular disorder, aortic, NOS

Vascular
796.2	Elevated BP w/o hypertension
401.1	Hypertension, benign
458.9	Hypotension, orthostatic
443.9	Peripheral vascular disease, unspec.
451.9	Thrombophlebitis, unspec.
459.81	Venous insufficiency, unspec.

Respiratory System
Lower Respiratory Tract
493.90	Asthma, unspec.
466.0	Bronchitis, acute
496	COPD, NOS
486	Pneumonia, unspec.

Upper Respiratory Tract
462	Pharyngitis, acute
477.9	Rhinitis, allergic, cause unspec.
461.9	Sinusitis, acute, NOS
465.9	Upper respiratory infection, acute, NOS

Digestive System
564.00	Constipation, unspec.
562.10	Diverticulosis of colon
562.11	Diverticulitis of colon, NOS
535.50	Gastritis, unspec. w/o hemorrhage
558.9	Gastroenteritis, noninfectious, unspec.
530.81	Gastroesophageal reflux, no esophagitis
455.6	Hemorrhoids, NOS
564.1	Irritable bowel syndrome
578.1	Melena

Genitourinary System
Urinary System Diseases
592.9	Calculus, urinary, unspec.
595.0	Cystitis, acute
599.7	Hematuria
593.9	Renal insufficiency, acute
599.0	Urinary tract infection, unspec./pyuria

Male Genital Organ Diseases
607.84	Impotence, organic
302.72	Impotence, psychosexual dysfunction
601.9	Prostatitis, NOS
257.2	Testicular hypofunction

Breast Diseases
611.72	Breast lump

Female Genital Organ Diseases
616.0	Cervicitis
622.10	Dysplasia, cervix, unspec.
625.9	Pelvic pain, unspec. female disease
616.10	Vaginitis/vulvitis, unspec.

Disorders of Menstruation
626.0	Amenorrhea
627.9	Menopausal disorders, unspec.
626.2	Menstruation, excessive/frequent
625.3	Menstruation, painful
626.6	Metrorrhagia

Pregnancy, Childbirth
641.90	Hemorrhage in preg., unspec.
V24.2	Postpartum follow-up, routine
V22.2	Pregnant state, incidental
V22.0	Prenatal care, normal, first pregnancy
V22.1	Prenatal care, normal, other pregnancy

Skin, Subcutaneous Tissue
706.1	Acne
702.0	Actinic keratosis
682.9	Cellulitis/abscess, unspec.
692.9	Contact dermatitis, NOS
691.8	Eczema, atopic dermatitis
703.0	Ingrown nail
110.1	Onychomycosis
709.9	Other skin disease, unspec.
696.1	Psoriasis, other
695.3	Rosacea
706.2	Sebaceous cyst
702.19	Seborrheic keratosis, NOS
707.9	Ulcer, skin, chronic, unspec.
708.9	Urticaria, unspec.

Musculoskeletal and Connective Tissue
General
716.90	Arthropathy, unspec.
729.1	Fibromyositis
715.90	Osteoarthrosis, unspec.
733.00	Osteoporosis, unspec.
714.0	Rheumatoid arthritis
727.00	Synovitis/tenosynovitis, unspec.

Lower Extremity
729.5	Pain in limb
728.71	Plantar fasciitis

Spine/Torso
724.4	Back pain w/ radiation, unspec.
723.9	Cervical disorder, NOS

Upper Extremity
726.32	Lateral epicondylitis
726.10	Rotator cuff syndrome, NOS

Perinatal (Infant)
779.3	Feeding problem, newborn

Signs and Symptoms
789.00	Abdominal pain, unspec.
795.01	Abnormal Pap, ASC-US
719.40	Arthralgia, unspec.
569.3	Bleeding, rectal
786.50	Chest pain, unspec.
786.2	Cough
787.91	Diarrhea, NOS
780.4	Dizziness/vertigo, NOS
787.2	Dysphagia
788.1	Dysuria
782.3	Edema, localized, NOS
783.3	Feeding problem, infant/elderly
780.6	Fever, nonperinatal
271.9	Glucose intolerance
784.0	Headache, unspec.
788.30	Incontinence/enuresis, NOS
782.2	Localized swelling/mass, superficial
785.6	Lymph nodes, enlarged
780.79	Malaise and fatigue, other
787.02	Nausea, alone
787.01	Nausea w/ vomiting
719.46	Pain, knee
724.2	Pain, low back
785.1	Palpitations
788.42	Polyuria
782.1	Rash, nonvesicular, unspec.
782.0	Sensory disturbance skin
786.05	Shortness of breath
780.2	Syncope
788.41	Urinary frequency
787.03	Vomiting, alone
783.21	Weight loss

Injuries and Adverse Effects
Dislocations, Sprains and Strains
845.00	Sprain/strain: ankle, unspec.
845.10	Sprain/strain: foot, unspec.
842.10	Sprain/strain: hand, unspec.
844.9	Sprain/strain: knee/leg, unspec.
847.0	Sprain/strain: neck, unspec.
840.9	Sprain/strain: shoulder/upper arm, unspec.
842.00	Sprain/strain: wrist, unspec.

Other Trauma, Adverse Effects
919.0	Abrasion, unspec.
924.9	Contusion, unspec.
919.4	Insect bite
894.0	Open wound, lower limb, unspec.
884.0	Open wound, upper limb, unspec.

Supplemental Classification
V72.32	Confirm norm Pap after initial abn
V25.01	Contraception, oral
V25.02	Contraception, other (diaphragm, etc.)
V25.2	Contraception, sterilization
V58.30	Dressing change, nonsurgical
V01.9	Exposure, infectious disease, unspec.
V72.31	Gynecological exam
V06.8	Immunization, combination, other
V06.1	Immunization, DTP
V04.81	Immunization, influenza
V70.0	Well adult check
V20.2	Well child check

1500

HEALTH INSURANCE CLAIM FORM

APPROVED BY NATIONAL UNIFORM CLAIM COMMITTEE 08/05

| | PICA | | | | | | | | | | PICA | | |

| 1. MEDICARE | MEDICAID | TRICARE CHAMPUS | CHAMPVA | GROUP HEALTH PLAN | FECA BLK LUNG | OTHER | 1a. INSURED'S I.D. NUMBER | (For Program in Item 1) |
| (Medicare #) | (Medicaid #) | (Sponsor's SSN) | (Member ID#) | (SSN or ID) | (SSN) | (ID) | | |

2. PATIENT'S NAME (Last Name, First Name, Middle Initial)

3. PATIENT'S BIRTH DATE MM | DD | YY   SEX   M □   F □

4. INSURED'S NAME (Last Name, First Name, Middle Initial)

5. PATIENT'S ADDRESS (No., Street)

6. PATIENT RELATIONSHIP TO INSURED
Self □   Spouse □   Child □   Other □

7. INSURED'S ADDRESS (No., Street)

CITY   STATE

8. PATIENT STATUS
Single □   Married □   Other □

CITY   STATE

ZIP CODE   TELEPHONE (Include Area Code)
(   )

Employed □   Full-Time Student □   Part-Time Student □

ZIP CODE   TELEPHONE (Include Area Code)
(   )

9. OTHER INSURED'S NAME (Last Name, First Name, Middle Initial)

10. IS PATIENT'S CONDITION RELATED TO:

11. INSURED'S POLICY GROUP OR FECA NUMBER

a. OTHER INSURED'S POLICY OR GROUP NUMBER

a. EMPLOYMENT? (Current or Previous)
YES □   NO □

a. INSURED'S DATE OF BIRTH MM | DD | YY   SEX   M □   F □

b. OTHER INSURED'S DATE OF BIRTH MM | DD | YY   SEX   M □   F □

b. AUTO ACCIDENT?   PLACE (State)
YES □   NO □

b. EMPLOYER'S NAME OR SCHOOL NAME

c. EMPLOYER'S NAME OR SCHOOL NAME

c. OTHER ACCIDENT?
YES □   NO □

c. INSURANCE PLAN NAME OR PROGRAM NAME

d. INSURANCE PLAN NAME OR PROGRAM NAME

10d. RESERVED FOR LOCAL USE

d. IS THERE ANOTHER HEALTH BENEFIT PLAN?
YES □   NO □   If yes, return to and complete item 9 a-d.

READ BACK OF FORM BEFORE COMPLETING & SIGNING THIS FORM.

12. PATIENT'S OR AUTHORIZED PERSON'S SIGNATURE I authorize the release of any medical or other information necessary to process this claim. I also request payment of government benefits either to myself or to the party who accepts assignment below.

SIGNED _____   DATE _____

13. INSURED'S OR AUTHORIZED PERSON'S SIGNATURE I authorize payment of medical benefits to the undersigned physician or supplier for services described below.

SIGNED _____

14. DATE OF CURRENT: MM | DD | YY   ILLNESS (First symptom) OR INJURY (Accident) OR PREGNANCY(LMP)

15. IF PATIENT HAS HAD SAME OR SIMILAR ILLNESS. GIVE FIRST DATE MM | DD | YY

16. DATES PATIENT UNABLE TO WORK IN CURRENT OCCUPATION
FROM MM | DD | YY   TO MM | DD | YY

17. NAME OF REFERRING PROVIDER OR OTHER SOURCE
17a.
17b. NPI

18. HOSPITALIZATION DATES RELATED TO CURRENT SERVICES
FROM MM | DD | YY   TO MM | DD | YY

19. RESERVED FOR LOCAL USE

20. OUTSIDE LAB? $ CHARGES
YES □   NO □

21. DIAGNOSIS OR NATURE OF ILLNESS OR INJURY (Relate Items 1, 2, 3 or 4 to Item 24E by Line)
1. |___ . ___| 3. |___ . ___|
2. |___ . ___| 4. |___ . ___|

22. MEDICAID RESUBMISSION CODE   ORIGINAL REF. NO.

23. PRIOR AUTHORIZATION NUMBER

24. A. DATE(S) OF SERVICE						B. PLACE OF SERVICE	C. EMG	D. PROCEDURES, SERVICES, OR SUPPLIES (Explain Unusual Circumstances) CPT/HCPCS MODIFIER	E. DIAGNOSIS POINTER	F. $ CHARGES	G. DAYS OR UNITS	H. EPSDT Family Plan	I. ID. QUAL.	J. RENDERING PROVIDER ID. #
From MM	DD	YY	To MM	DD	YY									
1													NPI	
2													NPI	
3													NPI	
4													NPI	
5													NPI	
6													NPI	

25. FEDERAL TAX I.D. NUMBER   SSN □ EIN □

26. PATIENT'S ACCOUNT NO.

27. ACCEPT ASSIGNMENT? (For govt. claims, see back)
YES □   NO □

28. TOTAL CHARGE $

29. AMOUNT PAID $

30. BALANCE DUE $

31. SIGNATURE OF PHYSICIAN OR SUPPLIER INCLUDING DEGREES OR CREDENTIALS (I certify that the statements on the reverse apply to this bill and are made a part thereof.)

SIGNED _____   DATE _____

32. SERVICE FACILITY LOCATION INFORMATION
a.   b.

33. BILLING PROVIDER INFO & PH # (   )
a.   b.

NUCC Instruction Manual available at: www.nucc.org   **PLEASE PRINT OR TYPE**   APPROVED OMB-0938-0999 FORM CMS-1500 (08-05)

CARRIER

PATIENT AND INSURED INFORMATION

PHYSICIAN OR SUPPLIER INFORMATION

CHAPTER 7, CHAPTER REVIEW EXERCISE 8

Patient Information Form

Please complete information in the spaces provided. Be sure to complete and sign the statement at the bottom of this form.

Patient		
Last Name	First Name	M.I.
Doe	John	R

Home Address			
Street	City	State	Zip
1299 Locust	Anytown	IA	52111

Phone Numbers & E-mail			
Home	Work	Cell	E-mail
222-7812	223-5432	888-4444	doe@email.com

Identity & Employment Information		
Social Security Number	Date of Birth	Employer
626-54-8970	3-15-67	Lehman Brothers, Inc

Primary Insurance	
Company Name	Phone Number
Metropolitan Life	414-555-6666
Billing Address	
4213 Walnut Chicago, Il 42678	
Name of Insured	Relation to Patient
Same	Self
Insured's ID Number	Group Number
626-54-8970	none

Secondary Insurance	
Company Name	Phone Number
None	
Billing Address	
Name of Insured	Relation to Patient
Insured's ID Number	Group Number

Emergency Information		
Emergency Contact Name	Relation	Phone
Ed Doe	Father	223-9765

I authorize the release of any medical or other information necessary to process this claim.
I hereby authorize payment of medical benefits billed to my insurance to John Smith, DO. I hereby accept
responsibility for payment for any service(s) provided to me that is not covered by my insurance. I agree
to pay all co-payments, coinsurance, and deductibles at the time the service is rendered.

John Doe   2/4/1999
—————————————————————   ——————————————
Signature of Patient or Guardian   *Date*

Date of service: 09-12-XXXX	Employer: Lehman Bros, Inc.
Patient name: John Doe	Insurance: Metropolitan
	Subscriber name: Self
Address: 1299 Locust Anytown, IA 51111	Insurance ID #: 626-54-8970 · Group #: none · Previous balance: 0.00
	Copay: 0.00 · Today's charges: 200.00
Phone: 555-222-7812	Account #: · Today's payment: 0.00 · Check#
DOB: 3-15-67 · Age: XX · Sex: M	Physician name: Smith · Balance due: 200.00

Office visit	New	Est		Office procedures				Laboratory		
Minimal		99211		Anoscopy		46600		Venipuncture		36415
Problem focused	99201	99212		Audiometry		92551		Blood glucose, monitoring device		82962
Expanded problem focused	99202	99213		Cerumen removal		69210		Blood glucose, visual dipstick		82948
Detailed	99203	99214		Colposcopy		57452		CBC, w/ auto differential		85025
Comprehensive	99204	99215		Colposcopy w/biopsy		57455		CBC, w/o auto differential		85027
Comprehensive (new patient)	99205			ECG, w/interpretation		93000		Cholesterol		82465
Significant, separate service	–25	–25		ECG, rhythm strip		93040		Hemoccult, guaiac		82270
Well visit	**New**	**Est**		Endometrial biopsy		58100		Hemoccult, immunoassay		82274
< 1 y	99381	99391		Flexible sigmoidoscopy		45330		Hemoglobin A1C		85018
1–4 y	99382	99392		Flexible sigmoidoscopy w/biopsy		45331		Lipid panel		80061
5–11 y	99383	99393		Fracture care, cast/splint		29___		Liver panel		80076
12–17 y	99384	99394		Site: _____				KOH prep (skin, hair, nails)		87220
18–39 y	99385	99395		Nebulizer		94640		Metabolic panel, basic		80048
40–64 y	99386	99396		Nebulizer demo		94664		Metabolic panel, comprehensive		80053
65 y +	99387	99397		Spirometry		94010		Mononucleosis		86308
Medicare preventive services				Spirometry, pre and post		94060		Pregnancy, blood		84703
Pap		Q0091		Tympanometry		92567		Pregnancy, urine		81025
Pelvic & breast		G0101		Vasectomy		55250		Renal panel		80069
Prostate/PSA		G0103		**Skin procedures**		**Units**		Sedimentation rate		85651
Tobacco counseling/3–10 min		G0375		Burn care, initial	16000			Strep, rapid		86403
Tobacco counseling/>10 min		G0376		Foreign body, skin, simple	10120			Strep culture		87081
Welcome to Medicare exam		G0344		Foreign body, skin, complex	10121			Strep A		87880
ECG w/Welcome to Medicare exam		G0366		I&D, abscess	10060			TB		86580
Flexible sigmoidoscopy		G0104		I&D, hematoma/seroma	10140			UA, complete, non-automated		81000
Hemoccult, guaiac		G0107		Laceration repair, simple	120___			UA, w/o micro, non-automated		81002
Flu shot		G0008		Site: _____ Size: ____				UA, w/o micro, non-automated		81003
Pneumonia shot		G0009		Laceration repair, layered	120___			Urine colony count		87086
Consultation/preop clearance				Site: _____ Size: ____				Urine culture, presumptive		87088
Expanded problem focused		99242		Lesion, biopsy, one	11100			Wet mount/KOH		87210
Detailed		99243		Lesion, biopsy, each add'l	11101			**Vaccines**		
Comprehensive/mod complexity		99244		Lesion, excision, benign	114___			DT, <7 y		90702
Comprehensive/high complexity		99245		Site: _____ Size: ____				DTP		90701
Other services				Lesion, excision, malignant	116___			DtaP, <7 y		90700
After posted hours		99050		Site: _____ Size: ____				Flu, 6–35 months		90657
Evening/weekend appointment		99051		Lesion, paring/cutting, one	11055			Flu, 3 y +		90658
Home health certification		G0180		Lesion, paring/cutting, 2–4	11056			Hep A, adult		90632
Home health recertification		G0179		Lesion, shave	113___			Hep A, ped/adol, 2 dose		90633
Post-op follow-up		99024		Site: _____ Size: ____				Hep B, adult		90746
Prolonged/30–74 min		99354		Nail removal, partial	11730			Hep B, ped/adol 3 dose		90744
Special reports/forms		99080		Nail removal, w/matrix	11750			Hep B-Hib		90748
Disability/Workers comp		99455		Skin tag, 1–15	11200			Hib, 4 dose		90645
Radiology				Wart, flat, 1–14	17110			HPV		90649
				Wart, plantar, single	17000			IPV		90713
				Wart, plantar, each add'l	17003			MMR		90707

X	**Diagnoses**			**Medications**		**Units**		Pneumonia, >2 y		90732
1	Contusion R Upper Arm			Ampicillin, up to 500 mg	J0290			Pneumonia conjugate, <5 y		90669
2				B-12, up to 1,000 mcg	J3420			Td, >7 y		90718
3				Epinephrine, up to 1 ml	J0170			Varicella		90716
4				Kenalog, 10 mg	J3301			**Immunizations & Injections**		**Units**

Next office visit					Lidocaine, 10 mg	J2001		Allergen, one	95115	
Recheck · Prev · PRN · ___ D W M Y					Normal saline, 1000 cc	J7030		Allergen, multiple	95117	
Instructions:					Phenergan, up to 50 mg	J2550		Imm admin, one	90471	
					Progesterone, 150 mg	J1055		Imm admin, each add'l	90472	
					Rocephin, 250 mg	J0696		Imm admin, intranasal, one	90473	
					Testosterone, 200 mg	J1080		Imm admin, intranasal, each add'l	90474	
Referral					Tigan, up to 200 mg	J3250		Injection, joint, small	20600	
To:					Toradol, 15 mg	J1885		Injection, joint, intermediate	20605	
					Miscellaneous services			Injection, joint, major	20610	
Instructions:				X	Expanded Problem Focused, $200.00			Injection, ther/proph/diag	90772	
					Low Complexity, ER Visit			Injection, trigger point	20552	
Physician signature								**Supplies**		
X _____										

Infectious and Parasitic Diseases
053.9   Herpes zoster, NOS
054.9   Herpetic disease, uncomplicated
075   Mononucleosis
034.0   Strep throat
079.99 Viral infection, unspec.
078.10 Warts, all sites

Neoplasms
Benign Neoplasms
239.2   Skin, soft tissue neoplasm, inspec.
216.9   Skin, unspec.

Endocrine, Nutritional and Metabolic Disorders
Endocrine
250.01 Diabetes I, uncomplicated
250.91 Diabetes I, w/unspec. complications
250.00 Diabetes II/unspec., w/o complications, not uncontrolled
250.90 Diabetes II, w/unspec. complications
242.90 Hyperthyroidism, NOS
244.9   Hypothyroidism, inspec.

Metabolic/Other
274.9   Gout, unspec.
272.0   Hypercholesterolemia
272.2   Hyperlipidemia, mixed
272.1   Hypertriglyceridemia
278.01 Obesity, morbid
278.00 Obesity, NOS
278.02 Overweight

Blood Diseases
285.9   Anemia, other, unspec.

Mental Disorders
300.00 Anxiety state, unspec.
314.00 Attention deficit, w/o hyperactivity
290.0   Dementia, senile, NOS
311   Depression, NOS

Nervous System and Sense Organ Disorders
Nervous System Diseases
354.0   Carpal tunnel
345.90 Epilepsy, unspec., w/o status
346.90 Migraine, unspec., not intractable

Eye Diseases
372.30 Conjunctivitis, unspec.
368.10 Visual disturbance, unspec.

Ear Diseases
380.4   Cerumen impaction
389.9   Hearing loss, unspec.
380.10 Otitis externa, unspec.
382.00 Otitis media, acute

Circulatory System
Arrythmias
427.31 Atrial fibrillation
Cardiac
413.9   Angina pectoris, NOS
428.0   Heart failure, congestive, unspec.
414.9   Ischemic heart disease, chronic, unspec.
424.1   Valvular disorder, aortic, NOS
Vascular
796.2   Elevated BP w/o hypertension
401.1   Hypertension, benign
458.0   Hypotension, orthostatic
443.9   Peripheral vascular disease, unspec.
451.9   Thrombophlebitis, unspec.
459.81 Venous insufficiency, unspec.

Respiratory System
Lower Respiratory Tract
493.90 Asthma, unspec.
466.0   Bronchitis, acute
496   COPD, NOS
486   Pneumonia, unspec.

Upper Respiratory Tract
462   Pharyngitis, acute
477.9   Rhinitis, allergic, cause unspec.
461.9   Sinusitis, acute, NOS
465.9   Upper respiratory infection, acute, NOS

Digestive System
564.00 Constipation, unspec.
562.10 Diverticulosis of colon
562.11 Diverticulitis of colon, NOS
535.50 Gastritis, unspec. w/o hemorrhage
558.9   Gastroenteritis, noninfectious, unspec.
530.81 Gastroesophageal reflux, no esophagitis
455.6   Hemorrhoids, NOS
564.1   Irritable bowel syndrome
578.1   Melena

Genitourinary System
Urinary System Diseases
592.9   Calculus, urinary, unspec.
595.0   Cystitis, acute
599.7   Hematuria
593.9   Renal insufficiency, acute
599.0   Urinary tract infection, unspec./pyuria

Male Genital Organ Diseases
607.84 Impotence, organic
302.72 Impotence, psychosexual dysfunction
601.9   Prostatitis, NOS
257.2   Testicular hypofunction

Breast Diseases
611.72 Breast lump

Female Genital Organ Diseases
616.0   Cervicitis
622.10 Dysplasia, cervix, unspec.
625.9   Pelvic pain, unspec. female disease
616.10 Vaginitis/vulvitis, unspec.

Disorders of Menstruation
626.0   Amenorrhea
627.9   Menopausal disorders, unspec.
626.2   Menstruation, excessive/frequent
625.3   Menstruation, painful
626.6   Metrorrhagia

Pregnancy, Childbirth
641.90 Hemorrhage in preg., unspec.
V24.2   Postpartum follow-up, routine
V22.2   Pregnant state, incidental
V22.0   Prenatal care, normal, first pregnancy
V22.1   Prenatal care, normal, other pregnancy

Skin, Subcutaneous Tissue
706.1   Acne
702.0   Actinic keratosis
682.9   Cellulitis/abscess, unspec.
692.9   Contact dermatitis, NOS
691.8   Eczema, atopic dermatitis
703.0   Ingrown nail
110.1   Onychomycosis
709.9   Other skin disease, unspec.
696.1   Psoriasis, other
695.3   Rosacea
706.2   Sebaceous cyst
702.19 Seborrheic keratosis, NOS
707.9   Ulcer, skin, chronic, unspec.
708.9   Urticaria, unspec.

Musculoskeletal and Connective Tissue
General
716.90 Arthropathy, unspec.
729.1   Fibromyositis
715.90 Osteoarthrosis, unspec.
733.00 Osteoporosis, unspec.
714.0   Rheumatoid arthritis
727.00 Synovitis/tenosynovitis, unspec.

Lower Extremity
729.5   Pain in limb
728.71 Plantar fasciitis

Spine/Torso
724.4   Back pain w/ radiation, unspec.
723.9   Cervical disorder, NOS

Upper Extremity
726.32 Lateral epicondylitis
726.10 Rotator cuff syndrome, NOS

Perinatal (Infant)
779.3   Feeding problem, newborn

Signs and Symptoms
789.00 Abdominal pain, unspec.
795.01 Abnormal Pap, ASC-US
719.40 Arthralgia, unspec.
569.3   Bleeding, rectal
786.50 Chest pain, unspec.
786.2   Cough
787.91 Diarrhea, NOS
780.4   Dizziness/vertigo, NOS
787.2   Dysphagia
788.1   Dysuria
782.3   Edema, localized, NOS
783.3   Feeding problem, infant/elderly
780.6   Fever, nonperinatal
271.9   Glucose intolerance
784.0   Headache, unspec.
788.30 Incontinence/enuresis, NOS
782.2   Localized swelling/mass, superficial
785.6   Lymph nodes, enlarged
780.79 Malaise and fatigue, other
787.02 Nausea, alone
787.01 Nausea w/ vomiting
719.46 Pain, knee
724.2   Pain, low back
785.1   Palpitations
788.42 Polyuria
782.1   Rash, nonvesicular, unspec.
782.0   Sensory disturbance skin
786.05 Shortness of breath
780.2   Syncope
788.41 Urinary frequency
787.03 Vomiting, alone
783.21 Weight loss

Injuries and Adverse Effects
Dislocations, Sprains and Strains
845.00 Sprain/strain: ankle, unspec.
845.10 Sprain/strain: foot, unspec.
842.10 Sprain/strain: hand, unspec.
844.9   Sprain/strain: knee/leg, unspec.
847.0   Sprain/strain: neck, unspec.
840.9   Sprain/strain: shoulder/upper arm, unspec.
842.00 Sprain/strain: wrist, unspec.

Other Trauma, Adverse Effects
919.0   Abrasion, unspec.
924.9   Contusion, unspec.
919.4   Insect bite
894.0   Open wound, lower limb, unspec.
884.0   Open wound, upper limb, unspec.

Supplemental Classification
V72.32 Confirm norm Pap after initial abn
V25.01 Contraception, oral
V25.02 Contraception, other (diaphragm, etc.)
V25.2   Contraception, sterilization
V58.30 Dressing change, nonsurgical
V01.9   Exposure, infectious disease, unspec.
V72.31 Gynecological exam
V06.8   Immunization, combination, other
V06.1   Immunization, DTP
V04.81 Immunization, influenza
V70.0   Well adult check
V20.2   Well child check

1500

HEALTH INSURANCE CLAIM FORM

APPROVED BY NATIONAL UNIFORM CLAIM COMMITTEE 08/05

PICA						PICA

1. MEDICARE	MEDICAID	TRICARE CHAMPUS	CHAMPVA	GROUP HEALTH PLAN	FECA BLK LUNG	OTHER	1a. INSURED'S I.D. NUMBER	(For Program in Item 1)
(Medicare #)	(Medicaid #)	(Sponsor's SSN)	(Member ID#)	(SSN or ID)	(SSN)	(ID)		

2. PATIENT'S NAME (Last Name, First Name, Middle Initial)	3. PATIENT'S BIRTH DATE MM DD YY SEX M F	4. INSURED'S NAME (Last Name, First Name, Middle Initial)

5. PATIENT'S ADDRESS (No., Street)	6. PATIENT RELATIONSHIP TO INSURED Self Spouse Child Other	7. INSURED'S ADDRESS (No., Street)

CITY	STATE	8. PATIENT STATUS Single Married Other	CITY	STATE

ZIP CODE	TELEPHONE (Include Area Code) ( )	Employed Full-Time Student Part-Time Student	ZIP CODE	TELEPHONE (Include Area Code) ( )

9. OTHER INSURED'S NAME (Last Name, First Name, Middle Initial)	10. IS PATIENT'S CONDITION RELATED TO:	11. INSURED'S POLICY GROUP OR FECA NUMBER

a. OTHER INSURED'S POLICY OR GROUP NUMBER	a. EMPLOYMENT? (Current or Previous) YES NO	a. INSURED'S DATE OF BIRTH MM DD YY SEX M F

b. OTHER INSURED'S DATE OF BIRTH MM DD YY SEX M F	b. AUTO ACCIDENT? PLACE (State) YES NO	b. EMPLOYER'S NAME OR SCHOOL NAME

c. EMPLOYER'S NAME OR SCHOOL NAME	c. OTHER ACCIDENT? YES NO	c. INSURANCE PLAN NAME OR PROGRAM NAME

d. INSURANCE PLAN NAME OR PROGRAM NAME	10d. RESERVED FOR LOCAL USE	d. IS THERE ANOTHER HEALTH BENEFIT PLAN? YES NO *If yes*, return to and complete item 9 a-d.

READ BACK OF FORM BEFORE COMPLETING & SIGNING THIS FORM.

12. PATIENT'S OR AUTHORIZED PERSON'S SIGNATURE I authorize the release of any medical or other information necessary to process this claim. I also request payment of government benefits either to myself or to the party who accepts assignment below. SIGNED _____ DATE _____	13. INSURED'S OR AUTHORIZED PERSON'S SIGNATURE I authorize payment of medical benefits to the undersigned physician or supplier for services described below. SIGNED _____

14. DATE OF CURRENT: MM DD YY ILLNESS (First symptom) OR INJURY (Accident) OR PREGNANCY(LMP)	15. IF PATIENT HAS HAD SAME OR SIMILAR ILLNESS. GIVE FIRST DATE MM DD YY	16. DATES PATIENT UNABLE TO WORK IN CURRENT OCCUPATION MM DD YY MM DD YY FROM TO

17. NAME OF REFERRING PROVIDER OR OTHER SOURCE	17a. 17b. NPI	18. HOSPITALIZATION DATES RELATED TO CURRENT SERVICES MM DD YY MM DD YY FROM TO

19. RESERVED FOR LOCAL USE	20. OUTSIDE LAB? $ CHARGES YES NO

21. DIAGNOSIS OR NATURE OF ILLNESS OR INJURY (Relate Items 1, 2, 3 or 4 to Item 24E by Line) 1. ___ . ___ 3. ___ . ___ 2. ___ . ___ 4. ___ . ___	22. MEDICAID RESUBMISSION CODE ORIGINAL REF. NO. 23. PRIOR AUTHORIZATION NUMBER

24. A. DATE(S) OF SERVICE From To MM DD YY MM DD YY	B. PLACE OF SERVICE	C. EMG	D. PROCEDURES, SERVICES, OR SUPPLIES (Explain Unusual Circumstances) CPT/HCPCS MODIFIER	E. DIAGNOSIS POINTER	F. $ CHARGES	G. DAYS OR UNITS	H. EPSDT Family Plan	I. ID. QUAL.	J. RENDERING PROVIDER ID. #
1									NPI
2									NPI
3									NPI
4									NPI
5									NPI
6									NPI

25. FEDERAL TAX I.D. NUMBER SSN EIN	26. PATIENT'S ACCOUNT NO.	27. ACCEPT ASSIGNMENT? (For govt. claims, see back) YES NO	28. TOTAL CHARGE $	29. AMOUNT PAID $	30. BALANCE DUE $

31. SIGNATURE OF PHYSICIAN OR SUPPLIER INCLUDING DEGREES OR CREDENTIALS (I certify that the statements on the reverse apply to this bill and are made a part thereof.) SIGNED _____ DATE _____	32. SERVICE FACILITY LOCATION INFORMATION a. b.	33. BILLING PROVIDER INFO & PH # ( ) a. b.

NUCC Instruction Manual available at: www.nucc.org   **PLEASE PRINT OR TYPE**   APPROVED OMB-0938-0999 FORM CMS-1500 (08-05)

CHAPTER 8, CHAPTER REVIEW EXERCISE 20

Patient Information Form

Please complete information in the spaces provided. Be sure to complete and sign the statement at the bottom of this form.

Patient		
Last Name	First Name	M.I.
Johnson	Adeline	S

Home Address			
Street	City	State	Zip
1673 Palm Ct.	Anytown	IA	32555

Phone Numbers & E-mail			
Home	Work	Cell	E-mail
432-3623	None	None	None

Identity Information	
Social Security Number	Date of Birth
428-23-5467	4-12-XX

Primary Insurance	
Company Name	Phone Number
Medicare	800-555-5555
Billing Address	
123 Government Ln., Washington, DC 20002	
Name of Insured	Relation to Patient
Adeline Johnson	Self
Insured's ID Number	Group Number
428-23-5467A	None

Secondary Insurance	
Company Name	Phone Number
AARP	477-878-9898
Billing Address	
123 Ancient Blvd., Mature, FL 49876	
Name of Insured	Relation to Patient
Adeline Johnson	Self
Insured's ID Number	Group Number
A45234	None

Emergency Information		
Emergency Contact Name	Relation	Phone
Zelda Jones	Neighbor	223-1424

I authorize the release of any medical or other information necessary to process this claim.
I hereby authorize payment of medical benefits billed to my insurance to John Smith, DO. I hereby accept
responsibility for payment for any service(s) provided to me that is not covered by my insurance. I agree
to pay all co-payments, coinsurance, and deductibles at the time the service is rendered.

Adeline Johnson   3/10/XXXX
‾‾‾‾‾‾‾‾‾‾‾‾‾‾‾‾‾‾‾‾‾‾‾‾‾‾‾‾‾   ‾‾‾‾‾‾‾‾‾‾‾‾‾‾‾
Signature of Patient or Guardian   *Date*

Date of service: 3-10-XXXX	

Patient name: Adeline Johnson	Insurance: Medicare	
	Subscriber name: Self	
Address: 1673 Palm Ct. Anytown, IA 55555	Group #:	Previous balance:
	Copay:	Today's charges: 100.00
Phone: 432-3623	Account #:	Today's payment: check#
DOB: 4-12-32 Age: 78 Sex: F	Physician name: Smith	Balance due: 100.00

	Office visit	New	Est		Office procedures			Laboratory	
	Minimal		99211		Anoscopy		46600	Venipuncture	36415
	Problem focused	99201	99212		Audiometry		92551	Blood glucose, monitoring device	82962
X	Expanded problem focused	99202	99213		Cerumen removal		69210	Blood glucose, visual dipstick	82948
	Detailed	99203	99214		Colposcopy		57452	CBC, w/ auto differential	85025
	Comprehensive	99204	99215		Colposcopy w/biopsy		57455	CBC, w/o auto differential	85027
	Comprehensive (new patient)	99205			ECG, w/interpretation		93000	Cholesterol	82465
	Significant, separate service	−25	−25		ECG, rhythm strip		93040	Hemoccult, guaiac	82270
	Well visit	**New**	**Est**		Endometrial biopsy		58100	Hemoccult, immunoassay	82274
	< 1 y	99381	99391		Flexible sigmoidoscopy		45330	Hemoglobin A1C	85018
	1–4 y	99382	99392		Flexible sigmoidoscopy w/biopsy		45331	Lipid panel	80061
	5–11 y	99383	99393		Fracture care, cast/splint	29___		Liver panel	80076
	12–17 y	99384	99394		Site: _____			KOH prep (skin, hair, nails)	87220
	18–39 y	99385	99395		Nebulizer		94640	Metabolic panel, basic	80048
	40–64 y	99386	99396		Nebulizer demo		94664	Metabolic panel, comprehensive	80053
	65 y +	99387	99397		Spirometry		94010	Mononucleosis	86308
	Medicare preventive services				Spirometry, pre and post		94060	Pregnancy, blood	84703
	Pap		Q0091		Tympanometry		92567	Pregnancy, urine	81025
	Pelvic & breast		G0101		Vasectomy		55250	Renal panel	80069
	Prostate/PSA		G0103		**Skin procedures**		**Units**	Sedimentation rate	85651
	Tobacco counseling/3–10 min		G0375		Burn care, initial	16000		Strep, rapid	86403
	Tobacco counseling/>10 min		G0376		Foreign body, skin, simple	10120		Strep culture	87081
	Welcome to Medicare exam		G0344		Foreign body, skin, complex	10121		Strep A	87880
	ECG w/Welcome to Medicare exam		G0366		I&D, abscess	10060		TB	86580
	Flexible sigmoidoscopy		G0104		I&D, hematoma/seroma	10140		UA, complete, non-automated	81000
	Hemoccult, guaiac		G0107		Laceration repair, simple	120___		UA, w/o micro, non-automated	81002
	Flu shot		G0008		Site: _____ Size: _____			UA, w/o micro, non-automated	81003
	Pneumonia shot		G0009		Laceration repair, layered	120___		Urine colony count	87086
	Inpatient hospital care				Site: _____ Size: _____			Urine culture, presumptive	87088
	Initial hospital care		99221		Lesion, biopsy, one	11100		Wet mount/KOH	87210
	Problem focused subsequent hospital care		99231		Lesion, biopsy, each add'l	11101		**Vaccines**	
	Expanded problem focused sub. hosp. care		99232		Lesion, excision, benign	114___		DT, <7 y	90702
	Detailed subsequent hospital care		99233		Site: _____ Size: _____			DTP	90701
	Other services				Lesion, excision, malignant	116___		DtaP, <7 y	90700
	After posted hours		99050		Site: _____ Size: _____			Flu, 6–35 months	90657
	Evening/weekend appointment		99051		Lesion, paring/cutting, one	11055		Flu, 3 y +	90658
	Home health certification		G0180		Lesion, paring/cutting, 2–4	11056		Hep A, adult	90632
	Home health recertification		G0179		Lesion, shave	113___		Hep A, ped/adol, 2 dose	90633
	Post-op follow-up		99024		Site: _____ Size: _____			Hep B, adult	90746
	Prolonged/30–74 min		99354		Nail removal, partial	11730		Hep B, ped/adol 3 dose	90744
	Special reports/forms		99080		Nail removal, w/matrix	11750		Hep B-Hib	90748
	Disability/Workers comp		99455		Skin tag, 1–15	11200		Hib, 4 dose	90645
	Radiology				Wart, flat, 1–14	17110		HPV	90649
					Wart, plantar, single	17000		IPV	90713
					Wart, plantar, each add'l	17003		MMR	90707
X	**Diagnoses**				**Medications**		**Units**	Pneumonia, >2 y	90732
1	Bunion				Ampicillin, up to 500 mg	J0290		Pneumonia conjugate, <5 y	90669
2					B-12, up to 1,000 mcg	J3420		Td, >7 y	90718
3					Epinephrine, up to 1 ml	J0170		Varicella	90716
4					Kenalog, 10 mg	J3301		**Immunizations & Injections**	**Units**
	Next office visit				Lidocaine, 10 mg	J2001		Allergen, one	95115
	Recheck Prev PRN _____ D W M Y				Normal saline, 1000 cc	J7030		Allergen, multiple	95117
	Instructions:				Phenergan, up to 50 mg	J2550		Imm admin, one	90471
					Progesterone, 150 mg	J1055		Imm admin, each add'l	90472
					Rocephin, 250 mg	J0696		Imm admin, intranasal, one	90473
					Testosterone, 200 mg	J1080		Imm admin, intranasal, each add'l	90474
	Referral				Tigan, up to 200 mg	J3250		Injection, joint, small	20600
	To:				Toradol, 15 mg	J1885		Injection, joint, intermediate	20605
	Instructions:				**Miscellaneous services**			Injection, joint, major	20610
								Injection, ther/proph/diag	90772
				X	Bunionectomy, without sesamoidectomy, simple, exostectomy performed, 3-15-xxxx			Injection, trigger point	20552
	Physician signature							**Supplies**	
	X _____								

Infectious and Parasitic Diseases

053.9	Herpes zoster, NOS
054.9	Herpetic disease, uncomplicated
075	Mononucleosis
034.0	Strep throat
079.99	Viral infection, unspec.
078.10	Warts, all sites

Neoplasms

Benign Neoplasms

239.2	Skin, soft tissue neoplasm, inspec.
216.9	Skin, unspec.

Endocrine, Nutritional and Metabolic Disorders

Endocrine

250.01	Diabetes I, uncomplicated
250.91	Diabetes I, w/unspec. complications
250.00	Diabetes II/unspec., w/o complications, not uncontrolled
250.90	Diabetes II, w/unspec. complications
242.90	Hyperthyroidism, NOS
244.9	Hypothyroidism, inspec.

Metabolic/Other

274.9	Gout, unspec.
272.0	Hypercholesterolemia
272.2	Hyperlipidemia, mixed
272.1	Hypertriglyceridemia
278.01	Obesity, morbid
278.00	Obesity, NOS
278.02	Overweight

Blood Diseases

285.9	Anemia, other, unspec.

Mental Disorders

300.00	Anxiety state, unspec.
314.00	Attention deficit, w/o hyperactivity
290.0	Dementia, senile, NOS
311	Depression, NOS

Nervous System and Sense Organ Disorders

Nervous System Diseases

354.0	Carpal tunnel
345.90	Epilepsy, unspec., w/o status
346.90	Migraine, unspec., not intractable

Eye Diseases

372.30	Conjunctivitis, unspec.
368.10	Visual disturbance, unspec.

Ear Diseases

380.4	Cerumen impaction
389.9	Hearing loss, unspec.
380.10	Otitis externa, unspec.
382.00	Otitis media, acute

Circulatory System

Arrythmias

427.31	Atrial fibrillation

Cardiac

413.9	Angina pectoris, NOS
428.0	Heart failure, congestive, unspec.
414.9	Ischemic heart disease, chronic, unspec.
424.1	Valvular disorder, aortic, NOS

Vascular

796.2	Elevated BP w/o hypertension
401.1	Hypertension, benign
458.0	Hypotension, orthostatic
443.9	Peripheral vascular disease, unspec.
451.9	Thrombophlebitis, unspec.
459.81	Venous insufficiency, unspec.

Respiratory System

Lower Respiratory Tract

493.90	Asthma, unspec.
466.0	Bronchitis, acute
496	COPD, NOS
486	Pneumonia, unspec.

Upper Respiratory Tract

462	Pharyngitis, acute
477.9	Rhinitis, allergic, cause unspec.
461.9	Sinusitis, acute, NOS
465.9	Upper respiratory infection, acute, NOS

Digestive System

564.00	Constipation, unspec.
562.10	Diverticulosis of colon
562.11	Diverticulitis of colon, NOS
535.50	Gastritis, unspec. w/o hemorrhage
558.9	Gastroenteritis, noninfectious, unspec.
530.81	Gastroesophageal reflux, no esophagitis
455.6	Hemorrhoids, NOS
564.1	Irritable bowel syndrome
578.1	Melena

Genitourinary System

Urinary System Diseases

592.9	Calculus, urinary, unspec.
595.0	Cystitis, acute
599.7	Hematuria
593.9	Renal insufficiency, acute
599.0	Urinary tract infection, unspec./pyuria

Male Genital Organ Diseases

607.84	Impotence, organic
302.72	Impotence, psychosexual dysfunction
601.9	Prostatitis, NOS
257.2	Testicular hypofunction

Breast Diseases

611.72	Breast lump

Female Genital Organ Diseases

616.0	Cervicitis
622.10	Dysplasia, cervix, unspec.
625.9	Pelvic pain, unspec. female disease
616.10	Vaginitis/vulvitis, unspec.

Disorders of Menstruation

626.0	Amenorrhea
627.9	Menopausal disorders, unspec.
626.2	Menstruation, excessive/frequent
625.3	Menstruation, painful
626.6	Metrorrhagia

Pregnancy, Childbirth

641.90	Hemorrhage in preg., unspec.
V24.2	Postpartum follow-up, routine
V22.2	Pregnant state, incidental
V22.0	Prenatal care, normal, first pregnancy
V22.1	Prenatal care, normal, other pregnancy

Skin, Subcutaneous Tissue

706.1	Acne
702.0	Actinic keratosis
682.9	Cellulitis/abscess, unspec.
692.9	Contact dermatitis, NOS
691.8	Eczema, atopic dermatitis
703.0	Ingrown nail
110.1	Onychomycosis
709.9	Other skin disease, unspec.
696.1	Psoriasis, other
695.3	Rosacea
706.2	Sebaceous cyst
702.19	Seborrheic keratosis, NOS
707.9	Ulcer, skin, chronic, unspec.
708.9	Urticaria, unspec.

Musculoskeletal and Connective Tissue

General

716.90	Arthropathy, unspec.
729.1	Fibromyositis
715.90	Osteoarthrosis, unspec.
733.00	Osteoporosis, unspec.
714.0	Rheumatoid arthritis
727.00	Synovitis/tenosynovitis, unspec.

Lower Extremity

729.5	Pain in limb
728.71	Plantar fasciitis

Spine/Torso

724.4	Back pain w/ radiation, unspec.
723.9	Cervical disorder, NOS

Upper Extremity

726.32	Lateral epicondylitis
726.10	Rotator cuff syndrome, NOS

Perinatal (Infant)

779.3	Feeding problem, newborn

Signs and Symptoms

789.00	Abdominal pain, unspec.
795.01	Abnormal Pap, ASC-US
719.40	Arthralgia, unspec.
569.3	Bleeding, rectal
786.50	Chest pain, unspec.
786.2	Cough
787.91	Diarrhea, NOS
780.4	Dizziness/vertigo, NOS
787.2	Dysphagia
788.1	Dysuria
782.3	Edema, localized, NOS
783.3	Feeding problem, infant/elderly
780.6	Fever, nonperinatal
271.9	Glucose intolerance
784.0	Headache, unspec.
788.30	Incontinence/enuresis, NOS
782.2	Localized swelling/mass, superficial
785.6	Lymph nodes, enlarged
780.79	Malaise and fatigue, other
787.02	Nausea, alone
787.01	Nausea w/ vomiting
719.46	Pain, knee
724.2	Pain, low back
785.1	Palpitations
788.42	Polyuria
782.1	Rash, nonvesicular, unspec.
782.0	Sensory disturbance skin
786.05	Shortness of breath
780.2	Syncope
788.41	Urinary frequency
787.03	Vomiting, alone
783.21	Weight loss

Injuries and Adverse Effects

Dislocations, Sprains and Strains

845.00	Sprain/strain: ankle, unspec.
845.10	Sprain/strain: foot, unspec.
842.10	Sprain/strain: hand, unspec.
844.9	Sprain/strain: knee/leg, unspec.
847.0	Sprain/strain: neck, unspec.
840.9	Sprain/strain: shoulder/upper arm, unspec.
842.00	Sprain/strain: wrist, unspec.

Other Trauma, Adverse Effects

919.0	Abrasion, unspec.
924.9	Contusion, unspec.
919.4	Insect bite
894.0	Open wound, lower limb, unspec.
884.0	Open wound, upper limb, unspec.

Supplemental Classification

V72.32	Confirm norm Pap after initial abn
V25.01	Contraception, oral
V25.02	Contraception, other (diaphragm, etc.)
V25.2	Contraception, sterilization
V58.30	Dressing change, nonsurgical
V01.9	Exposure, infectious disease, unspec.
V72.31	Gynecological exam
V06.8	Immunization, combination, other
V06.1	Immunization, DTP
V04.81	Immunization, influenza
V70.0	Well adult check
V20.2	Well child check

1500

HEALTH INSURANCE CLAIM FORM

APPROVED BY NATIONAL UNIFORM CLAIM COMMITTEE 08/05

1. MEDICARE (Medicare #) · MEDICAID (Medicaid #) · TRICARE CHAMPUS (Sponsor's SSN) · CHAMPVA (Member ID#) · GROUP HEALTH PLAN (SSN or ID) · FECA BLK LUNG (SSN) · OTHER (ID)
1a. INSURED'S I.D. NUMBER (For Program in Item 1)

2. PATIENT'S NAME (Last Name, First Name, Middle Initial)
3. PATIENT'S BIRTH DATE MM DD YY · SEX M F
4. INSURED'S NAME (Last Name, First Name, Middle Initial)

5. PATIENT'S ADDRESS (No., Street)
6. PATIENT RELATIONSHIP TO INSURED — Self Spouse Child Other
7. INSURED'S ADDRESS (No., Street)

CITY · STATE
8. PATIENT STATUS — Single Married Other
CITY · STATE

ZIP CODE · TELEPHONE (Include Area Code) ( )
Employed Full-Time Student Part-Time Student
ZIP CODE · TELEPHONE (Include Area Code) ( )

9. OTHER INSURED'S NAME (Last Name, First Name, Middle Initial)
10. IS PATIENT'S CONDITION RELATED TO:
11. INSURED'S POLICY GROUP OR FECA NUMBER

a. OTHER INSURED'S POLICY OR GROUP NUMBER
a. EMPLOYMENT? (Current or Previous) YES NO
a. INSURED'S DATE OF BIRTH MM DD YY · SEX M F

b. OTHER INSURED'S DATE OF BIRTH MM DD YY · SEX M F
b. AUTO ACCIDENT? YES NO · PLACE (State)
b. EMPLOYER'S NAME OR SCHOOL NAME

c. EMPLOYER'S NAME OR SCHOOL NAME
c. OTHER ACCIDENT? YES NO
c. INSURANCE PLAN NAME OR PROGRAM NAME

d. INSURANCE PLAN NAME OR PROGRAM NAME
10d. RESERVED FOR LOCAL USE
d. IS THERE ANOTHER HEALTH BENEFIT PLAN? YES NO *If yes*, return to and complete item 9 a-d.

READ BACK OF FORM BEFORE COMPLETING & SIGNING THIS FORM.
12. PATIENT'S OR AUTHORIZED PERSON'S SIGNATURE I authorize the release of any medical or other information necessary to process this claim. I also request payment of government benefits either to myself or to the party who accepts assignment below.

SIGNED _____ DATE _____

13. INSURED'S OR AUTHORIZED PERSON'S SIGNATURE I authorize payment of medical benefits to the undersigned physician or supplier for services described below.

SIGNED _____

14. DATE OF CURRENT: MM DD YY — ILLNESS (First symptom) OR INJURY (Accident) OR PREGNANCY(LMP)
15. IF PATIENT HAS HAD SAME OR SIMILAR ILLNESS. GIVE FIRST DATE MM DD YY
16. DATES PATIENT UNABLE TO WORK IN CURRENT OCCUPATION MM DD YY FROM TO MM DD YY

17. NAME OF REFERRING PROVIDER OR OTHER SOURCE
17a.
17b. NPI
18. HOSPITALIZATION DATES RELATED TO CURRENT SERVICES MM DD YY FROM TO MM DD YY

19. RESERVED FOR LOCAL USE
20. OUTSIDE LAB? YES NO · $ CHARGES

21. DIAGNOSIS OR NATURE OF ILLNESS OR INJURY (Relate Items 1, 2, 3 or 4 to Item 24E by Line)
1. |___ . ___| 3. |___ . ___|
2. |___ . ___| 4. |___ . ___|

22. MEDICAID RESUBMISSION CODE · ORIGINAL REF. NO.

23. PRIOR AUTHORIZATION NUMBER

24. A. DATE(S) OF SERVICE					B. PLACE OF SERVICE	C. EMG	D. PROCEDURES, SERVICES, OR SUPPLIES (Explain Unusual Circumstances) CPT/HCPCS MODIFIER	E. DIAGNOSIS POINTER	F. $ CHARGES	G. DAYS OR UNITS	H. EPSDT Family Plan	I. ID. QUAL.	J. RENDERING PROVIDER ID. #
From			To											
MM	DD	YY	MM	DD	YY									
1													NPI	
2													NPI	
3													NPI	
4													NPI	
5													NPI	
6													NPI	

25. FEDERAL TAX I.D. NUMBER · SSN EIN
26. PATIENT'S ACCOUNT NO.
27. ACCEPT ASSIGNMENT? (For govt. claims, see back) YES NO
28. TOTAL CHARGE $
29. AMOUNT PAID $
30. BALANCE DUE $

31. SIGNATURE OF PHYSICIAN OR SUPPLIER INCLUDING DEGREES OR CREDENTIALS (I certify that the statements on the reverse apply to this bill and are made a part thereof.)

SIGNED _____ DATE _____

32. SERVICE FACILITY LOCATION INFORMATION

a. b.

33. BILLING PROVIDER INFO & PH # ( )

a. b.

PATIENT AND INSURED INFORMATION · PHYSICIAN OR SUPPLIER INFORMATION

CHAPTER 8, CHAPTER REVIEW EXERCISE 21

Patient Information Form

Please complete information in the spaces provided. Be sure to complete and sign the statement at the bottom of this form.

Patient		
Last Name	First Name	M.I.
Smith	Mary	H

Home Address			
Street	City	State	Zip
4590 Shoreline Drive	Anytown	IA	51222

Phone Numbers & E-mail			
Home	Work	Cell	E-mail
222-7643	None	101-4747	smith@mail.com

Identity Information	
Social Security Number	Date of Birth
515-26-7642	10-7-XX

Primary Insurance	
Company Name	Phone Number
Medicare	212-655-4545
Billing Address	
Name of Insured	Relation to Patient
Self	
Insured's ID Number	Group Number
487-34-7621B	None

Secondary Insurance	
Company Name	Phone Number
Blue Cross Blue Shield	
Billing Address	
636 Headache Ct., Des Moines, IA 57843	
Name of Insured	Relation to Patient
William Smith	Husband
Insured's ID Number	Group Number
487-34-7621	XQQ

Emergency Information		
Emergency Contact Name	Relation	Phone
William Smith	Husband	222-7643

I authorize the release of any medical or other information necessary to process this claim.
I hereby authorize payment of medical benefits billed to my insurance to John Smith, DO. I hereby accept
responsibility for payment for any service(s) provided to me that is not covered by my insurance. I agree
to pay all co-payments, coinsurance, and deductibles at the time the service is rendered.

Mary Smith   10/10/XXXX
_____   _____
Signature of Patient or Guardian   *Date*

Date of service: 10-10-XXXX	

Patient name: Mary Smith	Insurance: Medicare	
	Subscriber name: Mary	
Address: 4590 Shoreline Anytown, IA 51222	Group #: 487-34-7621B	Previous balance:
	Copay:	Today's charges: 180.00
Phone: 222-7643	Account #:	Today's payment: check#
DOB: 10-7-39 Age: 71 Sex: F	Physician name: Smith	Balance due: 180.00

	Office visit	New	Est		Office procedures				Laboratory	
	Minimal		99211		Anoscopy		46600		Venipuncture	36415
	Problem focused	99201	99212		Audiometry		92551		Blood glucose, monitoring device	82962
X	Expanded problem focused	99202	99213		Cerumen removal		69210		Blood glucose, visual dipstick	82948
	Detailed	99203	99214		Colposcopy		57452		CBC, w/ auto differential	85025
	Comprehensive	99204	99215		Colposcopy w/biopsy		57455		CBC, w/o auto differential	85027
	Comprehensive (new patient)	99205			ECG, w/interpretation		93000		Cholesterol	82465
	Significant, separate service	–25	–25		ECG, rhythm strip		93040		Hemoccult, guaiac	82270
	Well visit	**New**	**Est**		Endometrial biopsy		58100		Hemoccult, immunoassay	82274
	< 1 y		99381	99391	Flexible sigmoidoscopy		45330		Hemoglobin A1C	85018
	1–4 y	99382	99392		Flexible sigmoidoscopy w/biopsy		45331		Lipid panel	80061
	5–11 y	99383	99393		Fracture care, cast/splint		29____		Liver panel	80076
	12–17 y	99384	99394		Site: _____				KOH prep (skin, hair, nails)	87220
	18–39 y	99385	99395		Nebulizer		94640		Metabolic panel, basic	80048
	40–64 y	99386	99396		Nebulizer demo		94664		Metabolic panel, comprehensive	80053
	65 y +	99387	99397		Spirometry		94010		Mononucleosis	86308
	Medicare preventive services				Spirometry, pre and post		94060		Pregnancy, blood	84703
	Pap		Q0091		Tympanometry		92567		Pregnancy, urine	81025
	Pelvic & breast		G0101		Vasectomy		55250		Renal panel	80069
	Prostate/PSA		G0103		**Skin procedures**		**Units**		Sedimentation rate	85651
	Tobacco counseling/3–10 min		G0375		Burn care, initial	16000			Strep, rapid	86403
	Tobacco counseling/>10 min		G0376		Foreign body, skin, simple	10120			Strep culture	87081
	Welcome to Medicare exam		G0344		Foreign body, skin, complex	10121			Strep A	87880
	ECG w/Welcome to Medicare exam		G0366		I&D, abscess	10060			TB	86580
	Flexible sigmoidoscopy		G0104		I&D, hematoma/seroma	10140			UA, complete, non-automated	81000
	Hemoccult, guaiac		G0107		Laceration repair, simple	120____			UA, w/o micro, non-automated	81002
	Flu shot		G0008		Site: _____ Size: ____				UA, w/o micro, non-automated	81003
	Pneumonia shot		G0009		Laceration repair, layered	120____			Urine colony count	87086
	Inpatient hospital care				Site: _____ Size: ____				Urine culture, presumptive	87088
	Initial hospital care		99221		Lesion, biopsy, one	11100			Wet mount/KOH	87210
	Problem focused subsequent hospital care		99231		Lesion, biopsy, each add'l	11101			**Vaccines**	
	Expanded problem focused sub. hosp. care		99232		Lesion, excision, benign	114____			DT, <7 y	90702
	Detailed subsequent hospital care		99233		Site: _____ Size: ____				DTP	90701
	Other services				Lesion, excision, malignant	116____			DtaP, <7 y	90700
	After posted hours		99050		Site: _____ Size: ____				Flu, 6–35 months	90657
	Evening/weekend appointment		99051		Lesion, paring/cutting, one	11055			Flu, 3 y +	90658
	Home health certification		G0180		Lesion, paring/cutting, 2–4	11056			Hep A, adult	90632
	Home health recertification		G0179		Lesion, shave	113____			Hep A, ped/adol, 2 dose	90633
	Post-op follow-up		99024		Site: _____ Size: ____				Hep B, adult	90746
	Prolonged/30–74 min		99354		Nail removal, partial	11730			Hep B, ped/adol 3 dose	90744
	Special reports/forms		99080		Nail removal, w/matrix	11750			Hep B-Hib	90748
	Disability/Workers comp		99455		Skin tag, 1–15	11200			Hib, 4 dose	90645
	Radiology				Wart, flat, 1–14	17110			HPV	90649
					Wart, plantar, single	17000			IPV	90713
					Wart, plantar, each add'l	17003			MMR	90707
X	**Diagnoses**				**Medications**		**Units**		Pneumonia, >2 y	90732
1	Viral pneumonia				Ampicillin, up to 500 mg	J0290			Pneumonia conjugate, <5 y	90669
2					B-12, up to 1,000 mcg	J3420			Td, >7 y	90718
3					Epinephrine, up to 1 ml	J0170			Varicella	90716
4					Kenalog, 10 mg	J3301			**Immunizations & Injections**	**Units**

Next office visit

Recheck	Prev	PRN		____ D W M Y

Instructions:

Referral

To:

Instructions:

Physician signature

X _____

Medications (cont.)		
Lidocaine, 10 mg	J2001	
Normal saline, 1000 cc	J7030	
Phenergan, up to 50 mg	J2550	
Progesterone, 150 mg	J1055	
Rocephin, 250 mg	J0696	
Testosterone, 200 mg	J1080	
Tigan, up to 200 mg	J3250	
Toradol, 15 mg	J1885	

Miscellaneous services		
X Chest x-ray		

Immunizations & Injections		**Units**
Allergen, one	95115	
Allergen, multiple	95117	
Imm admin, one	90471	
Imm admin, each add'l	90472	
Imm admin, intranasal, one	90473	
Imm admin, intranasal, each add'l	90474	
Injection, joint, small	20600	
Injection, joint, intermediate	20605	
Injection, joint, major	20610	
Injection, ther/proph/diag	90772	
Injection, trigger point	20552	
Supplies		

Infectious and Parasitic Diseases

053.9	Herpes zoster, NOS
054.9	Herpetic disease, uncomplicated
075	Mononucleosis
034.0	Strep throat
079.99	Viral infection, unspec.
078.10	Warts, all sites

Neoplasms

Benign Neoplasms
239.2	Skin, soft tissue neoplasm, inspec.
216.9	Skin, unspec.

Endocrine, Nutritional and Metabolic Disorders

Endocrine
250.01	Diabetes I, uncomplicated
250.91	Diabetes I, w/unspec. complications
250.00	Diabetes II/unspec., w/o complications, not uncontrolled
250.90	Diabetes II, w/unspec. complications
242.90	Hyperthyroidism, NOS
244.9	Hypothyroidism, inspec.

Metabolic/Other
274.9	Gout, unspec.
272.0	Hypercholesterolemia
272.2	Hyperlipidemia, mixed
272.1	Hypertriglyceridemia
278.01	Obesity, morbid
278.00	Obesity, NOS
278.02	Overweight

Blood Diseases

285.9	Anemia, other, unspec.

Mental Disorders

300.00	Anxiety state, unspec.
314.00	Attention deficit, w/o hyperactivity
290.0	Dementia, senile, NOS
311	Depression, NOS

Nervous System and Sense Organ Disorders

Nervous System Diseases
354.0	Carpal tunnel
345.90	Epilepsy, unspec., w/o status
346.90	Migraine, unspec., not intractable

Eye Diseases
372.30	Conjunctivitis, unspec.
368.10	Visual disturbance, unspec.

Ear Diseases
380.4	Cerumen impaction
389.9	Hearing loss, unspec.
380.10	Otitis externa, unspec.
382.00	Otitis media, acute

Circulatory System

Arrythmias
427.31	Atrial fibrillation

Cardiac
413.9	Angina pectoris, NOS
428.0	Heart failure, congestive, unspec.
414.9	Ischemic heart disease, chronic, unspec.
424.1	Valvular disorder, aortic, NOS

Vascular
796.2	Elevated BP w/o hypertension
401.1	Hypertension, benign
458.0	Hypotension, orthostatic
443.9	Peripheral vascular disease, unspec.
451.9	Thrombophlebitis, unspec.
459.81	Venous insufficiency, unspec.

Respiratory System

Lower Respiratory Tract
493.90	Asthma, unspec.
466.0	Bronchitis, acute
496	COPD, NOS
486	Pneumonia, unspec.

Upper Respiratory Tract
462	Pharyngitis, acute
477.9	Rhinitis, allergic, cause unspec.
461.9	Sinusitis, acute, NOS
465.9	Upper respiratory infection, acute, NOS

Digestive System

564.00	Constipation, unspec.
562.10	Diverticulosis of colon
562.11	Diverticulitis of colon, NOS
535.50	Gastritis, unspec. w/o hemorrhage
558.9	Gastroenteritis, noninfectious, unspec.
530.81	Gastroesophageal reflux, no esophagitis
455.6	Hemorrhoids, NOS
564.1	Irritable bowel syndrome
578.1	Melena

Genitourinary System

Urinary System Diseases
592.9	Calculus, urinary, unspec.
595.0	Cystitis, acute
599.7	Hematuria
593.9	Renal insufficiency, acute
599.0	Urinary tract infection, unspec./pyuria

Male Genital Organ Diseases
607.84	Impotence, organic
302.72	Impotence, psychosexual dysfunction
601.9	Prostatitis, NOS
257.2	Testicular hypofunction

Breast Diseases
611.72	Breast lump

Female Genital Organ Diseases
616.0	Cervicitis
622.10	Dysplasia, cervix, unspec.
625.9	Pelvic pain, unspec. female disease
616.10	Vaginitis/vulvitis, unspec.

Disorders of Menstruation
626.0	Amenorrhea
627.9	Menopausal disorders, unspec.
626.2	Menstruation, excessive/frequent
625.3	Menstruation, painful
626.6	Metrorrhagia

Pregnancy, Childbirth

641.90	Hemorrhage in preg., unspec.
V24.2	Postpartum follow-up, routine
V22.2	Pregnant state, incidental
V22.0	Prenatal care, normal, first pregnancy
V22.1	Prenatal care, normal, other pregnancy

Skin, Subcutaneous Tissue

706.1	Acne
702.0	Actinic keratosis
682.9	Cellulitis/abscess, unspec.
692.9	Contact dermatitis, NOS
691.8	Eczema, atopic dermatitis
703.0	Ingrown nail
110.1	Onychomycosis
709.9	Other skin disease, unspec.
696.1	Psoriasis, other
695.3	Rosacea
706.2	Sebaceous cyst
702.19	Seborrheic keratosis, NOS
707.9	Ulcer, skin, chronic, unspec.
708.9	Urticaria, unspec.

Musculoskeletal and Connective Tissue

General
716.90	Arthropathy, unspec.
729.1	Fibromyositis
715.90	Osteoarthrosis, unspec.
733.00	Osteoporosis, unspec.
714.0	Rheumatoid arthritis
727.00	Synovitis/tenosynovitis, unspec.

Lower Extremity
729.5	Pain in limb
728.71	Plantar fasciitis

Spine/Torso
724.4	Back pain w/ radiation, unspec.
723.9	Cervical disorder, NOS

Upper Extremity
726.32	Lateral epicondylitis
726.10	Rotator cuff syndrome, NOS

Perinatal (Infant)

779.3	Feeding problem, newborn

Signs and Symptoms

789.00	Abdominal pain, unspec.
795.01	Abnormal Pap, ASC-US
719.40	Arthralgia, unspec.
569.3	Bleeding, rectal
786.50	Chest pain, unspec.
786.2	Cough
787.91	Diarrhea, NOS
780.4	Dizziness/vertigo, NOS
787.2	Dysphagia
788.1	Dysuria
782.3	Edema, localized, NOS
783.3	Feeding problem, infant/elderly
780.6	Fever, nonperinatal
271.9	Glucose intolerance
784.0	Headache, unspec.
788.30	Incontinence/enuresis, NOS
782.2	Localized swelling/mass, superficial
785.6	Lymph nodes, enlarged
780.79	Malaise and fatigue, other
787.02	Nausea, alone
787.01	Nausea w/ vomiting
719.46	Pain, knee
724.2	Pain, low back
785.1	Palpitations
788.42	Polyuria
782.1	Rash, nonvesicular, unspec.
782.0	Sensory disturbance skin
786.05	Shortness of breath
780.2	Syncope
788.41	Urinary frequency
787.03	Vomiting, alone
783.21	Weight loss

Injuries and Adverse Effects

Dislocations, Sprains and Strains
845.00	Sprain/strain: ankle, unspec.
845.10	Sprain/strain: foot, unspec.
842.10	Sprain/strain: hand, unspec.
844.9	Sprain/strain: knee/leg, unspec.
847.0	Sprain/strain: neck, unspec.
840.9	Sprain/strain: shoulder/upper arm, unspec.
842.00	Sprain/strain: wrist, unspec.

Other Trauma, Adverse Effects
919.0	Abrasion, unspec.
924.9	Contusion, unspec.
919.4	Insect bite
894.0	Open wound, lower limb, unspec.
884.0	Open wound, upper limb, unspec.

Supplemental Classification

V72.32	Confirm norm Pap after initial abn
V25.01	Contraception, oral
V25.02	Contraception, other (diaphragm, etc.)
V25.2	Contraception, sterilization
V58.30	Dressing change, nonsurgical
V01.9	Exposure, infectious disease, unspec.
V72.31	Gynecological exam
V06.8	Immunization, combination, other
V06.1	Immunization, DTP
V04.81	Immunization, influenza
V70.0	Well adult check
V20.2	Well child check

1500

HEALTH INSURANCE CLAIM FORM

APPROVED BY NATIONAL UNIFORM CLAIM COMMITTEE 08/05

CARRIER →

☐☐☐ PICA | | PICA ☐☐☐

1. MEDICARE ☐ (Medicare #)   MEDICAID ☐ (Medicaid #)   TRICARE CHAMPUS ☐ (Sponsor's SSN)   CHAMPVA ☐ (Member ID#)   GROUP HEALTH PLAN ☐ (SSN or ID)   FECA BLK LUNG ☐ (SSN)   OTHER ☐ (ID)
1a. INSURED'S I.D. NUMBER   (For Program in Item 1)

2. PATIENT'S NAME (Last Name, First Name, Middle Initial)

3. PATIENT'S BIRTH DATE MM | DD | YY   SEX   M ☐   F ☐

4. INSURED'S NAME (Last Name, First Name, Middle Initial)

5. PATIENT'S ADDRESS (No., Street)

6. PATIENT RELATIONSHIP TO INSURED   Self ☐   Spouse ☐   Child ☐   Other ☐

7. INSURED'S ADDRESS (No., Street)

CITY   STATE

8. PATIENT STATUS   Single ☐   Married ☐   Other ☐

CITY   STATE

ZIP CODE   TELEPHONE (Include Area Code)   (　　)

Employed ☐   Full-Time Student ☐   Part-Time Student ☐

ZIP CODE   TELEPHONE (Include Area Code)   (　　)

9. OTHER INSURED'S NAME (Last Name, First Name, Middle Initial)

10. IS PATIENT'S CONDITION RELATED TO:

11. INSURED'S POLICY GROUP OR FECA NUMBER

a. OTHER INSURED'S POLICY OR GROUP NUMBER

a. EMPLOYMENT? (Current or Previous)   ☐ YES   ☐ NO

a. INSURED'S DATE OF BIRTH MM | DD | YY   SEX   M ☐   F ☐

b. OTHER INSURED'S DATE OF BIRTH MM | DD | YY   SEX   M ☐   F ☐

b. AUTO ACCIDENT?   PLACE (State)   ☐ YES   ☐ NO

b. EMPLOYER'S NAME OR SCHOOL NAME

c. EMPLOYER'S NAME OR SCHOOL NAME

c. OTHER ACCIDENT?   ☐ YES   ☐ NO

c. INSURANCE PLAN NAME OR PROGRAM NAME

d. INSURANCE PLAN NAME OR PROGRAM NAME

10d. RESERVED FOR LOCAL USE

d. IS THERE ANOTHER HEALTH BENEFIT PLAN?   ☐ YES   ☐ NO   **If yes**, return to and complete item 9 a-d.

READ BACK OF FORM BEFORE COMPLETING & SIGNING THIS FORM.

12. PATIENT'S OR AUTHORIZED PERSON'S SIGNATURE I authorize the release of any medical or other information necessary to process this claim. I also request payment of government benefits either to myself or to the party who accepts assignment below.

SIGNED _____ DATE _____

13. INSURED'S OR AUTHORIZED PERSON'S SIGNATURE I authorize payment of medical benefits to the undersigned physician or supplier for services described below.

SIGNED _____

PATIENT AND INSURED INFORMATION

14. DATE OF CURRENT: MM | DD | YY ◄ ILLNESS (First symptom) OR INJURY (Accident) OR PREGNANCY(LMP)

15. IF PATIENT HAS HAD SAME OR SIMILAR ILLNESS. GIVE FIRST DATE MM | DD | YY

16. DATES PATIENT UNABLE TO WORK IN CURRENT OCCUPATION MM | DD | YY   FROM   TO   MM | DD | YY

17. NAME OF REFERRING PROVIDER OR OTHER SOURCE   17a.   17b. NPI

18. HOSPITALIZATION DATES RELATED TO CURRENT SERVICES MM | DD | YY   FROM   TO   MM | DD | YY

19. RESERVED FOR LOCAL USE

20. OUTSIDE LAB?   ☐ YES   ☐ NO $ CHARGES

21. DIAGNOSIS OR NATURE OF ILLNESS OR INJURY (Relate Items 1, 2, 3 or 4 to Item 24E by Line)

1. |___.___   3. |___.___

2. |___.___   4. |___.___

22. MEDICAID RESUBMISSION CODE   ORIGINAL REF. NO.

23. PRIOR AUTHORIZATION NUMBER

24. A. DATE(S) OF SERVICE						B. PLACE OF SERVICE	C. EMG	D. PROCEDURES, SERVICES, OR SUPPLIES (Explain Unusual Circumstances)		E. DIAGNOSIS POINTER	F. $ CHARGES	G. DAYS OR UNITS	H. EPSDT Family Plan	I. ID. QUAL.	J. RENDERING PROVIDER ID. #
From MM	DD	YY	To MM	DD	YY			CPT/HCPCS	MODIFIER						
1														NPI	
2														NPI	
3														NPI	
4														NPI	
5														NPI	
6														NPI	

25. FEDERAL TAX I.D. NUMBER   SSN ☐ EIN ☐

26. PATIENT'S ACCOUNT NO.

27. ACCEPT ASSIGNMENT? (For govt. claims, see back)   ☐ YES   ☐ NO

28. TOTAL CHARGE $

29. AMOUNT PAID $

30. BALANCE DUE $

31. SIGNATURE OF PHYSICIAN OR SUPPLIER INCLUDING DEGREES OR CREDENTIALS (I certify that the statements on the reverse apply to this bill and are made a part thereof.)

SIGNED _____ DATE _____

32. SERVICE FACILITY LOCATION INFORMATION

a.   b.

33. BILLING PROVIDER INFO & PH # (　　)

a.   b.

PHYSICIAN OR SUPPLIER INFORMATION

NUCC Instruction Manual available at: www.nucc.org   *PLEASE PRINT OR TYPE*   APPROVED OMB-0938-0999 FORM CMS-1500 (08-05)

CHAPTER 9, CHAPTER REVIEW EXERCISE 11

Patient Information Form

Please complete information in the spaces provided. Be sure to complete and sign the statement at the bottom of this form.

Patient		
Last Name	First Name	M.I.
Smith	Jane	P

Home Address			
Street	City	State	Zip
4590 Elm	Anytown	IA	52211

Phone Numbers & E-mail			
Home	Work	Cell	E-mail
221-3478	None	363-8686	None

Identity Information	
Social Security Number	Date of Birth
576-34-2358	7-9-XX

Primary Insurance	
Company Name	Phone Number
Medicaid	232-5858
Billing Address	
P.O. Box 23311, Everytown, IA 54211	
Name of Insured	Relation to Patient
Jane	Self
Insured's ID Number	Group Number
1234567A	None

Secondary Insurance	
Company Name	Phone Number
None	
Billing Address	
Name of Insured	Relation to Patient
Insured's ID Number	Group Number

Emergency Information		
Emergency Contact Name	Relation	Phone
Bonnie Clark	Mother	221-3478

I authorize the release of any medical or other information necessary to process this claim.
I hereby authorize payment of medical benefits billed to my insurance to John Smith, DO. I hereby accept
responsibility for payment for any service(s) provided to me that is not covered by my insurance. I agree
to pay all co-payments, coinsurance, and deductibles at the time the service is rendered.

Jane Smith   5/1/XXXX

Signature of Patient or Guardian   Date

Date of service: 5-1-XXXX					
Patient name: Jane Smith		Insurance: Medicaid			
		Subscriber name: Same			
Address: 4590 Elm Anytown, IA 52211		Group #: None		Previous balance:	
		Copay: None		Today's charges: ?	
Phone: 221-3478		Account #: None		Today's payment: 0.00	Check# None
DOB: ? Age: 41 Sex: F		Physician name: Smith		Balance due: ?	

Office visit	New	Est
Minimal		99211
Problem focused	99201	99212
X Expanded problem focused	99202	99213
Detailed	99203	99214
Comprehensive	99204	99215
Comprehensive (new patient)	99205	
Significant, separate service	–25	–25

Well visit	New	Est
< 1 y	99381	99391
1–4 y	99382	99392
5–11 y	99383	99393
12–17 y	99384	99394
18–39 y	99385	99395
40–64 y	99386	99396
65 y +	99387	99397

Medicare preventive services	
Pap	Q0091
Pelvic & breast	G0101
Prostate/PSA	G0103
Tobacco counseling/3–10 min	G0375
Tobacco counseling/>10 min	G0376
Welcome to Medicare exam	G0344
ECG w/Welcome to Medicare exam	G0366
Flexible sigmoidoscopy	G0104
Hemoccult, guaiac	G0107
Flu shot	G0008
Pneumonia shot	G0009

Consultation/preop clearance	
Expanded problem focused	99242
Detailed	99243
Comprehensive/mod complexity	99244
Comprehensive/high complexity	99245

Other services	
After posted hours	99050
Evening/weekend appointment	99051
Home health certification	G0180
Home health recertification	G0179
Post-op follow-up	99024
Prolonged/30–74 min	99354
Special reports/forms	99080
Disability/Workers comp	99455

Radiology	
X Sinus x-rays	

X Diagnoses	
1	Sinus infection
2	
3	
4	

Next office visit

Recheck	Prev	PRN	_____ D W M Y

Instructions:

Referral

To:

Instructions:

Physician signature

X _____

Office procedures	
Anoscopy	46600
Audiometry	92551
Cerumen removal	69210
Colposcopy	57452
Colposcopy w/biopsy	57455
ECG, w/interpretation	93000
ECG, rhythm strip	93040
Endometrial biopsy	58100
Flexible sigmoidoscopy	45330
Flexible sigmoidoscopy w/biopsy	45331
Fracture care, cast/splint	29 ____
Site: _____	
Nebulizer	94640
Nebulizer demo	94664
Spirometry	94010
Spirometry, pre and post	94060
Tympanometry	92567
Vasectomy	55250

Skin procedures		Units
Burn care, initial	16000	
Foreign body, skin, simple	10120	
Foreign body, skin, complex	10121	
I&D, abscess	10060	
I&D, hematoma/seroma	10140	
Laceration repair, simple	120 ___	
Site: _____ Size: ____		
Laceration repair, layered	120 ___	
Site: _____ Size: ____		
Lesion, biopsy, one	11100	
Lesion, biopsy, each add'l	11101	
Lesion, excision, benign	114 ___	
Site: _____ Size: ____		
Lesion, excision, malignant	116 ___	
Site: _____ Size: ____		
Lesion, paring/cutting, one	11055	
Lesion, paring/cutting, 2–4	11056	
Lesion, shave	113 ___	
Site: _____ Size: ____		
Nail removal, partial	11730	
Nail removal, w/matrix	11750	
Skin tag, 1–15	11200	
Wart, flat, 1–14	17110	
Wart, plantar, single	17000	
Wart, plantar, each add'l	17003	

Medications		Units
Ampicillin, up to 500 mg	J0290	
B-12, up to 1,000 mcg	J3420	
Epinephrine, up to 1 ml	J0170	
Kenalog, 10 mg	J3301	
Lidocaine, 10 mg	J2001	
Normal saline, 1000 cc	J7030	
Phenergan, up to 50 mg	J2550	
Progesterone, 150 mg	J1055	
Rocephin, 250 mg	J0696	
Testosterone, 200 mg	J1080	
Tigan, up to 200 mg	J3250	
Toradol, 15 mg	J1885	

Miscellaneous services	

Laboratory	
Venipuncture	36415
Blood glucose, monitoring device	82962
Blood glucose, visual dipstick	82948
CBC, w/ auto differential	85025
CBC, w/o auto differential	85027
Cholesterol	82465
Hemoccult, guaiac	82270
Hemoccult, immunoassay	82274
Hemoglobin A1C	85018
Lipid panel	80061
Liver panel	80076
KOH prep (skin, hair, nails)	87220
Metabolic panel, basic	80048
Metabolic panel, comprehensive	80053
Mononucleosis	86308
Pregnancy, blood	84703
Pregnancy, urine	81025
Renal panel	80069
Sedimentation rate	85651
Strep, rapid	86403
Strep culture	87081
Strep A	87880
TB	86580
UA, complete, non-automated	81000
UA, w/o micro, non-automated	81002
UA, w/o micro, non-automated	81003
Urine colony count	87086
Urine culture, presumptive	87088
Wet mount/KOH	87210

Vaccines	
DT, <7 y	90702
DTP	90701
DtaP, <7 y	90700
Flu, 6–35 months	90657
Flu, 3 y +	90658
Hep A, adult	90632
Hep A, ped/adol, 2 dose	90633
Hep B, adult	90746
Hep B, ped/adol 3 dose	90744
Hep B-Hib	90748
Hib, 4 dose	90645
HPV	90649
IPV	90713
MMR	90707
Pneumonia, >2 y	90732
Pneumonia conjugate, <5 y	90669
Td, >7 y	90718
Varicella	90716

Immunizations & Injections		Units
Allergen, one	95115	
Allergen, multiple	95117	
Imm admin, one	90471	
Imm admin, each add'l	90472	
Imm admin, intranasal, one	90473	
Imm admin, intranasal, each add'l	90474	
Injection, joint, small	20600	
Injection, joint, intermediate	20605	
Injection, joint, major	20610	
Injection, ther/proph/diag	90772	
Injection, trigger point	20552	

Supplies	

Infectious and Parasitic Diseases

053.9	Herpes zoster, NOS
054.9	Herpetic disease, uncomplicated
075	Mononucleosis
034.0	Strep throat
079.99	Viral infection, unspec.
078.10	Warts, all sites

Neoplasms

Benign Neoplasms
239.2	Skin, soft tissue neoplasm, inspec.
216.9	Skin, unspec.

Endocrine, Nutritional and Metabolic Disorders

Endocrine
250.01	Diabetes I, uncomplicated
250.91	Diabetes I, w/unspec. complications
250.00	Diabetes II/unspec., w/o complications, not uncontrolled
250.90	Diabetes II, w/unspec. complications
242.90	Hyperthyroidism, NOS
244.9	Hypothyroidism, inspec.

Metabolic/Other
274.9	Gout, unspec.
272.0	Hypercholesterolemia
272.2	Hyperlipidemia, mixed
272.1	Hypertriglyceridemia
278.01	Obesity, morbid
278.00	Obesity, NOS
278.02	Overweight

Blood Diseases

285.9	Anemia, other, unspec.

Mental Disorders

300.00	Anxiety state, unspec.
314.00	Attention deficit, w/o hyperactivity
290.0	Dementia, senile, NOS
311	Depression, NOS

Nervous System and Sense Organ Disorders

Nervous System Diseases
354.0	Carpal tunnel
345.90	Epilepsy, unspec., w/o status
346.90	Migraine, unspec., not intractable

Eye Diseases
372.30	Conjunctivitis, unspec.
368.10	Visual disturbance, unspec.

Ear Diseases
380.4	Cerumen impaction
389.9	Hearing loss, unspec.
380.10	Otitis externa, unspec.
382.00	Otitis media, acute

Circulatory System

Arrythmias
427.31	Atrial fibrillation

Cardiac
413.9	Angina pectoris, NOS
428.0	Heart failure, congestive, unspec.
414.9	Ischemic heart disease, chronic, unspec.
424.1	Valvular disorder, aortic, NOS

Vascular
796.2	Elevated BP w/o hypertension
401.1	Hypertension, benign
458.0	Hypotension, orthostatic
443.9	Peripheral vascular disease, unspec.
451.9	Thrombophlebitis, unspec.
459.81	Venous insufficiency, unspec.

Respiratory System

Lower Respiratory Tract
493.90	Asthma, unspec.
466.0	Bronchitis, acute
496	COPD, NOS
486	Pneumonia, unspec.

Upper Respiratory Tract
462	Pharyngitis, acute
477.9	Rhinitis, allergic, cause unspec.
461.9	Sinusitis, acute, NOS
465.9	Upper respiratory infection, acute, NOS

Digestive System

564.00	Constipation, unspec.
562.10	Diverticulosis of colon
562.11	Diverticulitis of colon, NOS
535.50	Gastritis, unspec. w/o hemorrhage
558.9	Gastroenteritis, noninfectious, unspec.
530.81	Gastroesophageal reflux, no esophagitis
455.6	Hemorrhoids, NOS
564.1	Irritable bowel syndrome
578.1	Melena

Genitourinary System

Urinary System Diseases
592.9	Calculus, urinary, unspec.
595.0	Cystitis, acute
599.7	Hematuria
593.9	Renal insufficiency, acute
599.0	Urinary tract infection, unspec./pyuria

Male Genital Organ Diseases
607.84	Impotence, organic
302.72	Impotence, psychosexual dysfunction
601.9	Prostatitis, NOS
257.2	Testicular hypofunction

Breast Diseases
611.72	Breast lump

Female Genital Organ Diseases
616.0	Cervicitis
622.10	Dysplasia, cervix, unspec.
625.9	Pelvic pain, unspec. female disease
616.10	Vaginitis/vulvitis, unspec.

Disorders of Menstruation
626.0	Amenorrhea
627.9	Menopausal disorders, unspec.
626.2	Menstruation, excessive/frequent
625.3	Menstruation, painful
626.6	Metrorrhagia

Pregnancy, Childbirth

641.90	Hemorrhage in preg., unspec.
V24.2	Postpartum follow-up, routine
V22.2	Pregnant state, incidental
V22.0	Prenatal care, normal, first pregnancy
V22.1	Prenatal care, normal, other pregnancy

Skin, Subcutaneous Tissue

706.1	Acne
702.0	Actinic keratosis
682.9	Cellulitis/abscess, unspec.
692.9	Contact dermatitis, NOS
691.8	Eczema, atopic dermatitis
703.0	Ingrown nail
110.1	Onychomycosis
709.9	Other skin disease, unspec.
696.1	Psoriasis, other
695.3	Rosacea
706.2	Sebaceous cyst
702.19	Seborrheic keratosis, NOS
707.9	Ulcer, skin, chronic, unspec.
708.9	Urticaria, unspec.

Musculoskeletal and Connective Tissue

General
716.90	Arthropathy, unspec.
729.1	Fibromyositis
715.90	Osteoarthrosis, unspec.
733.00	Osteoporosis, unspec.
714.0	Rheumatoid arthritis
727.00	Synovitis/tenosynovitis, unspec.

Lower Extremity
729.5	Pain in limb
728.71	Plantar fasciitis

Spine/Torso
724.4	Back pain w/ radiation, unspec.
723.9	Cervical disorder, NOS

Upper Extremity
726.32	Lateral epicondylitis
726.10	Rotator cuff syndrome, NOS

Perinatal (Infant)

779.3	Feeding problem, newborn

Signs and Symptoms

789.00	Abdominal pain, unspec.
795.01	Abnormal Pap, ASC-US
719.40	Arthralgia, unspec.
569.3	Bleeding, rectal
786.50	Chest pain, unspec.
786.2	Cough
787.91	Diarrhea, NOS
780.4	Dizziness/vertigo, NOS
787.2	Dysphagia
788.1	Dysuria
782.3	Edema, localized, NOS
783.3	Feeding problem, infant/elderly
780.6	Fever, nonperinatal
271.9	Glucose intolerance
784.0	Headache, unspec.
788.30	Incontinence/enuresis, NOS
782.2	Localized swelling/mass, superficial
785.6	Lymph nodes, enlarged
780.79	Malaise and fatigue, other
787.02	Nausea, alone
787.01	Nausea w/ vomiting
719.46	Pain, knee
724.2	Pain, low back
785.1	Palpitations
788.42	Polyuria
782.1	Rash, nonvesicular, unspec.
782.0	Sensory disturbance skin
786.05	Shortness of breath
780.2	Syncope
788.41	Urinary frequency
787.03	Vomiting, alone
783.21	Weight loss

Injuries and Adverse Effects

Dislocations, Sprains and Strains
845.00	Sprain/strain: ankle, unspec.
845.10	Sprain/strain: foot, unspec.
842.10	Sprain/strain: hand, unspec.
844.9	Sprain/strain: knee/leg, unspec.
847.0	Sprain/strain: neck, unspec.
840.9	Sprain/strain: shoulder/upper arm, unspec.
842.00	Sprain/strain: wrist, unspec.

Other Trauma, Adverse Effects
919.0	Abrasion, unspec.
924.9	Contusion, unspec.
919.4	Insect bite
894.0	Open wound, lower limb, unspec.
884.0	Open wound, upper limb, unspec.

Supplemental Classification

V72.32	Confirm norm Pap after initial abn
V25.01	Contraception, oral
V25.02	Contraception, other (diaphragm, etc.)
V25.2	Contraception, sterilization
V58.30	Dressing change, nonsurgical
V01.9	Exposure, infectious disease, unspec.
V72.31	Gynecological exam
V06.8	Immunization, combination, other
V06.1	Immunization, DTP
V04.81	Immunization, influenza
V70.0	Well adult check
V20.2	Well child check

1500

HEALTH INSURANCE CLAIM FORM

APPROVED BY NATIONAL UNIFORM CLAIM COMMITTEE 08/05

☐☐ PICA	PICA ☐☐

1. MEDICARE ☐ (Medicare #) **MEDICAID** ☐ (Medicaid #) **TRICARE CHAMPUS** ☐ (Sponsor's SSN) **CHAMPVA** ☐ (Member ID#) **GROUP HEALTH PLAN** ☐ (SSN or ID) **FECA BLK LUNG** ☐ (SSN) **OTHER** ☐ (ID) **1a. INSURED'S I.D. NUMBER** (For Program in Item 1)

2. PATIENT'S NAME (Last Name, First Name, Middle Initial)

3. PATIENT'S BIRTH DATE MM DD YY **SEX** M ☐ F ☐

4. INSURED'S NAME (Last Name, First Name, Middle Initial)

5. PATIENT'S ADDRESS (No., Street)

6. PATIENT RELATIONSHIP TO INSURED Self ☐ Spouse ☐ Child ☐ Other ☐

7. INSURED'S ADDRESS (No., Street)

CITY **STATE**

8. PATIENT STATUS Single ☐ Married ☐ Other ☐
Employed ☐ Full-Time Student ☐ Part-Time Student ☐

CITY **STATE**

ZIP CODE **TELEPHONE** (Include Area Code) ( )

ZIP CODE **TELEPHONE** (Include Area Code) ( )

9. OTHER INSURED'S NAME (Last Name, First Name, Middle Initial)

10. IS PATIENT'S CONDITION RELATED TO:

11. INSURED'S POLICY GROUP OR FECA NUMBER

a. OTHER INSURED'S POLICY OR GROUP NUMBER

a. EMPLOYMENT? (Current or Previous) ☐ YES ☐ NO

a. INSURED'S DATE OF BIRTH MM DD YY **SEX** M ☐ F ☐

b. OTHER INSURED'S DATE OF BIRTH MM DD YY **SEX** M ☐ F ☐

b. AUTO ACCIDENT? ☐ YES ☐ NO **PLACE (State)**

b. EMPLOYER'S NAME OR SCHOOL NAME

c. EMPLOYER'S NAME OR SCHOOL NAME

c. OTHER ACCIDENT? ☐ YES ☐ NO

c. INSURANCE PLAN NAME OR PROGRAM NAME

d. INSURANCE PLAN NAME OR PROGRAM NAME

10d. RESERVED FOR LOCAL USE

d. IS THERE ANOTHER HEALTH BENEFIT PLAN? ☐ YES ☐ NO *If yes*, return to and complete item 9 a-d.

READ BACK OF FORM BEFORE COMPLETING & SIGNING THIS FORM.

12. PATIENT'S OR AUTHORIZED PERSON'S SIGNATURE I authorize the release of any medical or other information necessary to process this claim. I also request payment of government benefits either to myself or to the party who accepts assignment below.

SIGNED _____ DATE _____

13. INSURED'S OR AUTHORIZED PERSON'S SIGNATURE I authorize payment of medical benefits to the undersigned physician or supplier for services described below.

SIGNED _____

14. DATE OF CURRENT: MM DD YY ◀ ILLNESS (First symptom) OR INJURY (Accident) OR PREGNANCY(LMP)

15. IF PATIENT HAS HAD SAME OR SIMILAR ILLNESS. GIVE FIRST DATE MM DD YY

16. DATES PATIENT UNABLE TO WORK IN CURRENT OCCUPATION MM DD YY FROM TO MM DD YY

17. NAME OF REFERRING PROVIDER OR OTHER SOURCE

17a.
17b. NPI

18. HOSPITALIZATION DATES RELATED TO CURRENT SERVICES MM DD YY FROM TO MM DD YY

19. RESERVED FOR LOCAL USE

20. OUTSIDE LAB? ☐ YES ☐ NO **$ CHARGES**

21. DIAGNOSIS OR NATURE OF ILLNESS OR INJURY (Relate Items 1, 2, 3 or 4 to Item 24E by Line)

1. ⌊___.___⌋   3. ⌊___.___⌋
2. ⌊___.___⌋   4. ⌊___.___⌋

22. MEDICAID RESUBMISSION CODE ORIGINAL REF. NO.

23. PRIOR AUTHORIZATION NUMBER

24. A. DATE(S) OF SERVICE						B. PLACE OF SERVICE	C. EMG	D. PROCEDURES, SERVICES, OR SUPPLIES (Explain Unusual Circumstances) CPT/HCPCS MODIFIER	E. DIAGNOSIS POINTER	F. $ CHARGES	G. DAYS OR UNITS	H. EPSDT Family Plan	I. ID. QUAL.	J. RENDERING PROVIDER ID. #
From MM	DD	YY	To MM	DD	YY									
1													NPI	
2													NPI	
3													NPI	
4													NPI	
5													NPI	
6													NPI	

25. FEDERAL TAX I.D. NUMBER ☐ SSN ☐ EIN

26. PATIENT'S ACCOUNT NO.

27. ACCEPT ASSIGNMENT? (For govt. claims, see back) ☐ YES ☐ NO

28. TOTAL CHARGE $

29. AMOUNT PAID $

30. BALANCE DUE $

31. SIGNATURE OF PHYSICIAN OR SUPPLIER INCLUDING DEGREES OR CREDENTIALS (I certify that the statements on the reverse apply to this bill and are made a part thereof.)

SIGNED _____ DATE _____

32. SERVICE FACILITY LOCATION INFORMATION
a.   b.

33. BILLING PROVIDER INFO & PH # ( )
a.   b.

NUCC Instruction Manual available at: www.nucc.org   ***PLEASE PRINT OR TYPE***   APPROVED OMB-0938-0999 FORM CMS-1500 (08-05)

CARRIER

PATIENT AND INSURED INFORMATION

PHYSICIAN OR SUPPLIER INFORMATION

CHAPTER 9, CHAPTER REVIEW EXERCISE 12

Patient Information Form

Please complete information in the spaces provided. Be sure to complete and sign the statement at the bottom of this form.

Patient		
Last Name	First Name	M.I.
White	Lynn	A

Home Address			
Street	City	State	Zip
1452 Adams	Anytown	IA	52223

Phone Numbers & E-mail			
Home	Work	Cell	E-mail
231-8961	None	896-1231	white@mail.com

Identity Information	
Social Security Number	Date of Birth
428-90-6431	6-2-XX

Primary Insurance	
Company Name	Phone Number
Medicaid	232-5858
Billing Address	
P.O. Box 23311, Everytown, IA 54211	
Name of Insured	Relation to Patient
Lynn	Self
Insured's ID Number	Group Number
0987654J	None

Secondary Insurance	
Company Name	Phone Number
None	
Billing Address	
Name of Insured	Relation to Patient
Insured's ID Number	Group Number

Emergency Information		
Emergency Contact Name	Relation	Phone

I authorize the release of any medical or other information necessary to process this claim.
I hereby authorize payment of medical benefits billed to my insurance to John Smith, DO. I hereby accept responsibility for payment for any service(s) provided to me that is not covered by my insurance. I agree to pay all co-payments, coinsurance, and deductibles at the time the service is rendered.

Lynn White   8/1/XXXX
_____   _____
Signature of Patient or Guardian   Date

Date of service: 8-1-XXXX				
Patient name: Lynn White	Insurance: Medicaid			
	Subscriber name: Self			
Address: 1452 Adams Anytown, IA 52223	Group #: 0987654J		Previous balance:	
	Copay:		Today's charges: 1025.00	
Phone: 231-8961	Account #:		Today's payment:	Check#
DOB: 6-2-72 Age: Sex: F	Physician name: Smith		Balance due: 1025.00	

Office visit	New	Est	Office procedures			Laboratory	
Minimal		99211	Anoscopy		46600	Venipuncture	36415
Problem focused	99201	99212	Audiometry		92551	Blood glucose, monitoring device	82962
Expanded problem focused	99202	99213	Cerumen removal		69210	Blood glucose, visual dipstick	82948
X Detailed	99203	99214	Colposcopy		57452	CBC, w/ auto differential	85025
Comprehensive	99204	99215	Colposcopy w/biopsy		57455	CBC, w/o auto differential	85027
Comprehensive (new patient)	99205		ECG, w/interpretation		93000	Cholesterol	82465
Significant, separate service	–25	–25	ECG, rhythm strip		93040	Hemoccult, guaiac	82270
Well visit	**New**	**Est**	Endometrial biopsy		58100	Hemoccult, immunoassay	82274
< 1 y	99381	99391	Flexible sigmoidoscopy		45330	Hemoglobin A1C	85018
1–4 y	99382	99392	Flexible sigmoidoscopy w/biopsy		45331	Lipid panel	80061
5–11 y	99383	99393	Fracture care, cast/splint		29___	Liver panel	80076
12–17 y	99384	99394	Site: _____			KOH prep (skin, hair, nails)	87220
18–39 y	99385	99395	Nebulizer		94640	Metabolic panel, basic	80048
40–64 y	99386	99396	Nebulizer demo		94664	Metabolic panel, comprehensive	80053
65 y +	99387	99397	Spirometry		94010	Mononucleosis	86308
Medicare preventive services			Spirometry, pre and post		94060	Pregnancy, blood	84703
Pap		Q0091	Tympanometry		92567	Pregnancy, urine	81025
Pelvic & breast		G0101	Vasectomy		55250	Renal panel	80069
Prostate/PSA		G0103	**Skin procedures**		**Units**	Sedimentation rate	85651
Tobacco counseling/3–10 min		G0375	Burn care, initial	16000		Strep, rapid	86403
Tobacco counseling/>10 min		G0376	Foreign body, skin, simple	10120		Strep culture	87081
Welcome to Medicare exam		G0344	Foreign body, skin, complex	10121		Strep A	87880
ECG w/Welcome to Medicare exam		G0366	I&D, abscess	10060		TB	86580
Flexible sigmoidoscopy		G0104	I&D, hematoma/seroma	10140		UA, complete, non-automated	81000
Hemoccult, guaiac		G0107	Laceration repair, simple	120___		UA, w/o micro, non-automated	81002
Flu shot		G0008	Site: _____ Size: _____			UA, w/o micro, non-automated	81003
Pneumonia shot		G0009	Laceration repair, layered	120___		Urine colony count	87086
Consultation/preop clearance			Site: _____ Size: _____			Urine culture, presumptive	87088
Expanded problem focused		99242	Lesion, biopsy, one	11100		Wet mount/KOH	87210
Detailed		99243	Lesion, biopsy, each add'l	11101		**Vaccines**	
Comprehensive/mod complexity		99244	Lesion, excision, benign	114___		DT, <7 y	90702
Comprehensive/high complexity		99245	Site: _____ Size: _____			DTP	90701
Other services			Lesion, excision, malignant	116___		DtaP, <7 y	90700
After posted hours		99050	Site: _____ Size: _____			Flu, 6–35 months	90657
Evening/weekend appointment		99051	Lesion, paring/cutting, one	11055		Flu, 3 y +	90658
Home health certification		G0180	Lesion, paring/cutting, 2–4	11056		Hep A, adult	90632
Home health recertification		G0179	Lesion, shave	113___		Hep A, ped/adol, 2 dose	90633
Post-op follow-up		99024	Site: _____ Size: _____			Hep B, adult	90746
Prolonged/30–74 min		99354	Nail removal, partial	11730		Hep B, ped/adol 3 dose	90744
Special reports/forms		99080	Nail removal, w/matrix	11750		Hep B-Hib	90748
Disability/Workers comp		99455	Skin tag, 1–15	11200		Hib, 4 dose	90645
Radiology			Wart, flat, 1–14	17110		HPV	90649
			Wart, plantar, single	17000		IPV	90713
			Wart, plantar, each add'l	17003		MMR	90707
X **Diagnoses**			**Medications**		**Units**	Pneumonia, >2 y	90732
1 Mitral valve prolapse			Ampicillin, up to 500 mg	J0290		Pneumonia conjugate, <5 y	90669
2			B-12, up to 1,000 mcg	J3420		Td, >7 y	90718
3			Epinephrine, up to 1 ml	J0170		Varicella	90716
4			Kenalog, 10 mg	J3301		**Immunizations & Injections**	**Units**
Next office visit			Lidocaine, 10 mg	J2001		Allergen, one	95115
Recheck Prev PRN _____ D W M Y			Normal saline, 1000 cc	J7030		Allergen, multiple	95117
Instructions:			Phenergan, up to 50 mg	J2550		Imm admin, one	90471
			Progesterone, 150 mg	J1055		Imm admin, each add'l	90472
			Rocephin, 250 mg	J0696		Imm admin, intranasal, one	90473
			Testosterone, 200 mg	J1080		Imm admin, intranasal, each add'l	90474
			Tigan, up to 200 mg	J3250		Injection, joint, small	20600
Referral			Toradol, 15 mg	J1885		Injection, joint, intermediate	20605
To:			**Miscellaneous services**			Injection, joint, major	20610
Instructions:			X M/Mode 2-D echo			Injection, ther/proph/diag	90772
						Injection, trigger point	20552
Physician signature						**Supplies**	
X _____							

Infectious and Parasitic Diseases

053.9	Herpes zoster, NOS
054.9	Herpetic disease, uncomplicated
075	Mononucleosis
034.0	Strep throat
079.99	Viral infection, unspec.
078.10	Warts, all sites

Neoplasms

Benign Neoplasms

239.2	Skin, soft tissue neoplasm, inspec.
216.9	Skin, unspec.

Endocrine, Nutritional and Metabolic Disorders

Endocrine

250.01	Diabetes I, uncomplicated
250.91	Diabetes I, w/unspec. complications
250.00	Diabetes II/unspec., w/o complications, not uncontrolled
250.90	Diabetes II, w/unspec. complications
242.90	Hyperthyroidism, NOS
244.9	Hypothyroidism, inspec.

Metabolic/Other

274.9	Gout, unspec.
272.0	Hypercholesterolemia
272.2	Hyperlipidemia, mixed
272.1	Hypertriglyceridemia
278.01	Obesity, morbid
278.00	Obesity, NOS
278.02	Overweight

Blood Diseases

285.9	Anemia, other, unspec.

Mental Disorders

300.00	Anxiety state, unspec.
314.00	Attention deficit, w/o hyperactivity
290.0	Dementia, senile, NOS
311	Depression, NOS

Nervous System and Sense Organ Disorders

Nervous System Diseases

354.0	Carpal tunnel
345.90	Epilepsy, unspec., w/o status
346.90	Migraine, unspec., not intractable

Eye Diseases

372.30	Conjunctivitis, unspec.
368.10	Visual disturbance, unspec.

Ear Diseases

380.4	Cerumen impaction
389.9	Hearing loss, unspec.
380.10	Otitis externa, unspec.
382.00	Otitis media, acute

Circulatory System

Arrythmias

427.31	Atrial fibrillation

Cardiac

413.9	Angina pectoris, NOS
428.0	Heart failure, congestive, unspec.
414.9	Ischemic heart disease, chronic, unspec.
424.1	Valvular disorder, aortic, NOS

Vascular

796.2	Elevated BP w/o hypertension
401.1	Hypertension, benign
458.0	Hypotension, orthostatic
443.9	Peripheral vascular disease, unspec.
451.9	Thrombophlebitis, unspec.
459.81	Venous insufficiency, unspec.

Respiratory System

Lower Respiratory Tract

493.90	Asthma, unspec.
466.0	Bronchitis, acute
496	COPD, NOS
486	Pneumonia, unspec.

Upper Respiratory Tract

462	Pharyngitis, acute
477.9	Rhinitis, allergic, cause unspec.
461.9	Sinusitis, acute, NOS
465.9	Upper respiratory infection, acute, NOS

Digestive System

564.00	Constipation, unspec.
562.10	Diverticulosis of colon
562.11	Diverticulitis of colon, NOS
535.50	Gastritis, unspec. w/o hemorrhage
558.9	Gastroenteritis, noninfectious, unspec.
530.81	Gastroesophageal reflux, no esophagitis
455.6	Hemorrhoids, NOS
564.1	Irritable bowel syndrome
578.1	Melena

Genitourinary System

Urinary System Diseases

592.9	Calculus, urinary, unspec.
595.0	Cystitis, acute
599.7	Hematuria
593.9	Renal insufficiency, acute
599.0	Urinary tract infection, unspec./pyuria

Male Genital Organ Diseases

607.84	Impotence, organic
302.72	Impotence, psychosexual dysfunction
601.9	Prostatitis, NOS
257.2	Testicular hypofunction

Breast Diseases

611.72	Breast lump

Female Genital Organ Diseases

616.0	Cervicitis
622.10	Dysplasia, cervix, unspec.
625.9	Pelvic pain, unspec. female disease
616.10	Vaginitis/vulvitis, unspec.

Disorders of Menstruation

626.0	Amenorrhea
627.9	Menopausal disorders, unspec.
626.2	Menstruation, excessive/frequent
625.3	Menstruation, painful
626.6	Metrorrhagia

Pregnancy, Childbirth

641.90	Hemorrhage in preg., unspec.
V24.2	Postpartum follow-up, routine
V22.2	Pregnant state, incidental
V22.0	Prenatal care, normal, first pregnancy
V22.1	Prenatal care, normal, other pregnancy

Skin, Subcutaneous Tissue

706.1	Acne
702.0	Actinic keratosis
682.9	Cellulitis/abscess, unspec.
692.9	Contact dermatitis, NOS
691.8	Eczema, atopic dermatitis
703.0	Ingrown nail
110.1	Onychomycosis
709.9	Other skin disease, unspec.
696.1	Psoriasis, other
695.3	Rosacea
706.2	Sebaceous cyst
702.19	Seborrheic keratosis, NOS
707.9	Ulcer, skin, chronic, unspec.
708.9	Urticaria, unspec.

Musculoskeletal and Connective Tissue

General

716.90	Arthropathy, unspec.
729.1	Fibromyositis
715.90	Osteoarthrosis, unspec.
733.00	Osteoporosis, unspec.
714.0	Rheumatoid arthritis
727.00	Synovitis/tenosynovitis, unspec.

Lower Extremity

729.5	Pain in limb
728.71	Plantar fasciitis

Spine/Torso

724.4	Back pain w/ radiation, unspec.
723.9	Cervical disorder, NOS

Upper Extremity

726.32	Lateral epicondylitis
726.10	Rotator cuff syndrome, NOS

Perinatal (Infant)

779.3	Feeding problem, newborn

Signs and Symptoms

789.00	Abdominal pain, unspec.
795.01	Abnormal Pap, ASC-US
719.40	Arthralgia, unspec.
569.3	Bleeding, rectal
786.50	Chest pain, unspec.
786.2	Cough
787.91	Diarrhea, NOS
780.4	Dizziness/vertigo, NOS
787.2	Dysphagia
788.1	Dysuria
782.3	Edema, localized, NOS
783.3	Feeding problem, infant/elderly
780.6	Fever, nonperinatal
271.9	Glucose intolerance
784.0	Headache, unspec.
788.30	Incontinence/enuresis, NOS
782.2	Localized swelling/mass, superficial
785.6	Lymph nodes, enlarged
780.79	Malaise and fatigue, other
787.02	Nausea, alone
787.01	Nausea w/ vomiting
719.46	Pain, knee
724.2	Pain, low back
785.1	Palpitations
788.42	Polyuria
782.1	Rash, nonvesicular, unspec.
782.0	Sensory disturbance skin
786.05	Shortness of breath
780.2	Syncope
788.41	Urinary frequency
787.03	Vomiting, alone
783.21	Weight loss

Injuries and Adverse Effects

Dislocations, Sprains and Strains

845.00	Sprain/strain: ankle, unspec.
845.10	Sprain/strain: foot, unspec.
842.10	Sprain/strain: hand, unspec.
844.9	Sprain/strain: knee/leg, unspec.
847.0	Sprain/strain: neck, unspec.
840.9	Sprain/strain: shoulder/upper arm, unspec.
842.00	Sprain/strain: wrist, unspec.

Other Trauma, Adverse Effects

919.0	Abrasion, unspec.
924.9	Contusion, unspec.
919.4	Insect bite
894.0	Open wound, lower limb, unspec.
884.0	Open wound, upper limb, unspec.

Supplemental Classification

V72.32	Confirm norm Pap after initial abn
V25.01	Contraception, oral
V25.02	Contraception, other (diaphragm, etc.)
V25.2	Contraception, sterilization
V58.30	Dressing change, nonsurgical
V01.9	Exposure, infectious disease, unspec.
V72.31	Gynecological exam
V06.8	Immunization, combination, other
V06.1	Immunization, DTP
V04.81	Immunization, influenza
V70.0	Well adult check
V20.2	Well child check

1500

HEALTH INSURANCE CLAIM FORM

APPROVED BY NATIONAL UNIFORM CLAIM COMMITTEE 08/05

☐☐ PICA ▢▢ | PICA ▢▢

| 1. MEDICARE ☐ (Medicare #) | MEDICAID ☐ (Medicaid #) | TRICARE CHAMPUS ☐ (Sponsor's SSN) | CHAMPVA ☐ (Member ID#) | GROUP HEALTH PLAN ☐ (SSN or ID) | FECA BLK LUNG ☐ (SSN) | OTHER ☐ (ID) | 1a. INSURED'S I.D. NUMBER (For Program in Item 1) |

2. PATIENT'S NAME (Last Name, First Name, Middle Initial)

3. PATIENT'S BIRTH DATE MM DD YY SEX M ☐ F ☐

4. INSURED'S NAME (Last Name, First Name, Middle Initial)

5. PATIENT'S ADDRESS (No., Street)

6. PATIENT RELATIONSHIP TO INSURED Self ☐ Spouse ☐ Child ☐ Other ☐

7. INSURED'S ADDRESS (No., Street)

CITY | STATE

8. PATIENT STATUS Single ☐ Married ☐ Other ☐ Employed ☐ Full-Time Student ☐ Part-Time Student ☐

CITY | STATE

ZIP CODE | TELEPHONE (Include Area Code) ( )

ZIP CODE | TELEPHONE (Include Area Code) ( )

9. OTHER INSURED'S NAME (Last Name, First Name, Middle Initial)

10. IS PATIENT'S CONDITION RELATED TO:

11. INSURED'S POLICY GROUP OR FECA NUMBER

a. OTHER INSURED'S POLICY OR GROUP NUMBER

a. EMPLOYMENT? (Current or Previous) ☐ YES ☐ NO

a. INSURED'S DATE OF BIRTH MM DD YY SEX M ☐ F ☐

b. OTHER INSURED'S DATE OF BIRTH MM DD YY SEX M ☐ F ☐

b. AUTO ACCIDENT? ☐ YES ☐ NO PLACE (State)

b. EMPLOYER'S NAME OR SCHOOL NAME

c. EMPLOYER'S NAME OR SCHOOL NAME

c. OTHER ACCIDENT? ☐ YES ☐ NO

c. INSURANCE PLAN NAME OR PROGRAM NAME

d. INSURANCE PLAN NAME OR PROGRAM NAME

10d. RESERVED FOR LOCAL USE

d. IS THERE ANOTHER HEALTH BENEFIT PLAN? ☐ YES ☐ NO If yes, return to and complete item 9 a-d.

READ BACK OF FORM BEFORE COMPLETING & SIGNING THIS FORM.

12. PATIENT'S OR AUTHORIZED PERSON'S SIGNATURE I authorize the release of any medical or other information necessary to process this claim. I also request payment of government benefits either to myself or to the party who accepts assignment below.

SIGNED _____ DATE _____

13. INSURED'S OR AUTHORIZED PERSON'S SIGNATURE I authorize payment of medical benefits to the undersigned physician or supplier for services described below.

SIGNED _____

14. DATE OF CURRENT: MM DD YY ILLNESS (First symptom) OR INJURY (Accident) OR PREGNANCY(LMP)

15. IF PATIENT HAS HAD SAME OR SIMILAR ILLNESS. GIVE FIRST DATE MM DD YY

16. DATES PATIENT UNABLE TO WORK IN CURRENT OCCUPATION FROM MM DD YY TO MM DD YY

17. NAME OF REFERRING PROVIDER OR OTHER SOURCE

17a. | 17b. NPI

18. HOSPITALIZATION DATES RELATED TO CURRENT SERVICES FROM MM DD YY TO MM DD YY

19. RESERVED FOR LOCAL USE

20. OUTSIDE LAB? ☐ YES ☐ NO $ CHARGES

21. DIAGNOSIS OR NATURE OF ILLNESS OR INJURY (Relate Items 1, 2, 3 or 4 to Item 24E by Line)

1. |___.___ 3. |___.___

2. |___.___ 4. |___.___

22. MEDICAID RESUBMISSION CODE | ORIGINAL REF. NO.

23. PRIOR AUTHORIZATION NUMBER

24. A. DATE(S) OF SERVICE From MM DD YY To MM DD YY	B. PLACE OF SERVICE	C. EMG	D. PROCEDURES, SERVICES, OR SUPPLIES (Explain Unusual Circumstances) CPT/HCPCS | MODIFIER	E. DIAGNOSIS POINTER	F. $ CHARGES	G. DAYS OR UNITS	H. EPSDT Family Plan	I. ID. QUAL.	J. RENDERING PROVIDER ID. #
1									NPI
2									NPI
3									NPI
4									NPI
5									NPI
6									NPI

25. FEDERAL TAX I.D. NUMBER SSN ☐ EIN ☐

26. PATIENT'S ACCOUNT NO.

27. ACCEPT ASSIGNMENT? (For govt. claims, see back) ☐ YES ☐ NO

28. TOTAL CHARGE $

29. AMOUNT PAID $

30. BALANCE DUE $

31. SIGNATURE OF PHYSICIAN OR SUPPLIER INCLUDING DEGREES OR CREDENTIALS (I certify that the statements on the reverse apply to this bill and are made a part thereof.)

SIGNED _____ DATE _____

32. SERVICE FACILITY LOCATION INFORMATION

a. | b.

33. BILLING PROVIDER INFO & PH # ( )

a. | b.

NUCC Instruction Manual available at: www.nucc.org

PLEASE PRINT OR TYPE

APPROVED OMB-0938-0999 FORM CMS-1500 (08-05)

CARRIER

PATIENT AND INSURED INFORMATION

PHYSICIAN OR SUPPLIER INFORMATION

Common Abbreviations

abnl	Abnormal
ad	Right ear
AgNO3	Silver
Anes	Anesthesia
angio	Angiography
ant	Anterior
AODM	Adult onset diabetes mellitus
APPY	Appendectomy
as	Left ear
ASHD	Arteriosclerotic heart disease
ASCVD	Arteriosclerotic cardiovascular disease
ASPVD	Arteriosclerotic peripheral vascular disease
AU	Both ears
A&W	Alive and well
BCC	Basal cell carcinoma
BCP	Birth control pills
bid	Twice a day
BM	Bowel movement
BMR	Basal metabolic rate
BNO	Bladder neck obstruction
BOM	Bilateral otitis media
BP	Blood pressure
BPH	Benign prostatic hypertrophy
BSOM	Bilateral serous otitis media
CA	Cancer
CAB	Coronary artery bypass
CBC	Complete blood count
CC	Chief complete
CHD	Congestive heart disease
CHF	Congestive heart failure
chol	Cholesterol
cm	Centimeter
CNS	Central nervous system
COPD	Chronic obstructive pulmonary disease
CP	Cerebral palsy
CTS	Carpal tunnel syndrome
CVA	Cerebrovascular accident
CVD	Cardiovascular disease
CXR	Chest x-ray
D&C	Dilation and curettage
D/C	Discontinue
decub	Decubitus

dep	Dependent
Dep	Depressed
DIFF	Differential
DM	Diabetes mellitus
DOB	Date of birth
DPT	Diphtheria, pertussis and tetanus
DUB	Dysfunctional uterine bleeding
Dr.	Doctor
DRG	Diagnostic related groups
DT	Diphtheria, tetanus
DX	Diagnosis
ECG or EKG	Electrocardiogram
EDC	Expected date of confinement
EEG	Electroencephalogram
EENT	Ears, eyes, nose, and throat
EMG	Electromyelogram
EUA	Exam under anesthesia
ext	External
5 FU	5-Fluorouracil
FBS	Fasting blood sugar
FH	Family history
FHR	Fetal heart rate
FHX	Family history
FTT	Failure to thrive
FU	Follow up
FUO	Fever of unknown origin
FX	Fracture
GB	Gallbladder
GC	Gonococcal gonorrhea
GI	Gastrointestinal
GR	Gravida
grp	Group
GTT	Glucose tolerance test
GYN	Gynecology
GU	Genitourinary
H&H	Hemoglobin and hematocrit
H&P	History and physical
HA	Headache
HBP	High blood pressure
HCT	Hematocrit
HCVD	Heart-cardiovascular disease
HEENT	Head, ears, eyes, nose, and throat
HGB	Hemoglobin
ht	Height
Hx	History
Hyst	Hysterectomy
IAR	Inhalant allergic reaction
I&A	Irrigation and aspiration
I&D	Incision and drainage
ICU	Intensive care unit
IM	Intramuscular
INJ	Injection
IOL	Intraocular lens
IV	Intravenous
IVP	Intravenous pyelogram

K+	Potassium
KUB	Kidneys, ureter, and bladder
L&W	Living and well
LLQ	Left lower quadrant
LUQ	Left upper quadrant
LMP	Last menstrual period
mg	Milligram
MI	Myocardial infarction
ml	Milliliter
MMR	Measles, mumps, and rubella
MP	Menstrual period
MR	Mental retardation
NBC	Newborn care
NSVD	Normal spontaneous vaginal delivery
NVD	Nausea, vomiting, and diarrhea
O&P	Ova and parasites
OB	Obstetrics
OBS	Organic brain syndrome
OC	Oral contraceptives
OD	Right eye
OM (L,R,S)	Otitis media (left, right, or serous)
OPV	Oral polio vaccine
OR	Operating room
Ortho	Orthopedics or orthopaedics
OS	Left eye
O.T.	Occupational therapy
OTC	Over the counter
OU	Both eyes
PA	Posteroanterior
PAT	Paroxysmal atrial tachycardia
PCN	Penicillin
PDA	Patent ductus arteriosus
PE or PX	Physical examination
PFT	Pulmonary function test
PI	Present illness
PID	Pelvic inflammatory disease
po	Phone order
PO	By mouth
PT	Patient
PTCA	Percutaneous transluminal coronary angioplasty
PUD	Peptic ulcer disease
PUPPP	Pruritic urticarial papules and plaques of pregnancy
PVC	Premature ventricular contraction
PVD	Peripheral vascular disease
qd	Every day
qh	Every hour
qid	Four times a day
QUAD	Quadriplegic
R	Respirations
RA	Rheumatoid arthritis
RBC	Red blood cells
RLQ	Right lower quadrant
R/O	Rule out
ROM	Range of motion
ROS	Review of systems

RUQ	Right upper quadrant
Rx	Prescriptions
S+	Sodium
S&S	Signs and symptoms
SLE	Systemic lupus erythematosus
SMA-12	Sequential multiple analysis, 12 tests
SOAP	Subjective, objective, assessment, and plan
SOB	Short of breath
SUB Q	Subcutaneous
T	Temperature
T&A	Tonsillectomy and adenoidectomy
TB	Tuberculosis
TIA	Transient ischemic attack
TM	Tympanic membrane
TMJ	Temporomandibular Joint
TPR	Temperature, pulse, and respirations
Tx	Treatment
UA	Urinalysis
UCHD	Usual childhood diseases
UGI	Upper gastrointestinal
URI	Upper respiratory tract infection
UTI	Urinary tract infection
VDRL	Venereal disease research laboratory test for syphilis
WBC	White blood cells

INDEX

Note: Page numbers followed by "b," "f," and "t" indicate boxes, figures, and tables, respectively.